BRITISH COLUMBIA AND THE
UNITED STATES

THE RELATIONS OF
CANADA AND THE UNITED STATES

═══════

A SERIES OF STUDIES
PREPARED UNDER THE DIRECTION OF THE
CARNEGIE ENDOWMENT FOR INTERNATIONAL PEACE
DIVISION OF ECONOMICS AND HISTORY

JAMES T. SHOTWELL, *Director*

BRITISH COLUMBIA AND THE UNITED STATES

THE NORTH PACIFIC SLOPE FROM FUR TRADE TO AVIATION

BY

F. W. HOWAY,

W. N. SAGE,

AND

H. F. ANGUS

EDITED BY

H. F. ANGUS, ed.

TORONTO : THE RYERSON PRESS

NEW HAVEN : YALE UNIVERSITY PRESS

LONDON : HUMPHREY MILFORD : OXFORD UNIVERSITY PRESS

FOR THE CARNEGIE ENDOWMENT FOR INTERNATIONAL

PEACE : DIVISION OF ECONOMICS AND HISTORY

1942

PRINTED AND BOUND IN CANADA
BY THE RYERSON PRESS, TORONTO

INTRODUCTION

THIS volume is unique in the Canadian-American series. It was originally intended to match it with a parallel volume dealing with the history of the northwestern states, with especial reference to their contacts and their joint interest with Canada in international problems. It has not been possible as yet to add this volume to the series, however, and the need for it is materially lessened by the wide sweep of the narrative of Judge Howay's history of the pioneering days. Indeed the most notable fact in the history of northwest exploration is the absence of a clear sense of the political border. The trappers and fur traders followed their hazardous trails in lands that still belonged to the Indian. Boundary lines become fixed when settlements appear and the forest gives way to the farm and the market town. When law and order have to be established according to set rules and with recognized magistrates, people begin to think in terms of the thing called government, rather than of rivalries of trading companies pushing into the open stretches of the wilderness. It is only then that politics steps in, bringing to the fore a different set of interests, those of sentiment and prestige as well as of national advantage. Sovereignty that brooks no rival tends to speak in unyielding tones of territorial claims and the prerogatives of power.

Nowhere else in the series of Canadian-American studies has this transition from the earliest exploration of the wilderness to the settlement of pioneering days been so fully documented as here, in the story of the trails through and beyond the Rocky Mountains. It is true that there are variations in the narrative from this general pattern of the emergence of political interest as a secondary stage of development. The sea captains of Spain and Britain were fully conscious of their mission as agents of the sovereigns overseas, and Lewis and Clark were commissioned rather as political explorers than as a part of the fur-hunting penetration of the wilderness then taking place. Nevertheless the story of the rivalries in the North-west did not take on the dangerous tone of national challenge until political leaders conceived of vast areas for settlement in terms of empire. As one follows the fortunes of the frontiersmen one sees how subordinate were their political interests to their interest in

v

reaping the harvest of the forest. The Oregon boundary dispute, on the other hand, with its slogan "Fifty-four Forty or Fight" was an issue of nineteenth-century imperialism and primarily an echo of sectional politics at Washington during the great period of American continental expansion.

When we turn from the intensely human incidents of the early days to the rise of British Columbia to provincial status in the newly-established Dominion of Canada, we come upon another set of problems, as scientific advance conquered the distance to the world markets and a new industrial system began to exploit the raw materials of mountain and river. Then the questions of rival railroad systems, mining, lumber, and fishing enterprises were tied in with larger entities of truly national proportion. Although still separated from the East by over a thousand miles of prairie and a wilderness untamed except by the national railway system, British Columbia found in federal union with the provinces farther east, a safeguard for the essentially British character of its traditions and institutions. At the same time its contacts with the western states increased. The last chapter of this volume deals with this paradox of the intimate neighbourhood of the two great communities of the Pacific Coast, American and Canadian, held in bond of friendship, but never losing a sense of distinct nationality, definite not only in the arts and science of government, but in the folkways of the people.

The volume is the work of three representatives of British Columbian scholarship. Judge Howay, who supplies the earlier sections, is a past master in the fields of early history and international relations on the Pacific Coast. Professor Sage, with equal competence, takes up the story from the era of Confederation. Three chapters, those dealing with the San Juan and Alaska boundary disputes and with the Fur Seals Arbitration, have a joint authorship; the original material was written by Judge Howay and the additions that take account of recent research were made by Professor Angus. Professor Angus has also welded these narratives together so as to bring out interpretative themes and establish uniformity in scale, and has written both the chapter on lumber and fish and the illuminating section which covers the period from 1912 to the present—"The Age of the Good Neighbours."

Thus, while the book reaches beyond the boundaries of the province to deal with the problems of northwestern America as a whole, its essential subject is British Columbian history. No better statement of its purpose and scope could be made than that which Professor Angus himself has expressed in the following words:

It is now a century and a half since white men first attempted to exploit the natural resources of what is now British Columbia. From the outset their techniques have been vastly superior to those of the Indians, but it is only in recent years that these techniques promise thoroughly to master the almost intractable difficulties of transportation. In this volume we have passed in review the progress of oceanic navigation from the days of the maritime fur trade, when British Columbia was first linked with the economic life of Europe and of China, to the age of steam and later to the opening of the Panama Canal. We have seen how the journeys by canoe and portage of the overland fur trade were superseded, in the days of the gold rush, by the first road age and, from the entry of the province into Confederation, by the epoch of railway building. But the full potentialities of the region have had to await not only the second road age, which followed by two decades the development of the automobile and which is still in progress, but the establishment of aerial transportation. The modern traveller, who has the good fortune to fly from Vancouver to Lethbridge on a clear summer evening, can take in at a glance this phase of economic history. Below him the famous sea of mountains continually baffles the highway engineer, distorting the lines of roads and railways and confining them to routes from west to east almost as tortuous as those followed by the overland fur traders; while cultivation seems to cling to the shores of lakes and rivers. It is true that the pleasure-loving motorist may welcome the deviations of the highway which enable him to prolong his holiday in a region of great natural beauty and that he may long for the day when the second road age shall open for him a path to Alaska. But in a work-a-day world, where time is money, the traveller by air is relieved to find himself, within two hours of leaving Vancouver, crossing the rugged crests of the Rocky Mountains. The lingering sunlight is reflected from the tawny clouds which frame the horizon and, shining through some gap in the mountain barrier, it still lights the upland plains of Alberta, where the roads run as straight as if they had been built by the Romans and where the fields are cultivated in strips as straight as the roads. It will be another hour before the sun sets over the ocean, beyond the province which has chosen the setting sun for its emblem, but for its device the words *Splendor sine occasu*.

Professor Sage wishes to thank the following research assistants: Mr. K. A. Waites on Annexation and Confederation; Miss H. Boutilier on Railways; Miss I. Bescoby on Mining; and Dr. Donald Davidson, general research. Dr. W. K. Lamb was of great help in obtaining material on the Klondike. Professor Chester Martin made many valuable suggestions.

Professor Angus wishes to thank Judge Howay and Professor Sage for their generous co-operation. To Dr. Hunter Miller he is deeply indebted for access to his unpublished manuscript on the San Juan boundary dispute. Several colleagues at the University of British Columbia: W. K. Lamb, G. G. Sedgwick, F. H. Soward, W. A. Clemens, J. M. Turnbull, and H. V. Warren have supplied constructive criticism. The maps were prepared by Mr. John Philip of the American Geographical Society, who has followed its spelling of place names. In assuming responsibility for the pattern of the book, he asks the reader to remember that since its aim was to contribute to the understanding of Canadian-American relations, space was freely accorded to those parts of the story which seemed to throw most light on this topic, while other parts were sharply abridged.

JAMES T. SHOTWELL

ANALYTICAL TABLE OF CONTENTS

BRITISH COLUMBIA AND THE UNITED STATES

CHAPTER I

ANGLO-AMERICAN COMPETITION IN THE MARITIME FUR TRADE

1785–1825

BRITISH-AMERICAN relations on the west coast of North America began with the maritime fur trade. Like the trade with China, to which it was ancillary, the maritime fur trade was a phase of the keen competition which developed between the two great sea-faring peoples soon after the establishment of the independence of the American colonies. In this trade the British laboured under handicaps which, in the end, proved decisive. During the period 1789–1815 there was almost constant warfare in Europe and in the last years of this period Britain was at war with the United States. Throughout the whole course of the maritime fur trade British traders were either controlled by one of two great trading monopolies, the South Sea Company and the East India Company, or were driven to subterfuges to evade this control. The first of these companies was in the final stages of decadence, the second was dominated by its trading interests in the Orient.

In the Orient itself the disadvantages suffered by the East India Company, partly through its obligation to export British manufactures to countries where there was not an eager market for them, partly through its inability to engage directly in the opium trade,[1] were offset by its power to bargain collectively with foreign governments and by its access to the British government. On the China coast these advantages were important because individual American traders had to rely on their own resources and had little influence with Congress;[2] but they meant nothing on the west coast of North America where the superior resourcefulness of the Americans and their natural aptitudes for trading had full scope.

1. C. P. Fitzgerald, *China: A Short Cultural History* (London, 1935), 555. Ships on Indian registry were by a fiction not considered British.

2. *Ibid.*

1

The maritime fur trade owed its origin to the third voyage of the great Captain James Cook. In 1776 this famous navigator undertook an expedition in search of the Northwest Passage. Early in 1778 he left the Sandwich (Hawaiian) Islands, which he had just discovered; on March 7 he sighted the coast of northwest America, and three weeks later he discovered Nootka Sound. He remained there nearly a month refitting his ships. For mirrors, beads, buttons, and trinkets his crew obtained from the natives many skins of bear, wolf, fox, deer, "and in particular of the sea-otters which are found at the islands east of Kamchatka."[3] After leaving Nootka he did not see land until he was in the vicinity of Sitka. Coasting along, he reached Prince William's Sound, Alaska, where more skins were obtained in exchange for beads: "They readily gave whatever they had in exchange for them [beads]; even their fine sea-otter skins."[4]

On the homeward voyage the ships visited Kamchatka where they glimpsed the value of the skins so casually procured. At Canton they learned their real value. Some prime skins brought $120 each; Captain King sold twenty sea-otter skins for $800; and the whole amount realized probably did not fall short of £2,000 sterling. The crew, intoxicated with this success, were on the verge of mutiny in their desire to return to the Northwest Coast to make their fortunes in the barter for peltry. The possibilities of such a trade so impressed Captain King that he drew up a detailed plan for its prosecution.[5]

The first to take advantage of Captain Cook's discovery were British adventurers from China and India, who seem at the outset to have been connected with the East India Company. But the monopolies of that company and the South Sea Company stood in the way of British effort.[6] Of the latter company Portlock says: "Without carrying on any traffic themselves, [they] stand in the way of more adventurous merchants." He adds, in praise of his employers: "This enterprise of the King George's Sound Company alone evinces what English co-partnership and English capital

3. James Cook and James King, *A Voyage to the Pacific Ocean . . . in the Years 1776, . . . 1780* (London, 1784), II, 270.
4. *Ibid.*, 357 f.
5. *Ibid.*, III, 431, 437, 438 f.
6. Lewis Melville, *The South Sea Bubble* (London, 1921), 3.

could undertake and execute were they less opposed by prejudice and restrained by monopoly."[7] British traders were compelled to obtain licences from the monopoly-holding companies. Charles Bishop in his manuscript journal states the terms on which the *Ruby* obtained her licence from the East India Company. They were these:

That the business of our voyage shall in no instance interfere to the prejudice of their trade.

That on the ship's arrival at Canton or any other place within the Empire of China, we are to obey all orders and instructions we may receive from the East India Company's supercargo or agents with respect to our behaviour to the natives.

That we must give a faithful manifest of our cargo before we attempt to dispose of it, to the supercargo; any stores, provisions, etc., not contained in the manifest to be liable to seizure.

We are not to obstruct their searching the ship when they please; none of the crew are to be left behind without permission of the supercargo.

We are not permitted to sell anything but the produce of the North-west Coast of America.

All gold or silver we receive from the natives is to be paid into the Company's treasury taking their bills at the usual rate of exchange.

We must not go to the southward and westward of Canton nor to the westward of New Holland.

We are not to ship any goods or merchandise without the express licence of the supercargo.

We are answerable, for any ill-behaviour towards the natives, to the super-cargo and must submit to his decision.

We must return direct to Great Britain at the expiration of the licence.

We must within fourteen days after our return to England deliver to the East India Company the original log book and journal of the voyage, which are not to be made public without our permission except to Government.

For the true and faithful performance of these we give bond of £25,000.[8]

The licence of the South Sea Company merely gave permission to fish or trade in the South Sea area. Few vessels troubled to obtain

7. Nathaniel Portlock, *A Voyage round the World . . . in 1785 . . .* (London, 1789), 4 f.

8. Charles Bishop, "Commercial Journal of the Ship *Ruby*, 1794-6," MS in the Archives of British Columbia, 5 f.

it.[9] It appears that some of the English traders took licences from both companies; others only obtained a licence from the East India Company and ran the chance of seizure by the South Sea Company; others had no licences at all.[10] A number of British vessels strove to evade the two monopolies by using the flags of other nations.

It will thus be apparent that these monopolies placed a great obstacle in the way of the British; but, besides the paternal oversight of their operations, the East India Company consistently refused permission to British vessels to buy teas and Oriental goods. Sir Alexander Mackenzie had chivalrously professed to believe that such permission would be granted by the "John Company," as the East India Company was called, to any unified British concern engaged in the American fur trade;[11] but the North West Company found the monopolists adamant in their refusal to abandon the least part of their exclusive privileges. After unsuccessful ventures in 1814, 1815, and 1816, the "Nor'Westers" realized that the only course was to conceal their trade under a foreign flag. For this purpose they made an arrangement with a Boston firm, that of J. & T. H. Perkins. The trading goods were sent from England to Boston; there they were placed in American bottoms and carried to the Columbia River. After discharging them, the ship loaded the company's furs and, arriving at Canton, disposed of them through the Perkins agents. The proceeds, in the form of teas, silks, and other Oriental goods, were taken back to Boston by the Perkins ships. The American firm retained a certain proportion of the net proceeds as payment for its services.[12] This exclusive attitude of the "John Company" was an important factor in the failure of the British to maintain control of the trade which they had inaugurated. The great profit lay in the final step:

9. *The Life and Adventures of John Nicol, Mariner* (London, 1822), 89.

10. John Meares, *Memorial*, dated April 30, 1790, in the Appendix to *Voyages Made in the Years 1788 and 1789* . . . by John Meares (London, 1790); James Colnett, MS journal (copy in library of F. W. Howay); "A New Vancouver Journal," *Washington Historical Quarterly*, VI, 59.

11. Alexander Mackenzie, *Voyages* . . . *through the Continent of North America* . . . *in the Years 1789 and 1793* (London, 1801), 412.

12. *Certain Correspondence of the Foreign Office and of the Hudson's Bay Company* (Ottawa, 1899), part II, 10 f.

the importation of Oriental goods. A British vessel was fortunate if she obtained a charter to carry to England a cargo for the East India Company.[13]

Another factor which militated against the success of the British was the article, in the early licences at any rate, requiring the trader to place the sale of his furs in the control of the East India Company and to submit to its supervision and direction in China. Portlock complains that, as a result of this control, his sea-otter skins brought less than $20 apiece while the market price was $80 or $90.[14]

An added factor was the war with France which, breaking out in 1793, continued with scarcely a lull down to 1815. In that life-and-death struggle such demands were made upon the resources and the man-power of Great Britain that little was left for this trade; but during those years the maritime fur trade was in its prime.

Other nations were attracted by it; but the real competitors were the British and the Americans. Massachusetts, whose sterile soil made her look to the fertile waters near and far, led the way in this branch of American foreign trade. Her difficulty had been to find some medium of exchange acceptable in Canton. Silver, the great purchasing agent of the East, was not available to her people for export in quantity. But enterprising Boston merchants, reading Captain Cook's *Third Voyage*, caught a vision of a new medium of exchange—sea-otter skins. Unhampered by ancient monopolies, the trade to the Northwest Coast and China gave promise of rich reward. In October, 1787, these Boston adventurers outfitted two vessels, the *Columbia* and the *Washington*, to make the attempt. When these arrived in Nootka Sound, in September, 1788, the trade had been in existence for three years, and some fifteen British vessels had been engaged in it. In August, 1790, the *Columbia* returned to Boston, the first ship to carry the Stars and Stripes around the world. The public imagination was fired, and a disappointing financial result was properly attributed to inexperience and an inefficient commander. Within three months the *Columbia* was refitted for a new effort, and two other ships left

13. Portlock, *Voyage round the World*, 4; Meares, *Memorial*, 2; Colnett, MS journal; *Oregon Historical Quarterly*, XXX, 205; *Certain Correspondence of the Foreign Office*, part II, 10 f.

14. Portlock, *Voyage round the World*, 382.

Boston to try their prentice hands in the new trade. Thereafter, and for year after year until about 1825, the United States, and especially the city of Boston, continued to send ships to the Northwest Coast as a part of the China trade: in 1799, seven vessels; in 1802, sixteen; in 1806, twelve; in 1811, fourteen; in 1816, eleven; and in 1819, eight.

To the Americans the maritime fur trade was a means to an end; to the British, owing to monopolies, it was an end in itself. After 1793, the British vessels ceased to come from Europe; any that were in the trade—and there were a few irregular sailings for about ten years—came from China. The figures are eloquent. Counting no vessel twice, and taking the period from 1785 to 1815, the hey-day of the trade, in decades, the result is:

	British	American
1785-1794............	25	15
1795-1804............	9	50
1805-1814............	3	40[15]

Of the three ships shown as British in the third of these periods, one may possibly have been a genuine British trading venture. After 1803 the British flag was not seen in the trade for more than a decade. Roquefeuil, in command of a French trading vessel on the coast in 1818, writes: "Hoisted American colors, these being the best known to the savages of the coast."[16]

When the trade passed beyond the beads-and-buttons stage, these American vessels became, in a way, pioneer general stores, carrying a varied assortment of hardware, copper, paint, clothing, cloth, domestic and culinary articles, and arms and ammunition. Much care was required in the selection of the goods, and great diplomacy in the trading. Here the New Englander's natural bent for "swapping" came to his aid and was a factor in his ultimate success. Joseph Ingraham, in 1791, invented iron collars and made them fashionable articles of dress, though the hideous things weighed about seven pounds; with these collars he secured in

15. F. W. Howay, "A List of Trading Vessels in Maritime Fur Trade," *Royal Society of Canada Transactions*, sec. II, for 1930, 1931, 1932, 1933, and 1934, covering the years 1785-1825.

16. Camille de Roquefeuil, *Voyage round the World* (London, 1823), 76; French ed. (Paris, 1823), II, 69.

forty-nine days more than 1,400 prime sea-otter skins, the rate of barter being three skins for one collar.[17] William Sturgis, another Boston captain, exchanged some 5,000 ermine skins, obtained on the Atlantic coast for thirty cents each, for sea-otter skins at the rate of three ermine for one sea-otter—about twenty dollars for ninety cents. Perhaps the best example of the Yankee as a coast trader is to be found in the case of the Boston ship *Jefferson*. That vessel entered her second season, 1794, with her trading goods practically exhausted. At Queen Charlotte Islands her captain found that the Indians had about 800 skins in their possession. Having little to offer them in the way of regular trade, he had the happy thought of turning his worn-out sails into women's garments, and of using the old clothing of his officers and crew, their trunks and boxes, seal oil, the ship's crockery, carpets, deep sea lines, old ropes, rigging, and anchors as means of barter. In fact, anything upon the ship for which the Indians expressed a fancy and which was not essential to her safety was exchanged for the coveted skins. Even the long boat went for thirty-five skins, worth, say, $700. As a result, the *Jefferson* obtained 300 of the 800 skins; and this in competition with the barque *Phoenix*, a well-found British trader of Bengal. The *Jefferson* had as tender the schooner *Resolution;* the Indians wished to purchase the small, swift-sailing craft, and the captain agreed that it should be theirs for fifty sea-otter skins.[18] To find suitable trade goods American vessels resorted to the Columbia River for tanned elk skins, the "armour" of the coast; they bartered for oolachan grease (the oil of a small fish) and exchanged it for skins with tribes that esteemed it a delicacy; and they trafficked in slaves with the natives.[19]

The Americans followed the British example in combining sealing

17. F. W. Howay, "The Voyage of the *Hope*," *Washington Historical Quarterly*, XI, 16 f.

18. F. W. Howay, "A Yankee Trader on the Northwest Coast," *Washington Historical Quarterly*, XXI, 83 ff.; Bernard Magee, "Log of the *Jefferson*," MS in the Massachusetts Historical Society, Boston.

19. Stephen Reynolds, *The Voyage of the New Hazard . . . 1810-1813*, ed. F. W. Howay (Salem, Mass., 1938). See Diamond Jenness, *The Indians of Canada* (Ottawa, 1932), 140-1, 373, 374. In the long run the fur trade destroyed slavery along with other social distinctions among the Indians of British Columbia, by making wealth accessible to all who could bring in furs for trade (*ibid.*, 257 f.).

with the fur trade. William Brown, the master of the *Butterworth* of London, had left a sealing party on Staten Island when outward bound in 1792, to be picked up on the homeward voyage. He was only following the precedent set by James Colnett, in 1786, in the London ship *Prince of Wales*.[20] The islands of Juan Fernandez, Masafuera, St. Felix, St. Ambrose, and the Galapagos lay close to the course taken by vessels bound to the Northwest Coast; from 1792 for ten years and more they were frequented by American maritime traders seeking to make a "safe" voyage by adding 10,000 or 15,000 seal-skins to their cargo for China. A delay of only a few weeks was necessary. In two months the *Jefferson* collected 13,000 at St. Ambrose; and the seal-skins, though selling in China for only fifty cents or a dollar each, made a respectable sum in the aggregate.[21]

The American traders did not overlook the possibilities of smuggling and illicit sales along the coast from Valparaiso to San Francisco, as soon as sea-otter became scarce in the lawful hunting grounds. Under the stale pretence of distress from the perils of the sea, their vessels entered the harbours of Spanish America and carried on a surreptitious trade.[22] They went further and openly defied the Spanish authorities. The *Dromo* in 1808, with the intention of forcing "a trade in the Spanish ports of the western continent then declared illegal except for Spanish vessels," carried twenty-six guns and a crew of a hundred men, for the purpose of overaweing or fighting it out with the Spanish *guardas costas*. On one occasion while illegally trading on the Chilean coast, she had an encounter with them in which two of her crew were killed and others injured.[23] In 1822, the schooner *Eagle* of Boston made a contract with the owners of the brig *Cossack* (which had been confiscated in 1818 for smuggling), whereby she undertook to

20. George Vancouver, *A Voyage of Discovery . . . in the Years 1790 . . . 1795 . . .* (London, 1801), V, 354; Colnett, MS journal.

21. Magee, "Log of the *Jefferson*"; Benjamin Morrell, *A Narrative of Four Voyages . . .* (New York, 1832), 130 f.

22. R. J. Cleveland, *In the Forecastle*, and *Voyages and Commercial Enterprises of the Sons of New England* (New York, 1855), 154 f., 196 f., 182. The two books appear to have been printed from the same plates.

23. George Little, *Life on the Ocean* (Boston, 1845), an account of the *Dromo*'s voyage by one of the crew.

recapture the brig and deliver her to her original owners. The high-handed act was carried through successfully.[24]

The *O'Cain* in 1803 opened up a new line of attack. Her commander, Joseph Burling O'Cain, contracted with the Russians in Alaska for the services of Aleuts who, transported to the Californian coast, hunted the sea-otter on shares. From 1803 to 1812, by means of this unholy alliance, the Americans carried on a continuous poaching in Californian waters.[25]

The Americans early made changes in the methods of trading. The British vessels, when the voyage occupied more than one season, had invariably wintered at the Hawaiian Islands. The *Columbia* and *Washington*, the first Boston traders, broke away from this custom; they spent the winter of 1788-9 in Nootka Sound. The *Columbia* on her second voyage remained during the winter of 1791-2 at Clayoquot Sound. The Americans resorted to the Hawaiian Islands for supplies; but those "summer isles of Eden" were never to them a mere wintering place. As the trade developed the American vessels ceased to go into winter quarters, and introduced the plan of trading steadily and flitting from village to village throughout their stay on the coast.[26]

British and American traders had both thought of making settlements. John Meares claimed that when his venture of 1789 was broken up by Spain he had on the *Argonaut* seventy Chinese artisans to form the nucleus of a settlement at Nootka Sound. The Spanish census of the prisoners shows only twenty-nine Chinese; but apart from this little discrepancy it may be doubted whether Meares' plans went beyond a mere temporary occupancy ancillary to the fur trade.[27] Portlock and Dixon, in 1785, carried instructions to establish factories for trade, and in that connection Nootka Sound was named. William Brown of the *Butterworth*, in 1793-4, had similar instructions; but in neither instance was any

24. S. E. Morison, "Boston Traders in Hawaiian Islands," *Washington Historical Quarterly*, XII, 196 f.

25. Adele Ogden, "Russian Sea-otter and Seal Hunting on the Californian Coast," in *The Russians in California* (San Francisco, 1933), 29.

26. F. W. Howay, "An Outline Sketch of the Maritime Fur Trade," *Annual Report of Canadian Historical Association* (Ottawa, 1932), 10.

27. Archives General of the Indies, Seville, Spain, Est. 90, Caj. 3, Leg. 18. Copy in library of F. W. Howay.

effort made to obey them.[28] Many of the Americans, as their manuscript journals show, also dreamed of settlements. For instance, John Boit, when at Masset Harbour, Queen Charlotte Islands, in 1791, speaks of it as a place "well calculated for a factory."[29] In 1809, the ship *Albatross* left Boston on a trading voyage with the additional purpose of planting a settlement at the mouth of the Columbia River. She carried all things necessary for clearing and planting the land and building the houses. At the Hawaiian Islands domestic animals and labourers were obtained. But owing to the hostility of the Indians the effort, after two attempts, was abandoned. Thus, two years before the Astoria venture, the Americans had taken steps to build a permanent trading settlement on the Columbia.[30]

As early as 1790 John Kendrick of the Boston vessel *Washington* and William Douglas of the British schooner *Grace* planned to establish a trade in sandalwood between the Hawaiian Islands and China and to unite it to the maritime fur trade. Though they each left sailors at "the islands" to collect this fragrant wood, their efforts ended in failure. It was not until about 1810 that sandalwood became an adjunct of the maritime trade. This phase of the trade grew in importance and lasted for more than ten years. It gave the traders a chance to barter merchandise and even ships to Kamehameha the Great and his successors. In the years 1815 to 1819 one British and six American vessels were so exchanged.

In their treatment of the Indians the maritime traders, whether British or American, acted in exactly the same manner. If a native stole or attempted to steal anything out of the ship, her guns were turned upon him or in his direction, and innocent and guilty alike felt the strength of the white man's weapons. Such was the conduct of Dixon in 1786 and of Meares in 1788, as well as that of Robert Gray in 1792, when in revenge for various thefts he destroyed the village of Opitsat.[31] John Kendrick in 1789 at Queen Charlotte

---

28. F. W. Howay, *The Dixon-Meares Controversy* (Toronto, 1929), 61 f., 117.

29. John Boit, "Log of the *Columbia*," *Oregon Historical Quarterly*, XXII, 287.

30. "Solid Men of Boston," MS in Bancroft Library, Berkeley, California; condensed account in H. H. Bancroft, *History of the Northwest Coast* (San Francisco, 1884), II, 130 ff.

31. Howay, "An Outline Sketch, . . ."; Boit, "Log of the *Columbia*," 303; Colnett, MS journal.

Islands tied some chiefs before his guns and threatened to blow them to pieces unless they ordered their people to bring him all their skins for trade. If the Indians refused to trade, the trader did not hesitate to use force. Such is the charge made by Joseph Ingraham of the Boston brig *Hope* against the British ship *Butterworth*. A similar charge is recorded by the Spaniards in 1792 against Captain Gray of the *Columbia*;[32] and Ingraham himself admits using force to compel the natives at Naden Harbour, Queen Charlotte Islands, to trade with him.

There was not only more initiative on the part of the Americans in the trading but also greater resourcefulness in overcoming difficult situations on the distant coast. In 1792 the ship *Columbia* struck a rock somewhere eastward of Cape St. James. The injury caused her to leak "one thousand smart strokes per hour." But Captain Gray continued his cruise to the northward and kept the leak under control by fothering it with a topsail. Ten days after the accident the ship reached Columbia's Cove. Finding the damage more serious than he could repair there, he proceeded to Nootka Sound. It being impossible to heave the *Columbia* down owing to her leaky upper works, Captain Gray laid her ashore on blocks. So quickly and efficiently was the work done that Don Quadra, the Spanish *Commandante*, "observed that he believed we could build a ship in a month."[33] Again, when in February, 1812, the American brig *New Hazard* struck upon a rocky islet in Clarence Strait, and was so damaged that she had five and a half feet of water in the hold, and "the water coming in as fast as we could clear it," yet by Herculean efforts the crew managed to keep the wrecked vessel afloat. A suitable place to effect repairs was found; the pumps were steadily kept going; the cargo was unloaded and everything of weight removed. In six days the brig was ready to lay on shore. In rain and sleet and snow the work went on, and so satisfactorily that three days later two hands had no difficulty in keeping her free of water. Sixteen sheets of copper were put on

32. Joseph Ingraham, MS "Journal of the *Hope*," in Library of Congress, December 25, 1791, and August 7, 1791; *Le viage hecho por las goletas Sutil y Mexicana* (Madrid, 1802), 24, and English translation (London, 1930), 22. See also H. R. Wagner, *Spanish Explorations in the Strait of Juan de Fuca* (Santa Ana, California, 1933), 229-30.

33. Boit, "Log of the *Columbia*," 319 f., 325, 326.

the hull and temporary repairs effected so that six or seven hundred strokes in twenty-four hours kept the leak under control. As no more could be accomplished, the cargo and other materials were taken aboard; the brig was back in the trade within a month after the accident; and so the leaky brig continued her work and successfully completed her voyage.[34]

In January, 1796, an accident occurred to the British ship *Ruby* which affords a marked contrast. This vessel had spent the season of 1795 on the coast and wintered in the Columbia River. She sailed thence in January, 1796, for the Hawaiian Islands to obtain provisions and extra men to enable her to continue her trade. The sea being exceedingly rough, the *Ruby* evidently pitched and strained in crossing the bar. The ship began to leak and when she reached Oahu was making from nineteen to twenty-two inches an hour. In order to heave her down, her captain tried to find H.M.S. *Providence*, which was then among "the islands" on her way to the coast. Unfortunately the *Ruby* was always behind the *Providence*, and finally ascertained that the man-of-war had sailed for Nootka. Instead of following her to the coast and continuing the season's trade, Captain Bishop sailed the *Ruby* to China. The voyage there occupied about six weeks; that to Nootka would have taken only three weeks; it seems strange that the longer was chosen. An American master would not have made such a choice. On the coast there were seven trading vessels at least besides the *Providence*, with many opportunities of obtaining assistance, and suitable coves in which to heave down. The result of this unwise action was to transform into a complete loss a voyage that should have yielded a profit. The first season's trade had resulted in furs worth in China about $20,000, which had cost in barter goods the invoice value of £658 12s. 4d. There was no reason to anticipate that the year 1796 would not be equally profitable.[35]

The maritime fur trade did not lead to a permanent settlement of the coast although it did promote thorough exploration. Forming settlements was talked of but not attempted. The trade was of a predatory character and at best constituted unequal trade with a primitive people. It did not develop the economy of the Indians by building up new and permanent sources of wealth. Indeed, it

34. Reynolds, *Voyage of the New Hazard*, February 10 to March 9, 1812.
35. Bishop, MS "Commercial Journal of the Ship *Ruby*," April 22, 1796.

was so destructive that it depleted the very basis on which it rested by practically exterminating the sea-otter;[36] while it seriously dislocated the finely balanced economic and social fabric of the Indians.[37] Governments had not yet realized that unequal trade should be regulated in the interests of humanity, or that they should intervene to enforce conservation.[38] Neither traders nor governments should be judged by the standards of today. Even the precarious control which might have been provided through the regulation of the trade by a far-sighted monopolistic company was absent. The importance of the maritime trade for later history of the Northwest Coast is that it led to efforts to establish overland trade which, in turn, led to settlement.

36. From 1826 to 1852 inclusive only 490 large skins, 150 pups, and one tail were traded at Fort Vancouver, Hudson's Bay Company's headquarters on the Columbia River. The greatest number of large skins traded in any one year was 55. See V. B. Scheffer, "The Sea Otter on the Washington Coast," *Pacific Northwest Quarterly*, XXXI, 375 f.

37. See Jenness, *Indians of Canada*, 261.

38. International co-operation in the interests of conservation came much later and it was not until 1911 that the hunting of the sea-otter was prohibited by international treaty. See Scheffer, "Sea Otter on the Washington Coast."

CHAPTER II

ANGLO-AMERICAN CONTACTS IN OVERLAND EXPLORATION AND IN THE OVERLAND FUR TRADE

1793-1818

ANGLO-AMERICAN contacts on land west of the Rocky Mountains will form the subject of this and the following chapters. They begin with exploration, which is not really competitive although the British explorations were undertaken by trading companies for the promotion of trade, and the government of the United States financed the expedition of Lewis and Clark. In the period before missionary effort and settlement began, conditions in the fur trade favoured large companies which had large resources at their disposal and could provide both experienced personnel and continuity of policy; for, even in its early stages, overland trading differs greatly from maritime trading which was essentially transitory in character and amounted to little more than a looting of the coast. For the purposes of overland trade, trading posts are established, permanent garrisons are maintained, settlement is always an eventual possibility, and it is recognized that some day there will be a boundary agreement assigning territorial sovereignty. Routes of access, whether by canoe, or pack, or waggon are of the utmost importance and must be kept fit for use. Relations with the Indians must be put on a permanent basis. It is of importance to all overland traders that none should sell arms or liquor to the Indians; and there has been a gradual improvement in this respect. Traders whose life is spent among the Indians come to know them well and indeed may intermarry with them. The problem of the half-breed arises. Sooner or later there will be missionary effort among the Indians, and sooner or later governments will recognize that the Indians have rights which must be respected. Depletion of natural resources may result from greed, or from reckless competition, and it may even on occasion be a deliberate policy, but normally there is some concern for the future of the trade. The cruder phase of predatory trading is recognized as temporary; but responsible trading companies do not expect to wind up their affairs when the economy develops.

This change in economic outlook is accompanied by some change in moral standards, though not by the apparent transformation of them which characterizes established economies in friendly competition with each other. Permanent traders have some elementary standards of decency in their dealings with competitors, analogous perhaps to the soldier's ideas of chivalry in war. They differ in this respect from the missionaries who may take their theological difficulties very seriously, and who may allow a belief in the guiding hand of Providence to destroy the obligation of gratitude which they might be expected to feel to the human agents whom Providence has employed. Permanent traders differ also from the pioneer settler whose sense of right and wrong is apt to be dominated by his land-hunger rather than by his theology.

Across these trade rivalries in no man's land fell the shadow of the War of 1812-14. In the preceding century it had sometimes happened that war began in trading outposts before it received official sanction from home governments. But, though the War of 1812 was in some respects a fur traders' war,[1] its immediate occasion lay in American protests against the British attitude towards neutrals on the high seas. West of the Rockies the incidents which occurred must have been almost unique in warfare. We find an American trading post with a British personnel, in the last stages of commercial failure, supplying its British rivals with food and then coercing them at the point of the cannon into concluding a bargain for the purchase of the whole concern before the arrival of British naval forces. Nor did the outcome of the war affect trading interests substantially. The territorial settlement was based on the restitution of conquests,[2] and in 1818 an agreement was made defining the status of the fur-trading territories in the West.[3] The boundary settlement which ultimately ensued will be described in a later chapter.

The French were the pioneers of the fur trade in America. Two renegade French adventurers brought its great possibilities to the attention of wealthy and aristocratic people in England. As a result "The Governor and Company of Adventurers of England trading into Hudson's Bay"—the Hudson's Bay Company, as it is

1. See D. G. Creighton, *The Commercial Empire of the St. Lawrence, 1760-1850* (Toronto, 1937), 175 ff.

2. *Ibid.*, 181.

3. *Ibid.*, 182.

usually called—was, in 1670, incorporated by Royal Charter. By that document it was granted the "Lordship" and the whole trade of the region that drained into Hudson Bay. A glance at the map will show how vast was this domain. Southward it extended to the height of land separating the rivers running into the Great Lakes from those flowing into Hudson Bay, and to the divide between those draining into Lake Winnipeg and those flowing into the Mississippi. Westward it reached to the Rocky Mountains, and northward to the head-waters of the Churchill.

The French, reaching out from the St. Lawrence, for many years drew the trade only from the southern side of the divide. Between 1732 and 1753 La Vérendrye and his successors built a chain of forts from Lake Superior to the Saskatchewan to intercept the trade flowing to Hudson Bay; but the effect of this opposition was scarcely felt by the Chartered Company. As the struggle in America between England and France became keener, these western trading posts were gradually abandoned. After Canada was ceded to Great Britain in 1763 the fur trade from Montreal was resumed. The British traders of that city from about 1765 made their way westward, following the old French routes. By 1768 James Finlay had reached the Saskatchewan. Others quickly followed.[4] The struggle, at the outset, was between the Hudson's Bay Company and individual traders. But in 1783-4 the majority of the Montrealers united in a partnership under the name of the North West Company. They refused to recognize the validity of their opponent's charter, and boldly and defiantly built trading posts and carried on trade in disregard of the Company's paper rights. It was a case of might *vs.* right.

Nevertheless the North West Company sought other parts of the unknown West where rivers might be found that did not flow into Hudson Bay. From the early French days vague stories had been told of a "Western Sea" and a westward-flowing river. In 1788 Alexander Mackenzie, one of the partners of the North West Company, set out to find the elusive "River of the West." A theory then existed that the water known as Cook Inlet was a river flowing out of Great Slave Lake. Such a river would offer a trading territory beyond the limits of the Hudson's Bay Company's

4. W. S. Wallace, "The Pedlars from Quebec," *Canadian Historical Review*, XIII, 387 ff.

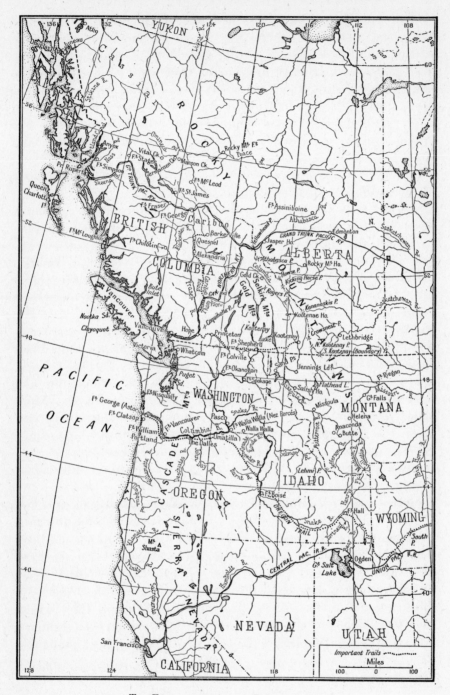

THE EXPLORATION OF THE PACIFIC SLOPE

charter. In June, 1789, Mackenzie, with his party of twelve men, began his search. He found the mysterious river, but instead of leading him to the Pacific it brought him to the Arctic Ocean. Though his first attempt had failed, Mackenzie, in 1792, made a second effort to find the "River of the West." He ascended the Peace River, wintered on its banks, and resumed his exploration in May, 1793. Arriving at the head-waters of the Peace, he crossed a low divide, and came upon the "Great River," now known as the Fraser. Descending that river, he turned westward up the Black-water, and reached the Pacific in July, 1793, the first crossing of the continent, north of Mexico.

Twelve years elapsed before the North West Company took any steps towards possessing the land which Mackenzie's intrepidity had laid open to them. But during that time they had slowly extended their trade westward. In 1798 and 1799 they had established Rocky Mountain Fort on the Peace River, some forty-five miles below the present Hudson's Hope.[5] In 1805 they instructed Simon Fraser, one of the partners who had been on the fur-trade frontier on Peace River since 1800 at least, to open new posts on its upper reaches and in the lands beyond. Late in the autumn of 1805 he founded Fort McLeod on its head-waters, the first trading post west of the Rocky Mountains. In 1806 and 1807 he and his lieutenant, John Stuart, established Fort St. James on Stuart Lake, Fort Fraser on Fraser Lake, and Fort George on Fraser River, the first posts on westward-flowing water.

The question of transportation to and from Montreal was becoming more acute with every mile of western advance. Mackenzie's exploration had shown the comparatively short distance from the Rockies to the Pacific; the Nor'Westers, believing as he did that his "Great River" was the Columbia, determined to ascertain its feasibility as a route to the Pacific. Under their instructions Fraser, in May, 1808, accompanied by Stuart and a party of twenty-two men, left Fort George to follow the river to the sea. It was freshet season and the Fraser was boiling angrily ocean-ward. After some days the attempt to proceed by water was abandoned, and the explorers took to the Indian trails along its banks. At

5. J. N. Wallace, *The Wintering Partners on Peace River* (Ottawa, 1929), 35 f.; Marion O'Neil, "The Peace River Journal, 1799-1800," *Washington Historical Quarterly*, XIX, 250 ff.

Yale the natives informed them that the river was navigable thence to the sea. Obtaining canoes, Fraser reached the mouth on July 3, 1808. There an observation showed the latitude to be about 49°. "The river, therefore," says Fraser in his journal, "is not the Columbia! If I had been convinced of this when I left my canoes I would certainly have returned."[6] The voyage showed that the Fraser River was not a feasible route for transport of goods and furs into and out of the interior.

It is sometimes suggested that this activity of the Montreal traders resulted from their knowledge of the departure of Lewis and Clark in 1804. This is improbable and there is nothing to support such a supposition but the coincidence in dates. The fact seems to be that the fusion with the XY Company—a group of traders who had seceded from the North West Company—in 1804 freed the Nor'Westers from a bitter opposition and afforded the desired opportunity to extend across the Rocky Mountains by pressing westward along the Peace and Saskatchewan, on whose upper reaches they had rested for six or seven years. There was no incitement to action in the despatch of an American government expedition, ostensibly scientific; for, so far as the world knew, President Jefferson's sole aim was the advancement of science.

We now know that Jefferson had secret springs of conduct. As early as December, 1783, he had become suspicious of the purpose of British western exploration. "They pretend," he wrote, "that it is only to promote knowledge. I am afraid they have thoughts of colonizing into that quarter." And he inquired about the prospects of raising an American expedition "to search that country."

In January, 1803, Jefferson sent a secret message to Congress in which he linked the possibility of ameliorating the condition of the Indians east of the Mississippi by ending private fur trade among them and introducing agriculture, with the opening of a route for the fur trader up the Missouri. The object of the Lewis and Clark expedition, as stated by Jefferson in June, 1803, was to explore the Missouri and its principal tributaries and discover the most direct and practicable water communication across the continent for the purpose of commerce. His purpose, so far as the public knew, was to avoid by land transport the long and dangerous voyage to and

6. L. R. Masson, *Les Bourgeois de la Compagnie du Nord-Ouest* (Quebec, 1889), I, 205.

from the Northwest Coast.[7] Louisiana then being French, and Spain
having some shadowy claims north of San Francisco, secrecy was
necessary regarding the course and object of the expedition. It was,
according to the article referred to, neither "before or after the
[Louisiana] purchase designed as a scientific exploring expedition,
but rather . . . it was an undertaking to develop the fur trade
along the Missouri in foreign territory." Nevertheless, seeing that
twenty years before Jefferson had visualized possible British
colonization in the Far West, it may well be that such a far-sighted
statesman entertained more than a vague thought of the possible
claims that might find a support in the work of the expedition.

The treaty for the purchase was made with France on May 2,
1803, and, before it was known in America, Lewis and Clark with
the nucleus of the party had left Philadelphia. The news reached
Washington on July 14, and on the next day President Jefferson
sent the information on to them. The treaty passed the Senate in
October, 1803. It was not until March, 1804, that the people of
St. Louis became aware of the change of national ownership.

After the arrival of Lewis and Clark at the Mississippi, the party
was completed. Besides twenty soldiers who had journeyed with
them it now included twenty *voyageurs* and hunters. On May 14,
1804, the expedition left their establishment near the mouth of the
Missouri, in a large keel boat and two small craft. So slow and
laborious was the passage up that river and so many were the
delays in meeting and pacifying the natives—to whom a party of
white men who had not come for trade was so unusual as to excite
their too easily aroused suspicions—that by October, 1804, they
had only reached the Mandan villages near what is now Bismark,
North Dakota. A fort—Fort Mandan—was built and the party
went into winter quarters. There they met Nor'Westers, under
François Larocque, who had come from Fort Assiniboine to trade
en derouine[8] with the Mandans and Assiniboines. Charbonneau,

7. R. B. Guinness, "The Purpose of the Lewis and Clark Expedition," *Mississippi Valley Historical Review*, XX, 90 ff.; instructions from President Jefferson
to Meriwether Lewis, June 20, 1803, in R. G. Thwaites, *Original Journals of the
Lewis and Clark Expedition* (New York, 1905), VII, 248.

8. In the Canadian West, this phrase came to mean the type of trading in
which the trader was outfitted at a trading post and carried his wares to the Indians,
instead of waiting for them to come to the post. See *Glossaire du parler français au
Canada* (Quebec, 1930).

a Canadian, the interpreter for Lewis and Clark, was allowed to
assist the Nor'Westers in their trade; but, says Larocque in his
journal, he was "strictly enjoined not to utter a word to the Indians
which might in any way be to the prejudice of the United States,
or any of its citizens, although I should order him to do so, 'which,'
said they, turning to me, 'we are far from thinking you would'."
The relations between the two parties were amicable and intimate.
"On all occasions [they] seemed happy to see us, and always
treated us with civility and kindness." Lewis and Clark claimed
that the northern boundary of Louisiana extended to the Assiniboine River and, while distributing flags and medals, forbade
Larocque in the name of the United States to give such tokens to
the Indians, saying that their government looked upon them as
sacred emblems of the attachment of the natives to their country.
Larocque adds that, having no such things, he ran no risk of
disobeying the order.

Charles MacKenzie, who was with Larocque, has also left a journal
which describes the intercourse as being most friendly; he mentions
many small acts of kindness on the part of Lewis and Clark that are
not recorded by them. Of Lewis, MacKenzie says he could speak
fluently and learnedly on all subjects, "but his inveterate dis-
position against the British stained, at least in our eyes, all his
eloquence." Clark, he states, was equally well informed, but his
conversation was always pleasant, for he seemed to dislike giving
offence unnecessarily. He records that the Indians "could not be
reconciled to these 'strangers' as they called them." On one
occasion he addressed them in an effort to explain the purpose of
the expedition; but Lewis and Clark complained that Lafrance,
one of the Nor'Westers, "spoke unfavourably of our intentions,"
and informed Larocque and MacKenzie of the consequences if they
did not put a stop "to the unfavourable and ill founded asser-
tions."[9] Here on the very first contact of British and Americans
on the Missouri are these suggestions of an effort on the part of the
former to arouse hostility in the Indians against the latter.

MacKenzie adds that the efforts of Lewis and Clark to compile
a vocabulary of the Mandan language aroused in those people a

9. François Larocque, "Missouri Journal" and Charles MacKenzie, "Missis-
souri Indians," both in Masson, *Les Bourgeois* . . ., I, 304, 330, 332, 334, 336 f.;
Thwaites, *Original Journals*, I, 227 f.

suspicion that the Americans had a wicked design upon their country. Possibly to have given an explanation might have calmed this childlike fear. That is what the British trader was accustomed to do, and with marked success. On April 7, 1805, the journey was resumed in six canoes and two pirogues, and the party reduced to thirty-one, exclusive of the two leaders. Two thousand miles yet lay between them and the Pacific Ocean. Toiling slowly with sail and oar and tracking line, it was not until May 26 that Lewis caught the first glimpse of the "Shining Mountains." About three weeks later, June 15, they reached Great Falls. Ten days were occupied in the portage at this spot and in building two boats in which they continued the laborious upward effort. July 15 saw them at the Three Forks of the Missouri. With horses obtained from the Snake Indians the explorers crossed the Rocky Mountains, though at times perilously near starvation. Obtaining canoes, they ventured down the Clearwater and the Columbia rivers, portaging where navigation was impossible, until on November 8, 1805, they reached the Pacific. On the south side of the Columbia they erected some seven buildings which they called Fort Clatsop. There they spent the winter of 1805-6 and, retracing their steps in a general way, arrived at St. Louis on September 23, 1806.[10]

As Alexander Mackenzie was the first on the upper Peace River, the first to cross the Rockies, the first on the Fraser, and the first to cross the continent north of Mexico, so Lewis and Clark were the first upon the upper Missouri, the first to cross the middle Rockies, and the first down the Columbia. From the reference in Lewis's journal to "Tacoutche Tesse," it seems plain that the explorers had with them a copy of Mackenzie's *Voyages*, which had been published in 1801.[11]

For some years prior to 1807 the North West Company had been anxious to reach out from the North Saskatchewan across the backbone of the continent. In 1799 they had built Rocky Mountain House, their most advanced post on that river.[12] It may be noted in passing that, though the two branches of the Saskatchewan rise in the Rockies, the advance to the West was along the North

10. Thwaites, *Original Journals*.
11. *Ibid.*, III, 60.
12. This post must not be confused with Rocky Mountain Fort, which was built about the same time on the Peace River.

Saskatchewan. A number of reasons, economic and social, operated to this end. A short portage from the Churchill waters led to the North Saskatchewan; similarly, a comparatively short portage from the Athabaska gave access to the North Saskatchewan; again, the North Saskatchewan flowed through a rich fur country; and, lastly, the Indians along its course were Cree, usually a friendly people. On the other hand, the South Saskatchewan flowed through the great plains, the buffalo country, where beaver and other furs were not so plentiful, and the Indians who inhabited it were Blackfeet, a warlike and treacherous race.

In 1800 came the first instructions to cross the Rocky Mountains from the head-waters of the North Saskatchewan. The attempt was made in June, 1801, but it was a complete failure. The party, under David Thompson, became entangled in the defiles of the mountains and the expedition was abandoned.[13]

The Piegans, one of the three tribes of the Blackfoot confederacy, kept close watch to prevent the Nor'Westers from crossing the mountains, lest arms and ammunition might be carried to their enemies. But in 1806, as Lewis and Clark were returning, they had an encounter with the Blackfeet in which two Indians were killed. The news travelled by "moccasin telegraph" to the Piegans, who at once set out for the Missouri, bent on retaliation. This afforded the long-awaited opportunity. In May, 1807, Thompson with a small party left Rocky Mountain House to pass the Rockies. Navigating the North Saskatchewan until the canoes could be taken no farther, he took horses, crossed the mountains, and reached the Columbia. There he made canoes and, embarking his outfit, continued up that river to Lake Windermere. About a mile from the lake, in July, 1807, he built Kootenae House, the first trading post in the Columbia watershed. From this centre he carried on his explorations in what are now British Columbia, Montana, Idaho, and Washington. In 1809 he built Kullyspell House and Saleesh House in Montana, and in 1810 Spokane House in Washington.[14]

13. F. W. Howay, "David Thompson's Account of His First Attempt to Cross the Rockies," *Queen's Quarterly*, August, 1933. This shows that, four years before the Lewis and Clark Expedition, the Nor'Westers had planned to cross the Rockies.

14. T. C. Elliott, "The Discovery of the Source of the Columbia River," *Oregon Historical Quarterly*, XXVI, 23 ff.; J. B. Tyrrell, *David Thompson's Narrative* (Toronto, 1916), Introduction.

During each of these years Thompson was here, there, and everywhere, exploring, trading, and, with an observant eye, recording in his voluminous note-books every matter of interest or importance. Over and above all this he each spring travelled from the tramontane country to Rainy Lake House with the proceeds of his winter's trade. His intercourse with the Kootenays brought to them fire-arms and ammunition. The result was soon felt by the Blackfeet, who resolved to cut off any further supplies to their enemies by preventing him from again crossing the mountains.

In consequence, when Thompson was returning in the autumn of 1810 from Rainy Lake with the goods for the next winter's trade, the watchful Piegans intercepted him and forbade him to proceed westward. After unsuccessful efforts to evade their sleepless vigilance, he was compelled to abandon his accustomed route. Reports had been received that a way to, or at any rate towards, the Columbia River existed by the head-waters of the Athabaska. Though "chill November's surly blasts" were at hand, he set out to find it. Crossing from the North Saskatchewan to the Athabaska, he and his party undertook to find a pass through the Rockies in a sub-zero temperature. In January, 1811, they reached the Columbia at the "Boat Encampment"; they had discovered the Athabaska Pass, the route of the British fur trade for nearly half a century. In April, having completed a canoe, Thompson and the remainder of his party, for some had deserted, made their way up the river to Kootenae House and on to Saleesh House. There, by June 5, he completed another canoe of split cedar in which he set out down Clark's Fork. He took horses to Spokane House, and continued his journey to the Columbia at Kettle Falls. There he remained from June 19 till July 3, meeting the Indians, examining the region, building another canoe, and preparing to descend the Columbia to the ocean. With prayers for a safe journey, for he was a devout man, he resumed his undertaking. That day he made ninety miles and encamped. To the Indians he told his purpose: "to open out a passage for the interior trade with the Pacific Ocean." Day by day he descended, making portages here and there, stopping to talk, smoke, and ingratiate himself with the natives. On July 8, for example, after travelling seven miles he came to an Indian village. He spent some hours with the Indians, re-embarked, and proceeded forty miles to another village near Pasco, where he put up for the night. Presents were exchanged mutually, the purpose of the journey explained, and the party entertained with songs and dances. The next day at the junction of the Snake River Thompson erected a pole bearing the following notice:

Know hereby that this country is claimed by Great Britain as part of its territories and that the N.W. Company of Merchants from Canada, finding the Factory for its people inconvenient for them do hereby intend to erect a Factory at this place for the commerce of the country around.

D. THOMPSON.

Later that day he met the chief of the Walla Walla tribe who had, says Thompson, "an American medal of 1801, Thomas Jefferson, and a small flag of that nation." These had been given him by Lewis and Clark on their outward voyage in October, 1805. The next day he learned from the Indians "of the American ship's arrival." Evidently this refers to the *Tonquin*, and shows that he was aware of Astor's plan. Nevertheless he continued the same easy-going gait that has been described, probably because his "object was to be at the Pacific Ocean before the month of August."[15] On July 15, having portaged across Tongue Point, he arrived with his eight *voyageurs*, "portant pavillon," as Franchère says, at "four low Log Huts, the far-famed Fort Astoria."[16]

John Jacob Astor had been connected with the fur trade since 1784. His earliest business was conducted from Montreal. There he met the partners of the North West Company. Indeed, he was in Montreal in September, 1808, and was entertained at the Beaver Club, the exclusive fur traders' club of Montreal. It may be that it was on this occasion he offered the North West Company a one-third interest in his gigantic venture.[17]

Astor's plan for the Pacific Coast trade[18] followed in a general way that outlined by Alexander Mackenzie.[19] A central establish-

15. Tyrrell, *David Thompson's Narrative*, 448.

16. Gabriel Franchère, *Relation d'un voyage* . . . (Montreal, 1820), 91; in the English ed. (New York, 1854), 120; Tyrrell, *David Thompson's Narrative*, 501.

17. L. J. Burpee, "The Beaver Club," *Annual Report of Canadian Historical Association* (Ottawa, 1924), 87; H. M. Chittenden, *The American Fur Trade of the Far West* (New York, 1902), 168; Washington Irving, *Astoria* (London, 1836), I, 51.

18. For Astor's other interests in the fur trade, see Creighton, *Commercial Empire of the St. Lawrence*, 166-7.

19. Alexander Mackenzie, *Voyages* (London, 1801), 410 f.

ment was to be erected at the mouth of the Columbia River, with trading posts scattered through the whole region drained by that river and its tributaries, and with vessels to gather the furs of the coast. The trading supplies were to be sent annually to the central depot, the returns of the trade to be carried to China and exchanged for Oriental goods for the American market—a golden round of profit. To carry out this ambitious plan, he organized the Pacific Fur Company. He was to supply the capital up to $400,000 and to bear all the losses for five years. Its one hundred shares were to be allotted fifty to Astor and the other fifty amongst his partners. At the end of five years if the trade proved unprofitable the partnership might be dissolved.

The North West Company, feeling strong in their own position, had refused Astor's offer. But in looking for the men who would be interested in his company as "winterers" (to employ the usual name) he went among its dissatisfied clerks. As has been pointed out, the North West Company was a partnership in which the clerks could look forward to advancement to membership; but of course they could not be admitted as quickly as they desired, and these delays made some who had waited long very impatient and disappointed.

Alexander McKay and Duncan McDougall left the company to join the new venture. David Stuart and his cousin, Robert Stuart, also Canadians, became partners in the new concern. These four, together with some thirteen Canadian *voyageurs* formerly in the employ of the company, sailed on Astor's vessel, the *Tonquin*, from New York in September, 1810. Members of another party which was to journey overland were also largely recruited in Montreal from among dissatisfied Nor'Westers, and the party was completed at Mackinac. The *Tonquin* arrived at the Columbia in March, 1811. A site was at once selected and the erection of Fort Astoria begun. After landing the party and their supplies at Astoria, the *Tonquin* sailed northward to trade along the coast. She never returned. At Clayoquot Sound, Vancouver Island, she was captured by the Indians and all on board except the interpreter were killed. The survivor reported that after her capture she was destroyed by an explosion of the powder magazine.

The land party, under Wilson P. Hunt and Donald McKenzie,

the latter a disgruntled Nor'Wester, left Mackinac in August, 1810, and arrived at St. Louis in the following September. Deciding not to remain there, the party pressed forward and on November 16 fixed their winter quarters near St. Joseph, Missouri. On April 21, 1811, they resumed their westward journey. New men had been added and some had deserted. Among the recruits was Pierre Dorion, whose enlistment roused the opposition of Manuel Lisa of the Missouri Fur Company. Then occurred a remarkable race which lasted two months and covered a distance of eleven hundred miles, and in which Lisa, by his knowledge, energy, and per-severance, was the winner, although Hunt had a start of about two hundred and forty miles. The antagonism reached a climax when one challenged the other to face him in a duel; but wiser counsels prevailed and the two parties went on together up the Missouri to the Arikaras.[20] There Hunt and his people, numbering sixty-four, left the river on July 18; and, travelling on horses, arrived at Andrew Henry's abandoned post on Henry's Fork of Snake River in October. Hunt also now unwisely determined to take to the river. Fifteen canoes were built and all went well until they reached Caldron Linn. Further navigation was impossible. The party broke up into smaller sections, two of which, numbering about forty in all, continued towards the Pacific overland. Those who were commanded by Hunt were at Grande Ronde on December 30, and there began to cross the Blue Mountains. January 8 saw them at the Umatilla; and on the twenty-first they reached the Columbia. Having passed the Dalles and the Cascades, they re-embarked and arrived at Astoria on February 15, 1812. Another section had reached that haven nearly a month before. One by one the different divisions of the original party, less losses and deser-tions, straggled into Fort Astoria.

In June, 1811, the Astorians heard reports that the Nor'-Westers were already established at Spokane; and when David Thompson arrived in July, 1811, the Astorians were preparing an expedition, under David Stuart, to locate a post at some convenient spot in that vicinity which would offer opposition to the Nor'-Westers and would be, moreover, a carrying out of Astor's plan.

Much has been written of the "race to the sea" between Thomp-

20. Chittenden, *American Fur Trade*, 185 ff.

son and the Astorians.[21] Unquestionably the North West Company was alarmed by Astor's expedition and urged the British government to send a ship to the Columbia River, promising that they would send an overland expedition.[22] But Thompson, whose leisurely journey has already been described, did not behave like a man running a race, and Alexander Ross says: "His [Thompson's] own visit had evidently no other object but to discourage us—a manoeuvre of the Northwest policy—to extend their trade at the expense of ours; but he failed."[23] Thompson was seeking a western outlet for the trade of the North West Company and this object did not involve an attempt to deny similar facilities to the Astorians in a land in which no territorial sovereignty had been established.

Personal relations with the American traders were friendly and cordial. The return of Thompson up the Columbia afforded a favourable opportunity to the Astorians to despatch the first trading party into the interior. In July, 1811, the combined parties, numbering twenty-one persons in all, set out. "We were to proceed together for the sake of mutual protection and safety, our party being too small to attempt anything of the kind by itself."[24] Nine days later Thompson and his men separated from the Astorians. He and David Stuart, who commanded them, made an exchange of men. Thompson took a Hawaiian and Stuart accepted in his place an experienced Canadian *voyageur* who had some knowledge of the Indian language. Yet these mutual kindnesses did not interfere with business. Thompson, according to Ross, had prevailed upon the natives at the confluence of the Snake River to urge the Astorians to locate on it instead of following the Columbia itself. But Stuart—an old Nor'Wester and up to all the tricks of the wilds—smoothed the situation and continued his way to the mouth of the Okanagan River.[25] Learning that there were white men ahead of him but a long way off, and knowing that they must belong to the North West Company, Stuart resolved to settle down and build Fort Okanagan.

21. The suggestion of a "race" owes its origin to Franchère. It does not appear in the original French edition published in 1820, but is made in a foot-note on page 122 of the English edition of 1854, published when Franchère was an old man.

22. See Creighton, *Commercial Empire of the St. Lawrence*, 164.

23. Alexander Ross, *Adventures . . . on the Columbia River* (London, 1849), 85.

24. *Ibid.*, 102.   25. *Ibid.*, 128 ff.

No sooner was it completed than he made his way to the Shuswap Indians on Thompson River. The trade prospects were so promising that he returned and established a post, sometimes called Shuswap or Kamloops. The Nor'Westers soon located alongside; whether they had preceded or merely followed Stuart is not known. At any rate, their clerk, Joseph Larocque, and Stuart were "open and candid and on friendly terms." The field was large enough for both and "they followed a fair and straightforward course of trade."[26]

So far as the interior was concerned, all went fairly well; but the coastal trade of Astoria had been handicapped by the destruction of the *Tonquin*, and by the utter uselessness of the *Dolly*, which had been intended as an auxiliary. In May, 1812, the *Beaver* arrived from New York with reinforcements of men and supplies of trading goods. She sailed from the Columbia to Alaska to traffic with the Russians; but, instead of returning as had been arranged, she proceeded to China, where owing to the outbreak of war she was interned. Astoria thus lost the guiding hand of Hunt, who had sailed on the *Beaver* and, after the visit to Alaska, had left her at the Hawaiian Islands. In the interval, Crooks, McLellan and Miller, three of the American partners, becoming disheartened, abandoned the undertaking and returned across the mountains; McKay had been lost on the *Tonquin;* Robert Stuart had been sent to New York with despatches for Astor; and John Clarke, a Canadian and a relative of Astor, had joined the concern. Thus, with the exception of Wilson P. Hunt, the only partners left on the Columbia in 1812 were Donald McKenzie, Duncan McDougall, David Stuart and John Clarke—all Canadians.

But if at Kamloops the Nor'Westers had come in to contest the trade with the Astorians, at Spokane the situation was exactly reversed. The North West Company had built there in 1810; the Astorians, whose resident partners, with the exception of Hunt, were now Canadians, resolved "to carry the war into Africa," and in 1812 sent parties under Donald McKenzie and John Clarke to establish posts above the forks of the Columbia and the Snake at points where most rivalry and opposition were apprehended.[27] Clarke settled down at Spokane within a short distance of the North West Company's post, and the struggle began. Ross visited

26. *Ibid.*, 206.
27. Irving, *Astoria*, III, 1.

Clarke at Spokane in December, 1812. He has something to say of "the sly and underhand dealings" of the competing traders. In their personal relations they professed friendship, but each had his scouts out in every direction, watching his opponent and the Indians, and striving, by fair means and foul, to outwit the other and secure the lion's share of the skins. To Ross, who had no previous knowledge of the fur trade, this conduct seemed strange; but it was merely a repetition of the tactics employed by the Hudson's Bay and Nor'West traders east of the mountains. Clarke held his own in the struggle, for he had had ten years' training in such artful devices when with the Nor'Westers, and in May, 1813, he set out for Astoria with twenty-eight horses loaded with the skins obtained in the winter's trade.

McKenzie, who had left Astoria with Clarke, separated from him and proceeded up the Snake River. Outposts were to be established among the Flatheads, Cœur d'Alènes, and Kootenays. Plainly the plan was to encircle the Columbia region with a line of protective trading posts. But the results of McKenzie's efforts were disappointing; though he sent men hither and yon, few furs could be obtained. Thoroughly downhearted, he repaired to Clarke's post at Spokane. There he met John George McTavish, a partner of the North West Company, who had just come across the Rockies, from whom he learned of the declaration of war in the preceding June. But this was not all. McTavish stated that he had fresh supplies of trading goods and was prepared vigorously to oppose the American company. As the keystone of the arch, he informed McKenzie that the armed ship, *Isaac Todd*, had been despatched to capture Astoria and was expected at the Columbia mouth in March, 1813. Loaded with all this bad news, McKenzie hurried to Astoria, where he arrived in January, 1813. He and McDougall talked the situation over with the clerks. McDougall, already despondent at the ill-luck that dogged the venture, was overwhelmed by this latest turn of the wheel. They assumed that the war would render it impossible for Astor to send out any vessel, and, as the only partners then at headquarters, they decided the undertaking must be abandoned by the following summer at the latest. They resolved that future trade should be confined to provisions and horses to enable the whole party to return overland with the furs already in hand.

Surely this resolution shows the courage of desperation. Hunt's overland party of Astorians, travelling comparatively light, had spent ten awful months in transit from St. Joseph and had straggled into Astoria, a wrecked and shattered body. A more hopeless scheme than the attempt to carry across the continent a body of one hundred persons, with three or four hundred packs of fur and the necessary supplies, could scarcely be conceived. The partners must have forgotten the attentions their people had received from the "gentry of Wishram."

A small bright spot appeared in June when Clarke and Stuart reached Astoria with 140 packs of furs. The four partners, McDougall, McKenzie, Clarke, and Stuart—to repeat, all Canadians—discussed the situation from every angle. Clarke and Stuart were not inclined to regard it as so hopeless as the others. On June 25, 1813, the four resolved to propose to their opponents a division of the trade: the Astorians should abandon the post at Spokane and its Kootenay outpost and their opponents leave them undisturbed in the remainder of the Columbia country; they also offered to supply their rivals with such few goods as they had applied for, payable in horses in the following spring or in other suitable value. The Nor'Westers were to forward their despatches to Astor "by their usual winter express, since," as they said, "it is beyond our power to fit out an express ourselves."[28]

It would appear that the proposed division of trading territory was approved, for in carrying out the next season's undertakings Clarke was to winter in the Flathead country, David Stuart at Okanogan, and a party in the Snake country. All were to direct their trade towards obtaining horses and provisions. Three of the clerks were to be released from their contracts and left free to "engage elsewhere," which in plain English meant that they could enter the service of the Nor'Westers. It must have been evident to their rivals that the Astoria venture was on the rocks.

On July 1, just before the partners set out for their respective winter quarters, the four drew up a memorandum in which, after setting forth their grievous condition owing to the non-return of the *Beaver*, which had left them without supplies, their failure to

28. Grace Flandrau, *Astor and the Oregon Country* (Great Northern Railway, 1926), 37; T. C. Elliott, "Sale of Astoria, 1813," *Oregon Historical Quarterly*, XXXIII, 44.

obtain any coastal trade, their inability to make a profit on the land trade, and the impossibility of recovering the losses or of over-coming the "powerful opposition," they declared that unless support and supplies soon arrived they must abandon the venture; and they fixed June 1, 1814, as the date of their departure on the forlorn hope of an overland journey homeward.

But on August 20 Hunt at last returned from the Hawaiian Islands on the *Albatross*. At first he was shocked by their decision; but he, McKenzie, and McDougall canvassed for six days the whole situation. As a result they, on August 25, prepared a lengthy manifesto, setting forth that, having found the trade unprofitable, they, in justice to Astor and themselves, must close the venture and convey the skins to market "with as little loss in our unfor-tunate undertaking as possible." They arranged that Hunt should return to the Hawaiian Islands and there charter some vessel to carry away their people, and the skins and other property of the concern. January 1, 1814, they fixed as the latest date at which he should leave the islands for Astoria. McKenzie was ordered to notify Clarke and Stuart of the change in plan and require them to forward their furs to headquarters by February 15, 1814. He was also instructed to ascertain whether the North West Company would take any of the Astorians into their employment and to sound McTavish as to whether the Nor'Westers would assume responsibility for the wages due them "and what goods and how many he would take in payment, the prices he would allow for beaver and for goods, and in fine to make a conditional arrangement to deliver the men and property at any given place, though by no means to bind ourselves (because we have no doubt we shall have a vessel to take them all off). But should Mr. McKenzie succeed in prevailing on Mr. McTavish to come with him to this place it is understood that he come to no arrangement whatever further than holding out such inducement as is necessary to bring him down."

Notwithstanding their assertion that Hunt would secure a ship to carry them away, they felt much doubt on the point, as is shown by the permission they gave to Clarke and Stuart either to return to Astoria or to make the best of their way homeward across the continent. They gave McKenzie "liberty to act at his dis-cretion in forming any arrangements with the said McTavish or the person acting for the North West Company." The memorandum also contained this somewhat cryptic expression: "It is also agreed that in case W. P. Hunt should not be able to return it is left solely with Mr. McDougall to finally conclude any arrangements we may be able to make with whoever may come forward on the part of the N.W. Co."[29]

Hunt departed the next day, leaving behind him dejected leaders not knowing what move to make. At the Marquesas he learned from Commodore Porter that the British frigate *Phoebe* and the sloops of war, *Cherub* and *Raccoon*, were on their way to the Columbia. "Here then," says Irving,[30] "was the death warrant of unfortunate Astoria. . . . He had been eager to extricate the property of Mr. Astor from a failing concern with as little loss as possible; there was now danger that the whole would be swallowed up." And so it would have been but for McDougall's action in selling the whole undertaking to the Nor'Westers.

But a further misfortune fell upon ill-fated Astoria. The *Lark*, Astor's third ship, which had left New York in March, 1813, by permission of the British admiral, Sir John B. Warren, upon the understanding that the goods and supplies were for the Russians at Sitka,[31] was wrecked upon the coast of Tahoorrowa (Kahoolawe), one of the Hawaiian Islands. Surely, one may ask: What was to be done?

To return to affairs at Astoria: McKenzie, as he journeyed to Spokane, met a strong party of Nor'Westers, under McTavish, John Stuart, Angus Bethune, and James McMillan. They had eight canoes loaded with furs to be shipped from the Columbia River, in accordance with the resolution of the annual meeting of 1812.[32] They bore a letter dated May 9, 1813, stating that the *Isaac Todd*, with Donald McTavish and John

29. A copy of the document from which these quotations are taken, and copies of the other agreements and resolutions, are given in Flandrau, *Astor and the Oregon Country*, 24-41. In chapters VII and VIII of K. W. Porter, *John Jacob Astor* (Cambridge, Mass., 1931) will be found the latest discussion of the Astoria undertaking. It is quite impartial. See also Elliott, "Sale of Astoria," 45.

30. Irving, *Astoria*, III, 214.

31. Porter, *John Jacob Astor*, I, 215.

32. G. C. Davidson, *The North West Company* (Berkeley, California, 1918), 135; W. S. Wallace, *Documents relating to the North West Company* (Toronto, 1934), 271; Franchère, *Narrative*, English ed., 191.

McDonald on board, was ready for sea on March 18, 1813. It added: "She is accompanied by a frigate, to take and destroy everything that is American on the N.W. Coast." The dark face of things was now black: nothing but certain disaster ahead. The war vessels might arrive at any moment: they had been seven months on the way.

Although the North West Company had urged the dispatch of men-of-war to capture the post, its representatives, who were now at the Columbia River mouth, were authorized to treat for the purchase of the whole Astoria undertaking. The North West party, numbering seventy-five men awaiting the arrival of their expected ship and the men-of-war and forced to obtain provisions from the Astorians, found themselves at last in a difficult situation. "Weary, at length, of applying to us incessantly for food (which we furnished them with a sparing hand), unable either to retrace their steps through the wilderness or to remain in their present position, they came to the conclusion of proposing to buy of us the whole establishment."[33]

The Astorians, disheartened to such an extent that they had resolved to abandon the enterprise and faced with the capture of their fort, listened to the proposition. No help had come from New York; it was impossible to carry their furs home overland. What else could they do? But, it is said, the Nor'Westers were loath to expend money in a purchase when capture would effect the same purpose, that of ridding them of their opponents. They therefore delayed. The Astorians urged on the negotiation. According to Ross, the latter finally manned the bastion, loaded and pointed the guns at the Nor'Westers' camp, and delivered an ultimatum requiring them to sign the documents within two hours or to end the negotiations and remove to some other spot.[34] Finally, on October 16, 1813, the bargain was concluded. The agreement recited that the Pacific Fur Company had been dissolved on July 1, 1813, with the intention of abandoning the trade on the Columbia River and vicinity. It provided for the future of the men at

33. Franchère, *Narrative*, English ed., 192. In the French edition, 144, Franchère puts the matter slightly more succinctly: "Las de recourir sans cesse à nous pour avoir des provisions ils nous proposèrent de leur vendre notre établissement et son contenu."

34. Ross, *Adventures on the Columbia River*, 254.

Astoria. The trading goods were valued at figures from 50 to 100 per cent above cost and the furs at a fixed price per skin.[35] The ink upon the document was hardly dry when, on November 30, 1813, the British ship of war *Raccoon* arrived to capture Fort Astoria. The Nor'Westers, at first uncertain of her nationality, sent the furs up the river in the hope of avoiding loss if the strange vessel should prove American.

Chittenden inclines to the view that the failure of the Astoria venture was due in part to the British nationality of the majority, but this is without foundation and is a reading into events of inferences derived from the subsequent situation. It will be plain from the simple facts of the case as already given and as follow that everyone connected with the undertaking—British and American alike—had become disheartened and discouraged owing to the losses sustained, and the difficulty of making headway against well-entrenched opponents. Chittenden suggests that Astor should have enlisted Americans instead of Nor'Westers in his venture.[36] He seems to forget that no American traders had then

35. The complete agreement is given in Davidson, *North West Company*, 293 ff.; and in Elliott, "Sale of Astoria," 48. There has been controversy as to the adequacy of the prices paid. Irving finds in the prices allowed for the furs evidence that they were sacrificed for one-third of their value: for example, 68 sea-otter skins were valued at $1,200, being about $18 apiece (the price in the agreement is 60*s.* each) and 30 others at $500, or $16.66 each, while according to him the value of the 68 was from $4,000 to $6,000 or $58 to $88 each, and that of the 30, $2,500 or $83.33 each. But this is quite wrong: sea-otter skins in Canton—the only market—brought in 1804, $24; in 1808, $30; and in 1811, $21.50 (Irving, *Astoria*, III, 2, 231; F. W. Howay, "A List of Trading Vessels in Maritime Fur Trade, 1805-13," *Royal Society of Canada Transactions*, sec. II, 1932, 46; Porter, *John Jacob Astor*, 228, 245 f., and chap. VIII, *passim*). Never since the days of Captain Cook and Captain Portlock had sea-otter brought such a figure as $88 in Canton. Again Irving complains of the price allowed for beavers, $2 a skin, which he says were worth $5. The normal price of beaver in St. Louis was $4 a pound; but in 1910 it was only bringing $2.50 a pound. See Chittenden, *American Fur Trade*, 145. When the immense cost of transportation to market is added it will be found that the price was fair. Moreover, according to Alexander Henry, Wilson Price Hunt, the principal agent of Astor, after an investigation of the prices at which the fort, the furs, and goods were sold assented to them and thus sanctioned the sale (Elliott Coues, *New Light on the Early History of the Greater Northwest*, New York, 1897, 852 f.). In that examination it was found that the prices of the goods were sometimes too high and sometimes too low.

36. Chittenden, *American Fur Trade*, 230.

even crossed the Rocky Mountains; and it cannot be said that their success in the trade on the upper reaches of the Missouri and in dealing with the Indians of that locality had marked them out as specially suited for such an undertaking. That McDougall and his associates were traitors to their employer is a gratuitous assertion, for which no shadow of foundation can be shown.[37] The effort was a failure; they abandoned it, and sold at a price agreeable to Astor's agent, W. P. Hunt.

With the purchase of Astoria by the North West Company, the first phase of Anglo-American rivalry in the fur trade ends. We must remember that east of the Rocky Mountains and to some extent west of them, several American trading companies were operating and that they came at some points into competition with the Hudson's Bay Company. The reputation of the British companies in the United States resulted in part from this competition.

To complete the picture of the rivalries of the fur traders, something must therefore be said of the principal American fur-trading concerns and of the leading fur traders in the first quarter of the nineteenth century. The three most important companies were: the St. Louis Missouri Fur Company, 1809-28; the Rocky Mountain Fur Company, the trade name of William H. Ashley, 1823-6, and of Smith, Jackson, and Sublette, 1826-31; and the American Fur Company, an incorporated name, first for John Jacob Astor, but later including others, trading first from Michilimackinac and, after 1823, from St. Louis.

The American fur trade was late in beginning an advance towards the Pacific. The great name in the early days of the trade was that of Manuel Lisa. In 1807, fired by reports brought back by Lewis and Clark, he resolved to open up trade with the Indians of the upper Missouri. In 1808 he formed the St. Louis Missouri Fur Company to take over his stock and that of his associates. In 1810 this company sent out its first expedition, a small army of 150 men, with full equipment for trade and defence. There were frequent reorganizations and by 1819 the company did not include any original shareholder except Manuel Lisa himself. He died in the following

---

37. The charge is made in the English edition of Franchère, *Narrative*, 368; but it does not appear in the original French edition. Porter in *John Jacob Astor*, 233 ff., emphasizes the fact that Hunt accepted the arrangement made by McDougall. It seems to follow that, if McDougall were a traitor, so was Hunt.

year and the management passed to Joshua Pilcher. In 1828 he set out with nine men for the Columbia River and with only one companion reached Fort Colvile, where he was hospitably received by the Hudson's Bay traders. "He was treated," says Chittenden, "with the hospitality so well understood by that company; but which when dispensed to rival traders, was always accompanied by a firm refusal to assist in any way in their trading operations."[38]

William H. Ashley began his fur trading in 1822 with Andrew Henry, who had earlier been a member of the Missouri Fur Company, as an associate. He founded the Rocky Mountain Fur Company and made a spectacular success of the venture. In his second expedition in 1823, he had with him three men to whom later, in 1826, he sold his business—Jedediah S. Smith, David E. Jackson, and William L. Sublette, later a member of the firm of Sublette and Campbell. In 1824 Smith with a small party of Ashley's men crossed the Rocky Mountains to the head-waters of the Snake River, where they met the Hudson's Bay trappers under Ross.[39] Imitating the Canadian practice of trading *en derouine*,[40] he abandoned the plan of building trading posts and substituted itinerant parties of traders and trappers—the "Mountain Men," as they were called—who met each year at an appointed time and place—the "rendezvous"—with the results of their trapping and trading.

The American Fur Company came from Michilimackinac to St. Louis in 1823 and its employees were largely recruited from Montreal. Of the Canadian *voyageurs*, Ramsay Crooks, Astor's right-hand man, wrote in 1817: "These people are indispensible to the successful prosecution of the trade, their places cannot be supplied by Americans who are for the most part . . . too independent to submit quietly to a proper controul, and who gain anywhere a subsistence much superior to a man of the interior."[41]

38. *American Fur Trade*, 157 f.

39. See *infra*, 49.

40. See *supra*, 20, f.n. 8.

41. Cited by Grace L. Nute, *The Voyageur* (New York, 1931), 203 ff., and quoted by H. A. Innis in "The Fur Trade of Canada and the United States," *Mississippi Valley Historical Review*, XX, 329.

It was not until 1828 that an advance was made by the American Fur Company towards the head-waters of the Missouri. Then Kenneth McKenzie, an old Nor'Wester, built Fort Union at the mouth of the Yellowstone. In the following year he sent a party over the mountains to trap. The American Fur Company was more successful than the Missouri Fur Company or Ashley's Rocky Mountain Fur Company in securing the goodwill of the Blackfeet Indians and a permanent foothold in their country. It is significant that its two leading men, McKenzie and Berger (who had been in the service of the Hudson's Bay Company), were trained in Canadian methods.

The British companies were, on the whole, more successful than the American in dealing with the Indians, and the American companies often attributed their own misfortunes to the intrigues of the Hudson's Bay Company.[42] This question of Indian animosity towards the Americans is one upon which it is difficult to dogmatize; but there are a number of points, consideration of which may throw some light upon the question. It may be that it originated in part in the conduct of the American traders themselves. The policy of terrorizing adopted by Lisa in 1809 against the Assiniboines may be contrasted with that of conciliation adopted by McKenzie, an old Nor'Wester, in 1829. Force breeds force, especially in a savage people. It is significant that the story of the fur trade north of 49° is one of peace and harmony, while south of that imaginary line it is crossed with trails of bloodshed, rapine, and plunder. When the Indians opposed the advance of the Americans, guns boomed and a way was made by force. But in 1793, when Alexander Mackenzie and his nine companions crossed the continent and on many occasions found the way barred by them, he landed, faced them boldly, explained his purpose, made them presents, won their friendship and passed on. In 1810 when the Piegans prevented Thompson from ascending the North Saskatchewan, he yielded and sought another route. When they besieged his Kootenae House, he and his people sat quietly (as the Americans, having learned from the British traders, did in 1831

42. Charges of this character are frequently made by Chittenden, *American Fur Trade*. See, for example, 124, 154, 335, 342.

at Fort Piegan) and waited till the storm blew itself out. The rivalry between the British companies, Hudson's Bay and North West, was most keen; for forty years they each strove by every means to outwit and out-bid the other, a far keener rivalry than ever prevailed between the British traders and the Americans, and yet there was no bloodshed. And the Indians had many guns.

Another fact which may bear upon the matter is the inherent difference between the British and American fur-trading concerns. Leaving aside the XY Company, which only lived for about six years (1798–1804), the North West Company existed for forty years and was then merged in the Hudson's Bay Company. The Hudson's Bay Company, incorporated in 1670, is still in existence, carrying on the fur trade in conjunction with broadened commercial activities. Their officers and employees came into the trade in subordinate capacities and, working upwards through many years of apprenticeship and experience with the different Indian tribes, ultimately reached the positions of command and responsibility. Living in the wilds from early boyhood and in daily contact with the natives, they came to understand them and learned the way to manage them. More than that, the very life of these companies depended on the conservation and the reaping of the fur harvest, and that again depended upon the establishment and maintenance of friendly relations with the natives.

The American traders on the other hand served no apprenticeship. Independent in spirit, self-reliant and resourceful, and acquainted with frontier life, they were yet, very largely, with little or no experience or previous knowledge of the trade or of the Indians. They refused to submit to the discipline which was cheerfully accepted by the employees of the British companies. The different American companies were short-lived. There was continuity in the British, but continual change in the American trade. In ten years the whole membership of the Missouri Fur Company was changed; Ashley's Rocky Mountain Fur Company existed only four years; the firm of Smith, Jackson and Sublette, which, as said above, traded under the same name, lasted for fifteen years. This may have led the American traders to lay particular emphasis on present profit; and the British traders, while by no means neglecting present advantages, to keep future profits and relations in view. As Porter in his *John Jacob Astor* says, having evidently in mind the Hudson's Bay Company,[43] "Being a permanent organization it would find it advantageous to treat the natives fairly."

43. Page 166; and see Innis, "Fur Trade of Canada and the United States," 321 f.

CHAPTER III

THE HUDSON'S BAY COMPANY AND THE AMERICAN OVERLAND FUR TRADERS

1818-1834

THIS chapter and the two which follow continue the account of Anglo-American competition in the overland fur trade, in the territory open to both countries under the terms of the Treaty of 1818. As the story goes further, it becomes clearer that the next stage in the economic development of the territory will be settlement by immigrants from the older communities of North America, and that there will eventually be a division of the territory between Great Britain and the United States. We find the rival companies anticipating, though not always correctly, the lines which this division will follow and making their plans accordingly. The period is still one of intense international rivalry, which is bound to continue while the economy is still in a predatory stage and while territorial sovereignty is still unsettled. The growth of colonization, in its earlier stages, is certain to embitter this rivalry as white settlers in a land of democratic traditions are sure to assume that the right of political self-determination is vested in them by some sort of divine or natural right, which excludes the Indians when heads are counted, although to outsiders the settlers may appear to have some difficulty in establishing even the right of appropriating the soil as against the indigenous population. But once the land has been appropriated, the way will be prepared for the steady growth of friendly feeling which happily marks the stage at which agricultural and industrial economies flourish. To mention this period is to anticipate; but there is a reason for anticipating. We must not judge people in the earlier predatory period by the standards of behaviour and of tolerance which have marked the later period. We must not be surprised if extravagant claims are made and intolerant language used. Indeed, there is rather reason for surprise that the difficult days of trade rivalries and of early settlement passed without recourse to armed conflict. When full account is taken of the difficulties of the situation, the behaviour of the actors who appear on the scene is creditable to their good

41

sense. But we must be prepared for words and deeds at which we should look askance today.

In considering the contacts of British and American traders on the Missouri and in Old Oregon, the political situation, which will be considered in detail in a later chapter, should be constantly kept in mind. Louisiana, the territory west of the Mississippi, before its acquisition by the United States in 1803 was a Spanish or French possession with undetermined boundaries, north and west. In it the North West Company and, to a small extent, the Hudson's Bay Company had been accustomed to trade. In 1816, probably at the instigation of John Jacob Astor, the United States passed a law declaring that "Licenses to trade with the Indians within the territorial limits of the United States shall not be granted to any but citizens of the United States, unless by the express direction of the President of the United States, and upon such terms and conditions as the public interest may, in his opinion, require." Goods of an unlicensed foreigner taken into the Indian country for trade were liable to confiscation, and severe penalties were provided for violation of the act.[1] In 1818 the 49th parallel was fixed as the northern boundary of the United States from the Lake of the Woods to the Rocky Mountains. The territory west of these mountains—Old Oregon—comprising the states of Oregon, Washington, Idaho, a part of Montana, and the Province of British Columbia, was then without sovereignty, a no man's land. Under the treaties of 1818 and 1827 it was to be free and open to British and Americans alike.

There was natural access to Old Oregon overland by the Missouri, the Saskatchewan, the Athabaska, and the Peace rivers. In 1803 when Louisiana was purchased, the British traders were far in the lead; and they were over the Rocky Mountains before an American trader had begun to stem the current of the Missouri. When, in 1810, Andrew Henry for the Missouri Fur Company crossed the Continental Divide, the North West Company had already seven or eight trading posts in operation in the tramontane region. To the American trader Old Oregon was a part of the United States, either as included in the Louisiana Purchase or by virtue of Captain Gray's discovery of the mouth of the Columbia River

1. K. W. Porter, *John Jacob Astor* (Cambridge, Mass., 1931), II, 694; *United States Statutes at Large*, III, chap. 165, April 29, 1816.

and the Lewis and Clark expedition; and treaty or no treaty, he looked upon the British traders as mere interlopers. The British trader regarded the area as one to whose trade he was lawfully entitled by the existing treaty, and that right was, in his eyes, strengthened by his prior occupation. These conflicting views show strongly in the clash between Ogden and Gardner in the trouble of 1825.[2] It is believed that national rights, present and future, bulked larger in the eyes of the individual American trader than in those of the individual British trader. The one was accustomed to act independently and form his own judgments; the other always acted upon instructions.

The Astoria venture and all that it possessed passed to the North West Company by the purchase of 1813; and from that time until 1821, the Nor'Westers were in undisputed possession of the fur trade west of the Rocky Mountains. The only occasion on which the Hudson's Bay Company crossed those mountains was in 1810, when Joseph Howse made his journey to the Columbia River, and on to Flathead Lake. Howse wintered, in 1810-11, not far from the site of Kalispell, Montana; in the spring he abandoned his post there and returned to the Saskatchewan country. The Hudson's Bay Company was not seen in the tramontane region again until after the union of 1821.[3]

The struggle between the Hudson's Bay Company and the North West Company, east of the Rocky Mountains, from 1812 onward, became gradually keener. The Nor'Westers had always shown in practice an utter disregard for the paper title of their rival. The Chartered Company on the other hand never seems to have taken any serious and determined step to maintain the exclusive rights and privileges purporting to be granted to it by the "Merry Monarch." Instead, the presence of the "pedlars"[3a] and their forts within the chartered territory was apparently accepted as a *fait*

2. H. M. Chittenden, *The American Fur Trade of the Far West* (New York, 1902), I, 277 n.; Frederick Merk, "Snake Country Expedition, 1824-5," *Oregon Historical Quarterly*, XXXV, 109. See *infra, 50*.

3. J. B. Tyrrell, *David Thompson's Narrative* (Toronto, 1916), li, 415, 458.

3a. For an explanation of the term "pedlars" cf. A. S. Morton, *The Canadian West to 1870-7* (London, 1939), 257. It was applied by the Hudson's Bay Company to the traders from Montreal. Morton confines the use of the term to the period before the formation of the North West Company.

accompli, and was only met by the establishment of opposition posts in close proximity. Among the servants of the two concerns there existed good fellowship and a genuine desire for mutual assistance; but also, side by side therewith, a keen rivalry for furs and a mutual determination to outwit and overreach in the peltry struggle. This was in marked contrast with the conduct of the American traders operating on the Missouri and in the Salt Lake country. The story of the American Fur Company and its rivals, Leclerc, and Sublette and Campbell, is illuminating on the point.[4]

This condition of "rivals in trade, but allies in danger" changed with the advent of Lord Selkirk's colony in Red River, into one of mutual aggression, engendering feelings of marked and mutual hostility. The struggle reached a crisis in June, 1815, in the skirmish at Seven Oaks, near Winnipeg, where fell Robert Semple, the Governor of the colony, and twenty others.[5] Then followed more aggressions, criminal prosecutions of officers and men of the North West Company for murder in connection with the bloody day at Seven Oaks, and civil actions against members of both the contesting companies for wrongs done in the last and heated days of the struggle. In 1820 Lord Selkirk died; and on March 26, 1821, the two companies, which on the trading grounds of the prairies, in the marts of the world, with voice and pen, and lastly with gun and cannon on the Red River, had struggled for nearly forty years, were united under the name of the Chartered Company—the Hudson's

4. Chittenden, *American Fur Trade*, 346 f., 352 f. Narcisse Leclerc, a former employee of the Company, invested his savings in a trading expedition, and in 1832 ascended the Missouri with an outfit, which included a quantity of liquor, just before the arrival of the official notification that the importation of liquor into the Indian country had been prohibited by law. An agent of the Company contrived to seize the liquor, hoping to see Leclerc prosecuted under the new law, but instead Leclerc went to law himself, carried the matter to Washington, and extracted a settlement from the Company.

William Sublette and Robert Campbell, both experienced traders, formed a partnership in 1832. The firm existed until 1842, and was the only serious opposition encountered by the American Fur Company during the ten years. In 1833 Kenneth McKenzie, acting for the Company, attempted to ruin the partners by buying up furs in their way, no matter what the cost. Knowing, however, that Sublette had ample credit at his command, the officers of the Company in St. Louis became anxious, and bought off their rival (*ibid.*, 254-6, 351-3).

5. W. S. Simpson, *Report of Proceedings . . . between the Earl of Selkirk and the North West Company* (Montreal, 1819).

Bay Company.[6] George Simpson, later Sir George Simpson, who had been in control of the old Hudson's Bay Company's trade in the Athabaska country,[7] soon became the head of the new concern in America. William Williams was appointed Governor of the Southern Department and Simpson, Governor of the Northern Department, of Rupert's Land, while R. P. Pelly was made Governor of Assiniboia, as Lord Selkirk's colony was called. Despite these divisions of authority, Simpson was the real power and practically the director of the Company's vast interests.[8]

One result of this union was to carry the Hudson's Bay Company's flag to the west of the Rockies, where it had flown but once— in the time of Joseph Howse, 1810-11—and to which it had been a stranger for a decade. The forts of the North West Company now became Hudson's Bay Company's establishments. In Old Oregon these appear to have been Astoria (Fort George), Walla Walla (Nez Percés), Okanogan, Spokane, Flathead House, Kootenae House, Fort McLeod, Fort Fraser, Fort Chilcotin, Fort Alexandria, Fort St. James, and Fort Kamloops.[9]

Of these posts, Astoria, Okanogan and Kamloops had been originally founded by the Pacific Fur Company; all the others were North West Company foundations. The Nor'Westers had always been accustomed to trade *en derouine*: that is, a trader would be outfitted with goods at one of the posts and, like a pedlar, would set out to visit the Indian villages and hawk his wares among them.[10] The Nor'Westers whom Astor took into his Pacific Fur Company naturally brought the custom with them. Thus *en*

6. For a précis of the agreement, see F. W. Howay, "Important Hudson's Bay Company Document," *Washington Historical Quarterly*, XXIII, 35 f.; W. S. Wallace, *Documents relating to the North West Company* (Toronto, 1934), 321 ff.

7. L. R. Masson, *Les Bourgeois de la Compagnie du Nord-Ouest* (Quebec, 1889), I, 140; E. E. Rich (ed.), *Simpson's Athabasca Journal* (Toronto, 1939).

8. E. H. Oliver, *The Canadian North-West* (Ottawa, 1914), I, 47; Frederick Merk, *Fur Trade and Empire* (Cambridge, Mass., 1931), 152 n.

9. Merk, *Fur Trade and Empire*, 194, 219, 229 f.; Alexander Ross, *The Fur Hunters of the Far West* (London, 1855), I, 170, 173.

10. See, for example, Norman McLeod, MS journal of Fort Alexandria, December 21, 1800 (in McGill University Library). Larocque and his party were *en derouine* when they met Lewis and Clark. See Masson, *Les Bourgeois . . .*, I, 299, 306. McLeod's journal is published in C. M. Gates (ed.), *Five Fur Traders of the Northwest* (University of Minnesota Press, 1933).

derouine was transplanted from the prairies to the Pacific Coast, and in 1812 we see Donald McKenzie setting out, pedlar-like, for the Snake River.[11] To this they had added the custom of sending out trapping expeditions on their own account, instead of relying entirely upon the natives for the furs.

The Snake country was known very early to be rich in fur-bearing animals, above all, beaver; and the first of these trading and trapping parties launched by the Astorians had been intended for that vicinity. Donald McKenzie, who after the fall of Astoria had joined the North West Company, was the pioneer of the Snake country expeditions. In 1818, the first of these efforts was launched. It left the recently established, but unfinished, Fort Walla Walla in September in formidable array: 55 men, 195 horses, 300 beaver traps, and a considerable stock of merchandise.[12] Other parties were sent to the Cowlitz and the Willamette, but the Snake undertakings will be followed in detail, inasmuch as they outlasted all the others. In July, 1819, the returns of the trapping and trading in the Snake country reached Fort Walla Walla. "The Snake expedition turned out well; it made up for all deficiencies elsewhere, and gave a handsome surplus besides."[13] Year by year the Nor'Westers sent parties to that vicinity. It was a dangerous service. The Indian tribes which frequented the territory—Nez Percés, Snakes, and Blackfeet—were in a constant state of tribal warfare; their war-parties roamed the land; roving bands of horse-thieves and warriors were ready to steal or kill at every opportunity. Constant vigilance, day and night: the least relaxation meant loss of animals, or merchandise, or peltry, or even life itself.

McKenzie commanded the Snake expeditions until the union of the two companies in 1821. He came back from his last effort in that land in July, 1821, with increased returns, and without having lost a man. He then left the service and, in the spring of 1822, crossed the mountains, never to return. He had by his perseverance and success in this trade and trapping turned the unfavourable balance against the Columbia River into a favourable one, and thus had planted his feet firmly on the ladder which reached to the

11. Gabriel Franchère, *Relation d'un voyage* . . . (Montreal, 1820), 121; English ed., 160.

12. Ross, *Fur Hunters of the Far West*, I, 184.

13. *Ibid.*, 212.

Governorship of Assiniboia, or the Red River Colony.[14] Such at any rate is Alexander Ross's statement; but Dr. McLoughlin, writing to Governor Simpson, March 20, 1846, says that when he came in 1824 the Snake country had been given up as hopeless by the late North West Company.

After Donald McKenzie left there was no officer to take charge of the Snake expeditions, but in order, as Alexander Ross puts it, that the trappers and hunters should not be without employment the party of 1822-3 was sent out under Finan McDonald, "a veteran of the North-west school." The dates of its departure and return are not exactly known. It was composed largely of "freemen," a considerable number of whom had with their families arrived at Spokane from the Saskatchewan.[15] Though McDonald lost in this expedition a number of men in encounters with the Piegans and Blackfeet, "everything considered the trip was as successful as could have been expected."[16]

In the following year, 1824, Alexander Ross took command of the venture, which left Flathead House in February. It consisted of 54 men of whom 43 were freemen, 25 women, and 64 children, and was provided with 62 guns, a brass three-pounder, 206 beaver traps, 231 horses, and ammunition and trading articles.[17] The whole

14. *Ibid.*, 280 f.; Oliver, *Canadian North-West*, 46.

15. Ross, *Fur Hunters of the Far West*, II, 2, 54; Merk, *Fur Trade and Empire*, 184. These freemen were Iroquois Indians or men whose term of service with the Company had expired, but who remained, having become enamoured of the wild life. By many they were regarded as worthless and of bad character. They, however, always formed a large part of the Snake country expeditions. The complaint was that though the region was rich in beaver the freemen were too indolent and careless to bring in the skins they had obtained, and that, for example, in April, 1823, seven hundred beaver skins trapped in the preceding year were lying *en cache* on the upper reaches of Snake River, awaiting transport. Some time in 1822 a number of these freemen deserted. "It is evident part of them have reached the American posts on the Yellowstone and Big Horn with much fur." Ross believed that the Americans had decoyed them from the Company's service. See T. C. Elliott, "Journal of Alexander Ross," *Oregon Historical Quarterly*, XIV, 385; "Letter of John McLoughlin," *ibid.*, XXXV, 121; Ross, *Fur Hunters of the Far West*, II, 129; T. C. Elliott, "Earliest Travelers on the Oregon Trail," *Oregon Historical Quarterly*, XIII, 78 ff.

16. Ross, *Fur Hunters of the Far West*, II, 5.

17. These figures are from Elliott, "Journal of Alexander Ross," 369 ff.; they differ slightly from those in Ross, *Fur Hunters of the Far West*, II, 7.

cavalcade when in marching order extended for a mile or more. Governor Simpson, in speaking of this expedition, requested that Ross be cautioned against opening a road for the Americans. Ross complains that the improvidence of the freemen in trading their equipment for "their bellies' sake" endangered the undertaking almost at the start. Of these men Governor Simpson wrote: "This band of Freemen, the very scum of the country and generally outcasts from the Service for misconduct are the most unruly and troublesome gang to deal with in this or perhaps any other part of the World, are under no control & feel their own independence; they therefore require very superior management to make anything of them, but I regret to find that Mr. Ross has not that talent and that his presence among them has been attended with little good."[18]

As the party advanced the trapping grounds were changed; and by the middle of April they were at the foot of the mountains. Crossing the continental divide by Gibbon Pass, the expedition was at the sources of the Missouri, and within the territory which the United States had acquired by the Louisiana Purchase. There they trapped until April 29, when they recrossed the divide probably by the Lemhi Pass to the Salmon River, a tributary of the Snake. Despite constant danger from Piegans and Blackfeet, the freemen would neither obey rules nor conform to discipline. During May the party trapped at and around the head-waters of the Snake River, but the returns were disappointing; and the Piegans were on their trail ready to cut off any stragglers.[19] On October 14, when Ross was at the head-waters of the Salmon River, some of the freemen returned from their hunt up Henry's Fork, claiming to have been attacked by the Indians and robbed of nine hundred beaver skins besides traps, guns, and horses. With them came seven American trappers from the Big Horn. Ross regarded these newcomers as spies rather than trappers, and suspected the Americans of intending to decoy his men away, as he believed they had done in 1822.[20] The constant intercourse between them caused him to suspect some knavery. Under pretence of fearing a night attack by the Indians, he doubled the guard and

18. Merk, *Fur Trade and Empire*, 198, 45.

19. Elliott, "Journal of Alexander Ross," 381, 383.

20. Ross, *Fur Hunters of the Far West*, II, 129; Elliott, "Journal of Alexander Ross," 385.

increased the speed of the homeward journey. He however admits that the great influence was the price of beaver: the Americans were paying more than he was. Yet Ross himself, on discovering that these seven American trappers had nine hundred beaver skins in two *caches*, had no scruples about trying to purchase them. He did not succeed; but only because they would not sell for less than $3 a pound. "The quarter," he says, "is swarming with trappers who next season are to penetrate the Snake country with a Major Henry at their head, the same gentleman who fifteen years ago wintered on Snake River."[21] These American trappers, led by the well-known Jedediah S. Smith, belonged to William H. Ashley's party, and when they encountered Ross's freemen were on their way to a rendezvous in the Green River country. The pillaging, of which these freemen told Ross, consisted of this: In some way or other, Smith had obtained all their catch of beaver, one hundred skins.[22] Despite Simpson's orders, Ross permitted the Americans to accompany him to Flathead House, where the party arrived on November 26, 1824. He nevertheless records his view that the Americans were advancing with hasty strides, scouring the country, and carrying off the cream of the trade, "and, if we do not speedily bestir ourselves the Yankees will reap all the advantages of our discoveries."[23] Ross claims that the trade of this year's expedition—the only one that he commanded—was, all things considered, the most profitable ever brought from the Snake country: amounting to five thousand beaver, exclusive of other peltry. He is pleased that Governor Simpson sent him "a letter of thanks on the success of the expedition."[24] Little did he know that at the moment he was penning these words Simpson was expressing to the London Board his real sentiments about Ross, whom he regarded as "a self-sufficient, empty-headed man . . . whose reports are so full of bombast and marvellous nonsense that it is impossible to get at any information that can be depended on from him."[25]

In 1824, before the return of Ross, Governor Simpson, "knowing

21. Elliott, "Journal of Alexander Ross," 385.
22. Chittenden, *American Fur Trade*, 271. See *supra*, 37.
23. Ross, *Fur Hunters of the Far West*, II, 143.
24. *Ibid.*, 143, 141.
25. Merk, *Fur Trade and Empire*, 46.

no one in the country better qualified to do it justice," had selected
Peter Skene Ogden to succeed him in the command of the Snake
expedition. Ogden, so appointed, remained in control from 1824 till
1829, leading in all five expeditions.[26] His first Snake expedition
left Flathead Post on December 20, 1824. It consisted of "25
lodges, 2 gentlemen, 2 interpreters, 71 men and lads, 80 guns,
364 beaver traps, 372 horses . . . the most formidable party that
ever set out for the Snakes."[27] With them went, much to Ogden's
disgust, Jedediah S. Smith and his men who had arrived at Flathead Post with Ross barely a month before. Chittenden is plainly
in error in his statement that Smith passed the winter of 1824-5
among the Flatheads.[28] Smith remained with Ogden's party until
April, 1825. Ross estimated that the expedition would secure
14,100 beaver. For five weeks it proceeded southeast, following,
probably, Ross's route "up the Missoula, to the Bitterroot, up the
Bitterroot to its East Fork and across the continental divide to
the sources of the Missouri." Thus Ogden was trespassing on
American territory, as Ross had done, and this in defiance of the
restrictive law of 1816.[29] Some time in April he reached Bear
River; there the Americans left the party. Ogden, freed of them,
followed Bear River to its mouth in Great Salt Lake.

On May 23, 1825, in Bear Valley, Johnson Gardner with a party
of Ashley's trappers, including some of those who had been at
Flathead House, arrived at Ogden's camp.[30] Accompanying the
new arrivals were fifteen of Ogden's freemen who had been absent
for a short time. Gardner and his people encamped about a hundred
yards away; above their position flew the American flag. They
"proclaimed to all that they were in United States Territories
and were all Free, indebted or engaged."[31] The next day an

26. They have been recorded as follows in the *Oregon Historical Quarterly:* That
of 1824-5, Frederick Merk, "Snake Country Expedition, 1824-25," XXXV, 93 ff.;
that of 1825-6, X, 331 ff.; that of 1826-7, XI, 201 ff.; that of 1827-8, XI, 355 ff.;
and that of 1828-9, XI, 381 ff., the last four all edited by T. C. Elliott.

27. Elliott, "Journal of Alexander Ross," 388.

28. Chittenden, *American Fur Trade*, I, 271.

29. Elliott, "Journal of Alexander Ross," 288; Merk, "Snake Country Expedition," 100; *United States Statutes at Large*, II, chap. 165, April 29, 1816—of which a
summary is given in Porter, *John Jacob Astor*, 694; and see *supra*, 42.

30. This is the incident mentioned on page 43, *supra*.

31. Merk, "Snake Country Expedition," 109.

interview took place whose repercussions extended over the whole West, but whose exact details have only recently been brought to light; and even these are in Ogden's account—Gardner has left none, so far as is known:

Gardner came to my tent and after a few words of no import, he questioned me as follows: "Do you know in whose Country you are?" to which I made answer that I did not, as it was not determined between Great Britain and America to whom *it* belonged, to which he made answer that it was, that it had been ceded to the latter, and as I had no license to trade or trap to return from whence I came without delay, to this I replied when we receive orders from the British Government to abandon the Country we shall obey, he then said remain at your peril, he then left my tent and seeing him go in an Iroquois Tent (John Gray) I followed him, on entering this villain Gray said, I must now tell you, that all the Iroquois as well as myself have long wished for an opportunity to join the Americans, and if we did not the last three years, it was owing to our bad luck in not meeting them, but now we go, and all you can say or do cannot prevent us. During this conversation Gardner was silent, but on going out he said you have had these men too long in your Service and have most shamefully imposed on them, treating them as *Slaves* selling them Goods at high prices and giving them nothing for their Furs, Gray then said that is all true and alluding to the Gentlemen he had been with in the Columbia, they are says he the greatest villains in the World, and if they were here I would shoot them, but as for you Sir you have dealt fair with us all. We have now been five Years in your Service, the longer we remain the more indebted we become altho' we give 150 Beaver a year, we are now in a free Country and have friends to support us, and go we will, and if every Man in the Camp does not leave you they do not seek their own interest, he then gave orders to raise Camp and in an instant all the Iroquois were in motion and ready to start this example was soon followed by others, a scene of confusion now ensued. Gardner at the head of the Americans accompanied by two of our Iroquois who deserted two years since, advanced to assist and support all who were inclined to desert. It was now that Lazard an Iroquois called out we are greater in number let us fire and pillage them, on saying this he advanced with his Gun cock'd and pointed at me. Old Pierre then seized two of the Company's horses but finding I was determined not to allow him or others to pillage, finding it sufficiently galling to see them going off with our Furs and enduring the most approbious [sic] terms they could think of, without allowing them to pillage us from both Americans and Iroquois. All this time with the exception of Mr. Kittson and McKay and two of the engaged men and not before the two latter were called did anyone come to my assistance. Thus we were overpower'd by numbers, and the greatest part of these Villains escaped with their Furs, in fact some of them had conveyed theirs in the night to the American camp they then departed.[32]

The next day Ogden made haste to remove from the scene, which despite Gardner's statement had not been ceded to the United States; that was deliberate falsehood—it was either in the Oregon Territory, where both had equal rights, or it was in Mexico. Before he could get away, however, two more of his freemen went over to the Americans, taking their catch and their equipment. The total number of freemen who thus deserted was twenty-three, leaving to Ogden but twenty trappers. Ogden concludes his story thus:

As we were on the eve of starting Gardner came forward and said you shall shortly see us in the Columbia and this Fall at the Flat heads and Kootenais as we are determined you shall no longer remain in our Territory to this I made answer when we receive orders from our own Government we shall but not before, in answer to this he said our Troops will reach the Columbia this Fall and make you, we then separated. I have been so far particular in giving you a true statement of the whole conversation that passed between Gardner and myself and leave you to form your own opinions.[33]

At once Ogden headed back for the Snake River; he felt that to remain would mean that he was trapping for the Americans and that more of his men would desert. He is frank enough to say:

Indeed the tempting offers made them independent of the low prices they sell their Goods and high rate they pay for their Beaver were too great for them to resist, and altho' I represented to them all the offers were held out as so many *Baits*, still without effect, indeed they were too well convinced of the contrary, as for a Beaver skin they could procure more for [sic] than they could with eight from us.[34]

Ogden reached the Snake River about June 12. His party began trapping, but the returns were poor. About ten days later he discovered five tents of Americans—thirty or forty men. Knowing the result of such a contact, he turned away to the northeast and determined to try the three forks of the Missouri—the confluence

32. *Ibid.*, 110.
33. *Ibid.*, 112.
34. *Ibid.*

of Jefferson, Madison, and Gallatin Rivers. It does not seem to have weighed with him that that was forbidden land—American territory. All he could see apparently was that it was rich in beaver. He must have known that it was east of the Rocky Mountains.

From this trespass Ogden returned to the Snake country, but learning that another party of Americans was trapping in the vicinity he set off for the northward. He felt that the Snake expeditions were ended; that it would be impossible to induce freemen to undertake them owing to dangers from Indians; and that, even if they did, they would desert to the Americans, because of the great difference in the prices both of goods and furs. The Americans, he said, had opened a communication by waggons from St. Louis to the first Spanish settlement of Taos, where they fit out their trappers and receive their furs; "and," he continues, "they say they intend reaching the Columbia also with Waggons not impossible so far as I have seen." Despite the loss of 700 beaver skins carried off to the Americans by the deserters in Bear Valley, Ogden returned to Fort Nez Percés with returns amounting to 4,000 beaver, and Dr. McLoughlin wrote: "You will see by the accounts sent out that its gains are very handsome."[35] John Work's journal helps to round out the story of these deserters.[36] In the summer of 1826 Work was in charge of the annual trading party to the Flatheads. It was not a special effort as a result of information as claimed by Lewis and Phillips,[37] but the usual *en derouine* to that tribe. To increase returns as well as to ingratiate themselves with the natives, these itinerant parties were frequently sent, not only to the Flatheads, but also to the Nez Percés and Kootenays. Before Work and his party left Fort Colvile they heard that some Americans were at Thompson's Prairie in Montana, west of the Rockies, trading with the Indians. Later Work

35. *Ibid.*, 116, 118 n.

36. John Work entered the service of the Hudson's Bay Company about 1814, came to the Columbia River in 1823, was appointed a chief trader in 1831, and the same year succeeded Peter Skene Ogden in charge of the Snake River expeditions (*see* this chapter, *infra*). He was appointed one of the managers of the Company's affairs west of the Rockies, moved to Victoria, Vancouver Island, in 1849, and died in 1861.

37. W. S. Lewis and P. C. Phillips, *The Journal of John Work* (Cleveland, 1923), 46.

was told that the Americans had been among the Flatheads with trading goods and it was said that they were going to build in the autumn on the upper waters of the Missouri. As Work progressed towards the Flathead country he was informed that "a lodge of Americans" was with those Indians but had only tobacco as trade. He learned that the deserters were still with them and had presented tobacco and scarlet cloth to two chiefs, "as from the chief of the American party Ashly [sic] who they said wished to see the Indians and that he was then off for a large quantity of supplies." The Americans, according to this information, had circulated a report that they were returning with a hundred and fifty horses loaded with goods, that another company was coming with an equal quantity, that five ships were to arrive at the Columbia's mouth, that this was to be the last year in which the British were to trade with the Indians, and that the Americans were now to get the country. Some of the deserters had already left their new employers and were living amongst the Flatheads. Work, however, did not meet the Americans, and, in consequence, had good trade. All this shows that after the meeting of 1825, Gardner had made good his threat to Ogden and had continued northward from Bear River through the Snake country to the Flatheads. The Hudson's Bay Company had intended to abandon Kootenae House and merely send trading parties amongst that tribe, but after this visit of the Americans they reconsidered their decision and strengthened the trading supplies both there and at the Flathead Post.[38]

The news of the desertion reached Dr. McLoughlin at Fort Vancouver in August, 1825. He lamented the loss of the horses and traps which he said were the Company's property (meaning, it would seem, that they had not been paid for), the probable consequent loss of the money due by the vanished freemen, and the loss of "furs to the amount of about three thousand pounds, and their future services."[39] This estimate is plainly very high. But the good doctor took umbrage especially at the threat to drive his Company from the territory as being American. In a letter of August 10, 1825, he points out that the lands west of the Rocky Mountains are, until 1828, free to both British and Americans.

38. This account is compiled from T. C. Elliott (ed.), "The Journal of John Work, July-September, 1826," *Washington Historical Quarterly*, VI, 26 ff.

39. Merk, *Fur Trade and Empire*, 254.

He adds: "By this you will see we are justified in resenting to the utmost of our power any attack on our persons and property or any assumption of authority over us by the Americans." He goes on to say that the sending of a force sufficiently strong to defy these threats and thus counteract the evil impression which the boastful words of Gardner and the desertion of the freemen might have made on the Indians and the remainder of the people, would be a good move and would have a beneficial effect.[40]

The London Committee of the Hudson's Bay Company, not knowing the geography, thought that the trouble had occurred east of the Rocky Mountains and hence within United States territory and regretted that their officer, Ogden, should have trespassed on American soil. On September 20, 1826, they wrote to Dr. John McLoughlin:

Had the spoliation taken place on the West side of the Mountains on the neutral ground which from the statement of Mr. Ogden appears not to have been the fact, we might have submitted such a case to the Ministers, as might have induced them to seek redress or a restitution of the property from the United States Government, but as the transaction took place on the United States territory we fear we must be compelled to bear the loss unless you are able to prove distinctly that it occurred on the West side of the Rocky Mountains, and we direct that you will by return of this vessel transmit the most full and particular information you can collect on the subject. We have most particularly to desire that all our officers will in future confine themselves and the Parties entrusted to their charge within the limits of the Company's Territories or the Neutral Ground till the Boundaries of the two Powers are defined, and any inattention to this instruction, on the matter being made known to us will be attended with our serious displeasure.[41]

Six months later the Committee advised Governor Simpson to pay as good a price as the Americans or even "something more" in order to prevent the recurrence of such an incident, and reminded him that in grasping too much all might be lost. The Committee further indicated that if, in the region west of the Rocky Mountains, their trading parties encountered any Americans an arrangement should, if possible, be made as to the localities where each would operate, and that there must be no aggression against them

40. *Ibid.*, 254.
41. Merk, "Snake Country Expedition," 119.

nor any violence except in self-defence.[42] In October, 1826, Ogden, writing the Governor, put his finger upon the spot:

From the exorbitant price the Trappers paid for their Goods and horses is solely to be attributed their desertion and former misconduct, indeed from the enormous prices they have been charged with, the difficulties they had to encounter and subject to so many losses, it was almost impossible however industrious a Man might be to clear his annual expences, in fact his four horses and traps alone cost him One hundred fifty large Beaver, nor could he depend on the latter for the year as they have been of late of an inferior quality, and seldom could a Trapper return to the depot without being obliged to renew both.[43]

Dr. John McLoughlin, investigating the trouble, stated that "it proceeded from the bad system in which the business was carried on and charging exorbitant prices for the supplies."

He added that he altered the whole system and, contrary to the advice of two of his colleagues, continued the Snake expeditions with such success that the opposition instead of gaining ground withdrew from the field.[44] The expedition of 1825-6 under Ogden left Fort Nez Percés or Walla Walla, on November 20, 1825, just twelve days after its return from the preceding. The route was up the Snake River, and thence to the head-waters of the Deschutes, then southward toward Klamath, and on to the John Day River country and the Blue Mountains, then over the divide to Burnt River which was followed to the Snake, and thence up that river. The experience of 1825 had filled Ogden with dread of American influence on his men. On March 20, 1826, while on Snake River, above the site of the future Fort Boisé, he learned from the Indians that some American traders and Iroquois Indian freemen were not more than three days' march distant. "If this be the case," says he, "our hunts are damned, and we may prepare to return empty-handed. With my discontented party I dread meeting the Americans. That some will attempt desertion I have not the least doubt, after the sufferings they have endured."[45] It

42. *Ibid.*, 120.

43. Merk, *Fur Trade and Empire*, 283-4.

44. Merk, "Snake Country Expedition," 121 f.; Lewis and Phillips, *Journal of John Work*, 45 n.

45. T. C. Elliott, "Peter Skene Ogden Journals," *Oregon Historical Quarterly*, X, 356.

was not long before the expected happened. On April 9, Ogden writes: "About 10 A.M., we were surprised by the arrival of a party of Americans and some of our deserters of last year, 28 in all. If we were surprised they were more so from an idea that the threats of last year would have prevented us from returning to this quarter, but they find themselves mistaken."[46] The next day the deserters visited Ogden: he had a busy time settling accounts with some of them, and trading. Evidently his price was higher than in the preceding year. He traded seventy-three beaver skins, large and small, and two seasoned otter at a "reasonable rate" and what was, doubtless, even more satisfactory obtained "81.12 beaver" in part payment of the debts owing and two promissory notes for balances due by three of these freemen. "Our deserters," says he, "are already tired of their new masters and from their manner will soon return to us. They promised to reach the Flat-heads this fall." Then he adds quite illogically: "I cannot imagine how the Americans can afford to sell their beaver to reap profit when they pay $3 per pound for coarse or fine, but such is the case."[46a]

It does not strike him, apparently, that in trading with these men he is doing the same thing for which he denounces the Americans. On the following day his unwelcome visitors departed. One of his men—"a worthless scamp"—wished to join them, and his new masters having paid his debt, Ogden consented. Two of the Americans joined him with their traps and horses. He accepted the accretion without any question of its propriety or as to the consistency of his own conduct. And as the visitors vanish, he joyfully records: "Not one of our party seemed the least inclined to desert; so much to their credit."[47] A tribute, one might add, to Dr. McLoughlin's good sense in improving the conditions under which they worked. Ten days later, learning that three half-breeds were bent on desertion to the Americans, Ogden secured their horses, arms, and blankets. He states that one of them being impudent received a drubbing from him. Yet Ogden can bear witness to the sturdy character of these men: "Many of the trappers came in, almost froze, naked as the greater part are, and destitute

46. *Ibid.*, 359.
46a. *Ibid.*, 360. The "81.12 beavers" is explained by Elliott as meaning eighty-one pounds, twelve shillings (£81 12s. 0d).
47. *Ibid.*

of shoes, it is surprising not a murmur or complaint do I hear;
such men are worthy of following Franklin. Two-thirds without a
blanket or any shelter, and have been so for the last six months."[48]
So, the expedition gradually makes its way homeward. Leaving
the party to return to Walla Walla along the usual route by way
of Powder River and Grande Ronde Valley, Ogden proceeded
westerly across the Blue Mountains and the Cascades to the Willamette River and thence to Fort Vancouver. The year's work had
produced, besides a few otter and other skins, 3,577 beaver, large
and small. The apparent gain was £2,533 18s.[49]

In 1826-7, the expedition under Ogden, though called a
Snake Expedition, had little contact with the Snake River country.
It operated principally in the Klamath region and in the vicinity
of Mount Shasta—territory theretofore unknown to the white man.
During the whole extent of its absence from Fort Nez Percés—
September, 1826, to July, 1827—it did not meet any of the
American trappers and traders from the Missouri, nor indeed with
opposition from any source.

Ogden's fourth Snake expedition, 1827-8, left Fort Walla
Walla, September 5, 1827. About ten days later, on the Grande
Ronde River, he learned that a party of American trappers were
on their way to that fort. Just beyond the present border of Idaho,
near the Weiser River, his men reported the finding of strange traps.
The Americans were there, as he soon discovered; though it was
farther west than he had thought to encounter them. That day,
September 25, he met an American who informed him that he and
five others were trapping on that river and that the party numbered
forty; Ogden had but twenty-eight and they were scattered.
He laments: "My sanguine hopes of beaver here are blasted. . . .
Encamped in company with the Americans. The trappers were in
every direction in quest of beaver. The Americans will not part
with one." The two parties encamped in company; and later continued together along the Snake River. On the twenty-eighth
Ogden writes, without the least comment: "The Americans
informed me it was their intention to follow me to the Columbia.
I informed them I could not offer them better terms than my own

48. *Ibid.*, 361.
49. *Ibid.*, 365.

men had. With this they were satisfied."[50] Almost despondingly,
about a week later, he writes: "I have little hope as the American
trappers are everywhere." The Americans needing supplies, he
furnished them at "¼ less than Indian tariff." One of the deserters
of 1825 who was still with the Americans delivered thirty-five
large beaver in payment of his debt to the Company. Ogden notes
that the Indian chief has an American flag. "It is my intent to
amuse the American party now with us so that McKay's men may
have time to trap the beaver where the Americans purpose going,"
he writes with charming ingenuousness. The Americans remained
with Ogden until November 30, when they set out for Utah Lake,
where General Ashley had his headquarters; in that time—some
six weeks—he had received from them more than a hundred
beaver skins in trade. Detachments of Ogden's men occasionally
met American trapping parties and sometimes one or two, to use
his word, "remained" with the Hudson's Bay people.[51] On
December 24, while ascending the Snake River, Tulloch, an
American, met Ogden's party. "He informed me," says Ogden,
"his company would readily enter into an agreement regarding
deserters." Tulloch further told him that "the conduct of Gardner's at our meeting 4 yrs. since has not been approved"; and spoke
highly of the treatment he had received from Ogden's lieutenant,
Thomas McKay, who was a step-son of Dr. McLoughlin. He notes
on January 5, 1828, that one of the proprietors of the Rocky
Mountain Fur Company (Jedediah S. Smith, D. E. Jackson, or
William L. Sublette) will probably arrive to arrange about deserters.
The Americans are paying $5 for a beaver skin; but he can only
pay $2 for large and $1 for small; yet on the other hand the
American trappers pay 150 per cent dearer for goods than do the
British. In these facts lies the root of the desertions. The relations
between the opposing trappers appear friendly, though each is
willing to take advantage of the other in matters of trade. The
Americans are anxious to obtain snowshoes, but Ogden, fearing
that they intend to bring other trappers, orders his men not to
supply them; and the men hold firm even though offered as high
as $25 for a pair. Ogden wished to prevent the Indians from

50. T. C. Elliott, "Journal of Peter Skene Ogden: Snake Expedition, 1827-1828,"
Oregon Historical Quarterly, XI, 362.
51. *Ibid.*, 367.

carrying messages for the Americans; "but," says he, "it is impossible for me to bribe so many Indians with my party."[52] One of the American *caches* is looted by the Snakes, and there is talk of declaring war on them; Ogden does not know what stand to take for his Company, though personally he would exterminate them. He supplies his opponents with meat as he knows that they cannot obtain it without snowshoes. He writes: "The American is now very low spirited. He cannot hire a man to go to his cache, nor snowshoes, nor does he suspect that I prevented. This day he offered 8 beaver and $50 for a pair and a prime horse to anyone who would carry a letter to the American camp. In this also he failed."[53] He fears that the Americans will bring in liquor, and admits quite freely that liquor would be most advantageous to them, saying that were he in their shoes: "Long since I would have had a good stock of liquor here and every beaver in the camp would be mine." The handicap of which Ogden complains arose from the discouragement of the use of liquor by the Hudson's Bay Company in compliance with the terms of the Company's licence to trade, 1821, which required it to diminish or ultimately prevent its sale or distribution to the Indians.[54] It has, however, been frequently alleged that the Company used liquor freely in its struggle with American traders.

At the same time Ogden discusses the situation with himself: The Americans have only ten traps; if they reach their camp they may return with twenty or thirty trappers; but they have a mountain to cross which is not usable by horses until April, and in the interval very little property can be transported on men's backs. The Americans, not being able to purchase snowshoes, had fabricated some "poor make-shifts," and were to start on January 28 for their depot at Utah Lake. The journey would occupy a month and, chucklingly, says Ogden, "Meantime there will be no beaver skins left among the Snakes." This attempt failed, but a second was successful. However, when the Americans returned they brought three more trappers of their party. Now they were

52. *Ibid.*, 369-70.

53. *Ibid.*, 370-1.

54. *Ibid.*, 371; see the Licence of Exclusive Trade, December 5, 1821, in E. O. S. Scholefield and F. W. Howay, *British Columbia from the Earliest Times to the Present* (Vancouver, 1914), I, 669 ff.

playing cards in the camp, and Ogden mentions that some of the American trappers had lost upwards of $400. He tells of one of his deserters who, with the results of his hunts and the sale of his horses and traps, has $2,100 and is going to St. Louis an independent man. "In the H. B. service," he adds, "with the strictest economy barring accidents in the course of 10 years he might collect that sum. Is it surprising men give preference to the American service and [who] pay extravagant prices for beavers?"[55] He goes on to say that one of the new arrivals informed him that the two American trappers who had joined him on April 11, 1826, were heavily indebted to his concern: "I replied," continues Ogden, "I had no knowledge of the same and that it was his duty to secure his men and debts also. I said my conduct to them was far different from theirs to me four years since. He said it was regretted; that there was no regular company otherwise I shd. have received compensation. It may be so. At all events, dependent on me, they cannot acknowledge less. I have acted honorable and shall continue so."[56] It would seem from the last words that Ogden regarded his conduct in preventing the Americans from obtaining assistance as "honorable." However, he permitted the men to return to the American party. On February 23, 1828, some of the Americans "left for the Flatheads and perhaps the Kootenays." Ogden adds that he believes "they intend trapping the Forks of the Missouri for which they are strong enough in numbers." On March 17, 1828, he writes: "The Americans now 5 in number more or less starving do not attempt to take beaver, but gamble from morning to night. May they continue. My trappers are not idle."[57] The remaining Americans separated from Ogden on March 26, having been with him from the preceding December. He began to think of his return. On April 24, he had 2,000 beaver skins. A fortnight later McKay arrived with 440 more. Two months later another detachment of his party was encountered; it had "650 beaver concealed in a cache, on Sickly [Malade] River." This would seem to make the returns of this expedition about 3,100 beaver skins. The party reached Fort Walla Walla on July 22, 1828. Ogden closes his

55. Elliott, "Journal of Peter Skene Ogden: Snake Expedition, 1827-1828," 374-5.

56. *Ibid.*, 375.

57. *Ibid.*, 376.

journal with regret for the loss of life, but adds: "The returns far exceed my expectations."

After a delay of two months, Ogden set out on his fifth and last Snake River expedition. He took the same general course as in the preceding year: by way of Grande Ronde, Powder, and Burnt rivers, throwing off detachments here and there. He pressed to the southward on this venture; and into a section of country that had become very familiar to, and popular with, the Americans—the vicinity of Great Salt Lake. He discovered during this expedition the river which we now know as the Humboldt; he travelled thence to Great Salt Lake, which he followed northward. The story is the usual one: difficulties with the Indians, loss of horses and traps by theft, and scarcity of food; but it has no clashes nor even meetings between the rival traders.

It will be noted that in Ogden's five Snake country expeditions he usually left Fort Nez Percés (Walla Walla) and returned to it. As early as July, 1826, he had suggested to Governor Simpson that as two-thirds of the time was occupied in travelling to and from the trapping grounds, he might consider and adopt the American plan: "Far different is the mode the Americans conduct their trapping expedition, their trappers remain five and six years in their hunting grounds and their equippers meet them annually secure their furs and give them their supplies and although great the expence and danger they have to encounter to reach the Missouri, still they find it to their advantage to conduct their business in this way and surely there is a wide difference in the prices they pay for their Furs and sell their Goods compared to us a difference of 200 p.C."[58]

John Work commanded the expedition of 1830-1. It followed in a general way Ogden's track of 1827. On the Snake River in October, Work met twenty Americans, a detachment from the American Fur Company's party of two hundred. They were headed for the Flathead country to establish a post but the advanced season forced them to defer their visit until the next spring. The relations were amicable; the persistent trapping had scarcely left enough fur to fight about. In its travels the expedition, stretching away to the southward as far as Utah Lake, covered

58. Merk, *Fur Trade and Empire*, 276.

more than two thousand miles, setting its traps at all likely places, but the result was the same—very few beavers or none at all. Fifty and sixty-five beavers were big days—the usual record is four, eleven, or twelve, with 150 traps set. It returned to Walla Walla, July 20, 1831.

Plainly the region was depleted. The expedition of 1832-3 under Work went southward towards California. The establishment of Wyeth's Fort Hall in 1834, followed by the Hudson's Bay Company's Fort Boisé, ended the Snake expeditions. In March, 1833, by agreement the British and American traders determined their spheres of operation. Writing in March, 1833, Dr. McLoughlin said, "Snake country is ruined and there are at present 400 Americans in it, and I see nothing that they can do to live but to go in a body to the Piegan Lands which will be a Death blow to the Saskatchewan." And on February 1, 1834, he wrote: "As to the Snake country we have hunted it up and also the country between this and California."[59]

The freemen, their trapping days ended, turned their attention to the rich lands of the Willamette, and became the early agriculturists of Oregon. They are included in the "Canadians" so frequently mentioned in the political discussions leading up to the provisional government of 1843. This annual and persistent trapping had in about twelve years transformed "a country richer in beaver than any they had ever seen" into a fur-desert. Three motives underlay these trapping and trading expeditions. The first and obvious one was the desire of the Hudson's Bay Company to reap the great fur-harvest, with consequent increase of returns and profits. But underneath this lay two others—one a commercial; the other a political motive—but both of them connected with the boundary question.

The Snake country lay west of the Rocky Mountains. It formed a part of Old Oregon—the territory which from 1818 to 1846 was in dispute between Great Britain and the United States. While the sovereignty was undetermined British subjects and American citizens had equal rights in that vast region. But the Hudson's Bay

59. The facts in this paragraph are culled from MS letters of McLoughlin to Edward Ermatinger in Ermatinger Papers, Public Archives of Canada, and from other letters published in *Washington Historical Quarterly*, II, 163 ff., 168, 233; "Journal of John Work," *Oregon Historical Quarterly*, XIII, 368 ff., XIV, 281 ff.

Company and its employés were, until the 1840's, the dominant civilized power therein. This showed that their superior organization had prevailed over the looser organization of the Americans in companies no one of which could secure a legal monopoly or be required to accept the responsibilities of a monopoly trader. We have seen American individualism as a factor in arousing hostility in the Indians along the Missouri and thus blocking the natural road from St. Louis to the Snake country by the Lemhi Pass and other passes from Missouri head-waters to those of the Snake. And thus it was that American effort in the Snake country was merely occasional and sporadic. But the Hudson's Bay Company, to protect their trade on the Columbia, set to themselves the task of making the Snake country a fur-break, hoping by trapping it out to prevent the ingress of the St. Louis traders. How far they succeeded in their ultimate aim has been already shown. "It helped," says Professor Merk,[60] "to sterilize the southern and eastern sides of the Columbia Valley, to insulate the northern side against Saint Louis influence. It helped to convert the lower Columbia into a principality of the Hudson's Bay Company, governed until the day of pioneers by Fort Vancouver and London." The other motive—the political—was more directly connected with the vexed question of the future boundary line between British and American possessions west of the Rockies. Governor Simpson put the policy plainly in his report on his first journey to the Pacific (1824): "If properly managed no question exists that it [Snake Country] would yield handsome profits as we have convincing proof that the country is a rich preserve of Beaver and which for political reasons we should endeavor to destroy as fast as possible."[61] Even before 1825 when the Hudson's Bay Company notified Dr. John McLoughlin, its Superintendent in Old Oregon, that the British would lay no claim to the territory south of the Columbia River, it was felt that in the division that region must fall to the United States. But in the meantime the Treaty of 1818 left the territory open to both nations. From the Company's point of view it was necessary that they should reap the fur-harvest while they had the right. Such reaping, while increasing their profits, would leave untouched the fur-lands of the north.

60. Merk, "Snake Country Expedition," 107.
61. Merk, *Fur Trade and Empire*, 46.

This policy was enunciated by the London Committee of the Company in a letter dated February 23, 1826: "In the meantime the deficiency might be made up by keeping all the frontier country hunted close, and by trapping expeditions in those countries likely to fall within the Boundary of the United States." These instructions were reiterated on March 12, 1827: "It is extremely desirable to hunt as bare as possible all the Country South of the Columbia and West of the Mountains."[62]

62. *Ibid.*, 286; "Snake Country Expedition," 120.

CHAPTER IV

THE HUDSON'S BAY COMPANY IN OLD OREGON
1818-1835

WE come now to the first American efforts to obtain a foothold in the valley of the Columbia, since the days of Astoria. This movement had two facets: trade and agriculture. In this chapter we shall deal with the former and its failure. The success of the latter will be told in the next chapter. Bonneville, Wyeth, and Kelley represent the first trading attempts. These novices pitted themselves against the Hudson's Bay Company, then supreme in the region. That concern had its line of trading posts as a support all the way from Hudson Bay, along the Saskatchewan and the Athabaska to the Columbia, its regular overland brigades, its coastal trading vessels, and its annual supply ships from London—an organization perfected by a hundred and fifty years of experience. Its posts on the Columbia were merely new links in its long chain. It had enormous capital, vast influence, and a field force bred in, adapted and trained to the service. Moreover its long existence and constant friendly treatment had ingratiated it with the Indians and solidified its position among them. The American effort was headed by men of no experience, no training, and no knowledge of the country, the natives, or the trade. They had no organization and no capital equal to the requirements of a struggle with the strongest Company in the fur trade. Their servants were raw recruits as ignorant of all essentials as themselves. The game was lost before a card was played. It is significant that neither the Rocky Mountain Fur Company nor the long-existing, strongly-capitalized American Fur Company was attracted by the possibilities of the Columbia trade in competition with such an opponent. But these novices rushed in where Astor feared to tread. The time was not ripe. Those companies would not enter a field in which their opponent had such distinct advantages.

Underlying all the contacts of the Hudson's Bay Company and the earliest American traders on the Columbia was the sovereignty of the domain west of the Rockies. Lewis and Clark, in 1804-6, though ostensibly only travelling in the interest of commerce, forbade Larocque to distribute flags and medals (of which he had none) among the Mandans on the Missouri, as being a portion of the United States, though the northern boundary had not then been fixed. They declared that their government regarded such things as "sacred emblems of the attachment of the Indians to their country." Yet their journals record that they themselves distributed medals and flags with lavish hand, both east and west of the Continental Divide—that is, outside as well as inside Louisiana. This failure to distinguish between the territory of the United States and the no man's land west of the Rocky Mountains continued. We have already seen it in the case of Gardner and his statements to Ogden in 1825. It will be seen in this chapter in the actions and words of Jedediah Smith and Hall J. Kelley. It is not suggested that the Americans as a whole were unaware of the distinction, but that the traders who came into contact with the British had an absolutely erroneous view of the situation; and that this view governed their conduct.

The Hudson's Bay Company on the other hand was resolved, as we have seen, to obtain every benefit from the legal rights assured it as a British corporation by the treaties of 1818 and 1827. At the same time it sought to protect itself against the "Boston pedlars" by a vigorous all-the-year-round opposition. If the Snake country were transformed into a fur-break and the maritime traders driven off the coast, the trade of Old Oregon would be secured to the Company whose trapping parties would exhaust the southerly portion ere the sovereignty was determined.

It was believed by the Company that when the sovereignty of Old Oregon came ultimately to be settled the Columbia would, for some portion of its course at all events, form the dividing line.[1] Throughout the period between 1825 and 1846 the Hudson's Bay Company, always closely in touch with the British government, strove by every legitimate means, therefore, to strengthen the British claim to the part of Old Oregon lying north of that river. These efforts will be apparent in this and the following chapter.

The union of 1821 brought the Hudson's Bay Company to the shores of the Pacific. It necessarily called for a re-orientation of

1. Letter of Governor J. H. Pelly to the Hon. Geo. Canning, of December, 1825, in Frederick Merk, *Fur Trade and Empire* (Cambridge, Mass., 1931), 257 ff.

ideas. From its inception in 1670 the Company had thought in terms of the Atlantic; now it must in addition think in terms of the Pacific. The red ensign of Great Britain with HBC in the field is seen west of the Rocky Mountains for the first time since its comet-like appearance in 1810-11, under Joseph Howse. The forts then actually existing and operating in the tramontane country and which had all been owned by the North West Company, were: McLeod (1805), St. James (1806), Fraser (1806), George (1807), Kamloops (1812), Alexandria (1821), Flathead or Saleesh House (1809), Kootenae House (1811), Spokane House (1810), Okanogan (1811), Fort George or Astoria (1811), and Nez Percés or Walla Walla (1818). Of these the first six were in what is now British territory (all except Kamloops being in the vaguely defined district of New Caledonia), and the latter six in what is now the United States.

George Simpson, the actual though not the nominal head of the new Hudson's Bay Company—for from motives of policy the united concern retained the name of the older and chartered company—arrived on the Columbia River in 1824 on his first visit. With him came the man whose name is revered in Old Oregon, Dr. John McLoughlin, the Superintendent of the Columbia Department from 1824 to 1845. As a result of that visit and its accompanying investigations, a number of changes were made: Spokane House was to be abandoned, as being off the line of travel, and to be replaced by Fort Colvile; Fort George or Astoria was also to be abandoned and Fort Vancouver to be erected in its stead; the tramontane region was to be supplied from the ocean—the long haul across Canada was to cease and give way to a Pacific outlet; the Boston maritime fur traders, who for more than twenty years had monopolized the sea-otter trade and who were now breaking into the land fur trade, were to be energetically opposed, to the end that the fur trade of Old Oregon should be entirely in the Company's hands.

Of these changes three call for attention. The removal from Fort George (or Astoria) to Fort Vancouver was to some extent the result of divergent views upon the effect of the return of that post to the United States in 1818, under the terms of the Treaty of Ghent. But it can be best explained by the following quotation from a letter from Sir J. H. Pelly, the Governor of the Hudson's

Bay Company, dated December 9, 1825, to George Canning: "In compliance with a wish expressed by you at our last interview Governor Simpson when at Columbia abandoned Fort George on the South side of the river and formed a new Establishment on the North side about 75 miles from the mouth of the River at a place called by Lt. Broughton "Belle Vue" point. Governor Simpson named the new Establishment 'Fort Vancouver' in order to identify our Claim to the Soil and trade with Lt. Broughton's discovery and Survey."[2]

The North West Company had from 1813 onward supplied their posts on the Columbia by annual ship at first from London but later from Boston. With the union the plan was continued but the annual ship came from London. The reason for the change was that the Nor'Westers had only employed the Boston vessels to evade the monopoly of the East India Company in China; but with the union the new Hudson's Bay Company carried practically all its furs to London. The New Caledonia posts had been supplied from, and had forwarded their returns to, Rainy Lake or, later, York Factory. The Governor determined to do the obvious, and connect them with the Pacific Ocean which was so close, instead of carrying to and from the distant eastern terminus. For this purpose he instituted a canoe and horse brigade which after 1826 would bring forts St. James, Fraser, George, and Alexandria into connection with the Columbia.

To drive away the Boston vessels the Governor determined to enter into a vigorous opposition. His plan included the building of trading posts on the coast and the placing of trading ships on the coastal waters. Out of this came Fort Langley which was built near the mouth of the Fraser River in 1827; Fort Simpson, erected on Nass River in 1831; Fort McLoughlin, established in 1833 on Lama Passage; and the trading vessels *Cadboro* (1827), *Llama* (1831), and the steamer *Beaver* (1836).

The location of Fort Vancouver at Bellevue Point, within the limit of Lieutenant Broughton's survey of the Columbia River, indicated a reliance upon Vancouver's work as a basis of claim to the sovereignty of the region. In selecting the exact site, a mile and a quarter from the river, Simpson had in mind his plan of a

2. *Certain Correspondence of the Foreign Office and of the Hudson's Bay Company* (Ottawa, 1899), 11 f.; Merk, *Fur Trade and Empire*, 258.

future main depot at the mouth of Fraser River. In the winter of 1824-5, Fort Vancouver was built. On March 19, 1825, Governor Simpson writes: "I baptized it by breaking a Bottle of Rum on the Flag Staff and repeating the following words in a loud voice: 'In behalf of the Hon'ble Hudson's Bay Co'y I hereby name this Establishment, FORT VANCOUVER. God save King George the 4th!' with three cheers."[3] Fort George (or Astoria) soon ceased to operate—all its activities being transferred to Fort Vancouver. On September 4, 1825, when Dr. John Scouler landed at the site, he found it "entirely abandoned by the settlers, and taken possession of by the Indians who are rapidly reducing it to a state of ruin and filth."[4] This change may possibly also be taken to indicate the belief of the Company that the Columbia River would be the boundary for a part, at least, of the distance between the ocean and the Rockies.

In November, 1824, Simpson sent James McMillan, whom he calls "my staunch and manly friend and fellow traveller," to examine Fraser River in pursuance of his plan to build there the headquarters of the Company on the coast.[5] It is believed that it was thought unwise to place the principal depot on the Columbia River, as being too near the probable line of boundary. McMillan's report showed that while the Fraser River might properly be the site of a trading post, its probable unnavigability for any distance inland prevented it from being considered as suitable for a main depot.[6] In consequence Fort Vancouver had forced upon it a greatness to which it was not born. When it blossomed from a mere trading post into the proud position of headquarters for the Columbia Department, a new site had to be found nearer the river bank. There the new fort rose in its majesty during 1828-9.[7]

The decision to abandon Fort George (or Astoria) was reconsidered and in 1829 it was reopened. This result was brought about

3. Merk, *Fur Trade and Empire*, 73, 124.

4. John Scouler, "Journal of a Voyage to N.W. America," *Oregon Historical Quarterly*, VI, 277.

5. Merk, *Fur Trade and Empire*, 154, 114.

6. *Ibid.*, 248, 258. For the complete account of the expedition see T. C. Elliott (ed.), "The Journal of John Work," *Washington Historical Quarterly*, III, 198 ff.

7. "Letter of Smith, Sublette, and Jackson, October 29, 1830," *Oregon Historical Quarterly*, IV, 396 f.

by the appearance in the Columbia River of the brigs *Owhyhee* and *Convoy* of Boston.[8] The palmy days of the maritime fur trade were gone; cargoes of sea-otter skins in a season were a thing of the past; now the maritime traders from Boston were willing and anxious to pick up every land skin that was offered. This brought them into direct opposition with the Hudson's Bay Company, especially as the coast Indians, in order to supply the trading vessels, visited the inland tribes to obtain furs which otherwise would have gone to the Company's posts. Josiah Marshall, the owner of these two brigs, had instructed them to "make a stand" on the Columbia and there seek beaver skins. Though Captain John Dominis, the commander of the expedition, had replied that he had not sufficient men to form a temporary post and would content himself with stationing one of the brigs in the river;[9] yet the log of the *Owhyhee* shows that on August 7, 1829, the mate and some of the crew were set ashore at Astoria to build a house for trade. The *Owhyhee*, with this party at Astoria, another at the Dalles, and the *Owhyhee* itself at Cassino's Camp, offered keen opposition to the Company, who met it with the old prairie policy of settling down to do business beside the aggressor.[10]

Donald Manson was sent in 1829 to reopen Fort George. Captain Dominis soon intimated that he was willing to sell out; Manson passed the word on to McLoughlin; but when the doctor and the Yankee captain discussed a sale they found themselves far apart. The captain wanted a high price for his goods, payable in large beaver skins, at $4.50 each; the doctor wished to buy only such goods as he required and to pay therefor in lumber at $10 per M. Later the captain reopened the matter, offering all his goods at a price payable in bills and guaranteeing no further opposition from *his* employers for two years. This offer the doctor also refused, saying that in view of the uncertainty of the Company's tenure the amount involved was too great, and that it was bad policy in any case to buy off opposition. For about a year the *Owhyhee* was in the Columbia River, sometimes alone, at others in company

8. F. W. Howay, "The Brig *Owhyhee* in the Columbia, 1829-30," *Oregon Historical Quarterly*, XXXV, 11.

9. S. E. Morison, "New England and Opening of Columbia River Salmon Trade, 1830," *Oregon Historical Quarterly*, XXVIII, 114.

10. Merk, *Fur Trade and Empire*, 323; Howay, "Brig *Owhyhee*," 14.

with the *Convoy*. These two American vessels gave Dr. McLoughlin, as he said, "an immensity of trouble." At their arrival the
Company was getting six large beaver for one blanket and twenty
for a musket (if Captain Thompson, the master of the *Convoy*,
be correct), but their sharp opposition reduced these rates by
75 per cent.[11] To this trade the *Owhyhee* added the first export of
salmon from the Columbia River; in August, 1830, when she left
the river she carried away fifty-three barrels of salted salmon
for the Boston market.[12] From the Columbia these two Boston
brigs sailed to the Strait of Juan de Fuca and its connecting waters,
where they spent about a month to the annoyance of the Company's
agent at Fort Langley—Archibald McDonald. Writing from Fort
Langley in February, 1831, McDonald says that "in the face of
two vessels" his trade of 1830 was nearly as good as that of 1829;
and he adds: "If the Americans are off this year I hope things will
be still better."[13]

It may be added that the *Owhyhee* had been in the Columbia
River for a few weeks in May and June, 1827; indeed, she was the
first American vessel in the Columbia fur trade since 1814, but she
was then more interested in spars than in furs. In 1788 John
Meares, an Englishman, had taken the first spars from the Northwest Coast to China; in 1818 the Boston ship *Mentor* is believed
to have carried some to China; and in 1819 the ship *Arab* of Boston
had sailed from the Columbia with a cargo of spars for Valparaiso.
Here appears to be the commencement of the trade of the Columbia
River in salmon and lumber. The Hudson's Bay Company had
frequently discussed the possibility of exporting salted salmon
as a sort of by-product from Fort Vancouver or Fort Langley,
and action in a small way was taken in 1830, if not before.
The Hudson's Bay Company was exporting lumber to the Hawaiian Islands in 1829 from the Columbia, and lumber and salmon to
California in 1830.[14]

11. Morison, "New England and Columbia River Salmon Trade," 123.
12. *Ibid.*, 115; Howay, "Brig *Owhyhee*," 18.
13. *Washington Historical Quarterly*, I, 259.
14. For the statements in this paragraph, see: Howay, "The Brig *Owhyhee* in the
Columbia, 1827," *Oregon Historical Quarterly*, XXXIV, 326 ff.; Morison, "New
England and Columbia River Salmon Trade," 112, 116; *Washington Historical
Quarterly*, I, 259, 261; and Merk, *Fur Trade and Empire*, 319.

In connection with the visit of these two brigs, *Owhyhee* and *Convoy*, John Dunn tells of an interesting incident:[15]

On one occasion an American vessel, Captain Thompson, was in the Columbia, trading furs and salmon. The vessel had got aground, in the upper part of the river, and the Indians, from various quarters, mustered with the intent of cutting the Americans off, thinking that they had an opportunity of revenge, and would thus escape the censure of the company. Dr. McLoughlin, the governor of Fort Vancouver, hearing of their intention, immediately despatched a party to their rendezvous; and informed them that if they injured one American, it would be just the same offence as if they had injured one of his servants, and they would be treated equally as enemies. This stunned them; and they relinquished their purpose; and all retired to their respective homes. Had not this come to the governor's ears the Americans must have perished.

The story rings true and it gives an account of Dr. McLoughlin's conduct which accords with his whole life in Oregon.

Frances Fuller Victor relates a story arising out of the same visit. While the *Owhyhee* was in the Columbia a deadly, devastating epidemic broke out among the Indians. As it originated among those living near the brig, the superstitious savages believed that Captain Dominis, her commander, had intentionally caused it by emptying a vial of "bad medicine" into the river with the deliberate purpose of destroying them. "It probably would have gone hard with the *Owhyhee's* crew," she says, "but for the influence of the Hudson's Bay Company, and the attentions of Doctor McLoughlin, who laboured faithfully, but in vain, to arrest the disease."[16]

In 1827 Jedediah S. Smith, of the American fur-trading concern of Smith, Jackson, and Sublette, made a trapping and trading jour-

15. Dunn was a strong supporter of the Hudson's Bay Company; but the story is quoted, apparently with approval, by the late F. V. Holman in his *Dr. John McLoughlin* (Cleveland, 1907), 36, and even by the anti-British W. A. Slacum in his "Report on Oregon," *Oregon Historical Quarterly*, XIII, 189 f. The accident to the *Convoy*, Captain D. W. Thompson, mentioned below, occurred early in April, 1830; but Dunn did not arrive on the Columbia in the barque *Ganymede* until about May, 1831. It would appear, then, that he is merely repeating some story that was current at the time.

16. John Dunn, *History of the Oregon Territory* (London, 1844), 162; F. F. Victor, "Flotsam and Jetsam of the Pacific," *Oregon Historical Quarterly*, II, 39 f.; and W. A. Slacum, "Report on Oregon."

ney into California. He is the same man who in 1824 had fallen in with the Hudson's Bay Company's Snake expedition and, accompanying it to Flathead House, had returned to the Snake country with the party under Peter Skene Ogden. The Mexican authorities ordered him out of California, but as a concession permitted him to leave by travelling northward instead of retracing his steps eastward. In the last days of December, 1827, Smith and his party of nineteen men with their traps, trading equipment, and horses left San Francisco. Their route was up the Sacramento River, across the mountains to Trinity and Klamath Rivers, and by the coast to Umpqua River. It was Smith's purpose to take his horses through to Great Salt Lake where he could easily sell them to the trappers and traders at $50 each. On the Umpqua his camp was attacked by Indians who killed fifteen of his men and stole all his property, including trading goods, horses, equipment, traps, and some one thousand beaver skins. Smith, with the survivors, on August 10, 1828, limped into the Hudson's Bay Company's headquarters at Fort Vancouver.[17]

By a fortunate circumstance Dr. McLoughlin had arranged to send a trapping and trading party under Alexander Roderick McLeod into the southerly part of Oregon and its preparations were well advanced when Smith arrived. Trade and trade rivalries gave way to humanity; and under Dr. McLoughlin's instructions McLeod, early in September, led his party to the Umpqua to recover the stolen property and to punish, if possible, the murderers. Some of the subordinates at Fort Vancouver objected to the expenditure in aid of an opposition trader, and especially Smith, whose name was associated with the desertions of Ogden's men in the Snake country in 1825, "as it was thought we would have difficulty enough to hold our own, being already at war to the northward, but the Dr. would have his own way."[18]

By another fortunate circumstance George Simpson, who had been appointed Governor-in-Chief of the Hudson's Bay Company's

17. M. S. Sullivan, *The Travels of Jedediah Smith* (Santa Ana, California, 1934), 108, 146 f.

18. "Letter of William Todd, July 15, 1829," *Washington Historical Quarterly*, I, 257. This letter contains a short account of the tragedy. The "war to the northward" refers to the punitive expedition against the Clallam Indians on Puget Sound in June, 1828.

Territories in 1826, reached Fort Vancouver on October 25, 1828, on his second journey to the Pacific Coast. He heartily approved of Dr. McLoughlin's action. The expedition was composed of thirty-eight men. After some three months of effort and an expense of £1,000 to the Company, it succeeded in recovering thirty-eight horses and more than seven hundred beaver skins. In a fine spirit of humanity Governor Simpson wrote to Smith: "We make no claims thereto [i.e., for salvage], on the contrary place the property which we have recovered at your disposal without any charge or demand whatsoever." The Company offered to buy the horses at $10 apiece "which is a higher price than we ever pay";[19] the beaver at $3 per skin, land-otter at $2, and sea-otter at $10, prices that they claimed to be fair, considering the damaged condition. "But," the Governor added, "if these prices be not satisfactory to you, and that you prefer leaving your property here until a favourable opportunity should present itself for removing it, we shall with pleasure retain it for you and deliver it when and to whom you may direct."[20] While writing as above, the Governor knew that McLeod had made enquiries into the cause of the massacre, inasmuch as these Indians had theretofore been well-behaved and friendly. He had learned that a report had reached the Umpquas that Smith's party "were enemies, destroying all the natives that came within their reach"; that this information was apparently confirmed by the severe treatment meted out to one of their own tribe who had stolen an axe; and that Smith's party declared themselves of a different nation and enemies of the Hudson's Bay Company whom, as being trespassers, they proclaimed their intention of driving from the Columbia region. When these statements were placed before Smith, he denied some of them; but, says Governor Simpson, "the whole story is well told and carries the probability of truth along with it."[21]

The entire proceedings were fully reported to London, and met with the heartiest approval of the Governor and Committee there.

We are much gratified to hear that every hospitable attention and assistance were offered to Mr. Smith the American and his Companions

---

19. Merk, *Fur Trade and Empire*, 304 f.; Sullivan, *Travels of Jedediah Smith*, 138.
20. Sullivan, *Travels of Jedediah Smith*, 142.
21. *Ibid.*, 148.

in distress after the horrible massacre of his party by the natives of the Umpqua, and from the humane feeling you have already manifested it is scarcely necessary to desire, that you will on all occasions render any protection in your power to Americans, Russians, or any other strangers who may be in the Country against the treachery or violence of the natives whatever may be the objects of the visits of such strangers, be they competitors in trade or otherwise, as all feelings of self interest must be laid aside when we can relieve or assist our fellow creatures.[22]

Smith informed the Hudson's Bay Company's people that flattering reports of the fertility of the Willamette Valley had reached St. Louis, the centre of the American fur trade, and that in consequence many eyes were turned longingly towards the western land of promise. He remained at Fort Vancouver as the guest of the Hudson's Bay Company until March 12, 1829, a period of more than seven months. From the Company and its representatives he had received nothing but kindness. When he departed he carried their draft for the sale price of the articles they had recovered for him and without the deduction of one cent. Moreover they furnished him with transportation to Flathead Post, whence he easily made his way to his partners: he met Jackson on his way to the Snake country, and Sublette near Henry's Fork.

On October 29, 1830, Smith joined his two partners in a letter to the Secretary of War, the greater part of which is a report by him of his *observations* while a guest at Fort Vancouver. He describes in considerable detail the conditions there and the various activities of his hosts, the Hudson's Bay Company. He stresses the fact that the fort is to be "a permanent establishment." Then, although aware of the Convention of 1818, he treats the Columbia River region as United States territory—much in the way that Johnson Gardner had done in the Snake country in 1825.[23] He says that the goods imported from London there "enter the territories of the United States, paying no duties." He speaks of the great quantity of furs shipped out by the Columbia, the number of which "could not be exactly ascertained, but Mr.

22. "Letter from London Committee to Dr. McLoughlin, October 28, 1829," in *ibid.*, 151.

23. See Ogden's report in chapter III, 51, *supra;* for Smith's letter see *Oregon Historical Quarterly*, IV, 395 ff.

Smith was informed indirectly that they amounted to about thirty thousand beaver skins besides otter skins and small furs."[24] He goes on to state that the Company does "not trap north of latitude 49 degrees, but confines that business to the territory of the United States." He continues with the statement that the British have taken possession of the Columbia River and the country south of it; "while no Americans have ever gone or can venture to go on the British side."[25] The interest of the United States and its citizens (including therein, of course, Smith, Jackson, and Sublette), requires, he says, that the Convention of 1818 "should be terminated and each nation confined to its own territories."[26] It would seem that Smith, like Gardner and other American traders, understood that Convention as a grant by the United States to Great Britain of trading rights within American territory; though it cannot be doubted that during his seven months' residence in Fort Vancouver he must have learned otherwise.

The movements of the American trader, Joshua Pilcher, formerly of the Missouri Fur Company, in 1828 and 1829, have been sketched in the preceding chapter. While he was at Flathead Lake, in 1829, Pilcher made Governor Simpson a proposition for a joint trading and trapping venture to the head-waters of the Missouri—the scene of Ogden's trespass in 1825. Simpson replied on February 18, 1829, that the region was within the territorial rights of the United States: "These rights," he said, "we as British subjects cannot infringe openly, and although the protecting laws of your Government might be successfully evaded by the plan you suggest still I do not think it would be reputable in the Hon'ble Hudson's Bay Co'y to make use of indirect means to acquire possession of a trade to which it has no just claims. Under these circumstances I cannot fall in with your views, and as regards Mr. Ogden he cannot without acting in direct opposition to his instructions cross the height of land."[27]

24. This is a mere guess or worse; for the annual returns of all the region south of 49°, the richest section, were only about nine thousand; the returns of the Snake expeditions have already been given (Merk, *Fur Trade and Empire*, 44).

25. Forgetting or in ignorance of the maritime traders who for forty years had swept the coast from Mexico to Alaska.

26. *Oregon Historical Quarterly*, IV, 395 ff.

27. Merk, *Fur Trade and Empire*, 307; and see W. I. Marshall, *Acquisition of Oregon* (Seattle, 1911), I, 318 ff.

In the early 1830's the increased interest in the Columbia River region resulted in two pioneering movements: those of Nathaniel J. Wyeth and Hall J. Kelley, the first attempts since the days of the Winships and Astor to found permanent trading settlements. Though in no way connected with them, and of small importance from any point of view, yet as occurring at the same time, the fur-trading expedition of Captain Bonneville should be mentioned. It had one trait in common with Wyeth's and Kelley's ventures: the leader's inexperience and utter ignorance of the difficulties and dangers of the task attempted.

Captain Bonneville was an officer of the United States Army, a soldier of fortune, whose imagination had been caught by the lure of the great open spaces of the West, but who was totally unacquainted with the fur trade and with the conditions under which it must be carried on. He, however, succeeded in organizing an expedition of 110 men, with the necessary goods and equipment, which set out on May 1, 1832, from Independence, Missouri, for the Rocky Mountains and the trapping grounds beyond. In preparation for the winter he, after reaching the Snake country, divided his party into three sections, which trapped in different parts of that rich but dangerous fur ground. During 1833, he became involved in disputes and contentions with the well-organized and powerful American traders: the American Fur Company and the "Mountain Men." That winter he spent on Portneuf River, a southern tributary of the Snake River. Early in March, 1834, Bonneville and three companions reached the Hudson's Bay Company's post, Nez Percés or Walla Walla. P. C. Pambrun, the officer in charge, received them kindly, welcomed them heartily, and treated them generously, as men, but made it very plain that as competing traders they could obtain no goods or materials for barter, nor any assistance that would strengthen them in the competition for furs.[28] Later in that year Bonneville strove again, but unsuccessfully, to secure trading goods from the Hudson's Bay Company at Nez Percés. Wherever he went in that vicinity he found the Company snugly ensconced and their influence paramount. After spending the winter of 1834 on Bear River he returned eastward and reached the frontier settle-

28. H. M. Chittenden, *The American Fur Trade of the Far West* (New York, 1902), I, 424.

ments in the middle of August, 1835. Bonneville's expedition was a failure, commercially and scientifically. He had, however, done one thing: he had taken waggons through South Pass and to Green River, thus making the fertile lands of Oregon somewhat more accessible from the eastward.[29] But Bonneville's greatest influence arose from the fact that his journals fell into the hands of Washington Irving, whose captivating story made his name a household word and raised Bonneville upon a pedestal to which neither his scheme nor its results gave him any claim. Bonneville in reporting to the War Department on July 29, 1833, pointed out the advantages which he claimed the Hudson's Bay Company had over the Americans in their cheaper goods, etc., and recommended that the American government occupy Oregon with a full company; but though he felt personally aggrieved that the Company had not been willing to sell him goods to be used in competition for furs he did not express one word of censure on their conduct.[30]

But the two expeditions of real importance and of direct influence are those already mentioned: Wyeth's and Kelley's. They originated in the dreams of Hall J. Kelley, a Boston schoolmaster, who, from the end of Astor's ill-starred undertaking, kept before the American people the value and importance of the Oregon territory and its necessity as a part of the United States.

Wyeth caught Kelley's vision; his practical mind saw a great opportunity. Kelley dreamed his dreams and failed; Wyeth strove to execute a trading plan and failed. The one, an impractical man with an impractical plan, failed; the other, a practical man with a workable plan, failed because he had insufficient capital, no previous experience, and no knowledge of trade methods and trade conditions.

Wyeth's plan was to form a trading concern to carry on business in the wild and distant region "where flows the Oregon." The nature of that business was left undetermined: "The company go out for trade in such branches as may be expedient"; but Wyeth added that "probably the fur-trade will be selected."[31] He intended

29. *Ibid.*, 431.

30. Marshall, *Acquisition of Oregon*, I, 322. For further details of Bonneville's expedition consult Chittenden, *American Fur Trade*, and Washington Irving, *The Adventures of Captain Bonneville* (1837).

31. Chittenden, *American Fur Trade*, I, 437.

to send his party with their equipment, horses, waggons, etc., overland from the Mississippi, to obtain his trading goods and market his returns by ship to and from the Columbia River. There was nothing new or brilliant in the idea; it had been Astor's plan; the Nor'Westers had so acted during their whole existence on the Pacific slope; and the Hudson's Bay Company were, even then, carrying on in exactly that way. But neither the management of a pleasure resort nor an acquaintance with the ice industry of New England is especially fitting as a training for the direction of fur trade and salmon curing on the Columbia. However, the scheme was launched; but the party that was to have been fifty numbered only twenty-four when the Mississippi was reached. At St. Louis the realities to be faced in the undertaking were seen without romantic glamour, the difficulties and dangers took on their true colours, and the inexperience of the leader became painfully apparent. With the assistance of William L. Sublette, of the Rocky Mountain Fur Company, the party, less deserters, on July 8, 1832, reached Pierre's Hole, near Henry's Fork of Snake River. There they met the true wild west: lodges of Indians, trappers of the American Fur Company and the Rocky Mountain Fur Company, and many freemen or free traders. The situation was desperate: for the leader in whom they had trusted knew as little, or as much, of this wild life as they did. Seven of the eighteen wisely resolved to turn back at this point.[32] The remaining eleven stuck to Wyeth, and for some three months they wandered and trapped in the Snake country, until, obtaining a guide to conduct them across the Blue Mountains, they on October 14, 1832, reached that haven of rest—Fort Nez Percés or Walla Walla. There P. C. Pambrun befriended Wyeth, as, indeed, did all the agents of the Hudson's Bay Company during his residence among them. From Walla Walla, Wyeth descended the Columbia to Fort Vancouver and then on to Astoria. On October 29, 1832, he writes: "I find myself involved in much difficulty on account of my men some of whom wish to leave me and whom the Co. do not wish to engage nor to have them in the country without being attached to some Co. able to protect them alledging that if any of them are killed they will be obliged to avenge it at an expense of money

32. John Ball, *Autobiography* (Glendale, California, 1925), 75 ff.

and amicable relations with the Indians. . . . The Co. seem disposed to render me all the assistance they can."[33]

Wyeth now learned that his ship, the *Sultana*, had been wrecked among the Society Islands. This, coupled with the disaffection of the few who had stood by him, led to the dissolution of his company. It was a case of *sauve qui peut*. Of the eleven who came on from Pierre's Hole, two died at Fort Vancouver, five went home by sea, two remained in Old Oregon, and two started on the return journey in 1833 with Wyeth. Those who clung to Wyeth and reached Fort Vancouver would have starved to death had it not been for the Hudson's Bay Company who lodged them and fed them throughout the winter. "We were received," says John Ball, one of the party, "with the greatest kindness as guests, which was very acceptable, or else we would have had to hunt for subsistence."[34] And what that would have meant to such novices may be easily imagined.

In the spring of 1833 the two men who still clung to Wyeth were, with him, given transportation by the Company to Flathead House with the brigade under Ermatinger. In the Snake country Wyeth met that other inexperienced adventurer, Captain Bonneville, whose story has been already outlined. They agreed to undertake a hunt to the southward as far as the Spanish settlements of California. Luckily for both it was only a dream. Wyeth now set his face homeward. He did not even collect the furs he had in *caches*, but pressed on to Green River, the rendezvous of that year for the American traders. The gathering ended, Wyeth crossed by South Pass to the Big Horn. There he made a bullboat in which he and his companions voyaged from the head of navigation on that river to the mouth of the Missouri: an adventure which gives Washington Irving fine scope for his pen.[35] This short sketch shows that the root of Wyeth's complete failure lay in his attempting an undertaking for which neither he nor any of his companions had the least training.

On November 7, 1833, Wyeth was back in Cambridge, Mass., his home. Despite his total failure he succeeded in securing capital to support another scheme: the Columbia River Fishing and

33. *Correspondence and Journals of N. J. Wyeth* (Eugene, Oregon, 1899), 176.
34. C. H. Carey, *History of Oregon* (Chicago, 1922), I, 299.
35. Irving, *Captain Bonneville*, chap. XLI.

Trading Company. Again he would cross the continent with a party and send a vessel, the *May Dacre*, around Cape Horn to the Columbia. This time his party consisted of seventy persons. It arrived in St. Louis in March, 1834, and at Independence in April. There Wyeth complained that the American companies had made him pay high prices for his horses. With the party were John K. Townsend and Thomas Nuttall, two scientists, and also several missionaries under Jason Lee and Daniel Lee. Townsend in his *Narrative* has left us a day-by-day account of the journey. When after much tribulation Wyeth on June 19, 1834, reached the rendezvous on Green River with the goods, which in accordance with his contract with Sublette he had brought to that spot, they were refused by the Rocky Mountain Fur Company and left on his hands. He, perforce, continued his route westward with the goods and, reaching Snake River, built there a fort known as Fort Hall—the first permanent post in that rich fur country. Leaving the establishment in charge of a subordinate, Mr. Evans, with eleven men, he pressed onward and, on September 2, 1834, he reached Fort Nez Percés; a fortnight later he was at Fort Vancouver.[36] There Dr. McLoughlin greeted him "with a frank and unassuming politeness which was most peculiarly grateful to our feelings." Townsend goes on to bear witness to what has been testified by every honest person who came to that post: "He [Dr. McLoughlin] requested us to consider his house as our home, provided a separate room for our use, a servant to wait upon us, and furnished us with every convenience which we could possibly wish for. I shall never cease to feel grateful to him for his disinterested kindness to the poor houseless and travel-worn strangers."[37] Wyeth writes: "I found Dr. McLaughlin [*sic*] in charge who received us in his usual manner. He has the power and uses it as a man should to make those about him and those who come in contact with him, comfortable and happy."[38]

The following day Wyeth's vessel, the *May Dacre*, was in the river, having been delayed owing to an accident. Her late arrival

36. Wyeth, *Correspondence*, 232; J. K. Townsend, *Narrative of a Journey across the Rocky Mountains* (Philadelphia, 1839), 168. See also L. S. Grant, "Old Fort Hall," M.A. Thesis in University of British Columbia Library.

37. Townsend, *Narrative of a Journey*, 169.

38. Wyeth, *Correspondence*, 233.

prevented her from taking part in the salmon season of 1834; but Wyeth loaded her with lumber in December and sent her to the Hawaiian Islands. He busied himself in seeking a site for a farm and in making preparations for a campaign into the Snake country. Though actively in opposition to the Hudson's Bay Company, he nevertheless returned on October 13, 1834, to Fort Vancouver "and was received with great attention by all there";[39] yet they knew whither he was bound and for what purpose. Wyeth's journal of that trip is a perfect Book of Lamentations: accidents happen to his horses and his boats; his Kanakas desert and he spends valuable time seeking them; he is taken down with fever and has seven men ill out of his twenty-one; he is deserted by his guide near the Blue Mountains, and when he sets his traps in likely places the returns are shamelessly disappointing. He mentions one creek, of which "several Indians with me say that once there was much beaver on this creek, but that the British Cos. have trapped it out."[40] With his Fort Hall operating in the Snake country, his Fort William in existence on Wappato or Sauvie's Island below the mouth of the Willamette River, his own trapping effort up the Deschutes River and with another party left trapping above the Dalles—all in opposition to the Hudson's Bay Company,—Wyeth yet records: "I arrived at Vancouver in the morning 23rd Feb. and met a reception such as one loves to find in a country such as this."[41]

Fort Hall had its difficulties. Some of its men were murdered; others were robbed of horses, traps, ammunition, clothing, and furs. Wyeth was too weak in force to punish such atrocities; he was, moreover, without experience with Indians. All he could do was to record that: "Mr. Pambrun the Hudson's Bay Company's agent at Fort Nez Percés is acquainted with the ringleader of this band of marauders, and intends to take the first opportunity of inflicting upon him due punishment, as well as to compel him to make ample restitution for the stolen property, and broken heads of the unoffending trappers."[42] And so Wyeth passes from the scene, leaving to his opponents the duty or privilege of punishing those who have done him wrong.

39. *Ibid.*, 234.
40. *Ibid.*, 250.
41. *Ibid.*, 251.
42. Townsend, *Narrative of a Journey*, 249.

Again Wyeth had failed. The fishing venture came to naught; in 1834 the *May Dacre* arrived too late and in 1835 only half a cargo of salmon was secured. The trading at Fort Hall fared no better. The trapping parties did not succeed. The mortality was heavy. On September 22, 1835, Wyeth wrote: "We have lost by drowning and disease and warfare 17 persons to this date and 14 now sick."[43] He was ready to leave the mouth of the Columbia by the end of September, 1835. He was to spend the winter at Fort Hall. On leaving he simply abandoned Fort William, on Sauvie's Island. He succeeded in selling Fort Hall to the Hudson's Bay Company, who maintained it until they withdrew from the territory after it had become part of the United States by the Treaty of Washington, 1846. Again Wyeth returned to Cambridge and re-entered the ice business—in which he prospered. His ventures on the Pacific were ahead of their time, lacked capital, and were managed by a man without the least experience of such business or even of the conditions and people of the West.

Wyeth had nothing but good to say of Dr. McLoughlin. When in 1850 S. R. Thurston, the first Delegate from the Territory of Oregon, was engineering through Congress the Oregon Donation Land Law with its iniquitous clause eleven depriving McLoughlin of his land claim, he wrote to Wyeth that McLoughlin's name had become odious to the people of Oregon because of his endeavours to prevent its settlement and cripple its growth. Wyeth replied stating the doctor's kindness to him and the early settlers. He did more. He wrote to the Honorable R. C. Winthrop, a member of the Senate, to enquire what matter was pending that concerned McLoughlin and offering to send a memorial on his conduct. Winthrop answered that he had seen Thurston, who would give him no information. Wyeth then wrote to McLoughlin enclosing the correspondence and saying: "Should you wish such services as I can render in this part of the United States I shall be pleased to give them in return for the many good things you did years since, and if my testimony as regards your efficient and friendly actions towards me and the other earliest Americans who settled in Oregon will be of use in placing you before the Oregon people in the dignified position of a benefactor, it will be cheerfully rendered."[44]

43. Wyeth, *Correspondence*, 154.
44. Holman, *Dr. John McLoughlin*, 256 ff.

It seems fitting to conclude this outline of Wyeth's activities with a quotation from John Dunn's *History of the Oregon Territory*, as that writer was on the spot at the time.

A Mr. Wyeth, of Boston, having heard much of the salmon fishery in the Columbia, and thinking it would afford a profitable trading speculation, chartered a vessel, in 1835; and on his way took a number of the Sandwich Islanders as fishermen; supplying himself also with a cargo of fishing nets, and a great variety of other fishing apparatus, on the most approved principles. On arriving at the Columbia he set vigorously to work, dead sure of making a fortune. But his nets were totally unfit for the occupation; and his exotic fishermen, notoriously familiar as they are with the watery element, were no match for the natives, pursuing their natural occupation in almost their indigenous element, and so familiar with the seasons, the currents, the localities, and all the many other circumstances that ensure success. He set up for a fur trader as well, and imagined that he would make up his loss in competition against the savages by his successful competition against the company. But his trappers were not more successful than his fishermen; although the company afforded him every facility; and he was obliged to quit the country a disappointed adventurer, having disposed of his goods and chattles to the company; who, according to his own written statement, treated him with generosity. To this fact, which I now state, Mr. W. Irving bears honourable testimony.[45]

Reference has been made to the wild dreams of Hall J. Kelley, the Boston schoolmaster, to whom Wyeth owed his information. Impracticable and visionary as were his schemes, they yet served to set people in the eastern United States thinking and talking of the new Land of Goshen beyond the Rockies. As one reads his writings and notices his strange obsessions and the stories he has to tell of his constant persecutions, the plottings and plannings of his "enemies" to do him purposeless harm, and finds these enemies pursuing him like furies everywhere, one feels that the "near approximation to insanity" of which he speaks[46] has gradually grown into insanity itself.

From 1824 onward—in season and out of season—Kelley worked to convince the public of the United States of the possibility of

45. Dunn, *History of the Oregon Territory*, 139 f.

46. Hall J. Kelley, *A History of the Settlement of Oregon* (Springfield, Mass., 1868), 15, cited by F. W. Powell, "Hall Jackson Kelley," *Oregon Historical Quarterly*, XVIII, 46.

settling the Oregon country. He claimed to have succeeded in securing four hundred prospective emigrants each of whom had pledged himself to pay $20 towards the expenses of reaching that land. These people with their equipment were to transport themselves to St. Louis. There Kelley was to take them in hand—the blind leading the blind—and guide them to the Columbia River, where each was to receive two hundred acres of land. He expected Congress to aid the movement by paying all or part of the expenses of the journey westward from the Mississippi. He managed to interest some religious and missionary societies in the scheme, which of course included the conversion of the Indians. He secured free transportation for himself on the Ohio and Mississippi rivers to New Orleans, and a passport permitting him to travel across Mexico. Some of his prospective settlers were to join him in New Orleans. He left Boston on November 1, 1832, for Oregon by this round-about route through Mexico, which no person had theretofore attempted. On May 11, 1833, he had reached Vera Cruz, but only after many difficulties, real or imaginary. In Mexico he had trouble, as he had everywhere; but he does not lose the chance to dream of a railroad in that land, and he even writes to President Santa Anna advocating it. In the end, after alleged adventures of different kinds, he reached San Blas. Thence he made his way to San Diego, California, where he arrived on April 14, 1834.[47] In June he was at Monterey; all his companions had fallen by the wayside. But there Ewing Young and his associates joined him: for wherever Kelley went he preached the attractiveness of Old Oregon. The party, now numbering, besides Kelley and Young, nine persons with horses and equipment, set out on July 8, 1834, on the last stage of the long journey to the Columbia. Again, in California, he dreamed of a railroad that was to run from some undetermined point to San Francisco. Somewhere on his route, after entering Oregon, Michel la Framboise of the Hudson's Bay Company, who was returning from San Francisco, came upon him and his party. Kelley was suffering from malaria. This servant of the detested Company administered curative medicines, befriended him, and guided him and his party to Fort Vancouver. On October 27, 1834, after a journey of six thousand miles, Kelley at last reached the

47. Powell, "Hall Jackson Kelley," *passim* and n. 45.

river of his dreams. To his intense surprise Dr. McLoughlin, the
Superintendent of the Company which he had been bitterly attack-
ing for years, while receiving him hospitably, and rendering him
medical aid, would not permit him to live within the fort. Instead
of being grateful for kindness from a stranger upon whom he had
no claim but that of common humanity, Kelley, forgetting very
conveniently his demented attacks upon the Company, says:
"I was led to the place assigned me, outside the stockade; and so
was cast out from the fort, as though unworthy to breathe the same
air or to tread the same ground as its proud and cowardly in-
mates."[48] While applying this language to those who had saved
his life and even then were ministering to his needs, it never seems
to have dawned upon him that it was Hall J. Kelley "as colonizer
and defamer of the company who was unwelcome, even after it was
evident that there was no stain on his character."[49] Part of
McLoughlin's action was doubtless due to the bad characters which
the Governor of California had given to Kelley and Young; he had
charged that they were horse and cattle thieves. Wyeth visited his
old friend Kelley on February 12, 1835. He is probably the person
who, according to Kelley's *Narrative*, "called to abuse me—to
say that he was against me—I should find no friends in that country
and I had better hasten out of it." Wyeth's entry says that,
arriving at Fort Vancouver, he found to his great astonishment,
Hall J. Kelley. "He came in co. with Mr. Young from Monte El
Rey and it is said stole between them a bunch of Horses. Kelley
is not received at the Fort as a gentleman a house is given him
and food sent him from the Gov. table but he is not suffered to
mess here."[50] One of the great difficulties with Kelley, as with
Johnson Gardner in 1825 and Jedediah Smith in 1830, was that he
believed that the Columbia River region was United States
territory. Kelley's actions show this, and his words also. It was not
difficult for them to reach this belief, especially where the British
were concerned, for "It must be remembered in all Oregon history

48. Quoted by Powell, "Hall Jackson Kelley," 126.
49. F. F. Victor, "Hall J. Kelley," *Oregon Historical Quarterly*, II, 394.
50. Wyeth, *Correspondence*, 250.

that the bitterness of Americans towards Great Britain was intense."[51]

> Had I been willing to place myself under the control and direction of the Company, all would have been peace; but so long as I was disposed to act independently, as an American on American soil, seeking authentic information, for general diffusion, and pursuing the avowed purpose of opening the trade of the territory to general competition, and the wealth of the country to general participation and enjoyment, so long was I an object of dread and dislike to the grasping monopolists of the Hudson's Bay Company. My abode in Oregon was thus rendered very disagreeable.[52]

Even leaving aside the charge made by Governor Figueroa, which Kelley denied and of which, it is clear, he was innocent, it is not difficult to understand how he, with these views and his strange, distorted mentality, should have been *persona non grata* with a man of the type of Dr. McLoughlin.

With Kelley arrived Ewing Young and nine other men, the first to come to Oregon for the sole purpose of settling on the land and making their homes.[53] Though Kelley's flighty schemes had failed, his effort had brought into Old Oregon the type of person he desired—the American pioneer. Before he left the Columbia Kelley dreamed of returning and forming a settlement at New Dungeness, on the southern side of the Strait of Juan de Fuca—a place he had never seen and whose suitability for such a purpose was quite unknown to him.[54]

Dr. McLoughlin, the Superintendent of the Company which he lost no opportunity of abusing and vilifying, aided his return to New England by the gift of a passage to the Hawaiian Islands, on its vessel the *Dryad*, and presented him with a draft for seven pounds sterling. Kelley records that he "felt grateful for it." But he showed his gratitude in complaints about his accommodation and his food: again everyone is conspiring to injure him.[55] From the Hawaiian Islands he obtained passage on the *Canton Packet* to Boston, where he arrived in 1836. He never revisited the Pacific

51. Katherine B. Judson, "The British Side of the Restoration of Astoria," *Oregon Historical Quarterly*, XX, 244.
52. Kelley, *Memoir*, quoted in Powell, "Hall Jackson Kelley," 134.
53. Powell, "Hall Jackson Kelley," 128.
54. *Ibid.*, 137.
55. *Ibid.*, 137 f.; Victor, "Flotsam and Jetsam," 399.

Coast. He made an effort to interest prospective emigrants in his scheme for a settlement on the Strait of Fuca: "But," says he, "the war of persecution continuing to rage, and the troops about me making daily attacks, and the hireling press again being turned against me, I was forced to abandon that enterprise."[56]

The rest of his life was spent in planning chimerical schemes, in preparing and presenting petitions to Congress for recognition of his services, in writing pamphlets on Oregon settlement and cognate subjects, and in an effort to put into shape for publication a narrative of his travels, but, to quote him, "a nervous affection in the head deranged the thoughts and enfeebling the pen, disabled him for the task."[57] One thing, however, it seems right to say of this visionary whose obsessions at times extended beyond the range of sanity, and that is well expressed by Frances Victor: "It is only justice to agree with him [Kelley] that he set (or aided in setting) on foot by his writings the immigration movement to the shores of the Pacific in all its forms whether missionary, commercial, or colonizing."[58]

In the latter part of this chapter we have seen the Hudson's Bay Company faced with the competition of various individual traders. It was relatively easy for the Company, pursuing a continuous policy guided by definite principles and directed by a man of character, to maintain its position. It was inevitable that it should come in for much dislike and much abuse. The Company stood for almost everything that Americans had been taught to dislike. It was a trading monopoly. It derived its authority from the government of Great Britain by a Royal Charter. Its organization was rather hierarchic than democratic. Its ultimate owners were absentees. Its personnel was largely Catholic. The American traders were rugged individualists and it is rare for rugged individualists to attribute their failures to their own shortcomings. In the next chapter we shall find the Company brought face to face with even harsher critics—Protestant missionaries and land-hungry settlers.

56. Powell, "Hall Jackson Kelley," 170 f.
57. *Ibid.*, 179.
58. Victor, "Hall J. Kelley," 399.

CHAPTER V

THE FUR TRADE AND SETTLEMENT IN OLD OREGON
1835-1846

PROBABLY it was as much a matter of policy for Americans, whether private citizens or government agents, to speak boldly and confidently of their "rights" and even to assume a somewhat truculent tone, as it was for the Hudson's Bay Company to adopt the conciliatory demeanour which it knew must be the one best calculated to please the British government.

For instance, W. A. Slacum, a lieutenant of the United States Navy, who was instructed by President Jackson to report on conditions in Old Oregon, spent almost a month on the Columbia in the winter of 1836. His report made in March, 1837, speaks of the Hudson's Bay Company as "claim [ing] the exclusive right to trade and commerce" in the region. The Company's monopoly, he must have known, was only against British subjects. Americans had by treaty the same right to visit, live, and trade there—a right exercised not only by the Boston ships, but also by the *Owhyhee* and *Convoy* in 1827 and 1829, and by Kelley and Wyeth. The difficulty the American trader faced was the strong opposition of the Company and not any exclusive right. He goes on to speak of "the influence the Hudson's Bay Company exercise over the Indian tribes within our acknowledged lines of territory" and of "their unauthorized introduction of large quantities of British goods within the territorial limits of the United States." The United States had no territory on the Columbia any more than had Great Britain, as he must have known. Again he speaks of the Snake country expeditions as "underselling the American fur-trader on *his own ground*" (the italics are his), well knowing that land to be west of the Rocky Mountains. This underselling he charges, in part, to the Company's paying no duties; but in a land like Old Oregon, without sovereignty or organized government, there could be no duties or taxes. He says that the Hudson's Bay Company supplied the Indians with arms; certainly they did and had done so for years, as had the American traders, both land

90

and maritime; and all supplied British guns—the Indian would take no other. Then he repeats the old charge that the Company instigated Indian atrocities. This has already been dealt with. Slacum knew nothing of the matter, and was merely repeating what he had heard. He says he expected the Company to throw every obstacle in the way of his navigating the Columbia; but they did not; on the contrary they welcomed him, even though they suspected that the story he told of his purpose in the country was not true. But Slacum certainly went beyond the bounds of truth and proper conduct when, on the Willamette, he "told the 'Canadians' that although they were located within the territorial limits of the United States their preëmption rights would doubtless be secured them when our Government should take possession of the country."[1] It is hard to justify such statements coming from a man in his position. Naturally they were believed by many Americans who based their conduct and opinions of the American rights thereon.

To the efforts of the Protestant missionaries was, largely, due the inception of the immigration movement which gave the Americans the ascendancy in the Oregon country. It is fitting therefore that the missionary effort and immigration should be linked in this chapter. The fur-trading effort of Bonneville had failed, save in so far as Irving's magic pen had used it as a text to stimulate the American spirit of adventure. Wyeth, after two attempts at trade, had retired, beaten. Hall J. Kelley's hare-brained schemes had ended disastrously. Nothing but bits of human flotsam and jetsam remained to bear witness to the failure of their flighty schemes. The missionaries, coming not as traders or colonizers (though some of them were in reality both), and supported by strong religious bodies, succeeded. Jason Lee (1839), and Elijah White (1841), both missionaries, returned from Oregon to the United States, seeking assistance in their spiritual work, but everywhere spreading the Gospel of Oregon. It is scarcely an exaggeration to say that they were more traders and colonizers than missionaries. Lee on his first visit in 1839 brought the petition of 1838 urging the United States to extend its jurisdiction over the Oregon country and encourage Americans to settle there. As a result, the United States did contribute to the expenses of sending

---

1. W. A. Slacum, "Report on Oregon, 1836-7," reprinted in *Oregon Historical Quarterly*, XIII, 184 f., 188 f., 197, 203, 220.

out the *Lausanne* party of 1840. The missionaries were behind the annual crop of petitions and resolutions. Lee did more: on his journey eastward he delivered an address on Oregon in Peoria, Illinois, which stimulated into being the first immigration (Peoria party) into Oregon, even though it was only partially successful. Oregon was not a new topic, but it was new to learn of it from those with knowledge and not from a dreamer like Hall J. Kelley. Elijah White in 1841 by his public addresses aroused an interest that resulted in the immigration of 1842, which he led across the plains to the Promised Land of Oregon.

It was Wyeth who had in 1834 brought the first missionaries. These were the Rev. Jason Lee and his nephew, the Rev. Daniel Lee, both natives of Lower Canada, with three American laymen, all Methodists. When the missionary party reached Fort Vancouver, Dr. McLoughlin welcomed them so heartily that they felt they were in their "own native land." These Methodists, the first religious denomination in Oregon, established their mission in the Willamette Valley. To aid them in their work of Christianizing the natives, the officers and men of the Hudson's Bay Company, many of them Roman Catholics, subscribed £26; Dr. McLoughlin heading the list with £6. Upon the arrival in 1840 of the *Lausanne* with a reinforcement of fifty-two persons, Dr. McLoughlin invited them to partake of the hospitalities of the fort. In it they were comfortably accommodated.[2] Their sojourn was pleasant and enjoyable, and without any charge. The Rev. Gustavus Hines, who was one of those on the *Lausanne* and who remained until the mission was broken up in 1844, bears testimony to the uniform kindness of the Hudson's Bay Company's officers through those years: "Few persons, whether coming by land or sea, have ever visited Vancouver without being received with a hospitality which knew no bounds, until every want of the traveller was supplied. Innumerable have been the favors conferred by them upon the American missionaries, and their assistance has been rendered at times when great inconvenience and even suffering would have resulted from neglect."[3]

How these missionaries repaid the unwavering kindness of Dr.

2. Daniel Lee and J. H. Frost, *Ten Years in Oregon* (New York, 1844), 225.

3. Gustavus Hines, *Oregon, its History, Condition and Prospects* (Auburn, 1851), 389.

McLoughlin will be told later. As a mission the Methodist effort was a failure. It did not Christianize one Indian. It was in truth concerned more with material things than with things of the spirit, as the strife with Dr. McLoughlin for land at Willamette Falls attests. In the Willamette Valley it lasted ten years; but at the Dalles the station continued until 1847. The venture cost about a quarter of a million dollars. Senator J. W. Nesmith stated in an address[4] that each missionary claimed 640 acres of land individually.

The American Board of Commissioners for Foreign Missions sent out in March, 1835, the Rev. Samuel Parker and Dr. Marcus Whitman to examine the situation and decide upon locations for their missions. Dr. Whitman, however, soon after reaching the rendezvous at Green River returned to New England for reinforcements. On Parker's arrival at Fort Vancouver, October 16, 1835, Dr. McLoughlin received him with many expressions of kindness, and invited him to make the fort his home for the winter and thereafter as long as it suited his convenience.[5] The *Missionary Herald* of March, 1837, contained Parker's grateful acknowledgment of the kindness he had invariably received from the Company, whose hospitality he had enjoyed from October 6, 1835, when he reached Walla Walla, until July 14, 1836, when he stepped off their barque, *Columbia*, at Honolulu. In that interval Parker had been at Fort Colvile, Astoria, and up the Willamette, carried and lodged and fed everywhere without a cent of expense. At the Hawaiian Islands he found an American whaler which landed him at New London, in May, 1837.

In the meantime Dr. Whitman had, under the auspices of the American Board of Commissioners for Foreign Missions, in association with the Rev. H. H. Spalding and W. H. Gray, a layman, set out to found missions amongst the Nez Percés and the Flatheads, in Old Oregon. From the rendezvous at Green River, whither they had come with American traders, they were furnished with a safe and direct escort by the Hudson's Bay Company to Walla Walla and thence to Fort Vancouver. They were welcomed in the same hearty way as their predecessors, and, like them,

4. *Transactions of Oregon Pioneer Association*, 1880, 21 f.

5. Samuel Parker, *Journal of an Exploring Tour beyond the Rocky Mountains* (Auburn, 1846), 18, 87, 147.

received aid in building their stations. The best of feeling prevailed between them and the Company's officers and men, from Dr. McLoughlin downwards. Whitman established his station at Waiilatpu, twenty-five miles from Fort Nez Percés; Spalding located his at Lapwai, near the present city of Lewiston, Idaho. Their letters and diaries testify to the generous treatment they received at the posts of the Company and to the unfailing kindness of its agents, manifested by gifts of food and supplies. For example, Spalding praised Archibald McDonald, the officer in charge at Fort Colvile, saying, September 11, 1838: "The favors which we have received from Mr. McDonald and his wife have not been few nor of little consequence to us. Besides the supplies furnished us for a given price, which are no less favors for being sold, and frequent presents of a bag of fine flour, a ham, a side of pork, buffalo tongues, etc., etc., there has been no charge for the first supply of provisions in 1836, the amount of which I will give you when I am certain it is not to be charged."[6]

In August, 1838, a reinforcement, including the Rev. Cushing Eels, Elkanah Walker, and A. B. Smith, sent out by the same Board, reached Dr. Whitman's station at Waiilatpu. Eels and Walker placed their mission at Tshimakain, near Spokane, and Smith located his at Kamai, about sixty miles east of Spalding's. Disintegration soon set in; but the internal dissensions of these missionaries do not concern us. Their relations, however, with the Hudson's Bay Company's officers continued upon the same amicable basis that had existed from the beginning.

Late in November, 1847, after the boundary line had been drawn by the Treaty of Washington, 1846, a great tragedy occurred: the Whitman massacre, at Waiilatpu. The destruction of life and property continued for eight days, fourteen persons were murdered, and fifty-three others, mostly women and children, taken prisoners. This, of course, ended the Waiilatpu mission; the station at Tshimakain was abandoned, its founders, Eels and Walker, fleeing for protection to the Hudson's Bay Company's Fort Colvile, where they received the warmest welcome and remained safe—housed within its hospitable walls.

In the anonymous book, *Traits of American Indian Life and*

6. W. I. Marshall, *Acquisition of Oregon* (Seattle, 1911), I, 350.

Character,[7] the origin of the massacre is attributed to Dr. Whitman's humane but unsuccessful efforts to cure the Indians, suffering from a violent outbreak of measles and dysentery. Their superstitious minds regarded the increasing mortality as due to a conspiracy between him and others at the mission to exterminate them by poison.

The news of the terrible event reached the Hudson's Bay Company's post at Fort Vancouver on the evening of December 6, 1847. At once James Douglas and Peter Skene Ogden, who had succeeded Dr. McLoughlin in the superintendence of the Company's affairs on the coast, took steps for the rescue of the captives. Great expedition was necessary. The effort must be made before the Indians should become aware that the Americans were preparing to send troops to punish the miscreants. With a force of sixteen men belonging to the Company, Ogden set off for Waiilatpu, in whose adobé buildings the prisoners were confined. On December 19 he arrived at the bloody spot. Anxiously, untiringly, he laboured to effect his humane purpose. The Rev. Cushing Eels reported him as saying to the Indians, in a public address urging them to accept ransom and free the captives:

I have not come here to make you promises or hold out assistance. We have nothing to do with your quarrels. We remain neutral. On my return, if you wish it, I shall do all I can for you, but I do not promise to prevent war. If you deliver me up all the prisoners I shall pay you for them on their being delivered, but let it not be said among you afterwards that I deceived you. I and Mr. Douglas represent the company. But I tell you once more we promise you nothing. We sympathize with these poor people and wish to return them to their friends and relations by paying you for them. My request in behalf of the families concerns you, so decide for yourselves.[8]

By the thirtieth all the captives were in his hands, safe from the bloodthirsty natives. The goods given them as ransom consisted of 63 three-point blankets, 63 common cotton shirts, 12 common guns, 600 rounds of ammunition, 37 pounds of tobacco, and 12 flints: to the value, according to Spalding, of $500. On the day following their release, Ogden, writing to the Rev. Mr. Walker,

7. London, 1853. The author is undoubtedly Peter Skene Ogden, then a Chief Factor of the Hudson's Bay Company. See F. W. Howay, "Authorship of Traits of Indian Life," *Oregon Historical Quarterly*, XXXV, 42 ff.

8. Marshall, *Acquisition of Oregon*, II, 223.

said: "I have been enabled to effect my object without compromising myself or others, and it now remains with the American Government to take what measures they deem most beneficial to restore tranquillity to this part of the country. This, I apprehend, cannot be finally effected without blood being shed freely. So as not to compromise either party I have made a heavy sacrifice in goods, but these are indeed of trifling value compared to the unfortunate beings I have rescued from these murderous wretches, and I feel truly happy."[9] This humane effort was entirely on the Company's initiative, without consulting the American settlers or the provisional government which they had formed. No account was ever rendered by the Company to the United States or to the State of Oregon for the value of the ransom goods, nor for the services of its sixteen employees who spent a month in effecting the happy result and in journeying to and from Waiilatpu. Nor did the United States government or the government of Oregon ever pay a penny of compensation to the Company for its outlay in the matter.[10] Governor Abernethy on behalf of Oregon, in January, 1848, did, it is true, write to Ogden thanking him for his conduct. After mentioning the dangerous situation of the captives, he proceeds: "From this state I am fully satisfied we could not relieve them. A small party of Americans would have been looked upon by them [the Indians] with contempt, a large party would have been the signal for a general massacre. Your immediate departure from Vancouver on receipt of the intelligence from Waiilatpu, enabling you to arrive at Walla Walla before the news of the American party having started from this reached them, together with your influence over the Indians accomplished the desirable object of relieving the distress."[11] Spalding in his first report of the terrible disaster wrote on January 8, 1848: "We owe it under kind heaven to the efforts of Mr. Ogden and Mr. Douglas that we are alive and at this place today. May the God of heaven abundantly reward them. The property at Waiilatpu had all been plundered and the buildings demolished. . . . Messrs. Eels and Walker have been advised to flee to Colville."[12] At first Spalding

9. *Ibid.*, 221, 225.
10. *Ibid.*, 226.
11. *Oregon Spectator*, January 20, 1848.
12. Marshall, *Acquisition of Oregon*, II, 203.

gave as the incentive of the massacre the same reason as Ogden gave: the failure of Dr. Whitman to cure the Indians of the measles. But later he turned against the Hudson's Bay Company and the Catholics and brought charges against them.[13] He wrote that the causes of the bloody tragedy were the policy and course pursued by the Hudson's Bay Company, "which was an embodiment of the British Government at that time," to exclude the American settlers, combined with the antagonism of the Catholics against the Protestant missions. The whole history of the Company in its relations with the missionaries, the traders, and the settlers; its conduct in the matter, in rescuing the captives at its own expense, and its giving shelter to Spalding himself as well as his remaining co-workers; and the high character of its representatives; all combine to brand the charge as utterly false. To make the falsity more apparent, it is only necessary to recall the fact that, almost a year and a half before the gruesome tragedy, the Treaty of Washington (June 15, 1846) had settled the Oregon question and fixed the boundary line between the British and American possessions. Only an unbalanced person could imagine that, thereafter, the murder of a dozen persons—an isolated event—would be instigated to break up the settlements and obtain the territory.[14]

To complete the outline sketch of early missions in Old Oregon, reference must be made to the work of the Roman Catholics, even though their missionaries were not concerned in any of the political movements nor in stimulating immigration and settlement. Their aim was purely religious: to Christianize the heathen and to offer spiritual comfort and support to the servants of the Hudson's Bay Company, who, speaking generally, were of the old faith.

The first Roman Catholic missionaries in Old Oregon were the abbés Blanchet and Demers, who after a journey of about four thousand miles from Montreal reached Fort Vancouver on November 24, 1838. In the correspondence which preceded their departure, Governor Simpson had urged that they locate their stations in the Cowlitz country and not to the south of the Colum-

13. Senate Executive Document, no. 37, 41st Congress, 3rd Session; House of Representatives, Executive Document, no. 38, 35th Congress, 1st Session; M. D. Drury, *Henry Harmon Spalding* (Caldwell, Idaho, 1936), 354 ff.

14. The whole subject of the Whitman massacre has been discussed from every angle and at the greatest length by Marshall, *Acquisition of Oregon*.

bia River, as it was well understood at that time that the British claims would be restricted to the territory north of that river.[15] But, as many of the retired servants of the Company had settled in the Willamette Valley, the prohibition was soon removed. Nevertheless the greater number of the Catholic missions were established north of the Columbia.

In 1840 the well-known Father DeSmet, a Jesuit missionary, made his first journey to Old Oregon, over the plains by the regular route, as far as the head-waters of the Snake River. He returned in 1841 and began the establishment of missions, principally, so far as the region west of the Rocky Mountains is concerned, among the Flatheads, Kootenays, and Cœur d'Alènes. For nearly twenty years Father DeSmet travelled here and there over Old Oregon and the Missouri country in his untiring missionary efforts. He wrote voluminously upon his work and travels, which extended as far as Jasper House in Athabaska Pass. His influence upon immigration was, however, small in proportion to his religious work.

The mission stations of the Roman Catholics, being off the usual line of travel from Fort Hall to the Dalles, did not occupy important positions as aids to the immigration which from 1842 onward was pouring into Old Oregon. One of the Catholic missionaries—Vicar-General Brouillet—happened to arrive on the scene of the Whitman massacre, soon after the bloody occurrence. He hastened to warn the Rev. Mr. Spalding of the danger and urged him to flee for safety. Bishop Blanchet, on learning the terrible news, hastened to the scene and interceded for the lives of the fifty-three captives. As in the case of the help given by the Hudson's Bay Company's officials, Spalding's first response was becomingly grateful. On December 10, 1847, he wrote to the Catholic priests at Walla Walla saying that he owed his life to his "dear friend," Brouillet, and asking their assistance in restoring peace. In a somewhat later account, after acknowledging that the ringleaders in the massacre were Indians who had been received into his own church and regarded by him as good Christians, he added:

They were, doubtless, urged on to the dreadful deed by foreign influences, which we have felt coming in upon us like a devastating flood for the last

15. This correspondence is in the Archives of the Archbishop of Saint Boniface, Manitoba, and was published in *Les Cloches de St. Boniface*, June, July, and August, 1932.

three or four years; and we have begged the authors, with tears in our eyes, to desist, not so much on account of our own lives and property, but for the sake of those coming, and the safety of those already in the country. But the authors thought none would be injured but the hated missionaries —the devoted heretics—and the work of hell was urged on, and was ended, not only in the death of three missionaries, the ruin of our Mission, but in a bloody war with the settlements, which may end in the massacre of every family.[16]

Marshall, in his *Acquisition of Oregon*, has with infinite patience brought together all the documents bearing on this despicable statement and shown its utter falsity.

The first immigrants to Old Oregon—excepting of course the missionaries who came as a body—were those from Red River Settlement. They were all British and, principally, natives of that settlement. They consisted of twenty-three families, numbering eighty persons.[17] The men in the party were, mostly, retired servants of the Hudson's Bay Company. It was intended that the immigrants should settle in the Cowlitz country, and be a kind of "half-servants of the company."[18]

Leaving Fort Garry early in June, 1841, they followed the Company's route across the prairies—the women and children in Red River carts, the men and lads on horses. Each family had two or three carts for their necessary effects, together with horses, cattle, and dogs. On July 19, 1841, Governor Simpson, then bound for the Columbia River, overtook them near Fort Carlton on the North Saskatchewan. He advised them to continue along the regular route by way of the Athabaska Pass; but they ultimately concluded to follow that taken by the Governor himself and cross the Rocky Mountains by a more southerly pass. Somewhere on the Bow River their guide deserted them; they providentially obtained another who led them across the Rockies by Whiteman's Pass, southward of that taken by Governor Simpson and "infinitely

16. "Letter from Spalding, April 6, 1848," *Transactions of Oregon Pioneer Association*, 1893.

17. Sir George Simpson, *Narrative of a Journey round the World* (London, 1847), I, 89; Marshall, *Acquisition of Oregon*, II, 84.

18. Spalding's journal, September 10, 1841, quoted in Marshall, *Acquisition of Oregon*, II, 84.

superior."[19] The difficulties in the mountains were so great that they abandoned their carts and loaded their goods and supplies on their animals. Travelling slowly, they rejoined the Governor's route near the source of the Columbia River. Thence the immigrants took the regular trail to Fort Colvile, and on October 4, 1841, reached Walla Walla. Most of them settled in the Cowlitz country, though some soon removed to the open, fertile lands of the Willamette Valley. This was the first immigration from Red River—the first attempt to bring in British settlers; and there was no other until 1854, long after the boundary question had been settled by the Treaty of Washington, 1846.

It now becomes necessary to retrace our steps and sketch in outline the story of the first organized immigrations from the eastern United States. The American frontier of settlement began to move into Oregon.[20] The attention of these people had been directed to the Columbia River by the incessant and insistent, though chimerical, schemes of Hall J. Kelley; then by the debates in Congress upon the Oregon Question; and lastly by the lectures of the Rev. Jason Lee and Dr. Elijah White.[21]

To this increased knowledge of the potential richness of the land was added the belief that Old Oregon was American territory where an intruding foreign company held sway and garnered its wealth, and all that was necessary was to go out and possess it. The hard times following the panic of 1837 were a further impetus. People were land-poor and yet land-hungry; money was scarce; business, dull; and the outlook in the older states, none too reassuring. Emigration societies were formed in Massachusetts, Pennsylvania, Indiana, Illinois, Ohio, Michigan, Missouri, Iowa, and, of course, Kentucky. Knowledge, economic pressure, patriotism, and religion combined under the stimulus of organized effort to set in motion those successive waves of immigration which in a few years transformed the valley of the Columbia from a fur-trading land to a land of pioneer homes and industry. "They [were] almost all from the western provinces [sic] and chiefly from Missouri."[22]

19. Simpson, *Narrative*, I, 89, 126; J. N. Wallace, *The Passes of the Rocky Mountains* (Calgary, 1927), 5.

20. F. J. Turner, *The Frontier in American History* (New York, 1920).

21. C. H. Carey, *History of Oregon* (Chicago, 1922), I, 420.

22. "Report of Lieutenant Peel," *Oregon Historical Quarterly*, XXIX, 62.

The immigrations, for earlier spasmodic attempts cannot be so classed, began in 1842.

> The first low wash of waves
> Where soon shall roll a human sea.

The party of 1842 consisted of fifty-one men, and fifty-seven women and children. They left the Missouri frontier in May, 1842, with seventeen or eighteen waggons. The distance from Independence, Missouri, the usual rendezvous, to their land of promise— the Willamette Valley—was about two thousand miles. At Forts Laramie and John, posts of American traders, they disposed of some waggons, under the impression that they could not take them through to the Columbia River. When they reached Fort Hall, a post of the Hudson's Bay Company near the upper reaches of Snake River, their waggons numbered but seven. There the waggon journey ended, as it was believed that it was impossible at the late season to take them over the Blue Mountains. These immigrants reached Fort Nez Percés about the middle of September. At Fort Hall the Company's representative offered to supply provisions (and did sell them flour at one-half the price charged them by the American traders at Fort Laramie) and to render any assistance in his power. Dr. McLoughlin at Fort Vancouver proffered assistance, supplied them with goods on credit, and gave them employment upon the buildings then being erected at Oregon City—the falls of the Willamette. He furnished them with wheat for flour, and seed to be repaid out of next year's crop, and let them have cows and other cattle to be returned in kind out of the increase. Dr. Elijah White, who was the leader of this immigration, bears testimony to the kind and hospitable treatment accorded them by both Dr. McLoughlin and James Douglas.[23] Of them he wrote mentioning "the cordial and most handsome reception I met with at Fort Vancouver from Gov. McLoughlin and his worthy associate Chief Factor, James Douglas Esq."

The American immigration of 1843, though not the largest, has been called the "Great Immigration," because of its influence upon the subsequent political and economic growth of Old Oregon.

23. Marshall, *Acquisition of Oregon*, I, 90 ff., 376; Elijah White, *Ten Years in Oregon* (Ithaca, 1850), 164; T. C. Elliott, "Richard ('Captain Johnny') Grant," *Oregon Historical Quarterly*, XXXVI, 9.

Elwood Evans puts the number of immigrants at between 875 and 1,000; Charles H. Carey says that they consisted of "about eight hundred men, women, and children." Before the arrival of this migration some of the American settlers then in Old Oregon had built a schooner, the *Star of Oregon*, and sailed her to San Francisco, California, where they exchanged her for 350 cows, purchased other animals, and recruited a party of forty-two men for the Willamette Valley. They set out on their return in May, 1843, to drive to Oregon 1,250 head of cattle, 600 head of horses and mules, and nearly 5,000 head of sheep. After a toilsome journey of seventy-five days they reached their destination with comparatively small loss.[24] Cattle and domestic animals had been brought by the immigration of 1842; and that of 1843 brought some 1,300 more.

In the story of the latter migration a myth—the Whitman Legend—has found a place. Dr. Whitman in 1842, so runs one of the numerous variants, hearing the Red River immigrants declare that with their advent the country would soon become British, fired with patriotism, resolved to awaken the United States government to the desperate necessity of immediate action. To this end he made a lengthy and really remarkable ride on horseback across the continent to Washington. He left Waiilatpu in October, 1842, and travelling by way of Santa Fé reached the Capital in the following March. He, so runs the myth, aroused the government and the people to the urgency of the situation, formed and led the immigration of 1843, and thus saved Oregon to the Union. This legend was investigated in a painstaking and exhaustive manner by the late W. I. Marshall,[25] whose work destroyed the Whitman myth. He proved that Whitman's great ride had nothing to do with the migrations to Oregon; that its purpose was to obtain the recall of a drastic destructive order which had been made by the Board of Foreign Missions as a result of the discord and wrangling prevailing amongst their missionaries; and that any association that Whitman might have had with the migration of 1843 was accidental and incidental, not fundamental.

The immigrants of 1843 left the Missouri frontier about the end of May with their cattle and domestic animals, and, travelling in

24. *Transactions of Oregon Pioneer Association*, 1891, 181-92.
25. *Acquisition of Oregon*.

covered waggons along the route way-worn by the American fur traders, reached Fort Hall, 1,323 miles from their starting point, in August. The road thence to the Umatilla River and over the Blue Mountains was less plain and far more difficult, but the greater part of the settlers reached the mission at Waiilatpu before the middle of October. Lieutenant Frémont states that when, on October 26, he arrived at Fort Walla Walla, Mr. McKinlay, the Hudson's Bay Company's officer in charge, received him with great civility and "to both myself and the heads of the emigrants, who were there at the time, extended the rites of hospitality in a comfortable dinner to which he invited us." At Fort Vancouver early in November, Frémont found many of the party—others were arriving daily. He adds: "All of them had been furnished with shelter, as far as it could be afforded by the buildings connected with the establishment. Necessary clothing and provisions (the latter to be afterwards returned in kind from the produce of their labour), were also furnished. This friendly assistance was of very great value to the emigrants, whose families were otherwise exposed to much suffering in the winter rains, which had now commenced, at the same time that they were in want of all the common necessities of life."[26] The immigrants of 1843 were the first to bring their waggons through to the Columbia River.

It has been claimed by opponents of the Hudson's Bay Company that its officers, and especially Richard Grant, then in charge at Fort Hall, had, in order to prevent further immigration, represented that it was utterly impossible to take waggons through to the Dalles. The party of 1842 had left their waggons at Fort Hall; and there is no doubt that many persons honestly believed in the impossibility of taking them farther. Before 1843 the attempt had not been made; and from his conduct to the newcomers it is only fair to conclude that in expressing his view of the improbability of making the remainder of the journey by waggons he was merely stating his honest opinion; and this T. C. Elliott, in his paper quoted in the preceding note, has shown was exactly Grant's attitude. The difficulties of that section are acknowledged to have been very great. The whole conduct of the Hudson's Bay Company is utterly opposed to the existence of any ulterior motive. Moreover,

26. *Ibid.*, I, 373; Elliott, "Richard ('Captain Johnny') Grant."

long-headed men, such as even its opponents admit that the
Company's officers were, would realize the absolute futility of
attempting to stop a movement of hardy self-reliant men by
discouraging the use of waggons or anything else for which a
substitute could be found.

Before the immigrants of 1844 left the Missouri frontier, the
Democratic party had raised in Congress the claim to "all of
Oregon," later translated into the Jingo cry of "Fifty-four Forty
or Fight." Warre and Vavasour in their report state that the
American government had offered as an inducement the free gift
of 640 acres to each settler. The reference is probably to the Linn
bill of 1842 which, however, failed to become law; though its
introduction, doubtless, raised expectations that such a law would
be enacted if and when the United States obtained sovereignty.
The number who crossed the plains by covered waggon to Oregon
in 1844 was estimated at about seven hundred; though Holman[27] claims that it was double that figure; and Dr. McLoughlin himself states that it amounted to 1,475 men, women, and
children. Travelling by the old route, now well-marked and easily-
traversable, they reached the Dalles late in the fall. The families
and the waggons were brought down the Columbia River by boats
lent by Dr. McLoughlin,[28] who, in anticipation of their arrival and
the demand it must make upon the limited food supply of the
country, had, in 1843, urged the settlers then in Old Oregon, to
raise larger quantities of grain and other necessaries. John Minto,
one of the 1844 immigrants, in his address presenting the portrait
of the "Good Doctor" now in the Senate Chamber of the State
of Oregon, used these words: "To the assistance given to the
immigration of 1843 as described by Colonel Nesmith, I can
add as an eye-witness, that those of 1844 received the loan of
boats in which to descend the Columbia River from the Dalles
(there being no road across the Cascades); the hungry were fed,
the sick cared for and nursed, and, not the least, was the fact that

27. F. V. Holman, *Dr. John McLoughlin* (Cleveland, 1907), 78; "A Narrative by
Dr. McLoughlin," *Oregon Historical Quarterly*, I, 200; Joseph Schafer, "Documents
relative to Warre and Vavasour's Military Reconnaissance in Oregon, 1845-6,"
Oregon Historical Quarterly, X, 49.

28. *Transactions of Oregon Pioneer Association*, 1876, quoted in Marshall,
Acquisition of Oregon, I, 383 f.

many of the employees of the Hudson's Bay Company followed the Good Doctor."[29]

The immigration of 1845 was the largest of those that came before the Treaty of Washington settled the boundary line; it numbered about three thousand men, women, and children, with between five and six hundred waggons. Leaving Independence, they travelled the same route as their predecessors, the Oregon Trail, so-called. They arrived at Fort Hall early in August, and after a short stay continued on to the Dalles. The members of the party bear witness to the uniform kindness and humanity of Dr. McLoughlin. The Hon. Stephen Statts, who came with the 1845 party, in an address to the Oregon Pioneer Association, after stating that on reaching the Willamette they had been without food for two days, continued:

He [Dr. McLoughlin] immediately furnished us with provisions without money and without price, and extended to us favors which we were ever ready to reciprocate. I am not one of those who wish to cast reflections on the character of Dr. McLoughlin or wish to impute to him anything wanting in the kindest feelings towards the emigrants of 1845. For well do I know that but for him many would have been more embarrassed in making provision for the coming winter's necessities than they were, and I have yet to see the emigrant of 1845 who, when speaking of "the old man doctor," does not speak in high commendation of his action to the emigrants of that year.[30]

Year by year these migrations continued, but as in June, 1846, the boundary line was drawn by the Treaty of Washington, there seems no necessity to carry this sketch of the immigrations further. By 1852, according to Ezra Meeker, one of the immigrants of that year, the Oregon Trail had become a road. In the vicinity of South Pass, he says, "the ancient highway is here in all its primitiveness and solitude worn deep and wide into the flinty roadbed—twelve, twenty, seventy, ninety—aye, two hundred feet wide, and two, five, fifteen feet deep."

Long before the immigrants from the eastern United States began to arrive, the Hudson's Bay Company had expanded beyond mere fur trading and was utilizing the natural resources of Old

29. *Transactions of Oregon Pioneer Association*, 1888, 129.
30. *Ibid.*, 1877, 46-59.

Oregon. In 1828, Jedediah S. Smith reported[31] that they had raised at Fort Vancouver seven hundred bushels of wheat, and had in cultivation fourteen acres of corn, fourteen acres of peas, eight acres of oats, and four or five acres of barley. They had also a fine garden with apple trees and grape vines. There were two hundred cattle, fifty horses, three hundred hogs, and fourteen goats. They employed gunsmiths, carpenters, a cooper, a tinsmith, and a baker. Already the Company had built a good sawmill on the Columbia River five miles above the fort, and a grist mill, then operated by hand but intended later for water-power. Two coasting vessels had been built, one of which was then on a voyage to the Hawaiian Islands.

Each year saw an extension of these outside operations. Naturally, the success of these efforts served as practical evidence of the agricultural possibilities of the Columbia River region. When Governor Simpson was at Fort Vancouver in November, 1841, he stated that the farm there had upwards of 1,200 acres under cultivation, and produced 3,500 bushels of barley, oats, and peas, 4,000 bushels of wheat, and a very large quantity of potatoes and other vegetables. The wheat gave a ten-fold return and weighed from sixty-five to sixty-eight and a half pounds a bushel. There were also fifteen hundred sheep and between four and five hundred cattle.[32]

On the Willamette a settlement formed by the ex-employés of the Hudson's Bay Company in the early thirties became a retreat for the freemen and the retired servants of the Company. In 1841 it contained about sixty Canadian families and sixty-five American. The whole population then amounted to about five hundred souls, besides Indians employed as agricultural labourers. The farms numbered about one hundred and twenty and varied from one hundred to five hundred acres each.[33] North of the Columbia River the Hudson's Bay Company or its subsidiary, the Puget Sound Agricultural Company, had two larger farms at Cowlitz and at Nisqually, Puget Sound. The former was on the Cow-

31. Letter dated October 29, 1830, *Oregon Historical Quarterly*, IV, 395 ff.

32. Simpson, *Narrative*, I, 247; Slacum, "Report on Oregon," 186. Slacum's figures deal with the period 1836-7 and do not agree with Simpson's for 1841. Production may have declined.

33. Simpson, *Narrative*, I, 249.

litz River some forty-five miles from its mouth. It embraced 3,500 acres, of which 600 acres were under cultivation in 1841 and 1,400 in 1845, and produced more than 10,000 bushels of grain. The settlement contained nineteen Canadian families, a part of the immigration from Red River in 1841. Large herds of cattle, flocks of sheep, and bands of horses were raised and pastured there. At Nisqually were centred the cattle-raising and farming activities: 5,800 sheep, 200 horses, and 1,850 head of cattle. Large crops of wheat, peas, and oats were raised, under the direction of a farmer from England.[34] It was not until October, 1845, that the first American settlers arrived in the territory north of the Columbia River, now the State of Washington. This was a party of six families, and two single men—thirty-one in all—headed by one M. T. Simmons, a stalwart Kentuckian. The immigrants of 1842, 1843, 1844, and 1845 had found their homes south of the river, mostly in the Willamette Valley. The Hudson's Bay Company still clinging to the hope, fast-fading, that the Columbia River would form the boundary, did all in its power to dissuade the American immigrants from going into the heavily-wooded region to the northward, and was equally urgent in persuading British subjects to choose that section. Yet when these first Americans set out for the vicinity of Puget Sound they carried a letter from Dr. McLoughlin requesting the Company's agent at Nisqually to supply them with grain and potatoes and charge the accounts to the Fort Vancouver office. His letter concluded: "They have all conducted themselves in a most neighborly, friendly manner, and I beg to recommend them to your kind assistance and friendly offices."[35] As a result they obtained the desired assistance, including ten head of beef cattle. Without this aid it is doubtful if they could have remained in the land, two hundred miles from the nearest source of supply, Fort Vancouver, and that owned by the same Company, which also controlled the only modern means of transportation and offered the only market. As Snowden says: "It

34. *Ibid.*, 178; Charles Wilkes, *Narrative of the United States Exploring Expedition . . . 1838 . . . 1842* (London, 1845), IV, 306 f., 316; Schafer, "Warre and Vavasour's Military Reconnaissance," 90 f.; Frederick Merk, "Oregon Pioneers and the Boundary," *American Historical Review*, XXIX, 683 f.; reprinted in *Oregon Historical Quarterly*, XXVIII, 366 ff.

35. C. A. Snowden, *History of Washington* (New York, 1909), II, 429 ff.

is apparent therefore, that in the end, the Company treated this party with much the same liberality it had shown to the settlers on the Willamette."[36] These settlers found in the cedar—that blessed tree of the Indian—a similar blessing: it supplied the materials for their houses and for the rude furniture they required. From it they made shingles which they disposed of to the Company in satisfaction of their debts and to obtain blankets, provisions, and materials for clothing.[37]

The British subjects in Old Oregon before 1846 were almost all employés of the Hudson's Bay Company, past or present. There were also the two Rev. Mr. Lee's of 1834 who were Canadians, two Englishmen and an Irishman who came in 1835, two more Englishmen who had drifted in about 1840, and, possibly, one or two more; but they were all connected with, and usually regarded as, Americans. By an act of the Imperial Parliament, provision was made for the trial and punishment of British subjects for crimes committed and for any infringement of civil rights in the unorganized territory west of the Rocky Mountains; no similar action as regards its citizens had been taken by the United States government, though the Americans, not to be outdone, had in 1838 elected justices of the peace for themselves.[38] But in practice the authority, position, and personality of Dr. John McLoughlin contributed the real peace-keeping power. The American has always had a *penchant* for public meetings and organizations for law-making. This instinct appears in the provisional government of 1772 in eastern Tennessee and in the miners' laws of California, Oregon, and Idaho. As early as 1838, when there were only about forty Americans in the Willamette Valley, they held a meeting and petitioned Congress to take "energetic measures to secure the execution of all laws affecting Indian trade and the intercourse of white men and Indians." Plainly such a request could only be aimed at the Hudson's Bay Company, their friend and assistant as has been shown. In 1840 and again in 1843 similar petitions were sent urging the enactment of laws for their government and

36. *Ibid.*, 430.

37. *Ibid.*, 434.

38. See the Act of 1821 in Robert Greenhow, *The History of Oregon and California* (Boston, 1844), 459 ff.; R. C. Clark, "How British and American Subjects United," *Oregon Historical Quarterly*, XIII, 141.

protection.[39] It does not seem to have struck them that legislation of that kind could only mean that the region they occupied was a part of the United States. Apparently they could not see that the United States could do what Great Britain had done and no more; legislate for its own subjects. But as there was no sovereignty in the region the United States Congress had no jurisdiction over either the Hudson's Bay Company or the Indians. In 1841 when there were some 137 Americans and 63 Canadians in the Willamette Valley, the occasion of the death of Ewing Young and the impossibility of disposing of his estate were seized upon to emphasize the absence of civil laws, and steps were taken to prepare a constitution and draft a code of laws. Commodore Wilkes of the United States Exploring Expedition was in Old Oregon at the time. The matter was referred to him and on his advice the proposed action was abandoned. The organizers of the movement plainly showed that they were favourable to the United States and hostile, or at any rate opposed, to the British in general and the Hudson's Bay Company in particular. In 1842, the United States government appointed Dr. Elijah White, originally a member of the Methodist mission but now separated from it, as "Sub Indian Agent," though by what right they did so, in view of the treaties of 1818 and 1827, does not appear, and his powers and jurisdiction were equally vague. Dr. McLoughlin refused to recognize his authority; and both he and the Canadians opposed the formation of a provisional government.[40]

But the American settlers pressed for some form of government and, after a number of preliminary meetings including the famous camouflaged "Wolf Meetings," which were ostensibly called to discuss the granting of bounties for wolves' heads, it was agreed on May 2, 1843, at Champoeg, in the Willamette Valley, by a vote of 52 to 50, that a provisional government be established. As was to be expected, its first form, settled in July, 1843, was crude and unsatisfactory. It depended on voluntary contributions and had no power

39. F. V. Holman, "A Brief History of Oregon Provisional Government," *Oregon Historical Quarterly*, XIII, 100 f.; C. J. Pike, "Petitions of Oregon Settlers," *ibid.*, XXXIV, 316 ff.

40. The facts in this paragraph are from: Wilkes, *Narrative*, IV, 350, 352; Clark, "How British and American Subjects United," 147 ff.; "Address of Canadian Settlers," *Oregon Historical Quarterly*, XIII, 338 ff.

to levy taxes, an essential of every government. In truth it was a government in name rather than in reality. As Bancroft says: "After all, there appeared to be no great need of law in Oregon." The root of the movement was feeling and sentiment, not necessity; the object was to oppose the Hudson's Bay Company and to assert and assure that Oregon was, or should become, a portion of the United States. This is shown by the phrase in the report of the committee adopting laws and regulations, "until the United States of America extend their jurisdiction over us."[41] The effect of such out-spoken aims was to intensify the opposition of the Company and the Canadians.

The increasing immigrations, bringing American citizens in hundreds, resulted in alterations that placed the provisional government on a more solid foundation. In 1844, these changes recognized the rights of both nations in the territory, and the support of the people was asked as "citizens of Oregon," and not as Americans or British. The oath of office was to support the organic laws of the provisional government so far as they were "consistent with my duties as a citizen of the United States or a subject of Great Britain."[42] The Americans being now in a handsome majority, such a concession, fitting the existing condition, could be made without fear and with the probability that it would, as it did, widen the basis of support. On this change of front the Canadians in the Willamette Valley accepted the provisional government. The jurisdiction of the provisional government was at first limited to the region south of the Columbia River, though, late in 1844, it was extended to fifty-four forty, a plain echo of the Democratic party's slogan, "Fifty-four Forty or Fight," in the election of that year. Thus the dominance of American influence was still apparent, even under the concession; as also in the memorial to Congress, dated June 28, 1845, requesting that territorial government be established in Oregon, though it added that, if this were contrary to the spirit of the existing treaties, naval and military protection be granted.[43]

The territory covered on paper by the provisional government

41. Holman, "Oregon Provisional Government," 119, 121; H. H. Bancroft, *History of Oregon* (San Francisco, 1888), I, 444.

42. Holman, "Oregon Provisional Government," 127.

43. *Ibid.*, 128, 130.

now extended from the Rocky Mountains to the Pacific Ocean and from California, then a Mexican possession, to Alaska, then belonging to Russia—in other words, to the whole of Old Oregon. But practically it narrowed to the territory west of the Cascade Mountains and south of the Columbia River. Tacitly the Hudson's Bay Company was recognized as the ruling power north of that river. In 1845, a new organic law was adopted by vote of the people. It provided for a governor and a legislature elected by voters resident south of the Columbia. All this time the Hudson's Bay Company had kept itself aloof from the proceedings. But in August, 1845, Dr. McLoughlin and James Douglas, acting for the Company, agreed to become parties to the provisional government. They based their action on the facts that this government was merely a compact for mutual protection, as neither Great Britain nor the United States could exercise jurisdiction over the country, and that such accession did not conflict with their duty to their own government, or interfere with the Company's trading rights. They stipulated in their acceptance that the Company was only to pay taxes upon its sales to the settlers. This satisfied the provisional government, for it assured them of co-operation and, what was even more important, increased revenue. As a result, a new county, Vancouver, was created north of the Columbia, and the provisional government obtained its recognition in that locality. James Douglas, Chief Factor of the Hudson's Bay Company, and M. T. Simmons, the earliest American settler north of the Columbia, were elected as the representatives of the new county in the Legislature. Both Douglas and McLoughlin had in the meantime taken the oath already set out.[44]

On June 15, 1846, the Treaty of Washington settled the boundary line; but the provisional government remained in existence until the formation of the Territory of Oregon, or to March 3, 1849.

Warre and Vavasour in their report upon conditions in Oregon in 1845-6, while inferentially criticizing Dr. McLoughlin for his assistance to the American immigrants, commended his action

44. Bancroft, *History of Oregon*, I, 495, contains in a foot-note the letter of request and its acceptance; R. G. Montgomery, *The White Headed Eagle* (New York, 1935), 306; R. G. Clark, "Last Step in Provisional Government," *Oregon Historical Quarterly*, XVI, 315 ff.

in joining the provisional government.[45] But if he hoped that this action on behalf of the Hudson's Bay Company would smooth its path or his own, he soon found his error. F. G. Holman says:

  I regret to say that a few of these early immigrants, at times, without cause, were rude to Dr. McLoughlin and abusive of his Company and of his Country. Some of them did not care—others had been prejudiced by false information, which they had read or heard before they left their homes, or on the way to Oregon. Some, I still more regret to say, accepted the credit extended to them by Dr. McLoughlin and never paid. But the payment to the Hudson's Bay Company of these bad debts was assumed by Dr. Mc-Loughlin. The aggregate amount is not definitely known, for Dr. McLough-lin suffered, in many ways, in silence. But it was a very large sum.[46]

His difficulties with Governor Simpson on matters of policy and management of the Company, which after the murder of his son in April, 1842, became more keen and bitter, finally culminated in his resignation in November, 1845, from the position of Super-intendent of its affairs, which he had filled so satisfactorily for more than twenty years.[47] Freed of his official troubles and responsibili-ties, Dr. McLoughlin devoted himself to his own personal affairs. He settled down as a mere storekeeper at Oregon City. But his life was made miserable by the difficulties over his land claim. Until the Donation Land Law of 1850, there were no legal titles to land in Oregon, except those of the various missions under the law of 1849 establishing the Territory of Oregon. Before 1850, the only title of private individuals to land was possession. As therefore each man had exactly the same right of occupancy, possessory rights were recognized and respected. In 1829, Dr. McLoughlin had taken possession of land on the east side of the Willamette at the falls and begun the erection of a sawmill. He had also erected three houses there. In 1832 he had blasted a millrace through the rocks of the island at the falls, Abernethy Island. Openly and continuously he was in possession and asserted his claim to the land, including the island. Soon after the arrival of the Lausanne, in 1840, some of the Methodist missionaries who had been so

45. Schafer, "Warre and Vavasour's Military Reconnaissance," 48 f., 51.
46. Holman, Dr. John McLoughlin, 86.
47. See hereon, McLoughlin's letter to Simpson, March 20, 1844, in Oregon Historical Quarterly, XVII, 215 ff.; "McLoughlin's Last Letter to Hudson's Bay Company, November 20, 1845," American Historical Review, XXI, 104 ff.

kindly received and welcomed and so materially aided by Dr. McLoughlin, determined to lay claim to his land. In 1843 a petition filled with mis-statements, innuendoes, and worse was forwarded to Congress setting forth a garbled account of the situation, making it appear that the good doctor was a despot and a tyrant, and stating that he did not own the land at Oregon City (the falls of the Willamette), and "which we hope he never will own." His ownership was a mere possessory right—the same title as the signatories had to the land they claimed as theirs. The petition urged Congress to take immediate action in regard to Oregon and enact "good and wholesome laws," for the good of the resident American citizens.[48] About one-third of the petitioners were immigrants of 1842 who, like all the others, had received nothing but kindness and assistance at the hands of the doctor and the Hudson's Bay Company. In the same year the provisional government, in which was strong Methodist influence, had passed a law depriving him of his land claim. But in the following year, 1844, better counsels prevailed and the act was repealed. For a moment there was a lull. As Dr. Elijah White wrote: "Had any gentleman disconnected with the Hudson's Bay Company been at half the pains and expense to establish a claim on the Willamette Falls, very few would have raised any opposition."[49]

It is beyond the scope of this study to follow the tangled story in detail. At considerable sacrifice McLoughlin succeeded in settling with the Methodist mission. But individual members of the mission laid claim to a part of the land, and these he had to buy off; the island which formed a valuable portion of the property was "jumped" by persons connected with the mission. One great objection to Dr. McLoughlin was that he was a British subject. As soon as possible after the admission of Oregon as a territory, Dr. McLoughlin became a naturalized American citizen (September 5, 1851). By misrepresentations and false statements made by the territorial delegate to Congress (of which the following will serve as an example: "This company [the Hudson's Bay Company] has been warring against our government for these forty years. Dr. McLoughlin has been their chief fugleman, first to cheat our

48. The above statements and those that follow are based on Holman, *Dr. John McLoughlin*. The petition is set out in full in that work, 198 ff.

49. White, *Ten Years in Oregon*, 200.

government out of the whole country and next to prevent its
settlement. He has driven men from claims and from the country
to stifle the efforts at settlement"), the Donation Land Law was
passed containing a section depriving McLoughlin at one fell
swoop of any right to the land at Willamette Falls. Though his
land was gone, "the White-headed Eagle" fought for his character.
To the falsehoods he replied calmly:

American demagogues have been base enough to assert that I caused
American citizens to be massacred by hundreds by the savages. I, who
saved all I could. I have been represented by the Delegate from Oregon,
the late S.R. Thurston, as doing all I could to prevent the settling [of Oregon]
while it was well known to every American settler who is acquainted with
the history of the Territory if [*sic*] this is not a downright falsehood, and
most certainly will say that he most firmly believes that I did all I could
to promote its settlement, and that I could not have done more for the
settlers if they had been my brothers and sisters, and after being the first
person to take a claim in the country and assisting the immigrants as I have,
my claim is reserved, after having expended all the means I had to improve
it, while every other settler in the country gets his.

And McLoughlin spoke truth, as every honest man in Oregon well
knew. In a letter published in the *Oregon Spectator*, September 12,
1850, he wrote:

I am described as a "fugleman" of the Hudson's Bay Company; first to
cheat our Government out of the whole country and next to prevent its settlement. I am an old man, and my head is very white with the frosts of many
winters, but I have never before been accused as a cheat. I was born a
British subject—I have had for twenty years the superintendence of the
Hudson's Bay Company's trade in Oregon and on the North West Coast;
and may be said to have been the representative of British interests in this
country; but I have never descended to court popularity, by pandering to
prejudice, and doing wrong to anyone. I have, on the other hand, afforded
every assistance to all who required it, and which religion and humanity
dictated; and this community can say if I did so or not.[50]

His land gone, and called upon by the Company to pay the moneys
due by the settlers for goods supplied by him to them on credit,

50. The three quotations above will be found in Holman, *Dr. John McLoughlin*,
129, 156, 130. Dr. McLoughlin spent over $90,000 in improvements on this land up
to January 1, 1851; see his detailed statement in *Oregon Historical Quarterly*, XIV,
68 ff.

McLoughlin might well have thought of Shakespeare's Timon of Athens. Seven years after he was deprived of his land claim, the "Father of Oregon" died, borne down by the calumny and ingratitude of some of those whose lives he had saved. In all fairness it must be added that many of the American settlers who realized his great services to the immigrants strove for years to right the grievous wrong that had been done him, and, after his death, succeeded.

Passing from this sad picture, let us glance for a moment at the relations between the American settlers and the British subjects, including the Hudson's Bay Company. These settlers, the immigrants of the 1840's, were predominantly from Missouri and the neighbouring states. They were of the pioneer type; courageous, determined, self-reliant, but often coarse, contentious, and uneducated. To quote Dr. Merk:

Southern uplanders, contentious, ignorant, and suspicious, they went to Oregon inflamed against the Hudson's Bay Company by the charges of such men as Kelley, Slacum, and Spaulding, printed in government documents, that it oppressed American settlers in the Willamette, or the atrocious accusation of Benton that it incited Indians to murder American trappers, five hundred of whom had already been slain. Powerful emigrant trains arriving in Oregon destitute and starving, and believing such tales, were capable of attempting any mischief, and it was partly to avert disaster that McLoughlin gave such generous aid to the companies of 1843 and 1844. Residence for a year or two in the Willamette dispelled much hostility, but there were always abundant opportunities for friction in the economic relations of monopoly-hating pioneers with a foreign corporation that dominated, even if benevolently, the life of the community.[51]

With the French Canadians in the Willamette the relations of the American settlers were uniformly amicable, at any rate after the formation of the provisional government. These men, former servants of the hated Company, only claimed the same amount of land as themselves, and, like themselves, were struggling to make a home in the new land. Though as a whole opposed to the establishment of a government, for they were a peaceable people not interested in politics, two of them sided with the Americans in the "Great Division" of 1843, that brought into being the provisional government. Their votes gave the necessary majority on that momentous occasion. The promise that their claims to their lands

51. Merk, "Oregon Pioneers and the Boundary," 693.

would be respected—land is very dear to the heart of a French Canadian—induced the others gradually to line up in support of the American movement. When the Cayuse War of 1848 broke out as a result of the Whitman massacre, the French Canadians held a meeting at French Prairie in the Willamette Valley and resolved that: "The Canadian citizens of Champoeg county feel it their duty to assist their adopted country in the prosecution of the war against the Cayuse Indians for the horrible massacre committed by them upon American citizens at Waiilatpu."[52] Their company, says Carey, performed conspicuous service in the short war that followed.

But to the Hudson's Bay Company the Americans took a totally different attitude. Numbers of the immigrants who owed their lives to it, so far from being grateful for such help and for continued advances on credit which in 1844 had reached $30,000—Lieutenant Howison in 1846 reported the amount as $80,000—complained that it was a monopoly, a foreign, British company, unfair and greedy in its dealings. They even charged the Company with using a false bushel measure in buying their wheat; and they made it a grievance that the Company's sawmill was operating in competition with one erected by the settlers, or rather by the Methodist mission—a body, of whom it is no misstatement to say that it was more interested in making money than in making converts. Much of the antagonism against the Company was stimulated by this so-called missionary settlement.

The continuous effort of the Company to induce the Americans to settle, if settle they must, on the south side of the Columbia River, led some of the hot-headed Americans to urge that the French Canadians should be forced to move to the other side of the river. Early in 1845 it was reported to McLoughlin that some thirty or forty Americans were attempting the organization of a party to drive out of the Willamette Valley all the Canadians and others having Indian or half-breed families who held lands there.[53] Nothing came of the movement, which appears to have had its root in misguided patriotism and land-hunger.

The constantly increasing number of settlers and the large farms

52. *Oregon Spectator*, January 20, 1848, cited in Carey, *History of Oregon*, I, 547.
53. Merk, "Oregon Pioneers and the Boundary," 694.

claimed by each, forced newcomers to locate on less desirable land or at a considerable distance from the centres. The natural result was that envious eyes were cast on the 8,960 acres occupied by the Company at Fort Vancouver. In February, 1845, Williamson, a settler from Indiana, erected a log hut on the Company's claim and posted a notice that he had located on it as unoccupied land. McLoughlin ordered the house to be demolished and the notice removed. In the heated argument that followed, McLoughlin asserted the Company's right to occupy and use such land as it required. Williamson, angered, threatened, if interfered with, to burn the best building in Oregon, which was interpreted as meaning Fort Vancouver. McLoughlin replied that force would be met by force, but that any vacant land was open to settlement. He offered assistance to Williamson to establish himself on such land, but the Indianian, claiming that the land in question was unoccupied, asserted his right to locate on it. More hot words, more threats, and the matter ended. McLoughlin reported the trouble to the provisional government, and that body, in regretting the unwarranted liberties taken by Williamson, promised to use every effort to prevent a recurrence.[54] Other similar efforts were made to "squat" upon the Company's various land claims. All of these were religiously gathered up by it and placed before the Commission which dealt with its claims and rights in Old Oregon. Lieutenant Howison, who was detailed by Commodore Sloat of the United States Navy to examine the situation in Oregon, early in 1846, in his refreshingly impartial report deals with these trespasses made, as he says, by Americans of "but little judgment and less delicacy." He mentions an instance where a man "and a professor of religion, too," had been ejected by legal process from squatting on the Company's claim. Having nothing wherewith to pay the costs assessed against him, they were borne by the Company. He immediately resumed his squatting and "the same formula of law must be gone through to get rid of him, and so on, *ad infinitum.*"[55]

He thinks that the constant squattings on the Company's claim arose from a belief that this foreign concern would soon, by the

54. Bancroft, *History of Oregon*, I, 459 ff. "Meddle not with this house or claim, For under is the master's name. H Williamson"

55. Lieutenant N. M. Howison, "Report on Oregon, 1846," *Oregon Historical Quarterly*, XIV, 33.

treaty to be made, or otherwise, be expelled from the Columbia region, coupled with the desire to be then in possession and so in a favourable position to take advantage of the situation thus caused. When the terms of the treaty were known, there was much heart-burning among some of the settlers. They were grievously dis-appointed that the Company's rights had been protected, and in consequence at their inability to grasp at the enclosed fields and ready-made habitations, which they had expected the treaty would have obliged the Company to vacate. For, as Howison says, he found on his arrival "the settled conviction on the mind of every one that all Oregon belonged to us, and that the English had long enough been gleaning its products."[56]

But this was only a crystallization of views that we have found outcropping in the story from the days of Lewis and Clark. As we have seen, those explorers had treated the regions east and west of the Rockies in a similar manner. They distributed flags and medals —those "sacred emblems of the attachment of the natives"—with an equally lavish hand. Gardner in 1825 had ordered Ogden out of the Snake country, as being United States territory; and told the Flatheads that the Americans were to have the country and the British would not be allowed to trade after that year. Smith in 1828 informed the Umpquas that the British were trespassers who were to be driven out of Old Oregon; and in his letter to the United States Secretary of War spoke of all the region south of 49° being then (1830) "the territory of the United States." Kelley when on the Columbia River regarded himself "as an American on American soil." Slacum stated publicly that the Columbia country was "within the territorial limits of the United States." And the burden of many of the speeches in Congress was to the same effect. It is not surprising that Howison found among the immigrants a settled belief that the Old Oregon country was, even before the treaty of 1846, United States territory.

The broadest, and indeed, the only, interpretation of these facts seems to be that, throughout the whole history of settlement in Western America, the pioneers assumed what we should call today the right of self-determination. They formed a community, made and enforced laws, and felt that they were entitled to determine

56. *Ibid.*, 32 ff.

the political future of the territory. In a later chapter we shall find
a striking illustration of this tendency in British Columbia where
a small number of settlers made a choice of the political destiny
of a large province. It was natural that the Methodist missionaries
should fall in with this sort of manifestation of spontaneous
democracy; and almost equally natural that the Catholic missionaries should instinctively prefer the appeal to authority which
could be made by the Hudson's Bay Company and by the other
agencies of the British government from which the Company
derived its powers. But to settlers from the United States the idea
that a European power had some claim to exercise jurisdiction
over them, or to deny their jurisdiction over all those who found
themselves in the territory, must have seemed so preposterous as
to make the treaties establishing this state of things appear quite
incredible. On this point, too, it is instructive to compare the early
history of the British colonies on the north Pacific Coast. Governments, as the account of the boundary negotiations in the next
chapter will show, took more sophisticated views.

CHAPTER VI

THE OREGON BOUNDARY SETTLEMENT AND ITS EFFECT ON THE HUDSON'S BAY COMPANY

1846-1851

THE Oregon boundary dispute has been so fully and so frequently discussed in every history of Oregon or the Northwest Coast that only the barest outline is necessary. For a complete examination of the question reference may be made to the authorities cited hereunder.[1]

The Oregon Question is usually regarded as the dispute between Great Britain and the United States which was settled by the Treaty of Washington, in 1846. But in its original and broadest form it concerned the sovereignty of the territory from San Francisco, the most northerly Spanish settlement, to Sitka, the most southerly Russian occupation. At the outset four nations were interested, Spain, Russia, Great Britain, and the United States. In 1819 Spain obtained a northern boundary at 42°; and in 1824 and 1825, the southern limit of Russian America was fixed at 54° 40′. Thus Great Britain and the United States were left as claimants of the intervening region.

The discussion of their claims necessarily included the consideration of Spanish activities north of 42° and of the relations between Spain and Great Britain; for by the Florida Treaty, of 1819, Spain had ceded to the United States all her "rights, claims, and pretensions" to the territory beyond 42°. In the controversy the United States based her claims to the region between 42° and 54° 40′, which for convenience is called Old Oregon, upon two grounds:

1. Robert Greenhow, *The History of Oregon and California* (Boston, 1844); Travers Twiss, *The Oregon Question Examined* (London, 1846); C. H. Carey, *History of Oregon* (Chicago, 1922), I, 453 ff.; J. R. Wilson, "The Oregon Question," *Oregon Historical Quarterly*, I, 111 ff. More recent contributions to phases of the matter are: Joseph Schafer, "British Attitude towards the Oregon Question," *American Historical Review*, XVI, 296 ff.; Frederick Merk, "Oregon Pioneers and the Boundary" and "British Party Politics and the Boundary," *American Historical Review*, XXIX, 681 ff., and XXXVII, 653 ff.; R. C. Clark, "Aberdeen and Peel on Oregon," *Oregon Historical Quarterly*, XXXIV, 236 ff.

by Louis Houck, who says: "It is clear that all of Montana and the States of Idaho, Oregon, and Washington should be placed in the galaxy of the Louisiana Purchase States."[3] He was of the opinion that the arguments to the contrary are "principally borrowed from British sources." But he is alone in making such a claim. Jefferson always denied that Louisiana crossed the Rockies.

Thus, so far as discovery and settlement up to the 1840's were concerned, the claims of Great Britain and the United States were almost on an equality. Neither could make out a perfect title. It was eminently a case for a compromise; and the only question, until the foolish cry of "Fifty-four Forty or Fight" arose in 1844, was what would be an equitable division? In such a compromise one factor that could scarcely be disregarded was the absence of any good harbour in Old Oregon south of the Strait of Juan de Fuca.

Year after year in Congress the question was debated. It was plain that during the existence of the treaty for joint occupation no act of sovereignty on either side could be exercised within the area. The purpose of these discussions was, apparently, to crystallize the public opinion that the American claim was clear and indisputable; that Old Oregon was a portion of the United States; and that any so-called British right was merely another effort of the mother-land to grasp what was not hers. It would be tiresome to enumerate the various forms in which the subject was presented. Some may be given as examples: in 1820, it was as to the expediency of occupying the Columbia River; in 1821 the bill was for occupying the Columbia River "and the territory of the United States adjacent thereto"; and so on.

The British government objected to this propaganda as being in violation of the spirit of the treaty. In 1824 it offered as a dividing line the 49th parallel to the Columbia and thence down that river; the United States countered with a demand for the extension of that parallel through to the Pacific. Thus more than twenty years before the conclusion of the dispute the two nations were close together. The question had simmered down to the area between the Columbia River and the 49th parallel—in all about 58,000 square miles.

In 1825, according to a document found among the papers of

3. Louis Houck, *The Boundaries of the Louisiana Purchase* (St. Louis, 1901), 97.

Dr. McLoughlin, the Hudson's Bay Company had notified him that in no event would the British claim extend south of the Columbia River.[4] In that year a committee was appointed by Congress to consider the establishment of a military post at the mouth of the Columbia. Dealing with the title to Old Oregon, their report placed the American right upon occupation by Astor's Pacific Fur Company, "strengthened, as the committee believe, by purchase [alluding, it is presumed, to the Louisiana Purchase], by discovery and exploration." The British pretensions, the report continued, were "wholly unfounded," British navigators not being the discoverers of any portion of the coast between the Mexican and the Russian possessions; and this despite the discoveries of Drake, Cook, Vancouver, and the British traders. Yet magnanimously, though inconsistently, the report continued by stating that in view of the British explorations the offer of 49° was the utmost concession that could be made, compatible with American interest, honour, or rights.

In 1826, when the negotiations opened for the renewal of the convention of 1818, the instructions to Andrew Gallatin, while stating that Great Britain had not and could not make out even a colourable title to any portion of the coast, authorized him to propose, as had been done in 1824, the extension of the 49th parallel to the Pacific Ocean, as a dividing line between the two nations. "This is our ultimatum, and you may announce it. We can consent to no other line more favorable to Great Britain." The Americans pointed out that the British proposal left them only the dangerous entrance of the Columbia River, and in urging 49°, stressed the necessity of obtaining the safe and commodious harbours of Puget Sound. The British met this argument by offering a detached portion of the Olympic peninsula. Further in support of 49°, the Americans proffered the free navigation of the Columbia; but the British did not regard that as an equivalent for the abandonment of their claims to the triangle in dispute. In the course of the discussions the Americans put forward the principle of contiguity, claiming that the division east of the Rockies established their right to the prolongation of the boundary along the 49th parallel. The negotiations ended in a deadlock. In 1827

4. See *Transactions of Oregon Pioneer Association*, 1880, quoted in full in W. I. Marshall, *Acquisition of Oregon* (Seattle, 1911), I, 430 ff.

the Convention of 1818 was continued, terminable on twelve months' notice.

Then followed the period of private activity in the occupation of Old Oregon, with Kelley as the protagonist, the arrival of the missionaries, and the advent of the first American settlers. It was realized, as Gallatin wrote to Clay in July, 1827, that the British had no desire to colonize the territory and were willing to let the settlement of the country take its course. Such settlement would naturally come from the United States. What was the American attitude? Slacum, who was sent out in 1836 by the United States government to report on the situation in Old Oregon, subscribed $500 towards the purchase of cattle for the American settlers. Whose was the money? Greenhow's *History of Oregon*, in reality a brief on the American side of the dispute, was published at government expense. The secret service fund of the United States contributed to the cost of sending out the great reinforcement of the Methodist missionaries in the *Lausanne* in 1841.[5] In 1843 the report of the Senate Committee upon suitable measures for the occupation and settlement of Old Oregon urged American immigration and the adoption of a policy in its aid. It added: "The occupation and settlement of Oregon by American citizens will of itself operate to repel all European intruders except those who come to enjoy the blessings of our laws; this would secure us more powerful arguments than any diplomacy could invent or use to assert and maintain our just rights in that country if war should ever be necessary to preserve and protect them." This report and other reports upon Old Oregon and the speeches on the subject were printed and distributed by thousands over the length and breadth of the United States. Public opinion was industriously moulded into the belief that the territory in dispute belonged to that country and that the British were "intruders" upon American soil.

The American immigrations have already been dealt with, and it has been shown that there was no British immigration save the party from Red River in 1841. Yet the Senate Committee of 1843, from whose report we have quoted, said:

Every one acquainted with the insidious and steady policy of Great Britain is aware that in all questions of boundary disputes with her neigh-

5. E. S. Meany, "Secret Aid for Oregon Missions," *Washington Historical Quarterly*, XV, 211 ff.

bours she invariably pushes her pretensions to territory, however unfounded or absurd, to the utmost limits of what is occupied by her subjects, and sometimes so far as to claim as a right what is convenient to her settlements whether on her own soil or not. Our interest therefore is and our policy should be to adopt a counteracting policy and to meet her advancing tide of settlement with ours; and the sooner we do this the better, for experience shows that a people under the impulse and enterprise of republican institutions peacefully repel by their approach the subjects of monarchical or despotic government just as the aborigines of the country recede before the advance of civilized man.

No effort was made by the Hudson's Bay Company or any other British organization or person to equalize immigration; that would have been impossible. The Company contented itself with inducing the Americans to settle in Willamette Valley, not at all a difficult task as its natural advantages were most appealing. As a result, when the Oregon dispute entered its final stage the whole American population was south of the Columbia. The British public knew nothing of Old Oregon; no attempt was undertaken to interest them; they cared nothing about it. All this talk of British immigration was drawn from a strong imagination.

After 1835 the United States sent out Slacum, the United States Exploring Expedition under Wilkes, and Lieutenant Howison to report on the conditions in Old Oregon. The British government was kept fully posted by the Hudson's Bay Company. But when in 1845 the war clouds began to lower they sent Lieutenants Warre and Vavasour to examine the Columbia River and the vicinity from a military point of view; and they ordered a number of war vessels to the coast to be prepared for eventualities.

In the meantime the Oregon Question entered the last stage. In 1842, the two governments agreed to make it "a subject of immediate attention"; but owing to internal difficulties in the United States it was not until August, 1844, that the negotiations actually commenced. The obstruction which the diplomats faced was the declaration in the previous May by the Democratic party that the American title "to the whole of Old Oregon [that is up to 54° 40'] is clear and unquestionable; that no portion of the same ought to be surrendered to England or any other power." The British offered the 49th parallel to the Columbia and down that river to the ocean, with a free port or ports. This was declined; but the Americans would not make a counter proposition. After Polk's election on the cry of Fifty-four Forty or Fight, the British made an offer to refer to arbitration; this also was refused. President Polk in his inaugural address stated: "Our title to the country of Oregon is clear and unquestionable and already our people are preparing to perfect that title by occupying it with their wives and children." Despite these words, which aroused strong resentment in England, the Americans again proposed the 49th parallel to the ocean, with a free port or ports on Vancouver Island, which would be severed by the line. The British Ambassador, Richard Pakenham, without referring the offer, peremptorily rejected it.

When Congress met in December, 1845, a resolution to authorize the President to give the year's notice was introduced and passed. Then came a flood of bills: "to authorize and arm the militia of Oregon," "to organize a territorial government for Oregon," "to establish a line of stockade and block-house forts along the Oregon trail," and "to protect the rights of American citizens in the territory of Oregon"; but Congress seemed content with the resolution to abrogate the Convention. The notice was delivered on May 21, 1846.

The feeling had become fairly general among rational men that the boundary for which the Americans had stood consistently must be accepted, but that when the line reached the mainland shore it should be deflected so as to leave Vancouver Island intact to the British. Pakenham's abrupt rejection forced the British government to reopen the question on its own initiative. Accordingly he was instructed to propose to the Americans that the boundary should follow "The 49th parallel from the Rocky Mountains to the sea-coast and thence in a southerly direction through the centre of King George's Sound [sic] and the Straits of Juan de Fuca to the Pacific Ocean leaving the whole of Vancouver's Island, with its ports and harbours in the possession of Great Britain." Accompanying this suggestion was a draft of a treaty which varied but slightly in wording from the above quotation. The treaty was placed before the United States Senate on June 10, 1846; two days later it was accepted without an alteration by a vote of 38 to 12; and on June 15, 1846, the long-standing dispute was ended by the Treaty of Washington, 1846.

Inasmuch as the somewhat vague phraseology of its first article, defining the boundary, gave rise to a subsequent dispute, known as the San Juan Question, the exact language is reproduced:

From the point on the forty-ninth parallel of north latitude, where the boundary laid down in existing treaties and conventions between the United States and Great Britain terminates, the line of boundary between the territories of the United States and those of Her Britannic Majesty shall be continued westward along the said forty-ninth parallel of north latitude to the middle of the channel which separates the continent from Vancouver's Island; and thence southerly through the middle of the said channel, and of Fuca's Straits, to the Pacific Ocean; Provided, however, that the navigation of the whole of the said channel and straits, south of the forty-ninth parallel of north latitude, remain free and open to both parties.

The treaty also granted to the Hudson's Bay Company and all British subjects the free navigation of the Columbia River to the ocean on the same footing as American citizens. The possessory rights of the Company and of all British subjects in occupation of land and other property were to be respected; and the Puget Sound Agricultural Company was confirmed in its rights to its farms, land, and other property.

Much has been written in an endeavour to explain how, after rejecting the 49th parallel in 1818, 1824, 1826, and 1844, the British government proposed it in 1846. Settlement, which is sometimes said to make sovereignty, cannot account for it, because there were no American settlers north of the Columbia: the whole population there was British, with the possible exception of Simmons's small party. Dr. Keenleyside suggests that it was an application of the doctrine of contiguity, giving to each claimant west of the Rockies the portion that adjoined its eastern possessions.[6] If so, there is little evidence in the discussions to bear it out. Dr. Merk insists that it was because the Hudson's Bay Company had, in 1845, removed its headquarters to Fort Victoria, then recently established. He relies upon a letter from Simpson asking McLoughlin to be on his guard against possible lawlessness of the American settlers and as a precautionary move to send the trading goods held in reserve at Vancouver to Victoria, together with those intended for the northern posts. He claims that this conduct showed

6. H. L. Keenleyside, *Canada and the United States* (New York, 1929), 203 ff.

that the Columbia River was not so essential to their trade as they had constantly insisted.[7] This position is open to grave doubt. The removal of a large quantity of goods to ensure their safety is vastly different from a change of base. Dr. Sage has shown that the Company did not complete the transfer of its headquarters from Fort Vancouver to Fort Victoria until about 1849, long after the boundary dispute was settled.[8] But Dr. Merk is on far safer ground in claiming in a more recent study[9] that the British people knew nothing and cared less about Oregon—they had not been so continuously educated in the matter as the Americans. The British statesmen took little interest in what one described as "a few miles of pine swamp." The peace-loving Lord Aberdeen, the Secretary for Foreign Affairs, saw nothing worth fighting for in the comparatively small area that was really in dispute; it was in his opinion of trifling value. Believing that the Columbia River could not, except at great expense, be an outlet of trade, he regarded the American demand for harbours in Puget Sound as eminently proper and reasonable; and he had expressed his personal views as early as March, 1844. Lord John Russell, the Whig chieftain, saw no objection to the abandonment of the British claim to a boundary along the Columbia River; indeed he thought so little of the Oregon dispute that there is no reference to it in his *Recollections and Suggestions*. Speaking in Glasgow in January, 1846, he had expressed what was, without doubt, the British attitude: "The question of more or less territory—whether they were to obtain one-half, and the United States one-half—whether they were to obtain a harbour in a particular position, or the United States to have that harbour, these were questions on which it would be disgraceful for two such nations to go to war. (immense cheering.)" The only discordant note came from Lord Palmerston, the stormy petrel of British foreign politics, who in a letter to Lord John Russell thus unburdened himself: "The Americans appear to have but one formula for boundary negotiations which runs thus: we say that we have a clear title to the whole of the thing which is in

7. Merk, "Oregon Pioneers and the Boundary," 691.
8. W. N. Sage, *Sir James Douglas and British Columbia* (Toronto, 1930), 132, 136, 139, 149.
9. Frederick Merk, "British Party Politics and Oregon," *American Historical Review*, XXXVII, 653 ff.

dispute, but we will prove our moderation by ceding to you for ample equivalent a small and comparatively little valuable portion of it; we are all of us determined to seize and keep the remainder whether you will or no; and if you do not agree to these terms you will be the cause of the war which we shall make against you." But after the treaty was signed he fell into line saying: "In every quarter it will be learned with entire satisfaction that the unfortunate differences between this country and the United States have been brought to a termination which, as far as we can at present judge, seems equally favourable to both parties."[10]

The Hudson's Bay Company and its subsidiary, the Puget Sound Agricultural Company, complained that the treaty forced the abandonment of their seventeen establishments and the loss of their trade. Dispassionately examined their complaint will be found, in great part, baseless. They had built and established themselves in a no man's land whose sovereignty as they knew at the time was yet to be settled. They had carried on trade for years with practically no opposition. They had drained a goodly part of the region of its fur-wealth. And their property and possessory rights had been preserved. As soon as the terms were known one of their prominent officials, James Douglas, wrote:

It appears that the Oregon Boundary is finally settled, on a basis more favourable to the United States than we had reason to anticipate . . . . Business will of course go on as usual, as the treaty will not take effect for many years to come. . . . About the Treaty, I cannot say much, the Government and Committee appear satisfied, perhaps *par nécessité*, with the provision made for the protection of British interests, and they being satisfied so am I. All things considered, the yielding mood of the British Ministry, and the concessions made, we have come off better than I expected. I looked for nothing short of an utter sacrifice of our interests.[11]

At Governor Simpson's request Peter Skene Ogden and James Douglas, who together occupied the position previously held by McLoughlin, made a statement, in 1847, of the acreage occupied and claimed by the two companies in Old Oregon and an estimate

10. The latter part of this paragraph is founded on Merk, "British Party Politics and Oregon."

11. Letters, James Douglas to W. F. Tolmie, November 4, 1846, April 19, 1847, quoted in E. O. S. Scholefield and F. W. Howay, *British Columbia from the Earliest Times to the Present* (Vancouver, 1914), I, 456.

in detail of the building and other improvements. The land claimed at Fort Vancouver was 8,960 acres, of which 1,419½ were under cultivation: at Nisqually, 11,520 acres, including 220 under cultivation; and at Cowlitz, 1,920 acres, of which more than 1,400 were under cultivation.[12] Their incomplete valuation was £74,766; a complete statement in 1857 increased the claim to £466,600. This was still further expanded in 1865 to over £1,000,000 by the inclusion of £500,000 for loss of trade and navigation rights and £100,000 for loss of cattle and rents. In any claim for damages the Hudson's Bay Company could never be accused of omitting anything. Under a Convention of July 1, 1863, a Joint Commission, composed of British and American nominees, was established to investigate and adjust demands made by the two companies. In 1869 President Grant reported that the Commission had completed its labours and had awarded $650,000 in extinguishment of all their rights in Old Oregon.[13]

Throughout this chapter the Hudson's Bay Company and the Puget Sound Agricultural Company, though different entities, have been treated as one. They were so closely related in their operations, notwithstanding that one was a fur-trading and the other a farming corporation, that even their servants could scarce distinguish between them. In January, 1856, for example H. N. Peers, in charge at Cowlitz, wrote: "The inventory of goods on hand at the end of outfit '54 I presume you will charge to the H.B. Co., and credit the P.S.A. Co., therewith, as the simplest way of doing business, for it would be impossible for me to keep the goods apart."

This settlement ended a long-standing dispute in the Territory of Washington. Upon the Company's farm and property at Cowlitz, being quite near the Columbia River, the American settlers had long cast envious eyes. H. N. Peers writes in 1856 that its horses are constantly being stolen, but that having caught a settler in possession of a stolen animal he is taking criminal proceedings. In 1857 one of the American settlers squatted within the area fenced by the Company. Peers thought that vigorous

12. T. C. Elliott, "British Values in Oregon, 1847," *Oregon Historical Quarterly*, XXXII, 27 ff.

13. *Messages and Papers of the Presidents*, VII, 35, cited in Carey, *History of Oregon*, I, 279.

steps were necessary as "his success would as a matter of course be a signal for all the rest—whom I have hitherto kept at bay—to advance and practically take possession of their several claims."[14]

But matters were worse at Nisqually. The acreage there claimed by the Company was about twenty square miles. It had been used for grazing, and seemed to the American settlers preposterously large. Snowden says that the Company's claim "comprised all the land lying between the Puyallup and the Nisqually Rivers, from the Sound to the summit of the Cascades, something more than 167,000 acres and 3562 acres at the Cowlitz Farms in Lewis County."[15] This is a gross exaggeration and is only cited to show that false statements concerning the British companies were circulated and accepted as facts. From 11,520 acres to 167,000 is certainly a long cry. Even though the treaty provided that "The farms, lands and other property of every description belonging to the Puget's Sound Agricultural Company, on the north side of the Columbia River, shall be confirmed to the said company," the Americans proceeded to squat on it. It was fine land and well situated: for the whole country was open when the Company made the location. Being used as grazing land it was by them regarded as unoccupied. It belonged to a grasping monopoly, to an alien concern; and the American settler wanted it. But, because of the words of the treaty, the squatters could file no notice in the land office. If they made a "location" it could not be surveyed, as the United States government had forbidden the surveyors to do so. Here was a large area of good land to which the settlers could obtain no title, not even a possessory right. All this angered the Americans and they complained loudly and vigorously. The treaty, said some, should be abrogated, or disregarded, or set at defiance. They did more. They proceeded to commit all manner of illegal acts. They shot the Company's cattle and horses and destroyed the crops. They "were very fierce against the Co.y"; they even required it to reduce its claim to the one square mile which was the limit of a donation claim for an American citizen. The settlers in the vicinity of Olympia had induced the Company to withdraw its cattle to the north side of the Nisqually River, and the residents of Steilacoom strove to follow their steps. The treaty was only so

14. Copies in library of F. W. Howay.
15. C. A. Snowden, *History of Washington* (New York, 1909), IV, 186.

much waste paper in their eyes: it conflicted with their ideas of individual liberty, of their right to squat on any "unoccupied" land within the territory. They squatted by the dozen on the lands claimed by the Company. When the Company attempted to survey its lands the surveyors were stopped by them. The *Nisqually Journal* contains many records of their unlawful acts.[16] The lands were assessed and taxes levied; but as the Company, while "confirmed" in its rights, had no patent—the title being in the United States government—it opposed every attempt to collect such land taxes. For ten years the fight went on in the courts. In the meantime one of the buildings on the Cowlitz farm was burned to the ground; incendiarism was strongly suspected. By 1867, taxes to the amount of about $60,000 had accumulated, and as the litigation to test their validity was making no headway, one of the counties applied for an order to sell sufficient of the Company's property to satisfy the claim for the disputed taxes; but before the order could be obtained came instructions from Washington, D.C., forbidding such action.[17] It was probably felt that the contemplated proceeding would result in a further claim for damages and render the work of the Commissioners more difficult. The award of the Commissioners took no notice of these taxes, probably because, in their opinion, they were not "legally assessed." This also was regarded as a grievance; the grasping monopoly had evaded payment, while the Americans were compelled to pay taxes. As soon as possible after the award the two companies removed their live-stock and other portable property to British Columbia. And thus ended the long connection between the Hudson's Bay Company and Old Oregon. Recounting some of these incidents Snowden says: "By these several acts was the authority of the United States and the new territorial government of Oregon, established north of the Columbia, and the majesty of the law vindicated in the fruitful region that was soon to become Washington."[18] Comment is unnecessary.

Not alone on land did the Hudson's Bay Company and other British subjects have trouble with the Americans. After the formation of the Territory of Oregon British vessels were subjected

16. *Washington Historical Quarterly*, XIV, 300 f., and XV, 129 f., 139.
17. Snowden, *History of Washington*, IV, 187 ff.
18. *Ibid.*, III, 87.

to much annoyance by the newly appointed officers, men clothed with a little brief authority.

In 1850 the British ship, *Albion*, arrived on the south side of the Strait of Fuca, seeking spars for the British Navy. Finding no one from whom to purchase them the crew proceeded to cut 42 pieces, 60 to 96 feet long. For this trifling trespass United States revenue officers seized the ship. She was libelled, condemned, and sold. A joint Commission held the American government responsible and assessed the damages at $20,000.[19] The seizure, says Bancroft:

was not a very magnanimous proceeding on the part of the officers of the great American republic, but was about what might have been expected from Indian fighters like Joe Meek raised to new dignities. We smile at the simple savage demanding pay from navigators for wood and water; but here were officers of the United States government seizing and confiscating a British vessel for cutting a few small trees from land lately stolen from the Indians, relinquished by Great Britain as much through a desire for peace as from any other cause, and which the United States afterward sold for a dollar and a quarter an acre, at which rate the present damage could not possibly have reached the sum of three cents![20]

In April, 1850, the Hudson's Bay Company's vessel, *Cadboro*, was seized by United States revenue officers for carrying goods from Victoria direct to Nisqually, though the duties were paid under protest. Even the Company's post at Nisqually was seized as containing so-called smuggled goods. And this in the face of the Company's having notified the American authorities of its desire to import and pay duties at Nisqually, asked for a revenue officer to be placed there, and pleaded that it would be impossible to carry on business there if the goods had first to be taken to the port of entry on the Columbia. Certainly no impediments were being taken by the Americans out of the Company's path. The vessel and trading post were both soon released from seizure.[21] Bancroft's words quoted above are applicable to this incident. The hated foreign Company was finding the law strictly enforced against it; and the most trivial and technical omissions punished as serious crimes.

19. *Report of Decisions of the Commission for Settlement of Claims under the Convention of February 8, 1853* (Washington, 1856), 376 ff.

20. H. H. Bancroft, *History of Oregon* (San Francisco, 1888), II, 106 f.

21. Snowden, *History of Washington*, IV, 83 ff., 513 f.

Again in 1850, when the American troops were to be removed from Nisqually to Steilacoom the commanding officer employed the Company's vessel, *Harpooner*, to transport the men and supplies. The vessel also carried some shingles and insignificant freight belonging to the American settlers. For this technical violation of the revenue laws the United States officials seized her; but the Treasury authorities held that there was no justification for the seizure; and the *Harpooner* was released.[22]

Still another instance of this petty persecution may be given. In 1850, Portland and Nisqually were made ports of entry. Later, about February, 1851, at the instance of the Oregon delegate the office was removed from Nisqually to Olympia. In November, 1851, the Company's steamer *Beaver* with the *Mary Dare* in tow landed a passenger at Nisqually without first taking her to Olympia. For this technical and innocent infraction the collector of customs seized both vessels. The Company promptly took the matter into the courts; the vessels were "very justly" released and the seizure cost the United States $20,000. Public meetings were held in which the settlers charged that the judge was bribed.[23]

In conclusion a word may be said regarding the actions of the Hudson's Bay Company after the treaty of 1846. When in 1847 the provisional government of Oregon resolved to enlist five hundred men and borrow $10,000 to carry on the Cayuse War arising out of the Whitman massacre, they applied to the Company for provisions and supplies. These were furnished to the amount of $1,800. Of this sum $599 was paid by the Oregon government, but the remainder remained unpaid until 1854 when it was ordered paid by the Commission of Claims.[24] And again in 1855-6 when the Indian war broke out Governor Mason of Washington Territory appealed to Governor Douglas of Vancouver Island, the head of the Hudson's Bay Company on the Pacific, for arms and ammuni-

22. Bancroft, *History of Oregon*, 107; for a slightly different version, see Snowden, *History of Washington*, III, 70 ff.

23. Bancroft, *History of Oregon*, II, 107 f.; "The Nisqually Journal, Nov. 27, Dec. 23, 1851, Feb. 6, May 23, 1852," *Washington Historical Quarterly*, XIV, 147 f., 232 f., 300 f., 134. Snowden, *History of Washington*, III, 188 ff., says the *Beaver* declared herself in ballast and had $500 worth of trading goods on board and the *Mary Dare*, a package of 230 pounds of sugar; but even he says the seizure was on a mere technicality.

24. See *Report of Decisions of the Commission for Settlement of Claims*, 68, 164 f.

tion; an action which Elwood Evans designates as humiliating to him and to the settlers of his territory. "That application," says Mason, "was promptly and cordially responded to, to the extent of his power, he at the same time regretting that he had at that moment no vessel-of-war at his disposal and that his steamers the *Otter* and *Beaver* were both absent, but that on the arrival of either, she should be despatched to the Sound, to render such services as might be required of her. Since then the *Otter* has visited this place."[25] In December, 1855, the Legislative Assembly of Washington Territory formally expressed the thanks of the people to Governor Douglas for this kindly assistance.

The incidents which have been narrated to show the state of international relations after the boundary settlement fit in with the interpretation given at the end of the last chapter. The settlers on the spot were far more intolerant, jealous, and aggressive than governments at a distance. The British forms of control, whether by the chartered companies or by governors, naturally led to more circumspect and more decorous behaviour than could well be expected from the public opinion of pioneers and land-hungry settlers. In later chapters we shall show how both these elements changed with the advance of agriculture and industry until we find two friendly democratic communities, differing it is true in the form of their growth, but not fundamentally dissimilar.

25. Elwood Evans, *History of the Pacific North West* (Portland, Oregon, 1889), I, 497.

CHAPTER VII

THE SETTLEMENT OF BRITISH COLUMBIA
1849-1862

In the discussion of the Oregon Question the insistent influence of the immigrations of Americans into the Columbia region in 1842, 1843, 1844, and 1845 was always present. So strong was it that, after the conclusion of the Treaty of Washington, 1846, British statesmen felt the necessity of taking some step to secure to the Empire in fact the territory that had been legally obtained by that settlement.[1]

To forestall peaceful penetration it was decided to found a British colony on Vancouver Island. For that purpose the island was, on January 13, 1849, granted to the Hudson's Bay Company upon terms which required it to establish settlements of British subjects thereon within five years. The grant was strongly criticized upon the ground that a fur-trading company could not be a suitable colonizing agency.[2]

Richard Blanshard, an English barrister, was sent out as Governor. He arrived at Fort Victoria in March, 1850; but it was soon too evident that the terms upon which colonists could obtain land were so onerous that the distant island had no attractions for English settlers. Land was held at one pound per acre, and for every one hundred acres purchased a settler must at his own expense "take out with him five single men or three married couples."[3] The colony afforded no market for farm produce: the Puget Sound Agricultural Company, closely connected with the Hudson's Bay

1. E. O. S. Scholefield and F. W. Howay, *British Columbia from the Earliest Times to the Present* (Vancouver, 1914), II, 43.

2. J. E. Fitzgerald, *An Examination of the Charter and Proceedings of the Hudson's Bay Company with reference to the Grant of Vancouver's Island* (London, 1849); for the other side of the question, see R. M. Martin, *The Hudson's Bay Territories and Vancouver's Island* (London, 1849).

3. The Company issued a circular setting forth the terms. A complete copy is published in the Victoria *Gazette*, September 9, 1858; and see Alexander Begg, *History of British Columbia* (Toronto, 1894), 186.

Company, was engaged in agriculture on the island in a large way, and completely absorbed the small local market, while access to the neighbouring territory of the United States was closed by tariff walls. At the same time land in Washington and Oregon could be obtained as a gift or at a nominal price.

No settlement could grow in such barren financial soil. Moreover, just at that moment, the Californian gold fields were attracting world attention and drawing people from every quarter of the globe. The Company claimed, perhaps truly, that some of the sparse population of the island was lured away by the prospects of wealth to be obtained from those placer mines. Governor Blanshard, finding that very few colonists arrived and that the only inhabitants were the active and retired servants of the Company, resigned in November, 1850. The acceptance of his resignation reached him in August, 1851. He at once left the embryo colony. James Douglas, the representative of the Hudson's Bay Company, succeeded him as Governor. The discovery of coal at Nanaimo and other places on the island brought a few more inhabitants; but the colony remained, until the gold rush of 1858, to all intents and purposes merely a fur traders' colony, clustered around Fort Victoria.

On the mainland the Company had a licence of exclusive trade with the Indians. The only evidences of civilization were its trading posts; the only civilized persons, its servants. At these posts wherever possible the Company established small gardens; but at Fort Langley, which had been founded in 1827, farming on a comparatively large, though primitive, scale was carried on, and a beginning had been made in the curing of salmon for domestic use and export. On the Fraser and its tributaries the Company had, in 1858, eight forts or trading posts: Fort St. James and Fort Fraser built in 1806; Fort George, 1807; Fort Kamloops, 1812; Fort Alexandria, 1821; Fort Langley, 1827; Fort Yale, 1848 (abandoned); Fort Hope, 1849. From Alexandria to Kamloops and thence to Okanagan on the Columbia River, and later to Yale and Hope on the Fraser River, the Company had built trails, known as brigade trails, over which the furs were brought out and the trading goods taken into the interior.

Gold was destined to play a large part in the history of British Columbia. It is said that, as early as 1833, small deposits were found on the shore of Okanagan Lake by David Douglas, the botanist.[4] However, the first discovery of any importance was made in 1850. In that year, Richard Blanshard reported to the Colonial Secretary that he had seen rich ore specimens which had come from the Queen Charlotte Islands;[5] and in July, 1851, the Hudson's Bay Company sent one of its vessels to the islands to investigate. News of this discovery spread, and at least two ships carrying sixty men left Puget Sound for the Queen Charlottes. In the spring of 1852 a further six vessels, with several hundred miners on board, sailed from San Francisco. The work of the miners was hindered by the hostility of the Indians and, although small pockets of very rich ore were uncovered, they were too few and far between to be of commercial importance.

It was in the midst of this small excitement that Douglas succeeded Blanshard as Governor of Vancouver Island. In the light of his experience in Oregon, Douglas feared that an influx of Americans would endanger British sovereignty over the islands and injure the trade of the Hudson's Bay Company, of which he was still Chief Factor. He, therefore, urged the British Government to exclude foreigners from trade with the islands. This London declined to do, but the Colonial Office did grant Douglas a commission as Lieutenant-Governor of the Queen Charlotte Islands and gave him authority to require gold prospectors and miners resorting there to take out licences upon suitable terms.[6] Douglas acted on this authorization, but not before the whole excitement had subsided.[7]

When news came in 1856 of the discovery of gold on the Fraser, Douglas was thus in a position to know the attitude which the Home authorities were likely to take towards an attempt to exclude foreigners. Exaggerated stories of the discoveries reached the neighbouring states. A great excitement arose in Washington and Oregon; soon it spread to California, the home of miners and the mining school of the Pacific Coast. Mining there had long since failed to produce "an ounce a day!" The Sierra placers were

4. A. G. Harvey, "David Douglas in British Columbia," *British Columbia Historical Quarterly*, IV, 235.

5. *Correspondence relative to the Discovery of Gold at Queen Charlotte's Island* (Ordered by the House of Commons to be printed, July 19, 1853).

6. *Ibid.*, 13.

7. For accounts of the Queen Charlotte gold rush, see Scholefield and Howay, *British Columbia*, II, 1 ff., and T. A. Rickard, "Indian Participation in the Gold Discoveries," *British Columbia Historical Quarterly*, II, 5 ff.

almost exhausted; the era of capital had come—the era of hydraulic sluicing and quartz mining.[8] The news of this latest *el Dorado* was as match to tinder. In Oregon the conditions were graphically summarized by Dr. Carl Friesach. In August, 1858, he says: "In Portland we found the whole population in the greatest state of excitement on account of the news of the discovery of gold fields on the Fraser River; it was the only topic of conversation in the whole town."[9] In the adjoining Territory of Washington the excitement was even more evident. Its small settlements along Puget Sound were depleted of their population. Shipping was paralysed. Crews deserted and rushed for the Fraser placers. Manufacturing and all industry were at a standstill. Numbers of United States soldiers at Steilacoom, Townsend, and Bellingham forgot their duty and forsook their posts.[10] From April to August, 1858, the newspapers of the Pacific Coast, and especially those of San Francisco, were filled with news, often exaggerated and misleading, of the Fraser River gold fields. In the mountain counties of California everything was topsy-turvy, all the foundations of their fragile society being rocked by the unreasoning excitement.[11] Maps of the gold regions and advertisements of the sailing of vessels therefor appeared in the daily press, side by side with offers of property for sale by those leaving for the new mines. "Had a good time with the boys," wrote one diarist at Marysville, on June 11, 1858, "found them crazy about Fraser River"; and on July 7, he wrote: "A great many down from above on their way to Fraser."[12] A letter of the time says: "When I wrote you last from Forest City Cal I had Just been burned out but bussiness was Good & I felt well but Just then the Fraser River Fever Broke out & it caused a General Stampede & Broke Down all business all Bussness men lost confidence in themselves."[13] From all the Pacific Coast of the

8. C. I. Wheat, "California's Bantam Cock," *California Historical Society Quarterly*, IX, 287.

9. Carl Friesach, *Ein Ausflug nach British Columbia* (Graz, 1875), 1.

10. *Pioneer and Democrat*, Olympia, Washington Territory, April 9, 1858; *Correspondence relative to the Discovery of Gold in Fraser's River, presented to Parliament, July 2, 1858*, p. 16.

11. Wheat, "California's Bantam Cock," 378.

12. *Ibid.*, 265, 346.

13. "Diary and Letters of Cyrus Olin Phillips," *California Historical Society Quarterly*, XI, 153.

United States everyone was anxious to set out for the latest *el Dorado.* "None too poor and none too rich to go. None too young and none too old to go; even the decrepit go."[14]

This rush was in reality merely the transporting of a part of California and the Pacific states to a land under the British flag. Wherever born these men had learned mining in the Californian schools, the Feather, Yuba, and American Rivers, and had learned their business methods in, or adapted them to, Californian environment. Their experience, their theories and practices, their implements, their money, their newspapers, their interests, their very friendships and hatreds, all were Californian. In every sense of the word they were Californians. And it may be said, generally, that their serious crimes, which were few indeed, were rooted in Californian conditions: the old animosities between Law and Order men and Vigilantes flamed forth even in the cool North.

The steamer *Commodore* left San Francisco on April 20, 1858, with the vanguard of 450 adventurers from California; though small parties from Oregon and Washington had preceded them.[15] Thereafter they poured in in hundreds and thousands by every kind of waterborne craft and by every land conveyance. From San Francisco, from Portland and Walla Walla, and from all the settlements on Puget Sound they came. By the middle of August, when the great inrush had practically subsided, some twenty-five or thirty thousand modern Argonauts had set out for the Fraser River. These Americans were welcomed, protected in their liberty and property, and placed on an equality with British subjects. No one could truthfully say as did John Nugent, the special agent of the United States, that "the Americans must be kept out."[16] Whatever restrictions they encountered, as will later appear, were of general application and in no way connected with nationality.

At this time a joint survey of the boundary line between British and American possessions, which had been begun in 1857, was in progress. The great majority of the American newcomers knew

14. R. L. Brown, *Essay on British Columbia* (New Westminster, 1863), 3.

15. This vanguard included 65 negroes, themselves the vanguard of about 400 refugees from the racial persecution which had then developed in California. See F. W. Howay, "The Negro Immigration into Vancouver Island in 1858," *Royal Society of Canada Transactions*, XXIX, sec. II, 145 ff.

16. Victoria *Gazette*, November 16, 1858.

that the diggings were in British territory, though some, either in ignorance or determined blindness, pretended to doubt the fact. This affected uncertainty was frequently invoked to bolster up suggested opposition to some action of the Governor or to some law promulgated by him which did not meet their approval.[17] The population of Victoria before this inrush was only about five hundred, composed largely of the Company's employees, past and present, and their families. The few English inhabitants were completely swamped by this great wave of American immigration. Victoria became for a time American, but its administration remained in the hands of English officials. Shops, stores, and houses of every description arose in all directions, built by Californian capital and stocked with Californian goods. In six weeks 225 buildings were erected. Even at that, accommodations were insufficient. In the latter part of July more than six thousand American adventurers were encamped at Victoria, awaiting the recession of the Fraser's waters. The outskirts of the town resembled the encampment of an army. Land prices increased enormously. Town lots 60 feet by 120, sold by the Hudson's Bay Company for $50 or $75, changed hands a month later for from $1,500 to $3,000. Well-situated lots commanded a rental of $250 to $400 a month.[18]

The merchants of San Francisco joined in the rush. Some of them moved their stocks bodily to Victoria, which was then a free port; many others established branch stores. The advertisements of the time make frequent reference to the fact that the merchant or other person was formerly in business at such and such an address in San Francisco.

In the influx were not only miners, mechanics, artisans, and labourers, but also traders, large and small, jobbers, and speculators, with a fair seasoning of gamblers, swindlers, thieves, and the like. The misconduct of this bad element is naturally the material found in the records, letters, newspapers, etc., but the great body of the Californians was of the respectable class, decent, law-abiding, and hard-working, who came seeking to better their condition by industry and fair and honest means and who, simply

17. For a similar use of an unsurveyed boundary during the Klondike rush, see *infra*, chap. XIII.

18. *California Historical Society Quarterly*, XI, 153, 154; Alfred Waddington, *Fraser River Mines Vindicated* (Victoria, 1858), 19.

because they were attending to their own affairs, make no appearance in the records.

While the crowd awaited in idleness the subsidence of the waters, a number of small disturbances occurred. They are mentioned here as showing one part—a very small part—of this American immigration. Late in July some of these rowdies rescued a man who had been arrested by the police. In the *mêlée* the officer was badly and roughly used. The excited crowd then proposed to hoist the American flag upon the fort. Douglas, equal to every emergency, ordered H.M.S. *Plumper* to the scene. Quiet again reigned. The ringleaders were arrested, fined small amounts, and bound over to keep the peace.[19] "Frequently men might be seen crying through the streets that they were 'true Americans' or singing and shouting about the 'Stars and Stripes.' American flags, too, were plentiful." No one paid any attention to these little ebullitions, realizing that they arose from an ill-directed patriotism combined with an over-indulgence in strong drink. Even Waddington who records them adds: "Indeed the behaviour of the Americans here has been generally most orderly and law-abiding."[20] Included in the rowdy element was the notorious Ned McGowan, of whom we shall hear more later. He arrived in Victoria, July 3, 1858, with some 460 other adventurers from San Francisco, in the steamer *Pacific*. "He felt an uncontrollable itch to twist the Lion's tail, and accordingly marked his advent on Britannia's shores by touching off a salute of one hundred guns from the *Pacific's* two small cannon, which Ned had manned with a crew of gold-hunters, most of whom had just returned from Walker's disastrous filibustering jaunt to Nicaragua." Carl Wheat alleges that Douglas at once "issued an order forbidding further salvos without express permission"; but this prohibition did not appear until August 25, 1858.[21]

The Americans also brought with them newspaper men, express men, and bankers. The first newspaper in British Columbia, the Victoria *Gazette*, appeared on June 25, 1858. It was owned by

19. Victoria *Gazette*, July 31, August 3, 1858; Waddington, *Fraser River Mines Vindicated*, 20.

20. Waddington, *Fraser River Mines Vindicated*, 20.

21. C. I. Wheat, "Ned, the Ubiquitous," *California Historical Society Quarterly*, VI; Victoria *Gazette*, September 2, 1858.

James W. Towne and Company, of San Francisco. Its issues contain much news of California and columns of advertisements of San Francisco merchants. Yet, during its short life, it fought for British interests and institutions, and, though sometimes critical of Governor Douglas, presented the needs and the grievances of the people in a fair and straightforward manner. The pioneer express service was inaugurated in June, 1858, by William T. Ballou, a wild waif of French descent who since 1846 had been drifting about on the Pacific Coast. He had been an express messenger in the Californian mines and realized the opportunities of profit afforded by such an undertaking in a country devoid of roads, of any form of public transportation, and of any postal service. His express canoes and mules gave connection with the American settlements on Puget Sound and with the Fraser River mines as far as Lytton and Kamloops, carrying letters, parcels, newspapers, coin, and gold dust expeditiously, regularly, and safely. The miners on the bars looked eagerly for Ballou's express messengers—their contact with the outside world. One wrote: "News from California and the States is very scarce here. Yesterday we had the first chance to get hold of a San Francisco paper, for which we paid $1.00."[22] At Victoria his express connected with Freeman's for Californian and eastern points. Wells, Fargo and Company's express, another American institution, connected Victoria with San Francisco and the world. It was, of course, an old-established concern in California. There and in British Columbia it was, besides being a common carrier, a purchaser and transmitter of gold dust. It received money on deposit, and to a certain extent fulfilled some of the functions of a bank. The first bank—Macdonald's Bank—was established in Victoria in 1859. It was founded by Alex. D. Macdonald, a Scotsman who for some years had been in business in California's mines. He combined Scotch training with experience of California and its miners. His institution bought gold dust, received deposits, issued paper money, and transacted a general banking business.[23]

22. *Daily Evening Bulletin*, San Francisco, October 26, 1858.

23. On these matters, see: John Forsyth, "The Pioneer Press of British Columbia," *First Annual Report of British Columbia Historical Association*, 1923, 23; R. L. Reid, "The First Bank in Western Canada," *Canadian Historical Review*, VII, 294 ff.

Even before the arrival of the first contingent of miners from California James Douglas, the Governor of Vancouver Island, had taken steps to meet the probable situation. It must not be forgotten that Douglas, as a representative of the Crown, had no jurisdiction beyond the confines of Vancouver Island; he was not sworn into office as Governor of the mainland Colony of British Columbia until November 19, 1858. But he had a dual capacity until that date. He was the head of the Hudson's Bay Company on the coast; and that Company had a licence of exclusive trade with the Indians west of the Rocky Mountains. In December, 1857, as Governor of Vancouver Island, he issued a "proclamation" notifying the public that gold in place belonged to the Crown and warning all persons not to mine it without permission. The following day by a further proclamation he fixed the licence fee for mining at ten shillings a month; in January, 1858, he increased the fee to twenty-one shillings.[24] Because of his dual position some of the American miners believed, or pretended to believe, that this licence fee was levied by the Hudson's Bay Company. They also thought that it was in the nature of a Foreign Miners Tax. This was not an altogether unnatural assumption on their part in view of the discrimination against foreigners in California.

That the situation may be plain a short sketch of the legislation there against foreign miners is given. In 1849-50 the first Legislature of California passed a very drastic act providing that "no person, not a native or natural-born citizen of the United States or one under the peace treaty (native California Indians excepted)" should mine gold without paying a licence fee of $20 a month. Another section enacted that any *posse* of American citizens might forcibly prevent an unlicensed foreigner from mining, and if such individual sought a new location he should be liable to imprisonment *and* fine.[25] In 1852, this act was replaced by one which provided that no person not a citizen of the United States (Californian Indians excepted) should be entitled to mine gold unless he had paid a licence fee of $3 a month. Then followed a terrible clause declaring that "No foreign miner who shall not have a license under the provisions of this Act shall be allowed to prosecute

24. *Correspondence relative to the Discovery of Gold in Fraser's River*, 9, 10; Kinahan Cornwallis, *The New El Dorado* (London, 1858), 349 f.

25. *Statutes of California*, 1850, c. 97, p. 221, passed, April 13, 1850.

or defend *any action* in any of the courts of this State."[26] In 1853 the licence tax on foreigners was raised to $4 a month. The collector was empowered to seize the property of any foreigner who refused to pay the tax and sell it on giving one hour's public notice. All foreigners resident in the mining districts were to be considered as miners and liable to this tax unless they were directly engaged in some other lawful business. Slight alterations were made in succeeding years, principally dealing with the Chinese; but this will indicate in a general way the manner in which foreigners were treated in the mines of California.[27] It is only fair to add that the foreign licence fee does not appear to have been everywhere strictly collected. In one mining community, of about three hundred miners one-quarter were foreigners, but no foreign tax collector had been there for four months.[28]

Leaving California where these restrictions prevailed, the Americans entered a foreign land on a basis of equality with its own subjects. However irksome the regulations they met, there was no discrimination—one and the same law applied to all. The *Pioneer and Democrat*, of Olympia, made this clear, stating on March 5, 1858: "The same license (21*s.* a month) is demanded of British as well as Americans or subjects of any other government; no distinction whatever is made as regards nationality or color. British subjects and American citizens stand on lines of perfect equality as to the privilege of working the mines."

In May, 1858, Douglas, still acting as Governor of Vancouver Island, issued another "proclamation" notifying the public of the Hudson's Bay Company's licence of exclusive trade with the *Indians*, warning *all persons* who proposed to fit out vessels for trade in the mining country that such conduct was an infringement of the Company's rights (which it plainly was not), and declaring that any vessels found with trading goods on board in Fraser River or the waters of the mainland, without a licence from the Company and a sufferance from the Collector of Customs at Victoria, were liable to forfeiture, and would be seized and con-

26. *Ibid.*, 1852, c. 37, p. 84.
27. See Wheat, "California's Bantam Cock"; "The Journals of Charles E. De Long," *California Historical Society Quarterly*, VIII, 353 ff.; Ernest de Massey, *A Frenchman in the Gold Rush* (San Francisco, 1927), 96.
28. *Daily Evening Bulletin*, San Francisco, May 31, 1858.

demned. This law dealing with the mainland was plainly invalid. It was disallowed when it reached England, but more than four months intervened between its promulgation and the receipt of notice of its disallowance. During that period, despite all complaints, it was enforced. In it the miners saw, and rightly, Douglas speaking for the Company rather than for the Crown. But it was not aimed at Americans; it was general. Its manifest purpose was to extend the Company's monopoly of the Indian trade to that of the whole mining region. Douglas certainly deserved the rebuke which Sir E. B. Lytton administered, as will be seen, in his disallowance.[29]

The adventurers came by steamer to Victoria, or to some American port on Puget Sound: Port Townsend, Whatcom, or Semiahmoo. Though bound for gold mines in British possessions the feeling of the Californians was to give the preference to any port in the United States, suitable or unsuitable, in order to avoid the British port of Victoria. Ultimately to their cost they found that geographic conditions are stronger than patriotic leanings, and a navigable river is a better highway than a rude mountain trail. Wherever they disembarked about 150 miles lay between them and the mines. For the greater part of that distance no steamers were in operation. The best they could do was to reach Fort Langley by the Hudson's Bay Company's vessels, *Beaver* and *Otter*. Even then about sixty miles of painful river navigation were before them. Many built boats to carry them from Victoria or the towns of Puget Sound to the mines; some hired Indian canoes, or sloops, or "plungers." Considerable loss of life resulted; but, undeterred, they pressed onward. On May 19, 1858, Douglas made a proposal to the Pacific Mail Steamship Company to place American steamers on the run between Victoria and the mining region. The terms he offered were that they would carry no goods but those of the Hudson's Bay Company, nor any passengers who had not a miner's licence, and that they would pay to that Company as compensation $2 head money for each passenger taken to Fraser River. Yet, strangely enough, the permission was to be issued not by Douglas as Governor, but by "the Agents of the Hudson's Bay Company." Sir E. B. Lytton, the Secretary of State for the

29. *Papers relative to British Columbia* (London, 1859), part I, 12, 42.

Colonies, on July 16, 1858, disallowed both of these "Proclamations." He pointed out that the newcomers had a right to trade with any inhabitants except the Indians; that a miner's licence could only be exacted from one about to engage in mining and not as a prerequisite to entry into the country; and that the Hudson's Bay Company had no just claim for head money as compensation for such entry. He expressed the desire that no unnecessary obstacle be interposed to prevent American or other foreign vessels from obtaining permission to navigate the Fraser. He recognized that Douglas had no authority to legislate for the mainland, but, pending future regularization, authorized him to take such measures as the unusual situation required. He added, and this is significant as indicating Lytton's feeling that these proclamations reflected Douglas, the representative of the Company, rather than Douglas, the representative of the Crown:

But I must distinctly warn you against using the powers hereby intrusted to you in maintainance of the interests of the Hudson's Bay Company in the territory. The Company is entitled, under its existing license, to the exclusive trade with the Indians, and possesses no other right or privilege whatever. It is therefore contrary to law, and equally contrary to the distinct instructions which I have to convey to you, to exclude any class of persons from the territory or to prevent any importation of goods into it on the ground of apprehended interference with this monopoly—still more to make any Governmental regulations subservient to the Revenues or interests of the Company.[30]

In a later despatch, dated August 14, 1858, Lytton cautioned Douglas that no distinction must be made between foreigners and British subjects as to the amount of the miner's licence fee and that "it must be made perfectly clear to every one" that such licence was not levied on behalf of the Hudson's Bay Company but by the prerogative of the Crown.[31] He continues:

Farther, with regard to these supposed rights of the Hudson's Bay Company, I must refer you, in even stronger terms, to the cautions already conveyed to you by my former Despatches. The Hudson's Bay Company have hitherto had an exclusive right to trade with Indians in the Fraser's River territory, but they have had no other right whatever. They have

30. *Ibid.*, 12, 18, 42.
31. *Ibid.*, 47 f.

no right to exclude strangers. They have had no rights of Government, or of occupation of the soil. They have had no right to prevent or interfere with any kind of trading except with the Indians alone.

But these despatches did not reach Douglas until about the first of October. In the meantime Douglas set himself to the enforcement of the proclamations, so distasteful to the Californian miners. He stationed H.M.S. *Satellite* at the mouth of the Fraser River to collect the licence fee and to prevent the entry of boats and other vessels with trading goods. In May, 1858, Isaac I. Stevens, the delegate to Congress from Washington Territory, complained to the Secretary of State, Lewis Cass, that "The Hudson's Bay Company had it in contemplation to set on foot a blockade of the mouth of Fraser River and to make other impediments to the access of American citizens to the gold mines of Fraser and Thompson rivers."[32] Plainly the dual capacity of Douglas rendered it difficult for the general public to distinguish between his acts as representing the Crown and those in his capacity as the head of the Hudson's Bay Company. The reference by Stevens is, of course, to Douglas's intended action in regard to the *Satellite*. On June 17, the British Secretary of State for Foreign Affairs stated that: "Her Majesty's Government are, on their part, disposed as far as they can properly do so, to deal liberally with the citizens of the United States who may desire to proceed to that quarter of the British possessions." But he added that the Hudson's Bay Company had certain rights in the region whose extent must be ascertained. The *Puget Sound Herald*, of Steilacoom, when the intention of Douglas to place the *Satellite* at the Fraser River mouth was known, charged the action to the Hudson's Bay Company's desire to secure the exclusive trade of the mines. In that view it was right, though the action was by Douglas as the representative of the Crown. It doubtless expressed the prevalent opinion of the Americans: "We opine that the Hudson's Bay Company will have a fine time in monopolizing this trade; a few Yankees have gone in that direction, and unless they have become extremely dull-witted, we think they will have a hand in the 'swapping.'"[33]

32. Victoria *Gazette*, September 7, 1858.
33. Quoted in *Washington Historical Quarterly*, XVIII, 203.

The Americans did not at all relish Douglas's step to enforce his proclamations. The Fraser River has three mouths: Canoe Pass, the main river, and the North Arm. As there are large sandbars at the mouths, the *Satellite* was anchored far from shore. The first plan was to enter by Canoe Pass which was nearest the American boundary, and, when the tide was in, enabled the light-draft boats to creep along close to the shore, miles from the man-of-war. In June, 1858, sixteen canoes which had so evaded the *Satellite* were seized at Fort Langley, but were released on payment of a charge of $5 each for a pass or sufferance, as they contained only miners and their personal property; but in some were found goods intended for sale, which Douglas called "contraband goods." These he held under seizure for condemnation by legal process.[34] To prevent any future evasions Douglas placed the brig *Recovery* near Fort Langley, where the river runs in one stream, "to stop canoes, etc., to make them pay licences, etc." Thus he cut off what he was pleased to call the illegal entry.

But the Americans were not disconcerted by this move. On Puget Sound had sprung up two towns, Whatcom and Semiahmoo, both claiming to be entry points to the mines; both avoiding any mention of the fact that these were located under a different flag. Semiahmoo scarcely advanced beyond a mere "paper town"; it depended largely upon the surreptitious entry by water—although there was a so-called trail thence to Langley—and received its quietus when Douglas placed the *Recovery* at Fort Langley. Whatcom, however, strove energetically to make her wealth off these foreign mines by advertising herself as being on the shortest and easiest route. Her people would build a trail to Fort Hope, willy-nilly, thus avoiding the tax-collecting vessel and gathering into their lap the trade bound for Fraser River. Thousands of adventurers were lured to Whatcom by statements that the trail was short, easy to travel, and almost completed; when, as a matter of fact, it existed only as a dotted line on the map. Many advertisements in the San Francisco papers gave the departures of steamers "for the new Gold Mines on Fraser's River, Puget Sound," by way of "Victoria and Bellingham Bay"—with nothing to indicate

34. *Papers relative to British Columbia*, part i, p. 13.

that the mines were not in the United States.[35] This attitude prevailed amongst the adventurers; true, they recognized in theory that the mines were British, but practically they regarded them as in American territory. Whatcom, for example, never thought of asking permission to enter and build a trail over land belonging to the British Crown; her moving thought was simply that there was wealth in those mines, and she would build a trail and obtain it.

But despite all the promises and advertisements it was found impossible to complete, expeditiously, the trail from Whatcom to Fort Hope. Its route was changed, to reach the Fraser River at Sumas, about thirty miles below the intended terminus. Early in July some unwise adventurers were actually using the Whatcom Trail: "They curse the trail and the men who influenced them to go on it. The trail strikes the river about thirty miles below Fort Hope, and then they have to get Indians to bring them here [Fort Hope] in canoes, when they get here they have neither provisions, nor blankets, and their clothing all torn to shreds."[36] Pack trains were organized with horses and mules brought from California for the transport of merchandise over the much-advertised trail. The difficulty, outside of that of the trail itself, was that it ended nowhere—merely came to the bank of the Fraser and stopped where no organized means of further conveyance existed.

Another factor in the failure of this trail from Whatcom was that Douglas soon completed arrangements whereby American steamers could navigate the Fraser. The terms he offered, as already given, were accepted by the *Surprise*, *Sea Bird*, *Umatilla*, *Maria*, *Enterprise*, and *Wilson G. Hunt*. They thus afforded expeditious transport to the mines, even though the passengers must all pay the illegal levies of the $2 head tax and the miner's licence fee. In June, 1858, one visitor wrote: "We lost no time in repairing to the Government gold license office in Victoria where we tendered our five dollars each, in exchange for a monthly voucher privileging us to dig, which also was our necessary passport to travel up river, for without it we could not have proceeded along the mainland. This tax was frankly paid, but heartily

35. Letter, Dewdney to Hamley, December 19, 1859, in the Archives of British Columbia; Wheat, "Ned the Ubiquitous," 17.
36. Letter from Fort Hope in Victoria *Gazette*, July 7, 1858.

denounced."[37] One Californian merchant states that in July, 1858, in order to travel on the *Surprise* with 3,200 pounds of merchandise he was required by the steamer to purchase nine mining licences at $5 each, as only 400 pounds were allowed for each passenger, and also to buy nine tickets, one for each licence.[38]

It was very plain that this first Whatcom trail was a failure; but that town realized that its life depended upon a trail—that without it the trade of the Fraser River would be monopolized by the towns north of the boundary and nothing would be left for Bellingham Bay. In June the Whatcom people recast their schemes and formed a plan to connect their town with the Hudson's Bay Company's brigade trail near Fort Hope. Such a trail, after it crossed the Cascade Mountains, would run through a comparatively open country and afford easy access to the Fraser above the canyons. Into the new scheme Whatcom entered in earnest. Subscriptions were obtained from other places on Puget Sound; and the work of location and construction was put in charge of Captain W. W. DeLacy, a United States engineer.[39] Governor Fayette McMullin of Washington Territory, in addressing a meeting at Whatcom in August, 1858, alluded to the rivalry between Victoria and Puget Sound for the trade of Fraser River and expressed the hope that Americans would give the preference to American soil. To this end he urged the early construction of the trail from Whatcom to the mines.[40]

Through the summer the work on the trail went on, and in August it was reported as completed. There was great jubilation in Whatcom. The distance to the connection with the brigade trail was given as 173 miles and thence to Kamloops another 100 miles. But Douglas met the situation by making a trail from Fort Hope to Fort Yale and improving the access to the Fraser River above that point. Whatcom had been steadily sending boats and canoes to the Fraser; these craft had obtained sufferances at Fort Langley;

37. Cornwallis, *New El Dorado*, 185 f.

38. C. O. Phillips, letter in *California Historical Society Quarterly*, XI, 154.

39. R. L. Reid, "Whatcom Trails to Fraser River Mines," *Washington Historical Quarterly*, XVIII, 201 ff. See this article for a detailed account of the whole effort.

40. Victoria *Gazette*, August 4, 1858. See also State of Minnesota, *Overland Emigration from Minnesota to Frazer River* (St. Paul, 1858), 42 f.

Douglas now ordered that all vessels navigating that river obtain the necessary authority at Victoria. This move aroused the ire of the *Northern Light*, a short-lived newspaper of Whatcom. It stated that the effect "should be to induce every American who has the least spark of national pride to avoid Victoria and everything British."[41] And yet the *raison d'être* of Whatcom was the trade of these British mines. The much-vaunted trail was as complete a failure as its predecessor. One company of twenty-two men who essayed the journey over it to the Fraser River mines was eight weeks in the transit. Grass grew in Whatcom's streets. The effort of the American towns on Puget Sound to draw the trade through their portals had ended in complete failure.

An attempt was also made by the Americans to establish a route from Portland, Oregon, by way of the Dalles, Walla Walla, Okanagan, and Similkameen to Thompson River. The first party consisted of 160 men with 400 horses and mules, and a herd of beef cattle. They reached Lytton about the middle of August, 1858, after a journey of thirty days over a trail which was described as so bad that once travelled it would never again be taken. Though the Hudson's Bay Company had used that route for the transport of furs and goods from 1826 to 1848 and had yearly thereafter passed through a part of the region with their brigades, they had had no difficulties with the Indians; yet when these adventurers from the United States sought to travel by that way they were attacked by the natives, three men killed and six wounded, and some sixty of the beef cattle stolen.[42] This trouble may have been a result of the hostilities between Indians and whites in Washington Territory. For two years this route was used spasmodically, but it never became a general line of travel. There being no port of entry on the mainland except Langley (or, later, New Westminster) goods imported by this southern route frequently escaped customs duties. In December, 1860, Douglas, whose position had been regularized in November, 1858, when he was sworn in as Governor of the new mainland colony of British Columbia, issued a proclamation ordering that all merchandise brought in over it should pay not only the regular customs, but also

41. Quoted in Victoria *Gazette*, September 8, 1858.
42. Letter from Fort Yale in *ibid.*, August 24, 1858.

a toll of $13 a ton and a fine of three per cent on the market value.[43]
Joel Palmer, an American, the spokesman for this route, wrote:
"In the collection of these duties and taxes, no discrimination is
made between British subjects and American citizens, or in favor
of English manufactures over American, or other foreign goods;
the collection of revenue seems to be the only object in view."[44]

It may be added that in June, 1858, the people of St. Paul and
other cities in Minnesota became interested in the possibility of
directing the trade of the new gold fields through that state by
an overland route up the Mississippi and the Red Rivers to Lake
Winnipeg and thence following in a general way that used by the
Hudson's Bay Company. In July the matter was crystallized, after
many meetings, into a resolution urging the state Legislature
to pass an act authorizing the cities of Minnesota to advance
money or guarantee payments up to $3,000 to any persons organiz-
ing and carrying through expeditions for such overland journeys
to Fraser River. A Select Committee of the House of Representatives approved the scheme and introduced in the session of 1858
a bill for that purpose.[45] Nothing practical, however, resulted.

Everywhere the miners looked for evidences such as had existed
in the Californian gold fields. One wrote: "Gold does exist in the
new country and there is no doubt in my mind that the upper
mines are much like the upper mountain mines of California."
Another stated: "By those familiar with it we are informed that it
is very similar to the placer gold of California." And another
wrote: "An old California miner says that this place very closely
resembled the North Fork of the American River in California."[46]
An experienced miner informed Douglas in April, 1858, that "the
geological formation of Fraser River had the characteristics of the
gold fields of California." In another letter Douglas reported:
"They say that the country is as rich as any part of California."[47]

43. The Southern Boundary Act, December 22, 1860. Letter, Douglas to
Newcastle, October 9, 1860, in *Further Papers relative to British Columbia* (London,
1860), part III, 1861, 22.

44. Letter in the *Oregon Statesman*, Salem, Oregon, February 14, 1860.

45. *Overland Emigration from Minnesota*, 4 ff.

46. *Ibid.*, 45, 40, 41. Compare letter from Dennis Cain in *British Columbian*,
August 22, 1861.

47. *Correspondence relative to the Discovery of Gold in Fraser's River*, 11, 12, 17.

The names given to many of the gold-bearing bars of Fraser River show the predominance of Americans and especially of Californians: "Fifty-four Forty," "Union," "Santa Clara," "American," "Puget Sound," "Yankee Doodle," "Eagle," "Texas," "Ohio," "New York," "Washington," "Madison," "Tehama," "Boston," "Mormon," "Yankee Flat," "Angel's Flat," and not to make a catalogue, "Stranglers,"—the slang name applied in California to the members of the Vigilance Committee.

Before the great rush began Douglas had reported: "A great number of Americans have also gone towards Thompson River; and others are preparing to follow." When the vanguard arrived on the steamer *Commodore* on April 25, 1858, he stated that they were represented as being, with some exceptions, "a specimen of the worst of the population of San Francisco; the very dregs, in fact, of society." But he adds that their conduct led him to quite a different conclusion as, though there was a temporary scarcity of food and accommodation, few police, and many temptations to excessive indulgence in liquor, there was not a single committal for rioting, drunkenness, or other offences. At the same time he feared that their attitude and sympathies might be decidedly anti-British. Taken as a whole they were, he says, men of intelligence, well provided with mining tools and capital.[48] On July 1, 1858, Sir Edward Bulwer Lytton, the Secretary of State for the Colonies, informed Douglas that he intended to send out a force, the Royal Engineers, to maintain law and order in the gold region. He emphasized the point that it was no part of British policy to exclude Americans or other foreigners therefrom; and he instructed Douglas to oppose no obstacle to their resort thither so long as they recognized British authority and conformed to the law.[49]

The miners' licences in June, 1858, stated that the size of the claim to be mined was twelve feet square. But the miners at Fort Yale bar, following the Californian custom, passed a series of resolutions, which, after defining the bar, ordered that on it the claims should be twenty-five feet in width extending from the river channel to high water-mark; that no miner should hold

48. *Ibid.*, 12, 13.
49. *Ibid.*, 17.

more than one claim on the bar; that failure to work a claim for five days, unless by reason of illness or absence on public business, should render it vacant; that a recorder should be elected to record all claims on the bar; and that his book should be open to inspection.[50] In July the Fort Yale bar miners passed another series of resolutions, or laws. They prohibited the sale of intoxicating liquor on the bar, ordered the confiscation and destruction of any such liquor then in their midst, and forbade the sale of arms or ammunition to the Indians. Breach of these laws was to be punished with whipping. A committee of twelve prominent miners was appointed to enforce them, "until the Government sees fit to carry out its own laws."[51] In these instances, which are merely given as examples, the Californian atmosphere of Fraser River can be seen. Major Downie in his book sets out in detail the miners' laws enacted by a meeting at the Forks of the Yuba in March, 1850.[52] Such local legislation was a component part of Californian mining.

It will be observed that the Yale miners' resolutions were in conflict with existing general law; but that did not seem to worry the Americans. They thought the twelve feet square too small a claim and they attempted to enlarge it. Douglas having made no provision for failure to work a claim continuously, they purported to do so. Though such resolutions might bind those who accepted them, their validity as regarded a stranger was more than doubtful. At any rate there was at the time no constituted judicial authority at Yale, and no tribunal in which to test any such question, the jurisdiction of the courts of Upper and Lower Canada in civil and criminal matters being practically non-existent.[53] In June, 1858, Douglas appointed Richard Hicks as revenue officer at Yale, and George Perrier as Justice of the Peace at Hill's Bar. In July, he appointed O. Travaillot, a Frenchman, as revenue officer

50. Cornwallis, *New El Dorado*, 402 f.

51. Victoria *Gazette*, August 4, 1858.

52. William Downie, *Hunting for Gold* (San Francisco, 1893), 80 f. Information on these meetings can be found in C. H. Shinn, *Mining Camps* (New York, 1885).

53. See W. N. Sage, *Sir James Douglas and British Columbia* (Toronto, 1930), 218. Special jurisdiction was given to the courts of Upper Canada to try cases arising in the Indian territory, in so far as they affected British Columbia, by two imperial statutes, 43 Geo. III, c. 138, and 1 and 2 Geo. IV, c. 66. These were repealed in 1858 by 21 and 22 Vict., c. 99.

for Lytton; and in September, 1858, Robert T. Smith as Justice of the Peace and revenue officer for Hope.[54] These men represented the public authority, for no legal government existed until the formation of the Colony of British Columbia in November, 1858. Their titles were no index to their jurisdiction. The so-called revenue officers, later known as Gold Commissioners, attended to and settled all matters relating to land, mining claims, records, water rights, collection of licence fees, and other revenue, and almost every other question. They were, as one expressed it, "court, customs, recorder, and coroner." In the primitive conditions much was necessarily left to their discretion. They dealt with and settled disputes regarding boundaries of claims, conflicting claims to water privileges, and similar matters concerning mining operations. Police officers were also appointed and a semblance of authority appeared. When the colony was formed in November, 1858, their appointments and all their acts were regularized. Matthew (later, Sir Matthew) B. Begbie, the Judge of British Columbia, did not arrive from England until November, 1858. In the meantime serious crimes were tried by Commissioners appointed by Douglas.

The Yale miners' resolutions seem to have borne fruit, for, in July, 1858, Douglas issued a proclamation containing new mining laws, by which he increased the size of alluvial claims to twenty-five feet frontage in rivers, and twenty-five feet of the beds of creeks and ravines, with a provision for forfeiture for failure to work them.[55] It is noteworthy that, though the Victoria *Gazette* was then being published in Victoria, this proclamation appeared in the *Evening Bulletin* of San Francisco and was thence copied into the local paper.

The miners on Hill's Bar on May 22, 1858, had also established a set of local laws dealing with the size of claims and similar matters. These they sent to Douglas for approval. They claimed that he had accepted them and that he had stated that they would not be altered until he received orders to that effect from the Home government. This seems improbable on its face, in view of the fact that he had already fixed twelve feet square as the size of a

54. *Papers relative to British Columbia*, part i, pp. 16, 17, 19; part ii, 1860, p. 4.
55. Victoria *Gazette*, August 5, 1858.

mining claim. In September, 1858, Richard Hicks, the revenue officer at Yale, settled the limits of claims on the bar by defining the high water-mark on the ground. A heated dispute arose, the miners declaring that Hicks was depriving them of their claims. They held the usual meeting—Ned McGowan among them—and passed a series of resolutions in which they declared that their laws "are the only laws that we will take as our guide until further evidence shall be furnished us from the proper source that the aforesaid laws have been legally changed, altered, or amended."[56] The United States government had appointed John Nugent as special agent to assure the Americans of the protection of their government, but not to interpose in civil questions between them and the British authorities. A more unsuitable choice could scarcely have been made.[57] Fortunately his stay was very short; he arrived on September 20 and left on November 13, 1858—less than two months. To him the Hill's Bar miners sent a copy of their resolutions, but the document did not reach him until he was on the verge of departure, and in consequence no action was taken. The Victoria *Gazette* pointed out the impropriety of such action, as the matter was purely one of a domestic nature. In any event the Americans soon discovered that the general law, and not their own local law, would be applied.

Of these local mining laws and their conflict with the general law De Groot wrote early in 1859: "These regulations, however, have been little regarded, the miners going on and fixing the size of their claims, and establishing such rules for holding and working them as they deemed expedient, a practice with which the Commissioner and his assistants have not interfered to any great extent. It is probable, however, that the authorities will assume a greater control when affairs shall become a little more settled...."[58] Even when De Groot wrote, the authorities had already stepped in and shown that the laws enunciated by the proper law-making authority were to govern and not those of any body of individuals.

56. *Ibid.*, September 28, November 6, 1858.

57. *Ibid.*, September 14, 22, 1858. Compare his farewell address in the same paper, November 13, with his Manifesto in it, November 16, 1858, and see editorial thereon in same issue and correspondence and advertisement in issue of November 18, 1858.

58. Henry De Groot, *British Columbia* (San Francisco, 1859), 20.

The effort to introduce the Californian practice had failed. Yet Douglas bowed to the American desire for local popular government. By his proclamation of 1859 he authorized the creation of local mining boards. Such boards were to be constituted by a Gold Commissioner at the direction of the Governor, whose action was to be set in motion by a petition signed by 101 miners of any locality. The mining boards were to consist of from six to twelve members, depending on the number of miners, and to be elected by the miners, regardless of nationality. The boards were empowered to enact local laws regulating the size of claims and sluices, the mode in which claims might be registered, worked, held, and forfeited, and generally all matters relating to mining in their districts. A law passed by a bare majority was to be valid if the Gold Commissioner assented thereto, otherwise it required a two-thirds majority. These local laws were, moreover, to have no force unless and until they were approved of by the Governor. "The mining boards," wrote Douglas, "will be fostered and encouraged as long as they confine their influence to its legitimate object, that of improving the conditions of the gold fields."[59]

As an example of the self-reliance of the American miners the Indian troubles of August, 1858, may be mentioned. The centre was the Big Canyon, about twenty miles up the Fraser River from Yale. For twenty years and more the Hudson's Bay Company had traversed the vicinity without any difficulties beyond the petty pilferings of the natives. The roots of the trouble are to be found in the Indian successes in the war then being waged in the neighbouring United States territory, in the Indian hostility to the Americans whose entrance into their country they steadfastly opposed, in the arrogance of the Californian miners who believed that "the only good Indian was a dead one," and in their interference with the Indian women. The miners in the Big Canyon, the disturbed region, fled to Yale, frequently despoiled of their tools and outfits. A number were killed and their bodies, in some instances scalped or decapitated, came floating down the swollen river. The usual public meetings were held at Hope, Yale, and other places to fix upon a course of action. As a result about 150 miners, well armed,

59. Gold Fields Act, 1859, ss. 29-37; *Further Papers relative to British Columbia*, part III, 51.

set out in three parties from Yale. One body, under Captain Graham, declared for "war to the knife"; but the majority, commanded by H. M. Snyder, favoured securing peace by a demonstration of force. The militant party burned a number of native villages, and had encounters with the Indians in which, it was alleged, thirty of the savages were killed, but in which they lost their leader and his lieutenant. The peace party marched from Yale to Lytton, some sixty miles, met the hostile Indian bands, and succeeded in making "treaties of peace" with them. Owing to a report that the Chinese had been supplying arms and ammunition to the natives, a miners' meeting was held at China Bar, at the head of the Big Canyon, and resolutions were passed ordering the Orientals from that bar for four weeks. This proceeding smacked of the miners' meetings of California. After an absence of eight days Snyder's party returned, bringing with them five of the principal chiefs that they might see the number and strength of the miners. There was no further difficulty with the Indians.

In the meantime Douglas had been informed of the hostilities, and a delegation of miners had interviewed him regarding the steps to be taken. He at once started for the scene, accompanied by a force of thirty-five men from the Boundary Survey and H.M.S. *Satellite;* but by the time he arrived the trouble was ended. Believing that liquor lay at the root, he issued a proclamation forbidding its sale or gift to Indians. He did not at all approve of the miners' action in sending an armed force to the scene of trouble. Armed force in his view could only be organized and authorized by one acting as Governor, and not by an irresponsible body of foreigners. Instead of thanking the Americans for stepping in and keeping order he criticized them. He told them that those who had shot the Indians were guilty of high treason. At a meeting at Hope when the subject was being discussed a speaker said: "No man could say where the 49th parallel was—and that for all any one knew as yet—and it was more than probable not only Fort Langley, but even Fort Yale was most likely on American soil."[60] Whenever the Americans resented any action of Douglas or clashed with him the supposed uncertainty of the boundary line was brought for-

60. Victoria *Gazette*, September 14, 1858; and that some believed that Fort Langley was in American territory, *ibid.*, August 17, 1858.

ward as a challenge to his jurisdiction, even though the boundary survey had located the 49th parallel on the coast and for some miles inland.[61]

To show the stern way in which Douglas looked upon any acts of lawlessness of the American miners the story of the Ned McGowan *opera bouffe* war will be given in outline. On Christmas Day, 1858, two miners from Hill's Bar brutally assaulted, at Yale, a negro named Dickson. He complained to P. B. Whannell, the local magistrate, who issued a warrant for the arrest of the miners and ordered the negro to be imprisoned and held as a necessary witness —a high-handed act, totally unjustified in the circumstances. The assailants were arrested at Hill's Bar, but George Perrier, its magistrate, refused to send them to Yale for trial. Instead, he ordered Hickson, the Hill's Bar constable, to Yale to obtain the negro complainant. Whannell not only refused to hand the negro over, but also in the end placed the constable, Hickson, in gaol at Yale for contempt of court. Perrier, angered, then issued a warrant for the arrest of his brother magistrate for contempt of his court in arresting his constable. He issued other warrants for the forcible release of the negro and the constable from their confinement at Yale, and for bringing them to Hill's Bar. These warrants were placed in the hands of Ned McGowan and some twelve or fourteen other Americans resident at Hill's Bar, who, fully-armed, came to Yale, seized Whannell and his gaoler, released the negro and the constable from confinement and brought the four before Perrier at Hill's Bar for trial. After dealing with the others Perrier fined Whannell $25 for his contempt.

On his return to Yale Whannell sent a fiery letter to Governor Douglas in which he stated that McGowan "at the head of a lawless band of ruffians broke open the Jail and liberated a prisoner,"— Hickson, the Hill's Bar constable. He added that Perrier had also issued a warrant for his arrest and "despatched a band of sworn-in special constables composed of the most notorious characters in that locality, including McGowan" to execute it. In conclusion he stated: "The town and the district are in a state bordering on

61. For a full account of the Indian trouble, consult Scholefield and Howay, *British Columbia*, II, 34 ff.; Victoria *Gazette*, August 21, 24, 25, 26, 27, September 1, 14, 1858; see also J. G. Williams, *The Adventures of a Seventeen-Year-Old Lad* (Boston, 1894), 286 ff., though this account is exaggerated.

anarchy; my own and the lives of the citizens are in imminent peril. I beg Your Excellency will afford us prompt aid. I have applied to Captain Grant for assistance already, as troops can easily be billeted in this town. An effective blow must at once be struck on the operations of these outlaws, else I tremble for the welfare of the Colony."[62] McGowan was bad enough and so were his followers, but there was nothing in the circumstances as above detailed to justify a sane man in writing such half-truths and exaggerations.

McGowan's reputation in California, where he had been pitilessly hunted by the Vigilance Committee in connection with the murder of James King of William, caused the authorities to take this letter at its face value. Colonel R. C. Moody left immediately for Yale with a force of Royal Engineers, blue jackets, and marines. In mid-winter, up seventy miles of ice-encumbered river, Moody and his men slowly made their way. As they approached the scene of the supposed rebellion the truth gradually dawned upon them and it was soon learned that the whole affair was merely a petty squabble between two ignorant magistrates. McGowan showed that instead of prison-breaking he was merely obeying the magistrate's warrant. In fact he made quite a favourable impression upon some of the officers. Lieutenant Mayne, who was of the party, wrote: "Whatever opinion the Vigilance Committee of San Francisco might entertain of these gentlemen, I, speaking as I found them, can only say that, all things considered, I have rarely lunched with a better-spoken, pleasanter party."[63] The two testy magistrates lost their commissions, and the colony paid the expenses. Though the incident was both costly and ludicrous, it had another side; it showed the Californian miners that, regardless of expense, lawlessness would be put down in the new mines.[64] Of course the inevitable public meetings were held to discuss the whole matter and a series of resolutions passed by the miners:

62. F. W. Howay, *The Early History of the Fraser River Mines* (Victoria, 1926), 57.

63. R. C. Mayne, *Four Years in British Columbia and Vancouver Island* (London, 1862), 70.

64. *Ibid.*, 58 ff.; for a full account see the letters of Judge Begbie and others in Howay, *Early History of Fraser River Mines*, 32 ff., 54 ff. Upon the life of McGowan, see H. H. Bancroft, *Popular Tribunals* (San Francisco, 1887), II, chap. xiv, and Wheat, "Ned, the Ubiquitous."

those of Hill's Bar supporting, those of Yale condemning, the action of Perrier in fining his fellow magistrate; for underneath the incident lay the old difficulties and animosities of California. The miners at Yale were largely partisans of the Vigilance Committee of 1856 in San Francisco; the miners on Hill's Bar were chiefly those opposed to that Committee—the so-called Law and Order faction—in reality a lawless body of men. Judge Begbie states that the lives of the most prominent miners of Hill's Bar would not be worth "an hour's purchase in any street in San Francisco." And to increase the hard feelings between the two parties the Hill's Bar miners dreaded that something like the Vigilance Committee, which they so greatly feared, might be formed at Yale and directed against themselves. Such a thought shows how little they knew of either Governor Douglas or Judge Begbie who would not have tolerated for a moment any such organization or any conditions similar to those that might have called for it in California.

In California the miners' meetings had not only settled all matters relating to mining claims and rights therein, but had also taken upon themselves the trial of crimes committed on their bar. Major Downie sets out the code established by them in 1850 on the Yuba, for the neighbouring district. The ninth article reads: "That in case of trials for crime of any kind there shall be ten present, besides the jury and witnesses." And such trials continued after administrative organization had been formed. They were defended on the ground that the administration was too weak to keep in order the lawless spirits who abounded among the newcomers. The miners regarded their camp law, especially the criminal part of it, as absolutely necessary for their well-being.[65] It is difficult to distinguish such lawless and unauthorized trials from lynch law. Downie records the trial of a Mexican woman, by one of these miners' courts, for murder, her conviction by the jury, and her subsequent execution. Upon the perpetration of a crime, especially when attended by circumstances of aggravation, the tardiness of constitutional trials provoked the miners in California to return occasionally to the more summary dispatch of these primitive mining courts.[66]

65. Downie, *Hunting for Gold*, 81, 148 ff.; Josiah Royce, *California, from the Conquest . . . to the Second Vigilance Committee* (Boston, 1886), 316.
66. E. S. Capron, *History of California* (Boston, 1854), 228.

But though the Californian miners, on their arrival on Fraser River, attempted to make each bar autonomous in mining matters, as has been shown, they never undertook to enforce criminal law for serious offences. Such an effort would have fallen still-born while Douglas was at the helm, and after the advent of Judge Begbie, in November, 1858, the greatest enthusiast for miners' law would not have dared to dream of introducing such illegal courts. Any attempt to create them and make them function would undoubtedly have landed the self-made judges and juries behind steel bars. Douglas's system of placing in each mining section an official who represented the law of the land, and his appointment, before Judge Begbie's arrival, of Commissioners to try persons accused of murder and other serious crimes, gave the miners an authority to which they could resort at once and obtain speedy justice. Even when, in 1858, King murdered Eaton at Cross Bar and Post murdered Miller at Madison Bar, the miners did not think of trying either of them in any self-constituted court, but were content to notify the authorities and rely upon them to deal with the criminals without delay.

When Judge Begbie arrived in November, 1858, the first moves were to swear him and Douglas into office as Judge and Governor respectively; to promulgate the Act of the Imperial Parliament creating the Colony of British Columbia, a separate entity from the Colony of Vancouver Island; to issue proclamations revoking the Hudson's Bay Company's licence of exclusive trade with the Indians, indemnifying Douglas and his appointees for all their actions, and declaring English law in force in the colony.

Judge Begbie immediately entered upon the duties of his office which included not only those of a strictly judicial nature but also those of an Attorney-General. At his first murder trial in March, 1859, when an American, Neil, was tried for killing a man in a dispute over a gambling game, half the jury was, under the law, comprised of foreigners and, as Judge Begbie says, the jury was, by the necessity of the case, composed in part of American citizens.[67] A verdict of manslaughter having been returned, he in sentencing the criminal to four years' imprisonment, took occasion to dwell upon the enormity of the crime and, luckily finding an American

67. F. W. Howay, *Early History of Fraser River Mines*, 44, 46.

law book, read from it some of the more decisive passages. In March, 1860, because of the difficulty of procuring a sufficient number of British subjects to serve on juries, Governor Douglas issued a proclamation authorizing the sheriff to summon for that purpose the required number of persons "whether British subjects or not."[68]

In his advisory capacity Begbie in March, 1859, reported that a boat from Puget Sound had been seized at Langley for failure to enter at the customs at New Westminster. The proclamation making that port one of entry had been only recently passed. It seemed to him "hard that the country should lose the industry of five men and the men themselves $150 of property where no fraud was clearly shown to have been intended." He accordingly authorized the collector of customs to release the seizure on payment of $50, being one-third of the value. By this course the revenue would lose $15, "which, if you think I am doing very wrong, you may make me repay." However, the Americans would not accept the offer. "This refusal," Begbie wrote, "releases me from any responsibility in the matter."[69] Begbie is so frequently painted as the hard and stern judge that such an incident as this, which shows the kindly heart of the man, is worth recording.

Until November, 1858, there was no Supreme Court of British Columbia, and hence there could be no bar; but on Vancouver Island a Supreme Court had been established in 1853. The bar on Vancouver Island was limited to British subjects. This aroused the ire of Mr. John Nugent, the special agent of the United States, who applied to Governor Douglas of Vancouver Island to permit American lawyers to appear in the courts of that colony in defence of Americans charged with crime. The Governor refused upon the ground that the rules of court were made by the Judge and were not under his jurisdiction. When the correspondence is examined a feeling arises that a different tone on Nugent's part might have evoked a favourable answer.[70] But Judge Begbie, soon after the Colony of British Columbia was formed, promulgated rules of court by which reputable lawyers entitled to practise in the

68. Proclamation, March 8, 1860.

69. Howay, *Early History of Fraser River Mines*, 45.

70. John Nugent's *Report*, in Senate Executive Document no. 29, 35th Congress, 2nd Session, 21 ff.

Supreme Court of any of the states of the American union were entitled to be enrolled for six months in the bar of that colony. This was another of those temporary measures which, owing to the nature of the migration, the propinquity of the United States, and the distance from England or any British colony, the public interest necessitated or at any rate rendered desirable. The rules provided that any American lawyers so enrolled should apply for naturalization as soon as possible, and that the number of Americans on the roll should never exceed that of the British.[71] Sir E. B. Lytton, as Secretary of State for the Colonies, while regretting the conditions that made such a rule necessary, offered no objection to it. However the rule was never invoked; no American lawyers asked for the privilege, one cause of which, said Douglas, might be assigned to the fact "that the country has enjoyed a singular degree of quiet, and almost an exemption from troublesome litigation."[72] The permission expired on June 30, 1859, and was not renewed.

As Judge Begbie did not arrive until after the departure of John Nugent he was free from his caustic and largely-unfounded criticisms, but Judge Cameron of Vancouver Island came under his fire, as, for that matter, did almost every official of either colony. Nugent cites some of Judge Cameron's alleged remarks as evidence of "the animus with which they dealt out law to American citizens."[73] Judge Cameron, it may be added, was not a trained lawyer, but a sugar planter from Demerara; he, however, was endowed with good common sense and a judicial mind. The attack upon him caused the *Puget Sound Herald*, of Steilacoom, Washington, to say:

We have formed a very favorable opinion of his [Judge Cameron's] ability, integrity, and purity. There seems to be a manifest desire on the part of the Judge to dispense Justice not only with rigidness and exactness, but with despatch. The manner in which Justice is meted out to parties litigant and all of the transactions of the tribunal are apparently very much at variance with the wholesale denunciations heaped upon the

71. Rules of Court, in *British Columbia Proclamations*, 1858; and in *Victoria Gazette*, December 30, 1858.

72. *Papers relative to British Columbia*, part II, 52, 81; Douglas to Lytton, in *Further Papers relative to British Columbia*, part III, 25.

73. Nugent, *Report*, 14. For Nugent's life and character, see Bancroft, *Popular Tribunals* II, 223 ff.

authorities of the colony by Mr. Special Commissioner John Nugent. We make these remarks on the principle of giving "honour to whom honour is due."[74]

The mines being on Fraser River, in the Colony of British Columbia, Judge Begbie was naturally the person with whom the American miners came into contact in the courts. In him they found a fearless judge, upright, stern, and even severe in his official capacity. But there was never any suggestion that he discriminated on the ground of nationality. To Judge Begbie a crime was a crime and it received its punishment, whether the criminal were red, white, yellow, or brown. A Chinese was charged with assaulting another Mongolian; an American miner was alleged to have deliberately destroyed an Indian's canoe; another miner was suspected of having sold liquor to an Indian: all these comparatively trifling matters, as well as the more serious and capital offences, he dealt with exhaustively and yet without time-wasting, and dispensed in every case the same speedy and honest, if somewhat rough-and-ready justice. He was the great force in maintaining law and order in the country; but beneath him were the local magistrates, by whatever name they might be called, men, if not so well learned in the law, yet as fully determined that lawlessness should obtain no footing in the land. Above them all was Governor Douglas, thoroughly imbued with the same determination. In the words of Bancroft: "Considering the circumstances surrounding the beginning, the unruly, wild men and the unruly gold-gatherers, society during these incipient stages was, I say, a marvel of order and obedience to law."[75]

As there were no miners' courts trying capital offences in British Columbia, so there were no lynchings—a form of proceeding but slightly removed. In a book called *Very Far West Indeed*, will be found a story of an alleged lynching at Jack of Clubs Creek, in Cariboo, in December, 1862. The author does not pretend that he was present; he merely retells what may, or may not, have been told him; but even if he actually heard the story it is none the less untrue. Briefly, an American miner is said to have told him how his partner drew up the bucket, left him at the bottom of the shaft

74. *Puget Sound Herald*, Steilacoom, Washington Territory, February 11, 1859.
75. H. H. Bancroft, *History of British Columbia* (San Francisco, 1890), 425.

and decamped with his goods, how he escaped, and, securing aid, followed and overtook the fugitive, who was then unceremoniously hanged from the limb of a tree.[76] Interviews many years ago with miners working on Jack of Clubs in 1862 and 1863 show that no such lynching ever occurred. Moreover the contemporary newspapers, which featured Cariboo news, contain no reference to such an event.

There was, however, one real lynching in British Columbia and, though it occurred in 1884, it is mentioned for the sake of completeness. In February of that year, a murder was committed in the State of Washington, near the boundary. The murderer fled into British Columbia. The British Columbian law officer arrested him and placed him in custody. That night a mob of about eighty men from the United States surrounded the place where the prisoner was confined. Their demand for him being refused, they showed force and his custodians surrendered him. The lynchers departed with the supposed criminal. The next morning he was found hanging from a tree about a mile from the boundary line. All the factors, except the scene of the lynching, belonged to the United States. Complaint of this breach of national rights was made and the matter became the subject of correspondence between the two governments.[77]

The American miners imported from California the practice of duelling, which was quite common in the Golden State; but it was a plant that did not flourish north of 49°. There is one recorded duel in British Columbia. In September, 1858, in Victoria, two men, John B. Collins and William Morris, alias "Tipperary Bill," a San Francisco boatman, had a warm dispute which grew from threats into bad language and culminated in a blow. At once a duel was arranged. The combatants, armed with pistols and accompanied by their friends, met by agreement on Vancouver Street, near Kanaka Row, a short distance from the fort. At the third shot, Collins fell, mortally wounded. Morris immediately fled to his Whitehall boat and with a companion made all haste for the American side of the line. The police from Victoria followed in hot pursuit, but, despite their best efforts, failed to overtake the fleeing

76. R. B. Johnson, *Very Far West Indeed* (London, 1872), 180 ff.
77. *Mainland Guardian*, New Westminster, March 1, 15, 1884.

murderer. Morris continued his flight to California where he was arrested for murder and hanged in the following spring.[78]

On February 22, 1859, the Americans at Yale celebrated Washington's birthday. Having fired a salute of one hundred guns they spent the day in merriment and wound up with a grand ball. Ned McGowan, who has been already mentioned, and J. W. Bagley, both of Hill's Bar and both in the black books of the San Francisco Vigilance Committee, got into a dispute, which became so keen that "satisfaction" was demanded. To Bagley's demand for a duel, McGowan, who had had experience with British justice, replied "that he would not fight in British territory, but was willing to meet him in United States territory." McGowan sold his mining claim on the bar in order to be on "the field of honour" in Washington Territory, but it is believed that the duel was not fought. He left Fraser River about the middle of March, showing with pride some $4,700 in gold dust, "pretty good," as he declared, "for an old man of fifty."

Another near-duel between Dolan and Burns, both of Hill's Bar and both of the lawless stripe of the so-called Law and Order party of San Francisco, was partly arranged. In this instance it appears that they actually thought of fighting the duel at Hill's Bar. "They had agreed to fight with revolvers at 30 paces, advancing a pace each shot, but Burns afterwards insisted that if there was no hit after the six shots a side, they should finish the business with Bowie knives. To this Dolan would not consent, as his right arm is weak from a wound, and so the matter stands."[79] So far as is known this duel never occurred. Dolan left the country with McGowan, a short time later.

When the Colony of Vancouver Island was formed in 1849, no currency, except possibly Hudson's Bay Company's tokens, was in use. All business was by barter; balances were adjusted and payments made by drafts on London. In that year a vessel arrived at Victoria, carrying American miners from California who were

78. Victoria *Gazette*, September 14, 15, 29, December 16, 1858. For a highly coloured account of this duel, in which the participants bear fictitious names, see D. W. Higgins, *The Mystic Spring* (Toronto, 1904), 231 ff.; *Daily Evening Bulletin*, San Francisco, April 8, 12, and June 10, 1859.

79. Howay, *Early History of Fraser River Mines*, 85, 87.

seeking supplies. They offered gold nuggets in exchange for goods. Roderick Finlayson, the officer in charge at Fort Victoria, had never seen native gold. Knowing, however, that gold was malleable he subjected the proffered nuggets to that test; as a result he offered, not without much hesitation, to take them at $11 an ounce. If this be thought unusually low it may be stated that it was the ruling price in Oregon, where gold dust brought from $10 to $14 an ounce. In 1858, Alfred Waddington says that the current price at Victoria was $14.50 an ounce. Captain Grant, the first settler in that colony, paid his Indian workers with tobacco. With the gradual settlement of the portion of Oregon north of the Columbia River, currency slowly displaced the primitive barter. The coin collected at Fort Vancouver and Nisqually was forwarded to Fort Victoria, the newly-established headquarters. In 1852, Fort Vancouver remitted to Victoria for shipment to London $60,000 in currency, ranging all the way from $50 gold pieces to dimes, and more than ninety-three ounces of gold dust.[80]

The discovery of coal at Nanaimo in 1852, gave employment to Indian workers. The Hudson's Bay Company, who were operating the coal mines, paid them in goods for the coal raised on the basis of 2s. 6d. a ton. The white colliers working at the same rate were settled with by draft on London, which was in reality a credit note. The produce of the mines found a market in San Francisco, to which port the first coal was sent in October, 1852. In September, 1853, the United States Steamer *Active* purchased at Nanaimo 100 tons of coal; payment was made by cash, $500, and draft on James King of William in San Francisco, for $600. Other vessels followed and, though there is no record, it seems fair to infer that some at any rate paid cash in whole or in part. Doubtless the sailors made purchases from the Company and paid therefor in American money. A customs officer had been appointed for Victoria in November, 1852, and a small charge made for entries and clearances; these also were probably paid in dollars. From such sources there appears to have drifted into Victoria—the only place then in contact with the outside world—a small supply of currency of a miscellaneous character. So long as the Company

80. For most of the facts in this and the succeeding paragraph I am indebted to Dr. W. Kaye Lamb, Librarian, University of British Columbia; Waddington, *Fraser River Mines Vindicated*, 43 f.

did not ship the currency to London it passed from hand to hand in exchange for goods or credit, and answered the needs of a circulating medium in the primitive conditions. In 1856, Nisqually sent to Fort Victoria a box containing various silver coins, aggregating $871.85.[81]

The government of the colony and the Hudson's Bay Company both carried their accounts in sterling, but the circulating medium, such as it was, was dollars. With the gold rush of 1858 American money in large quantities made its appearance. All the business of Vancouver Island and the mainland—later the Colony of British Columbia—whether public or private, was done in American money, but transmuted by the government and the Company for their records and accounts into English money. The first newspaper, the Victoria *Gazette*, which appeared in June, 1858, and was published in a colony whose official currency was sterling, placed its subscription at $20 a year, and single copies at 25 cents. All the prices published therein including those of the Hudson's Bay Company were in dollars. All sums of money mentioned in statutes or in government regulations were specified in sterling, but in such amounts as made an aliquot part of a dollar. Thus two forms of money existed in British Columbia. In April, 1861, the steamer *Tartar* brought out to British Columbia £6,900 in florins, shillings, sixpenny and threepenny pieces.[82] The latter did not circulate. The other coins passed readily from hand to hand, but not as sterling money; the florin was called half a dollar; the shilling, a quarter of a dollar; and the sixpenny piece, 12½ cents—"a bit" in ordinary parlance—though it was only taken as ten cents. For years the English sovereign passed current for $5.

Early in 1861 Governor Douglas proposed to raise £5,000, apparently for the purpose of meeting payments due to the contractors on the Cariboo Road, by an issue of government notes. It is not known whether the notes were actually issued; but later in that year the Governor did issue another series of notes. This time, however, they were in dollars and not in sterling. It is prob-

81. MS Journal of Nanaimo and letters between James Douglas and J. W. McKay, in charge of the mines there, especially those dated August 6, 14, September 5, 12, 1853. Copies in library of F. W. Howay.

82. *British Columbian*, New Westminster, April 11, 1861.

able, as R. L. Reid says,[83] that the paper being intended to pay the road contractors, the Governor thought that it would pass more readily if it were in terms of American money—the currency familiar to the people. The pressure of American influence shows plainly here when a man like Douglas who reverenced everything English, found it strong enough to cause him to issue notes of a British colony in terms of a foreign monetary unit; and that, too, in the face of an objection by the Colonial Treasurer to this "American Currency," as being unconstitutional.

The scarcity of coin was a constant cause of complaint. The Colonial Treasury had but little, and the banks were scarcely any better supplied. The result was that the American miners who desired to turn their gold dust into currency resorted to their own city of San Francisco.[84] This, it was urged, meant a great loss to British Columbia. At about the same time a notice appeared in the "Government Gazette" stating that the gold coins of the United States would thereafter be taken at $4.85 for the pound sterling. The same issue contained another notice signed by the merchants of New Westminster, then the capital, to the effect that thereafter they would only accept the sovereign for $4.85. "A funny kind of legislation," said the British Columbian.[85]

As a remedy Governor Douglas resolved to coin the gold of the country for use as money. On November 14, 1861, he wrote: "I propose to take immediate steps for the manufacture of gold pieces, equal in value to the 10 and 20 dollar American coins, and to bring them into general use as a circulating medium in both Colonies."[86] Accordingly a minting plant was obtained in San Francisco; but instead of coining sovereigns or any other pieces bearing the terminology of sterling it was to coin $20 and $10 pieces, which were to be American money in everything but the place of coining. The plan was carried out to the extent of manufacturing a few

83. R. L. Reid, *The Assay Office and the Proposed Mint at New Westminster* (Victoria, 1926), 14 f.

84. *British Columbian*, November 7, 1861; *Alta California*, San Francisco, November 29, 1861.

85. *British Columbian*, December 27, 1861. The "Government Gazette," as it was called, was then published on the fourth page of the *British Columbian*. The notice referred to appeared in issue of December 27, 1861.

86. *Papers relative to the Affairs of British Columbia* (London, 1862), part IV, 62.

sample coins, but the mint did not produce currency for circulation. However this undertaking and the issue of the notes in the same year, already mentioned, present the odd spectacle of a British colony whose official currency was sterling, whose public accounts were kept in that medium of exchange, issuing paper money and planning to issue gold coinage based on the American unit and expressed in its terms. That the notes were only a temporary expedient and that the gold coins were not actually produced for circulation are facts quite beside the point.

Until 1866, this strange situation continued. The colonies kept their official accounts in sterling; their statutes spoke in that currency also; but the people talked in terms of the dollar and all their business was in the American medium. In 1865 the Legislative Assembly of British Columbia ended the anomaly of two monetary systems in the colony. By Ordinance No. 8, it was declared that after January 1, 1866, the public accounts should be kept in dollars and cents; that the pound sterling should be equivalent to $4.85; the crown piece, $1.25; the half-crown, 62½ cents; the florin, 50 cents; the shilling, 25 cents; the sixpence, 12½ cents; and the threepenny piece, 6 cents; that the American eagle should be legal tender for $10, and its multiples or halves for proportionate sums; and that the American half-dollar, quarter-dollar, and dime should be legal tender for 50 cents, 25 cents, and 10 cents, respectively. The money in actual circulation was almost entirely American. Even as late as 1877 "the coins principally used were United States coins," both gold and silver.

An attempt will now be made to account for the situation described by gathering up and implementing scattered remarks. The Fraser River country was unprepared to receive such an influx as that of 1858. California from which the immigrants came being a mining state was the nearest, and to them the natural supply station. The horses and mules, the food, hardware, and mining utensils, the newspapers, postal and express services, the money, banks, and all other material requirements came from that state. From it too came, directly or indirectly, the light-draft river steamers for service on the Fraser. For everything they needed, for the solution of their every problem the miners looked to California and Californian experience.

The whole training of the Americans had been along the lines of independence and self-reliance; the British had been trained to refer every question to their superiors. The difficulties with the Indians encountered by the miners show this elemental difference; and it partly accounts for Governor Douglas's attitude to the miners in the trouble of 1858.

But the conduct of the Californian miners on Fraser River calls for more extended consideration. The steamer *Commodore* in April, 1858, landed in Victoria almost as many miners as its population, and they were, on the evidence of all witnesses, well-behaved. The rowdyism of San Francisco was absent; this was true even in July when the number had swollen to six thousand. The same obedience to law is found in the gold fields; and that even before the advent of Judge Begbie.

In that wild region with no roads, a few primitive trails, and practically only accessible by the Fraser River, thousands of American miners, many of whom had broken out of bounds in California, lived quietly under the law. The entire Colony of British Columbia had but seven Justices of the Peace, principally Gold Commissioners, and fifteen constables—a force ludicrously inadequate to cope with any serious criminal outbreak. Doubtless the lack of communications was in itself a passive deterrent.

Writing on August 6, 1860, Governor Douglas stated that since November 19, 1858, only two serious crimes had been committed by white men in the colony: "One burglary in which the criminals were seized and delivered up to the regular authorities by the inhabitants, and one murder committed at Lytton about a month ago, in which there is reason to believe that the criminal immediately escaped beyond the frontier. The only other cases have been petty thefts."[87] Judge Begbie, writing a short time before, referred to the spectacle afforded by the wild country and the wild miners all armed, with an inexperienced judge and magistracy, and a police force of less than twenty and yet there had been not one murder or attempted murder and only one assault with a deadly weapon. This unprecedented freedom from crime in a pioneer mining country he attributed to the firmness of the Governor and the unhesitating sternness with which one or two "difficulties" had been met and punished—meaning, it would seem, by himself.

87. Douglas MS Correspondence Book, 44 ff., in the Archives of British Columbia.

The miners had been impressed with the knowledge that any killings would "here consign the offenders without hope of mercy to the gallows or a life-long imprisonment." Of the Californian miners he wrote that they "Manifested a great desire to see justice firmly done, and great patience with the difficulties the judiciary have had to contend with. I have frequently complimented my rough auditory—sometimes 150 miners—on the good order and manly respect observed in my court."[88]

The whole matter can scarcely be disposed of merely by saying that the peaceful condition of the mines and the law-abiding behaviour of the miners, in such strange contrast with their conduct in California, were owing to Governor Douglas and Judge Begbie. There are other circumstances to be considered, though there may be divergent estimates of their relative force. The nature of the country and of the miners themselves must be taken into account. When the Californians reached Victoria they were upon an island, practically uninhabited, and from which escape was difficult; and from the mines the only egress was by the Fraser River; this, coupled with the absence of roads and the existence of primitive trails, rendered it almost impossible for a criminal to evade arrest. Many of the adventurers went no farther than Victoria. Owing to the disheartening reports of the gold fields the bad element, the professional gamblers, thieves, roughs and toughs, and such like, seeing no chance of "easy money" returned to San Francisco. Those who persevered to the bars of Fraser River were, speaking generally, real miners, naturally sober and industrious, even though some like McGowan, Bagley, and others of the gentry of Hill's Bar had been guilty of heinous crimes in the unrestrained licence of California. *Autres temps, autres mœurs.*

At first contact the Californians hooted Governor Douglas; for was he not the representative of the hated Hudson's Bay Company that had "tried to steal Oregon" from the United States? But when in November, 1858, he became Governor of British Columbia and severed his connection with the Company, they changed as they discovered his remarkable ability in managing men, and found that, underneath his ever-present dignity, was a man most approachable, jealous of the good name of the country he governed,

88. J. D. Pemberton, *Facts and Figures relating to Vancouver Island and British Columbia* (London, 1860), 128 ff.

earnestly desirous of enacting sound and beneficial legislation and of protecting every man's rights. "Many of my American acquaintances were astonished at the simplicity, promptness, and honesty with which government business was managed. Such a change from what they had been accustomed to in San Francisco."[89]

At first, too, they regarded Begbie as a persecutor. But his stern, severe, and impartial administration of rapid and even-handed justice, without fear, favour, or affection gradually won their admiration, as they realized that he gave to them what they had not found in California: a sense of protection not conferred by themselves and their weapons, but under the law. There is no greater incentive to respect for, and obedience to, the law than a well-grounded belief that it is fair and right and that breaches will be impartially investigated and punished. When the Californians came to know Governor Douglas and Judge Begbie they found in them a new kind of governor and a new kind of judge. From sure and impartial administration of the law the criminal, even the hardened one, flees. Bishop Sheepshanks relates that he asked a notorious American criminal, who was in gaol in New Westminster in 1860, what he would do when released: "Why, sir, I shall clear out of British territory without delay."[90]

The Californians found in British Columbia freedom under the law and safety under the law; a condition that any man not inherently bad appreciates. They found, too, that they had the same privileges as they had enjoyed in California and that the authorities were not insistent to interfere in small matters or to punish peccadilloes. They flew the American flag as and when they pleased; they celebrated Washington's birthday, year after year; they fired their "anvil salutes" annually on the Fourth of July;[91] and mere drunkenness was allowed to pass unheeded, so long as it did not trespass on others' rights. No one interfered with the Californian practice of carrying revolver and bowie-knife provided those lethal weapons were not used; it was left to them to learn, as soon they did, that with law properly administered such weapons were merely useless lumber. Bishop Hills, near Lytton in June,

89. MS letter from James Bell to John Thompson, dated San Francisco, February 27, 1859. Copy in library of F. W. Howay.

90. D. W. Duthie, *A Bishop in the Rough* (London, 1909), 34.

91. *British Columbian*, July 11, 1861.

1860, "overtook a miner from California with a revolver on one side and a bowie-knife on the other. I spoke about the former," said the Bishop, and he told me "they were needed in California, but not here."[92] The miners were permitted, or at any rate not prosecuted for, the practice of gambling, dear to the Californian heart, unless it caused some disturbance. These comparatively small matters were for the time being left to adjust themselves. But serious crimes—deadly assaults, robbery, and murder—were relentlessly prosecuted and severely punished. In those prosecutions these Californians sat as jurymen and thus became a part of law enforcement under new conditions. They found, too, that the presence of the Gold Commissioner in every mining district, to whom all complaints could be made and every difficulty brought for settlement, rendered the unlawful mining courts of California unnecessary; and their inherent desire for self-government was fully met by the institution of local mining boards. The combination of these influences it was that rendered the British Columbia mines free from the lawlessness which is so great a blot upon the story of California's mining days.

92. W. C. Hazlitt, *The Great Gold Fields of Cariboo* (London, 1862), 160.

CHAPTER VIII

BRITISH COLUMBIA IN THE BALANCE—ANNEXATION OR CONFEDERATION

1866-1871

ALTHOUGH Great Britain, in the treaty of 1846, had secured recognition of her claim to a sector of the Pacific Coast, the settlement of Vancouver Island and British Columbia during the two ensuing decades had not ensured the maintenance of this position by creating colonies which could be recognized as capable of life. It is the purpose of this chapter to trace the process by which the British territories on the Pacific Coast became an integral part of the Dominion of Canada and so definitively avoided the absorption into the American Union which to many in that country, in Great Britain, and, indeed, in British Columbia itself appeared to be its "Manifest Destiny."

The Hudson's Bay Company, of which James Douglas was the leading official west of the Rockies, legally held seisin of Vancouver Island. But constitutionally Vancouver Island was a Crown colony. The Governor was assisted by a Council and, after 1856, by a Legislative Assembly as well. The power of the Assembly was strictly limited and there was no approach to responsible government.

By the terms of the Royal Grant of 1849, all revenues from land sales, mineral royalties and licences, after the deduction of ten per cent from the gross proceeds for the use of the Hudson's Bay Company, were to be "applied towards the colonization and improvement of the island."[1] These revenues were placed in the so-called "colonial fund" which was administered by the Hudson's Bay Company. The Assembly in 1856 had enquired of Governor Douglas respecting information as to "what funds are subject to the control of this Assembly, if any; what is the amount, and from what source does it come, and what fund is the royalty on coal

1. *Papers relative to the Grant of Vancouver's Island to the Hudson's Bay Company* (1849, 103), 15-16.

paid into."[2] The members had received the reply that the only funds which could be controlled by the Assembly were those arising from liquor licences. Towards the end of Douglas's régime, as the result of agitation by the Assembly for the control of Crown lands and the entire revenue of the colony, the Duke of Newcastle, Secretary of State for the Colonies, proposed that the salaries of the Governor and the officials should be fixed by an act of the Legislature, and that in return, the Crown revenues of Vancouver Island, when a suitable settlement had been made of the claims of the Hudson's Bay Company, should be handed over to the Legislature of Vancouver Island.[3] The Assembly refused to agree to this proposal, and at the time of Douglas's retirement in 1864 the question remained unsettled.

The political structure of British Columbia was even simpler, and in the mainland colony Douglas was a virtual dictator. He issued "proclamations having the force of law" and ruled with the assistance of officials appointed by the British Colonial Office. It was not until shortly before his retirement that Douglas, acting upon instructions from the Duke of Newcastle, set up a Legislative Council of which one-third was elected and two-thirds composed of officials and magistrates.[4]

Sir James Douglas—he was knighted in 1863—was the only person to hold both governorships. On his retirement Downing Street appointed Albert Edward Kennedy for Vancouver Island and Frederick Seymour for British Columbia. Kennedy, a genial Irishman, inherited Douglas's squabble with the Assembly and a battle royal was waged over the vexed questions of Crown lands, Crown revenues, and the civil list which was to make permanent provision for the salaries of the Governor and the officials. The Assembly pleaded the poverty of the colony. The Governor upheld the policy laid down by the Duke of Newcastle and an impasse

2. Minutes of the House of Assembly, December 3, 1856, in *Memoir* no. III, Archives of British Columbia (Victoria, 1918), 22. Cf. W. N. Sage, *Sir James Douglas and British Columbia* (Toronto, 1930), 196.

3. Newcastle to Douglas, June 15, 1863, in the Archives of British Columbia. Cf. L. A. Wrinch, "Land Policy of the Colony of Vancouver Island, 1849-1866," M.A. Thesis in the University of British Columbia Library, 133.

4. *Papers relative to the Proposed Union of British Columbia and Vancouver Island* (London, 1866), 2.

was reached. Kennedy in the end was forced to borrow to pay the salaries which the Assembly had refused to vote. No solution of Vancouver Island's problem was found until the union of the colonies in 1866 when the Colonial Office transferred Governor Kennedy to a less turbulent colony and the Legislative Assembly was abolished.

In the mainland colony of British Columbia Governor Frederick Seymour met with less opposition. The "popular" or elected element in the Legislative Council could not hope to constitute a majority and Seymour was on the whole greatly influenced by the "official" members. The Governor was a well-meaning, easy-going mediocrity who seems to have owed his position to family influence in Great Britain. When he took office in 1864 the gold mines of Cariboo were still producing well and the gold colony was fairly prosperous. But by 1865 the gold stream had commenced to dry up and the colony was in financial difficulties.

The two colonies were not equally advanced politically or economically. British Columbia during the gold rushes had been the wealthier colony, but her population was unstable and liable to great fluctuations in numbers. Governor Seymour once wittily described British Columbia as a "road with a gold mine at one end and a city in a neighbouring colony at the other." The Cariboo road, constructed between 1862 and 1865, was the artery of the colony. Along it ran the gaily painted Concord stages, but by 1865 they were running empty. Vancouver Island, although by no means fully self-governing, had advanced farther towards that goal than had British Columbia. It was also more mature economically and was not so completely dependent on gold mining. Governor Douglas had in 1860 declared Victoria, including Esquimalt, a "free port." This meant that all goods came into Victoria free and after being warehoused there could be trans-shipped to British Columbia or to Washington Territory. Vancouver Island was a free trade colony and the British Columbia tariff was lower than the American. Victoria was also the centre of the white population on Vancouver Island and its connection with the Hudson's Bay Company was important.

There was really no valid reason for the continuance of two British colonies on the far west coast. The British government in

1866 decided to unite the two colonies, and legislation to that effect
was introduced into Parliament. The union was unpopular on the
mainland, especially in New Westminster. On Vancouver Island
the majority seems to have favoured union as facilitating a solution
of constitutional and financial difficulties. But Vancouver Island
paid a high price. She lost her Legislative Assembly and Victoria
ceased to be a "free port." Governor Kennedy, as has been stated,
was transferred to a new appointment and Governor Seymour
remained in charge of the united colony.

The first problem was the selection of the capital. Since Vancouver Island had been united to British Columbia, New Westminster rather naturally claimed to be the capital. Governor
Seymour at first supported the claims of New Westminster, but
when on home leave he changed his mind and favoured Victoria.
It has been suggested that the attitude of the Hudson's Bay
Company was a factor in the final choice of Victoria as capital.
Be that as it may, the island city became the capital in 1868 and
is today the capital of the Province of British Columbia.

The union of 1866 was a palliative not a cure for the financial
and constitutional problems of British Columbia. Governor
Seymour did not possess the strength of character necessary to
initiate drastic economies. He was unwilling to dismiss unnecessary
officials. In a few cases he did use the pruning knife, and there
is on record a rather pitiful letter in which the Governor pleaded
with the Colonial Office for a new position for the unfortunate
who had just been dismissed. It is not surprising to learn that
British Columbia's deficits continued, that its population steadily
diminished, and that taxation increased. The Legislative Council
of British Columbia had been enlarged to include representatives
from Vancouver Island, but the popularly elected members were
still in the minority. Responsible government was as far off as
ever.

British Columbia could expect no future as an isolated British
colony on the Northwest Pacific Coast with her nearest British
neighbour on the east the Red River Settlement and on the west
Hong Kong. In 1867 the United States purchased Alaska; and
British Columbia, as Attorney-General Crease stated in the Confederation debate in the Legislative Council of British Columbia in

March, 1870, was "sandwiched between United States Territory to the north and south."[5] Although British influences were strong they could not compensate for the hard facts of geography. British Columbia was separated from the settled portions of British North America not only by the towering peaks of the Rocky Mountains and by the broad open prairies but also by the rocks, lakes, rivers, and muskegs of the Canadian Shield. The Red River Settlement was isolated from Eastern Canada, and British Columbia was even more isolated from Red River. Although the Pacific colony held a strategic position on the Northwest Coast, and was Britain's little window towards the Orient, it was approximately fifteen thousand miles by sea from the motherland. In 1866 there was little, if any, direct immigration from Great Britain, and the decline of Cariboo led to emigration from the colony. Great Britain was faced by too many problems at home to pay much attention to faraway British Columbia.

The officials who ruled British Columbia during the years 1866-71 were in the main of British birth. Governor Frederick Seymour and his successor Governor Anthony Musgrave had both had experience in the British colonial service before coming to the Pacific Coast. Other prominent officials—Arthur N. Birch, Presiding Member of the Legislative Council, 1867, and during the absence of Governor Seymour the officer administering the government; W. A. G. Young, Presiding Member, 1868-9, and Colonial Secretary; Judge Matthew Baillie Begbie; Henry P. P. Crease, Attorney-General, to mention only a few—were natives of the British Isles. Of the members of the Legislative Council of 1870, which drew up the terms of union with Canada, three had been born in the eastern British North American provinces, and so might be classed as Canadians; nearly all the others had come to the colony from Great Britain and Ireland either directly or after a sojourn in California.

The Church of England was another link with the old country. To be sure no church was established in the colony, but in the early days of the former Colony of Vancouver Island an attempt had been made to inaugurate a policy of "clergy reserves," similar to those

5. *Debate on the Subject of Confederation with Canada* (Victoria, 1870), 5, hereafter cited as *Confederation Debates.*

existing in the old provinces of Canada.[6] The Rev. George Hills, D.D., of Great Yarmouth, was consecrated the first Bishop of Columbia in Westminster Abbey on February 24, 1859. He arrived in Victoria in January, 1860, and remained in office as Bishop until his retirement in 1892. Bishop Hills was a stiff Anglican and upheld all the traditions of his church. His controversy with Dean Cridge, the former chaplain of the Hudson's Bay Company at Fort Victoria, led to a schism in the church.

When the Colony of British Columbia had been formed in 1858 a special detachment of the Royal Engineers was sent out by the Secretary of State for the Colonies, Sir Edward Bulwer Lytton, to aid in the development of the mainland. The Royal Engineers were commanded by Colonel Richard Clement Moody, who was also appointed Commissioner of Lands and Works. The detachment was disbanded in 1863, the officers returning to England. Most of the men remained in the colony as settlers. The presence of these former British soldiers in the colony provided another link of empire. In addition there was the British naval establishment at Esquimalt which dated from the period of the Crimean War. British war vessels had been on the coast since the mid-forties when the Oregon Question was at its height. The presence of the Royal Navy in British Columbian waters had marked influence on the people of the colony.

There was little direct trade with Britain. Arthur T. Bushby, Acting Postmaster-General of the colony, writing to the Colonial Secretary on November 20, 1867, stated that the "entire trade of the Colony (with the exception of a few vessels during the year direct from England)" was "transacted with San Francisco."

On the whole the far-away Colony of British Columbia attracted relatively little attention in Downing Street. This was the period of Little Englandism. British Columbia was a poor, struggling, bankrupt colony off on the edge of things. *The Times* (London) on December 18, 1869, informed its readers in regard to the colony that "the way of getting at it is by the Isthmus of Darien and the Pacific, and the nearest civilized community is the State of California. With the exception of a limited official class, it receives

6. On the subject of the proposed "clergy reserve," see Alexander Begg, *History of British Columbia* (Toronto, 1894), 329-32, and Sage, *Sir James Douglas*, 281-5.

few emigrants from England, and a large proportion of its inhabitants consists of citizens of the United States who have entered it
from the South."[7] The attitude of the British government towards
British Columbia, as towards the other British colonies in North
America, was that of philosophical resignation to their following
the example of the United States by asserting their independence.
If this occurred before they were able to stand by themselves they
might be tempted to seek admission to the American Union. But
Great Britain was deaf to American suggestions that pressure
should be applied and, once Canadian Confederation was achieved,
British influence was directed to inducing British Columbia to
unite with Canada.

To the young colony the omnipresence of the United States
was a factor of vital importance. The metropolis of the Pacific
Coast was San Francisco; and Victoria, the capital and chief port
of British Columbia, was only its northern outpost, the gateway
to the rapidly declining gold fields of the Fraser Valley. British
Columbia was part of the great hinterland of San Francisco, a
hinterland which included Oregon and Washington, Nevada, Utah,
and Idaho as well as California. Victoria may have been the
San Francisco of British Columbia but its population in the 1860's
never rose above 4,000,[8] while that of San Francisco, the largest
and most important city west of the Mississippi, rose from 34,000
in 1850 to over 60,000 in the 1860's.[9]

San Francisco was Victoria's connecting link with the outside
world. The shipping lines to the Pacific Northwest, to Panama, and
across the Pacific had their headquarters in San Francisco, which
also became the terminus of the Union Pacific Railway in 1869.
Steamers began to come up to Victoria from San Francisco in 1854.
The gold rush of 1858 strengthened the hold of the American
steamship lines. The Pacific Mail Steamship Company, formed by

7. The *British Colonist*, Victoria, on January 27, 1870, took *The Times* severely
to task, pointing out the errors contained in the statement and claiming that the
American portion of the population did not amount to "more than one-fifth of the
civilized population of the Colony."

8. In 1860, 608; in 1867, 2,351; in 1869, 3,676; in 1870, 2,842. These figures
are quoted from Colonial Bluebooks by J. T. Marshall, *Vital Statistics of British
Columbia* (Victoria, n.d.), 189 ff.

9. Based on United States census figures for 1850 and on figures in H. H.
Bancroft, *History of California* (San Francisco, 1890).

William H. Aspinwall, Gardiner Howland, Henry Chauncey, and others, April 2, 1848, was the pioneer on the Northwest Coast. Its steamers had begun to call at Victoria before the gold rush and in 1858 Governor Douglas entered into a contract with this company to place steamers on Fraser River. But the terms were too favourable to the Hudson's Bay Company and the British Secretary of State for the Colonies, Sir Edward Bulwer Lytton, disallowed the contract.

In 1861 the Pacific Mail Steamship Company sold out its northern interests to Holladay and Flint. Ben Holladay, the owner of the Overland Stage Line, became a prominent figure in the ocean shipping of the coast. By degrees Holladay and Flint established their supremacy on the Northwest Coast. In 1862 they obtained a contract to run fortnightly mail steamers between Portland and Victoria. The American Civil War interfered but little with the prosperity of the Far West. The western movement continued unabated. Shipping lines reaped a rich harvest during the gold rushes of the early sixties. Ocean-going traffic between San Francisco, Portland, Victoria, and on Puget Sound remained in American hands, but the local trade in British Columbia was soon monopolized by ships of British registry. Holladay had organized the California, Oregon, and Mexico Steamship Company, commonly known as the "Holladay Line."

Until the union of 1866 Victoria possessed the advantage of being a "free port." American goods paid no duty there, although on the mainland a tariff existed. Victoria was thus an entrepot for Vancouver Island, British Columbia, and to some degree for the neighbouring states and Alaska. The transfer of Alaska to the United States in the year 1867 resulted in a great increase to American trade but had a consequently depressing effect on Victorian shipping.

In 1868 the Colony of British Columbia entered into a mail contract with the California, Oregon, and Mexico Steamship Company. In return for a subsidy of $1,000 a month, the company undertook to run one steamer a month direct from San Francisco to Victoria, and two a month by way of Portland. At this time traffic between Portland, Victoria, and the ports of Puget Sound justified a regular steamer, which was, of course, American owned. From 1866 the *Eliza Anderson*, a vessel operated by Captain

Duncan B. Finch, an American, held a monopoly of the traffic between Victoria and Olympia. During 1869, 1870, and 1871 rival American companies sought to obtain this prosperous trade. Rate wars, highly satisfying to the inhabitants of Vancouver Island and Washington Territory, resulted. For a time Victorians could travel to the Puget Sound ports for fifty and even for twenty-five cents!

Dr. J. S. Helmcken, speaking in the House of Assembly of Vancouver Island in 1864, remarked: "So far as direct steam communication is concerned . . . we have been more liberally treated by our American neighbours . . . far more so than by Her Majesty's Government."[10] But the American steamship companies were not animated by purely philanthropic motives. Naturally they expected profits, and the quality of service depended on the amount of the trade. Great Britain made no real attempt to compete in ocean-going trade. Among the sea captains and engineers were many of British birth, including even a few eastern Canadians, but the majority were American. It is interesting in this connection to recall that British Columbia laid down the maintenance of communication between Victoria, San Francisco, and Olympia as one of the terms of union, an eloquent tribute to her dependence upon the American steamship companies. After Confederation, and especially after the completion of the main line of the Canadian Pacific, Canadian vessels entered into the Puget Sound trade, but to this day trade with California is largely carried on by American vessels. This is particularly true of passenger traffic.

Reference has already been made to the mail contracts. The postal history of British Columbia prior to Confederation is another illustration of the isolation of the colony and its obligations to the great southern neighbour.[11] The following extract from a letter of Arthur T. Bushby, Acting Postmaster-General of British Columbia, to the Colonial Secretary, dated November 20, 1867, is illuminating:

Letters *from* British Columbia to Great Britain, in fact all correspondence between this Colony and other countries, is sent to San Francisco

10. *British Colonist*, January 12, 1864.

11. A. S. Deaville, "The Colonial Postal Systems and Postage Stamps of Vancouver Island and British Columbia, 1849-1871" is a definitive study of the

in a vessel subsidized by the Colony, is there treated as American mail matter, not being received (with a few exceptions) unless the full United States postage be prepaid, which causes the Post Office Department here to keep on hand a large supply of United States postage stamps, which are of course paid for in cash in advance, or to send down cash with the mail [*sic*]. The Postal Department of the Colony is thus in the position of a messenger entrusted with the Colony's correspondence to be posted in San Francisco.

Need one wonder that Governor Musgrave objected to this practice and declared that he had "never heard of anything so undignified in any other place as importing the stamps of another nation for use in a British Colony." But there was no other way. Even the American express companies, who had postal systems of their own, demanded the use of United States postage stamps. Mr. G. P. Bainbridge of Vancouver, who possesses one of the most complete collections of Vancouver Island and British Columbia postage stamps, has several examples of envelopes which bear Vancouver Island and British Columbia stamps along side of United States stamps. The colonial stamps were necessary to pay the local charges, the American to take the letters out of the colony. In 1868 an arrangement was made whereby letters for the United Kingdom might be pre-paid by use of colonial stamps, but letters for the United States, the Dominion of Canada, Prince Edward Island, which did not join Canada until 1873, and Newfoundland required United States stamps.

The express companies, most of which were of American origin, competed successfully with the local authorities in the handling of the local mails. Chartres Brew, Chief Inspector of Police for British Columbia, writing from Fort Yale in February, 1859, to Colonel R. C. Moody, bears eloquent testimony to this: "There are many complaints here of the irregularity and uncertainty of the mails. Merchants would rather send their letters by Bellor's [Ballou's] Express at the cost of half a dollar than put it in the post at a cost of 5 cents and remain in uncertainty when it would reach its destination."[12] Lieutenant R. C. Mayne praises the facilities

postal history of the two colonies and of the united colony. It forms *Memoir* no. VIII of the Archives of British Columbia and was published in Victoria in 1928. The quotations which follow are from pages 138 and 143.

12. Quoted in *ibid.*, 48, from the original in the Archives of British Columbia.

provided by the Wells Fargo Express Company and remarks, "I have never known a letter sent by them miscarry."[13] Billy Ballou, an American, as we have seen, began a local express company in British Columbia in 1858, operating to the Fraser River mines. His connections with "outside" were made through Freeman's Express Company. A rival, Kent and Smith, ran in connection with Wells, Fargo and Company. In 1860 F. J. Barnard, a Canadian, started Barnard's Express and six years later bought out his chief rival Dietz and Nelson. Barnard's company under the title of the British Columbia Express Company held the local field for many years.

Telegraphic communication between British Columbia and the outside world was at first by means of the American lines. For a brief period, until the Atlantic cable was successfully completed in 1866, the colony assumed an importance in the telegraph world which its geographical position would hardly seem to warrant. F. McDonough Collins of Washington, D.C., formulated a plan to construct a line from San Francisco through British Columbia to Alaska and by way of Bering Straits to the Amur River where it would connect with the Russian line across Siberia to St. Petersburg. Collins possessed a controlling interest in the California State Telegraph Company and in the Western Union. But a British company promoter, Sir Edward Watkin, whose interest in a transcontinental railway through British territory was well known, had visions of a telegraph line from Canada to British Columbia. His company, the Atlantic and Pacific Transit and Telegraph Company, received support from the British government and was also backed by Governor Douglas shortly before his retirement in 1864. The Legislative Assembly of Vancouver Island in 1864, however, passed an act in favour of the American scheme. This act was disallowed in Britain, but as satisfactory terms could not be arranged with Watkin's company, the American offer was accepted. On April 18, 1865, New Westminster was connected by wire with San Francisco. The first message received was the sad news of the assassination of President Lincoln. The line reached Cariboo that year and the Skeena River in 1866. But the deathblow to Collins's hopes came when the first triumphant flash crossed the Atlantic

13. R. C. Mayne, *Four Years in British Columbia and Vancouver Island* (London, 1862), 71.

cable. In 1868 Fort Stager on the Skeena, the end of the completed line in British Columbia, was abandoned. The Indians of the north-land fell heirs to the tons of wire and other materials left by the company. The British Columbia section remained in use and proved a boon to the inhabitants of Cariboo.

The year 1866 was tragic in the annals of the British colony on the Pacific Coast. An exodus to California set in. The *British Colonist* for June 5 recorded that the San Francisco steamer was taking away fourteen or fifteen families, and in its issue of January 16, 1867, lamented the continued movement to the south: "All leaving for other parts—mark! not by choice, but by the stern decrees of necessity, unable longer to make a living here. In 99 cases out of 100 people take their leave of us with heavy hearts, deploring that their destinies can no longer be cast with ours." A study of the population statistics for the united colony from 1867 to 1870 only partially bears out the contention of the *Colonist*. Until 1868 population declined, but increases are to be noted for 1869 and 1870.[14] It is impossible to guess what percentage of the population was American during this period, but it is probable that a fairly large proportion of those returning to the United States were American citizens.[15]

The Reciprocity Treaty of 1854 never applied to British Colum-bia or to Vancouver Island. The Pacific colonies, and after 1866 the united colony, felt the full effect of the American tariff. The "free port" at Victoria gave a certain impetus to the trade of Vancouver Island, but as has been noted, the union of 1866 entailed real hardship on the island by introducing the mainland tariff. From time to time agitations for reciprocity occurred, but nothing came of them. Strangely enough reciprocity was used as an argument both in favour of annexation and of Confederation. The annexationists showed that it would be impossible for British Columbia to obtain reciprocity alone and that she might as well

14. Marshall, *Vital Statistics*, 189-91. The totals, exclusive of Indians, but includ-ing Chinese and coloured, are as follows: 1867, 9,263; 1868, 8,594; 1869, 10,376; 1870, 10,586.

15. Much uncertainty exists on this point. One estimate places the number of American citizens in Victoria in 1870 as 100. The *British Colonist* for July 2, 1869, vigorously denies the claim of Charles Adderley, former Under-Secretary for the Colonies, that 98 per cent of the inhabitants were from the United States.

bow to the inevitable and come within the American tariff permanently by joining the United States. The argument used by the confederationists was that the Dominion of Canada would shortly secure an advantageous reciprocity treaty, and British Columbia by entering the Dominion would enjoy these benefits to the full. A coal strike in Nanaimo in 1870 was attributed to the effects of the American tariff, $1.28 a ton duty being charged on Vancouver Island coal at San Francisco. The coal owners attempted to cut the miners' wages by twelve and a half cents a ton. The miners struck, alleging that the imposition of the British Columbian tariff on the island had resulted in an increased cost of living. The *British Colonist* in discussing the situation stated that the opponents of federation were "the enemies of the coast miners, and indeed of every other class—the common enemies of general development and industrial progress."[16]

From the foregoing it may be seen that American economic influences were of paramount importance in British Columbia during this period. In common with all the mining areas of the Northwest the Pacific colony was really a northward extension of California. As James Truslow Adams has pointed out, the Pacific Coast "was always to remain differentiated from all the other frontiers." There was a much greater mingling of types, and the sudden accumulation of capital produced a new psychology. All gold seekers are, by nature, gamblers. On the Pacific slope the gambling spirit prevailed, and prevails. The professional gambler came north with the gold rush and was a noted figure in all the British Columbian mining camps. In the Legislative Library at Victoria hangs an oil painting of no artistic merit, but of some historical significance. It represents a noted card sharper, "Slim Jim," in the garb of a parson, taking the "pot" from his less astute opponents. From the setting of the painting it is evident that Jim and his fellows have come from south of the "line." It would be quite unfair to claim that Jim typifies the early history of the Pacific slope, or that he is to be classed as a major American influence, but he does represent the "easy come easy go" spirit of the mining camps.

But British influences cannot be neglected. The same miners

16. *British Colonist*, October 8, 1870.

who in California set up miners' meetings and invoked the power
of "Judge Lynch," when they came north respected British law
and order. As has been shown the wilder excesses of California were
not reproduced in British Columbia. The British fur traders had
left a tradition of fair dealing with the natives. This tradition was
strengthened by the efficient methods of Sir James Douglas, Judge
Begbie, and a group of able assistants. Although Canadians were
at first rather sharply distinguished from British Columbians,
their traditions were also British. British Columbia was a colony
and its political education proceeded along British rather than
American lines.

It became evident, as the years rolled on, that British Columbia
could not long remain an isolated British colony, and the colonists
had to give serious thought to the two lines of development which
lay open to them.[17] Neither Great Britain nor the United States
attempted to force their decision. Rarely has so small a population
in a British colony been in a position to make so momentous a
decision as that which confronted the less than ten thousand white
British Columbians, during the critical years between 1866 and
1871. In many ways the most natural line of political development
was annexation to the United States, but that would mean sever-
ance of the tie with the motherland and the end of *British* Columbia.
On the other hand Confederation presented almost insurmountable
geographic and economic difficulties.

To understand the political struggles of these few years we must
bear in mind the links with the British Isles and the omnipresence
of the United States. And we must examine the various groups
within the colony which aspired to determine the political future
of the land of their adoption. But there were other factors which
affected the issue: the attitude of Governor Seymour; the growing
demand for responsible government; the attitude of the government of the United States; the pressure exercised by Great Britain;
and the diplomacy of Canadian statesmen. In the end the con-

17. Independence was hardly a possibility, although Allan Nevins, in *Hamilton
Fish* (New York, 1936), 219, says that in June, 1869, Hamilton Fish was aware
of "a sentiment for independence in parts of Nova Scotia, Quebec and British
Columbia." In a letter to W. N. Sage, Mr. Willard E. Ireland, Archivist of British
Columbia, points out that this impression may have arisen from the fact that many
of the bitterest anti-confederationists in British Columbia were not annexationists.

federationists won, but their victory was not the result of their own unaided efforts. Sir John A. Macdonald succeeded in securing the appointment of Governor Musgrave as Seymour's successor. Musgrave, who had recently failed to bring Newfoundland into the Canadian union, was more than anxious to secure a victory for Confederation in British Columbia.

Our survey of opinion in the colony begins with the Canadian group. This group, in which of course natives of the Maritime Provinces are included, favoured Confederation. Prominent among the Canadians were Amor de Cosmos from Windsor, Nova Scotia, John Robson from Perth, Ontario, and F. J. Barnard from Quebec City. Mention should also be made of Dr. R. W. W. Carrall of Woodstock, Ontario, and J. Spencer Thompson also from "Old Canada." Both Carrall and Thompson supported the Confederation movement in Cariboo. Amor de Cosmos had been the "stormy petrel" of British Columbian politics ever since his arrival in 1858. He opposed Governor Douglas and denounced his illiberal rule. In his early days De Cosmos had come under the influence of Joseph Howe, the Nova Scotian reformer, and it has been suggested that De Cosmos aimed at becoming the Howe of British Columbia. But British Columbia was too immature politically for any such struggle for responsible government as had occurred in the Maritime Provinces or in the United Province of Canada in the 1840's. De Cosmos actively supported federation and was, as we shall see, prominent in the Confederation League and the Yale Convention of 1869. A newspaperman by profession De Cosmos wielded a telling pen.

John Robson, the original "Honest John" of British Columbian history, was De Cosmos's rival in the newspaper world. He also favoured Confederation and responsible government. Although he lived for a time in Victoria it was in New Westminster that Robson was really at home. New Westminster was essentially "British" in sentiment. It had been founded by the Royal Engineers and the annexationist movement made no headway there. Robson, as well as De Cosmos, never faltered in his opposition to annexation and in his championship of federation with Canada.

On the whole Canadians were none too popular in British Columbia. They were often termed "North American Chinamen," the implication being that they saved their money and sent it home to Canada. The Americans, on the other hand, were more generous and spent freely what they made. The "old country" born did not as a rule like either the Canadians, or Canada. J. D. Pemberton expressed this feeling clearly in a little verse included in a letter to the *British Colonist* in 1870 from which the following lines are taken.

> True Loyalty's to Motherland
> And not to Canada
> The love we bear is second hand
> To any step-mama.

In the Confederation debate of 1870 the Canadians were opposed by some of the "old country" members of the Legislative Council, who none the less recognized that it was natural that their Canadian colleagues should be attracted towards Confederation.[18]

But among those who had been born in the British Isles were numbered many supporters of Confederation. To them union with Canada was the best means of preserving the British connection. Others, including several of the leading "official" members of the Legislative Council of British Columbia, were at first either hostile or else lukewarm in their support, but when after the arrival of Governor Musgrave it became known that the British government favoured Confederation, they slowly rallied to Musgrave's support, recognizing that British Columbia could not long remain an isolated British colony. In the Confederation debate J. W. Trutch, Chief Commissioner of Lands and Works, supported Confederation as the only means of preserving British Columbia for the British Empire.

If you don't want Confederation, what do you want? To remain as you are? This I know you are not satisfied to do. What then? Establish a sort of Independent Government of about 6,000 people, connected with nobody, owing allegiance to nobody? The idea is absurd. There appears, then, to be no alternative to Confederation, but that suggestion which has been shadowed forth during the debate, and which I, for one, decline to consider as a possibility. And now we come to Confederation as our manifest destiny.

To sum up my argument in support of the motion of the Honourable the Attorney-General—I advocate Confederation because it will secure the continuance of this Colony under the British Flag, and strengthen British interests on this Continent; and because it will benefit this community, by lessening taxation and giving increased revenue for local expenditure; by

18. Cf. *Confederation Debate*, 1870, 37, speech of the Hon. D. B. Ring of Nanaimo.

advancing the political status of the Colony; by securing the practical aid of the Dominion Government, who are, I believe, able to—and whose special care it would be to devise and—carry into effect measures tending to develop the natural resources, and to promote the prosperity of this Colony; and by affording, through a railway, the only means of acquiring a permanent population, which must come from the east of the Rocky Mountains.[19]

The attitude of the British government was a factor of great significance during the crucial years from 1866 to 1871. Until the death of Governor Seymour in 1869 Downing Street was not pressing for British Columbia's entrance into the Canadian Dominion. There were, apparently, two reasons for this policy. Until the Hudson's Bay Company had relinquished its rights to the territory from the head of the Great Lakes to the Rocky Mountains and Canada had received these lands from the British Crown, British Columbia remained isolated from the Dominion of Canada. The second reason is not quite so definite but it seems to have been this. The British government was, so to speak, prepared to propose Canada as a suitor for the hand of British Columbia, but showed no intention of forcing a *mariage de convenance*. Seymour's opposition to Confederation was obvious from a perusal of his despatches. It was also clear that the governing group in British Columbia was opposed to the proposed union. But Governor Musgrave won over the officials, and the transfer of Hudson's Bay Territory to Canada cleared the way for federation.

That the British government favoured Confederation as early as the summer of 1869 is evident from Lord Granville's despatch to Governor Musgrave, dated August 14, 1869. The following paragraphs taken from this despatch are a very clear indication of the attitude of Downing Street.

In my despatch of the 17th June, in which I communicated to you your appointment to the Government of British Columbia, I informed you that I should probably have occasion to address you on the question then in

19. *Ibid.*, 22. The "suggestion shadowed forth during the debate" was, of course, annexation. Attorney-General H. P. P. Crease had on March 9, 1870, moved and Trutch had seconded: "That this Council do now resolve itself into Committee of the Whole, to take into consideration the terms proposed for the Confederation of the Colony of British Columbia with the Dominion of Canada, in His Excellency's Message to this Council" (*ibid.*, 3).

agitation of the Incorporation of that Colony with the Dominion of Canada. You are aware that Her Majesty's Government have hitherto declined to entertain this question, mainly, because it could not arise practically till the Territory of the Hudson Bay Company was annexed to the Dominion, but, also perhaps in the expectation that the public opinion of British Columbia might have opportunity to form and declare itself.

I have now to inform you that the terms on which Rupert's Land and the North West Territory are to be united to Canada, have been agreed upon by the parties concerned, and that the Queen will probably be advised, before long, to issue an Order in Council which will incorporate in the Dominion of Canada the whole of the British Possessions on the North American Continent, except the then conterminous colony of British Columbia.

The question therefore presents itself, whether this single colony should be excluded from the great body politic which is forming itself.

On this question the colony itself does not appear to be unanimous. But so far as I can judge from the Despatches which have reached me, I should conjecture that the prevailing opinion was in favor of union. I have no hesitation in stating that such is also the opinion of Her Majesty's Government.[20]

Lord Granville then proceeds to enumerate the advantages to British Columbia of union with Canada. Chief among them he lists the entrusting to the Dominion Parliament of national affairs and to the provinces "questions of local interest." He thus refers to the possibility of transcontinental communication or as he terms it "internal transit."

It is evident that the establishment of a British line of communication between the Atlantic and Pacific Oceans, is far more feasible by the operations of a single government, responsible for the progress of both shores of the Continent, than by a bargain negotiated between separate, perhaps in some respects rival governments and legislatures. The San Francisco of British North America would, under these circumstances, hold a greater commercial and political position than would be attained by the capital of the isolated colony of British Columbia.[21]

It should be noted that Granville does not in as many words refer to the construction of a transcontinental railway. None the less it is a fair inference. Sir Edward Watkin, Alfred Waddington, and

20. Granville to Musgrave, August 14, 1869, in *Sessional Papers of Canada,* 33 Vict., 1870, no. 31.

21. *Ibid.*

others, were already agitating for the building of such a railway through British territory.[22]

In his concluding paragraphs Lord Granville gives explicit directions to Governor Musgrave.

You will therefore give publicity to this despatch, a copy of which I have communicated to the Governor-General of Canada, and you will hold yourself authorized either in communication with Sir John Young, or otherwise, to take such steps as you properly and constitutionally can, for promoting the favorable consideration of this question.

It will not escape you that in acquainting you with the general views of the Government, I have avoided all matters of detail, on which the wishes of the people and the Legislature will of course be declared in due time. I think it necessary however to observe that the constitution of British Columbia will oblige the Governor to enter personally upon many questions, as the condition of the Indian tribes and the future position of government servants with which, in the case of a negotiation between two responsible governments, he would not be bound to concern himself.[23]

While the British government was at length making clear its attitude to the Governor of British Columbia, the United States Congress was considering the possible admission of western British North America into the American Union. As early as July, 1866, General Nathaniel P. Banks had introduced into the United States House of Representatives a bill directing the President "whenever notice shall be deposited in the Department of State that the Governments of Great Britain and the Provinces of New Brunswick, Nova Scotia, Prince Edward's Island, Newfoundland, Canada, British Columbia and Vancouver's Island have accepted the proposition . . . made by the United States, to publish by proclamation that, from the date thereof, the States of Nova Scotia, New Brunswick, Canada East and Canada West, and the Territories of Selkirk, Saskatchewan and Columbia . . . are con-

22. On this subject see Sir E. W. Watkin, *Canada and the States: Recollections, 1851-1886* (London, 1887); R. G. Trotter, *Canadian Federation: Its Origins and Achievement* (Toronto and London, 1924); R. L. Reid, "Alfred Waddington," *Royal Society of Canada Transactions*, XXVI, sec. II; and W. D. MacK. Sage, "Early Proposals for a Canadian Transcontinental Railway," MS in University of British Columbia Library.

23. *Sessional Papers of Canada*, 33 Vict., 1870, no. 31. Sir John Young was then Governor-General of Canada. He was raised to the peerage as Lord Lisgar and held office from 1869 to 1872.

stituted and admitted as States and Territories of the United States."[24]

This bill failed to attract much notice in Congress and did not pass. It is however interesting as an indication that the American annexationists dreamed of the inclusion of practically all of British North America in the United States. Vancouver Island and British Columbia were in this scheme to form the "Territory of Columbia" and to be granted the same representation as Montana Territory.

The question of the annexation of the territory west of the Great Lakes was brought before the Senate of the United States on December 9, 1867, when Senator Ramsey of Minnesota moved that the Committee on Foreign Relations be directed to enquire into the expediency of a treaty between the United States and the Dominion of Canada which would deal with the following topics: the question of *ad valorem* duty on exports and imports to the United States from Canada; excise duties "assimilated by concurrent legislation"; the navigation of the St. Lawrence and its tributaries; as to whether Canadian vessels in American ports should have all the privileges accorded to American ships in Canadian ports; the freedom of the Atlantic fisheries to citizens of both countries; a common system of law regarding copyrights, rates of postage, and so forth. The last of these topics dealt with annexation. The Senator's proposal was:

That Canada with the consent of Great Britain shall cede to the United States the districts of North America west of Longitude 90° on conditions following, to wit.

1. The United States will pay $6,000,000 to the Hudson Bay Co. [*sic*] in full discharge of all possessory rights and of all claims to territory or jurisdiction in North America whether founded on the charter of the company or any treaty, law or usage.

2. The United States will assume the public debt of British Columbia not exceeding the sum of $2,000,000.

3. To aid the construction of a railroad from the western extremity of Lake Superior to Puget Sound, the United States in addition to the grant of land heretofore made, will guaranty dividends of 5% upon the stock of the Northern Pacific Railroad Company: Provided that the amount of stock guaranteed as aforesaid shall not exceed $20,000 per mile and Congress shall regulate the securities for advances on account thereof.

24. *Congressional Globe*, 39th Congress, 1st Session, 3548. Cf. L. B. Shippee, *Canadian-American Relations, 1849-1874* (New Haven, 1939), 192, n. 27.

4. The Northwest Territory shall be divided and organized into Territories of the United States, not less than three in number; with all the rights and privileges of the citizens and government of Montana Territory; so far as the same can be made applicable.[25]

Senator Ramsey in introducing his resolutions stressed the importance of the proposals for British Columbia's entry into the Canadian federation as follows:

We are informed that a member of the Government of Canada is about to present to Parliament a bill for the extension of the dominion of Canada to the Pacific Ocean. The authorities of British Columbia having applied for admission to the Canadian federation, the passage of such an act by the Parliament at Ottawa, with the assent of the queen in council will consummate the annexation of northwest British America to Canada. The people of the Selkirk settlement, north-west of Minnesota, and the people of British Columbia on the Pacific coast would prefer admission to the American Union; and I believe it has become the duty of the American Congress to indicate openly and distinctly the terms and conditions which we are willing to offer as an alternative to the Canadian overture.[26]

Objection was raised to these proposals by Senator Grimes of Iowa who stated his opposition to anything "looking to another reciprocity treaty." The resolutions were laid on the table for the time being, but Senator Ramsey on January 31, 1868, returned to the fray with amendments on the subject of reciprocity. On July 27, 1868, Ramsey spoke at length on the subject of the amended resolutions. Senator Sumner objected to the suggestion that a treaty be made between the United States and Canada. Since Canada was not "a sovereign power" the treaty had to be made between the United States and Great Britain. Senator Ramsey accepted the amendment and the resolutions passed.[27] Their subsequent fate is none too clear, but they seem to have been brought to the attention of the Senate Committee on Pacific Railroads. This Committee was much impressed with the necessity for the construction of the Northern Pacific Railroad which would be another step in the securing of western British North America for the United States. The following passage from its report makes this clear.

25. *Congressional Globe*, 40th Congress, 2nd Session, 79.
26. *Ibid.*
27. *Ibid.*, 4506.

The line of the North Pacific runs for 1500 miles near the British possessions and when built will drain the agricultural products of the rich Saskatchewan and Red River Districts east of the mountains, and the gold country of the Fraser, Thompson and Kootenay Rivers west of the mountains. From China (Canton) to Liverpool it is 1500 miles nearer by the 49th parallel of latitude, than by the way of San Francisco and New York. This advantage in securing the overland trade from Asia will not be thrown away by the English, unless it is taken away by our first building the North Pacific road, establishing mercantile agencies at Puget Sound, fixing mercantile capital there, and getting possession on land, and on ocean, of all machinery of the new commerce between Asia and Europe. The opening by us first of a North Pacific Railroad seals the destiny of the British possessions west of the 91st meridian. They will become so strongly Americanized in interests and feelings that they will in effect be severed from the new Dominion and the question of their annexation will be but a question of time.[28]

In the autumn of 1869 an annexationist petition was circulated in Victoria and obtained over forty signatures. It was taken to Washington by Vincent Collyer, special Indian Commissioner for Alaskan tribes, and presented to President Grant. The San Francisco *Morning Bulletin* in its issue of November 17, 1869, reported Collyer as stating that in British Columbia "the feeling in favor of annexation" had "received new impulse from the recent note of Earl Granville, urging the British Columbians to affiliate with the Canadian Dominion." This the British Columbians regarded "as little less than insulting, as it would increase their burdens without affording them either political protection or material relief."[29]

Vincent Collyer duly handed the petition to President Grant on December 29, 1869. Next day the President "returned Collyer a verbal reply that he had received it with great interest and sent it to the Secretary of State."[30] Collyer also showed the petition to

28. *United States Congress*, 40th Congress, 3rd Session, Committee on Pacific Railroads. Necessity of two or three railroads to the Pacific, including a northern Pacific railroad; desirability of government aid; majority and minority reports; map. Serial 1362, February, 1869.

29. San Francisco *Morning Bulletin*, November 17, 1869, quoted in W. E. Ireland, "The Annexation Petition of 1869," *British Columbia Historical Quarterly*, IV, 270. This valuable article publishes for the first time the text of the petition and analyses the signatories.

30. *British Colonist*, January 11, 1870, quoted in Ireland, "Annexation Petition," 271.

Senator Sumner, Chairman of the Senate Committee on Foreign Relations, who declared that "the movement was important and could have but one termination." An additional list of sixty-one signatures was forwarded to President Grant in the summer of 1870, but by that time the Confederation movement was gaining headway in British Columbia.

The text of the petition and an analysis of signatories must be reserved for later treatment, but it would be well here to trace briefly the subsequent history of the petition. According to Mr. Ireland, the American government was "loath to take direct official notice of British Columbia's plea."[31] A copy was sent to John L. Motley, the American Minister in London. Motley talked over the matter with Lord Clarendon, the British Foreign Secretary, on February 19, 1870. Clarendon expressed no dissent from Motley's view that "the independence of all the British Colonies in North America . . . would lead naturally to amicable annexation to the Union" but observed that "attempts at conquest and violent annexation of those territories by the United States were much to be deprecated."[32] Whatever Lord Clarendon's personal views may have been, he must have known that the British government was urging British Columbia to join Canada.

Annexation was supported by many Americans on the Pacific Coast. Bishop Thompson of California in an address to a church conference shortly after the purchase of Alaska expressed himself as follows:

May we not by getting British Columbia, extend our territory in an unbroken line from Mexico to the Arctic Sea? How natural when one has four volumes of a work to desire the fifth! Moreover we shall need a large city on Puget Sound, and Victoria is the place for it. The people of that region are not averse to annexation; and although Great Britain is covetous of land, and may desire an outlet for her transmontane American possessions, yet she can derive no advantage from British Columbia comparable to that which it would confer upon us. It is not at all surprising that our Government is already negotiating for it, and if she can obtain it by can-

31. *Ibid.*, 285.

32. *Ibid.*, 286-7, quoting from Motley to Fish, February 21, 1870, confidential, *Despatches from the United States Minister in London to the Secretary of State,* Department of State Archives, Washington, vol. 102.

celling the claims for damages to our country during our great rebellion, each party will make a good bargain.[33]

This veiled reference to the Alabama Claims was by no means the first proposal that Great Britain hand over her Pacific Coast colony to the United States in settlement of this vexed question. In 1867 the New York *Herald* had commented on the movement towards annexation both in British Columbia and in California and Oregon. It claimed that "the press and people of Victoria are outspoken in favour of annexation." Its reference to the Alabama Claims is very definite: "It is said, also, that Mr. Seward has his eye on British Columbia, and that he wishes to make a settlement with England for the Alabama Claims by the annexation of that Territory."[34]

President Grant was firm on the subject of the Alabama Claims. "He believed that great wrongs had been done the United States, and that reparation must go far beyond a small money payment. He also believed the absorbtion of Canada by the Union to be inevitable and for both peoples highly desirable."[35] Grant, therefore, would probably raise no objection to the proposal that British Columbia become the victim on the altar of Anglo-American friendship. Secretary Seward was an expansionist and the annexation of British Columbia would close the gap between Washington Territory and Alaska. In British Columbia, as we shall see, this proposal strengthened the annexationist agitation and, at the same time, rallied the anti-annexationists to continue their efforts to preserve the British connection. By the terms of the Treaty of Washington of 1871, the Alabama Claims were submitted to arbitration. Long before the Geneva Tribunal had met British Columbia was a Canadian province.

Canada, as well as Great Britain and the United States, was interested in the fate of British Columbia. As early as the 1850's Canada had become aware of the possibilities for settlement in the

33. *British Columbian*, New Westminster, January 15, 1868, quoting from the *Christian Advocate*.

34. New York *Herald* quoted in Montreal *Gazette*, June 18, 1867. See H. L. Keenleyside, "British Columbia—Annexation or Confederation?", *Canadian Historical Association Report*, 1928, 33-40; Shippee, *Canadian-American Relations*, 199-200.

35. Nevins, *Hamilton Fish*, 216.

Hudson's Bay territories and to a less extent in Vancouver Island. When in 1857 the British House of Commons established a Select Committee to investigate into the affairs of the Hudson's Bay Company the Canadian government sent over Chief Justice W. H. Draper as a delegate. In his instructions Draper was told "to urge the expediency of marking out the limits [of the Northwest Territory], and so protecting the frontier of the lands above Lake Superior, about the Red River, and thence to the Pacific, as effectually to secure them against violent seizure or irregular settlement, until the advancing tide of emigrants from Canada and the United Kingdom . . . fairly flow into them and occupy them as subjects of the Queen on behalf of the British Empire." "The future importance of Vancouver's Island as the key to all British North America on the Pacific" was also stressed.[36]

George Brown of the Toronto *Globe* was also conducting a campaign in favour of Canada's annexation of the Hudson's Bay territories. He was more interested in the Red River than in the Pacific Coast. But Vancouver Island was so strategically placed that it would become a tempting bait for Canadian annexationists. If Canada were to take over the Hudson's Bay territories it would be well also to secure the Company's colony on the Pacific.

Canada's real interest in British Columbia dated, however, from the gold rush of 1858. Even before the gold seekers had arrived in their thousands on Fraser River, Alexander Morris had delivered his well-known lecture on Nova Britannia in which he envisaged in North America "a great Britannic Confederation, thoroughly imbued with the true principles of liberty, and reflecting the character of that great parent country from which their inhabitants have mainly sprung, and rising to power and strength under her guiding influence."[37] In his lecture Morris described Vancouver Island as "a British possession, improvidently leased to the Hudson's Bay Company, whose lease will expire in 1859."[38] In a second lecture delivered in Montreal during the winter of 1858 also before the Mercantile Library Association, Morris described

36. Minute of Council, February 18, 1857, in Public Archives of Canada, State Book R, 223 ff., quoted in Trotter, *Canadian Federation*, 236-7.

37. Alexander Morris, *Nova Britannia* (Toronto, 1884), 39. This lecture was delivered on March 18, 1858, before the Mercantile Library Association of Montreal.

38. *Ibid.*, 33.

the possibility of building a railway to the Pacific Coast and quoted with approval the report of Queen Victoria's speech to Parliament in 1858 during the session in which the act establishing the Colony of British Columbia was passed. "Her Majesty hopes that this new colony on the Pacific may be but one step in the career of steady progress by which Her Majesty's dominions in North America may ultimately be peopled, in an unbroken chain from the Atlantic to the Pacific, by a loyal and industrious population of subjects of the British Crown."[39] The Cariboo gold rush in the early 1860's also focussed attention upon British Columbia and a number of Canadians reached the new El Dorado. Conspicuous among them were the Overlanders of 1862, the only large party who came "the plains across" through British territory from Fort Garry to the Rocky Mountains and through the Yellowhead Pass to Cariboo.[40]

Canadians who came to British Columbia usually wrote back glowing accounts to their relatives and friends. These letters were often published in the local newspapers and had a certain influence. Charles G. Major of New Westminster, for example, wrote letters which were published in the Toronto Globe. Of more importance was the correspondence of Dr. R. W. W. Carrall and Dr. I. W. Powell, two Canadians who were prominent in British Columbia, with Sir John A. Macdonald. Powell's brother was a personal friend of Macdonald. John Robson kept up a correspondence with the Hon. Malcolm Cameron who passed the letters on to Macdonald. The Hon. S. L. Tilley kept in touch by letter with several New Brunswickers on Vancouver Island.[41]

39. Ibid., 90; Watkin, Canada and the States, 57, gives the speech in the first person, "I hope," etc.

40. The story of this overland expedition is best told in M. S. Wade, The Overlanders of '62 (Victoria, 1931). See also F. W. Howay, "The Argonauts of 1862," Royal Society of Canada Transactions, XIII, sec. II, 37-56.

41. This correspondence may be found among the Macdonald Papers and the S. L. Tilley Correspondence in the Public Archives of Canada. Valuable letters are Tilley to Macdonald, February 29, 1868; I. W. Powell to Macdonald, June 26, 1869; Carrall to Macdonald, January 10, 1871; Macdonald to M. Cameron, December 1, 1869. Dr. J. S. Helmcken also corresponded with Sir John A. Macdonald. Macdonald offered Helmcken the office of Premier of the Province of British Columbia but Helmcken refused it. Cf. Macdonald to Helmcken, July 17, 1871, and Helmcken to Macdonald, August 23, 1871. Cf. Trutch to Macdonald, October 9, 1871: "We

Mention should also be made of the Methodist missionaries from Canada who arrived in British Columbia in 1859. By their letters and reports they stimulated interest in the Pacific Coast colony. As early as 1838 Roman Catholic missionaries from Canada had been in Oregon and several priests had begun work in British Columbia. The annual reports published by the Societies for the Propagation of the Faith in Montreal and Quebec attest the interest felt in French-speaking Canada for the missions on the far west coast.

During the negotiations which led to the federation of four of the eastern provinces of British North America, the possible inclusion of the Hudson's Bay territories and British Columbia was often discussed. At the Quebec Conference in 1864 the motion of the Hon. George Brown for a federation with three local governments was amended on October 17 to include one "for each of the Canadas and for the Provinces of Nova Scotia, New Brunswick and Prince Edward Island, charged with the control of local matters in their respective sections, provision being made for the admission into the Union on equitable terms of Newfoundland, the North-West Territory, British Columbia and Vancouver."[42] Section 146 of the British North America Act provided for the admission of the Colony of British Columbia.[43] In 1868 the House of Commons of Canada asked for a "copy of all correspondence had with the Government respecting the North West Territory, including British Columbia, since the 5th December 1867."[44] The Canadian Cabinet on March 6, 1868, gave consideration to a memorial sent by certain citizens of Victoria favouring Confederation with Canada. The first signature was that of James Trimble, Mayor of Victoria and Chairman of the Committee appointed at the public meeting at which the resolutions were passed. Other members of the Committee were Amor de Cosmos, Dr. I. W. Powell, R.

all did our best to persuade Helmcken that it was his duty to take part in the government of the Province but he persists in declining to have anything further to do with Politics . . . ." Helmcken also refused the offer of a senatorship (Trutch to Macdonald, telegram, October 16, 1871).

42. Quoted in W. M. Whitelaw, *The Maritimes and Canada before Confederation* (Toronto, 1934), 244; Macdonald Papers, Confederation, I, 66.

43. 30 Vict., c. 3.

44. *Sessional Papers of Canada*, 31 Vict., 1868, no. 59.

Wallace, and H. E. Seelye. Ottawa was already preparing to negotiate terms of federation, but no negotiations could be successful until the Hudson's Bay Territory was taken over and the Legislative Council of British Columbia was prepared to offer proposals for union. The first obstacle was removed in 1870 and by that time Governor Musgrave had made his influence felt in British Columbia.

But the Canadian overtures had to meet the competition of the United States. Geographical and economic factors favoured the inclusion of British Columbia in the American Union. The international boundary cut across the natural lines of communication from north to south. In the Confederation debate of March, 1870, in the Legislative Council of British Columbia, the Hon. Dr. John Sebastian Helmcken, that doughty opponent of Confederation, clearly stated the dependence of British Columbia on the Great Republic: "The United States hems us in on every side; it is the Nation by which we exist; it is the Nation which has made this Colony what it is; but, nevertheless, it is one of our greatest drawbacks. We do not enjoy her advantages, nor do we profit much by them; we do not share her prosperity, and we are far too small to be her rival."[45]

From the union of the colonies in 1866 until the entrance of British Columbia into the Canadian federation in 1871 there was a distinct possibility that the colony on the Pacific Coast would yield to "Manifest Destiny" and become part of the American Union. Annexationist sentiment in British Columbia came to a head late in 1869 when the second annexationist petition was circulated and signed. As a result of the researches of Mr. W. E. Ireland, Provincial Archivist of British Columbia, it is now possible to quote from the text of the petition and to record his analysis of the signatories.

The petition is addressed "To His Excellency, the President of the United States of America" and preamble states that the memorialists are "residents of the Colony of British Columbia—many of us british subjects, . . . penetrated with the most profound feelings of loyalty to Her Majesty and Her Majesty's Government and that all entertain for Her, feelings of the greatest

45. *Confederation Debate*, 1870, 8.

respect as well as attachment to the country."[46] The colony, the memorialists submit, "is now suffering from great depression, owing to its isolation, a scarcity of population and other causes too numerous to mention." The petitioners then state their opposition to Confederation with Canada as follows:

That we view with feelings of alarm the avowed intention of Her Majesty's Government to confederate this Colony with the Dominion of Canada, as we believe such a measure can only tend to still further depression and ultimate injury for the following reasons, viz.:—

That confederation cannot give us protection against internal enemies or foreign foes, owing to the distance of this Colony from Ottawa.

That it cannot open to us a market for the produce of our lands, our forests, our mines or our waters.

That it cannot bring us population (our greatest need) as the Dominion itself is suffering from lack of it.

That our connection with the Dominion can satisfy no sentiment of loyalty or devotion.

That her commercial and industrial interests are opposed to ours.

That the tariff of the Dominion will be the ruin of our farmers and the commerce of our chief cities.[47]

The following reasons are advanced for "the *Acquisition of this Colony* by the *United States*":

It would result at once in opening to us an unrestricted market for our produce, bring an influx of population and with it induce the investment of capital in our Coal and Quartz Mines and in our forests.

It would insure us regular Mails and communication with the adjoining States and Territories and through them with the World at large.

It would lessen the expense of Government, by giving us representative Institutions and immediate control of our domestic concerns, besides giving us protection against foreign enemies. And with all these, we should still be united to a People of our own kindred, religion and tongue and a people who for all time, must intimately affect us in all our relations for weal or woe.

The petition was signed by H. F. Heisterman, Emil Sutro, Jacob Morris, Leopold Lowenberg, and thirty-nine others. The

46. Ireland, "Annexation Petition," 271. There are several indications that this petition was drawn up by persons more conversant with the German than the English language, e.g., the use of "british" as an adjective without a capital letter and the capitalization of "Her" when referring to Queen Victoria. As we shall see a large number of the signers was composed of Germans and German Jews.

47. *Ibid.*

additional list of sixty-one names, to which reference was made above,[48] brings the total to 104, very roughly one per cent of the white population of British Columbia. The most interesting point in connection with the original forty-three signatories is the large proportion of Germans and Jews among them. Heisterman was born in Bremen, but had lived long enough in England to take out naturalization papers. Sutro was a German Jew and Lowenberg was a native of Potsdam, Prussia. Two former officers of the Hudson's Bay Company, William H. McNeill and John Swanson, signed the petition. McNeill was an American, born in Boston, Mass., and Swanson was a native of Rupert's Land. Of those whose birthplace or nationality is known thirteen were Germans or Jews—it is unfortunately impossible to distinguish clearly between them. Ten others seem to fall into this category but their place of birth or nationality has not been discovered. Of the forty-three two were born in England, one being of Jewish extraction. There were two Irishmen, and three were born in the United States, one of Jewish parentage. Allowing for duplicates, those of Jewish descent born in the United States and Great Britain, it is clear that over fifty per cent of the total were either Germans or Jews. Mr. Ireland has been able to identify forty of the sixty-one additional signatures. He finds that "they are representative of much the same elements of the population of the colony as is indicated by the preceding analysis of the original signatories."[49]

Few of the signatories were men whose roots struck deep into British soil. They are quite distinct both from those natives of the British Isles who were attached to the British connection, and from the Canadian group who thought of British Columbia as the territory needed to round out the new Dominion of Canada. The petitioners express no dislike of Great Britain. They speak as pioneers with no background of tradition to sustain them and to make them conscious of their mission as empire builders. After Confederation they for the most part accepted loyally the arrangements against which they had protested and settled down as good citizens of Canada. Their protest was a natural one; but the historian cannot accept it, as an American president seems carelessly to have done, as indicative of the general opinion of British

48. *Supra*, 200.
49. Ireland, "Annexation Petition," 280.

Columbia. Even communities far more mature than this young colony may at times speak with two voices. But seldom has diversity of opinion been carried to a point at which the British government could be blamed for not protecting the interest of the colony in boundary negotiations with its powerful neighbour; while almost at the same time a group was pressing for annexation by that neighbour; and the Legislature was discussing Confederation with Canada. The truth seems to be that Washington appeared no more foreign than London and that Ottawa appeared to many more foreign than either. The colony might approach each centre in turn for favours just as a promoter might approach several rival bankers.

The annexationist movement was almost entirely confined to Victoria. It had no strong support on the mainland.[50] Even on Vancouver Island it represented only a fraction of the population. In this connection it is necessary to distinguish between the annexationists and the anti-confederationists. Dr. John Sebastian Helmcken did not sign the petition. Although often accused of being an annexationist—his speeches in the Confederation debate in 1870 may be thus interpreted—Dr. Helmcken stoutly maintained that he was *not* an annexationist but an anti-confederationist.[51] Joseph Despard Pemberton, the former Colonial Surveyor of Vancouver Island, was another important anti-confederationist. His three letters to the *British Colonist*[52] supported annexation by inference rather than by direct statement. To him the only dissimilarity between Canada and the United States was that "Canada is an English colony which has obtained its independence by peaceful means, and the States an English colony which has obtained its independence forced upon it by tyranny and injustice." Pemberton did not believe that Canada could finance the cost of a transcontinental railway and Great Britain was unwilling to take

50. Cf. W. N. Sage, "The Annexationist Movement in British Columbia," *Royal Society of Canada Transactions*, XXI, sec. 2, 97-110.

51 In his later life Helmcken clearly stated his position as follows: "Of course my being an Anti-Confederationist led to my being dubbed an 'Annexationist,' but really I had no idea of annexation, but merely wished the colony to be let alone under Her Majesty's Government and to prevent her many anxious periods. I had nothing whatever to do with Annexationist petitions and I do not know who signed them" (Helmcken Papers, in the Archives of British Columbia).

52. *British Colonist*, January 26, January 29, February 1, 1870.

on such a tremendous obligation. Without the railway, he added sarcastically, British Columbia "might as well for all practical purposes be confederated with the Pyramids of Egypt."

Thus the annexationists did not obtain the support of the so-called Family-Company-Compact, the conservative group of Hudson's Bay Company officials and their friends which tended to dominate the political situation on Vancouver Island. This group was, in the main, anti-confederationist. Annexation may thus be considered to have been a forlorn hope in British Columbia and the annexationists, although they were active in a year in which there was something approaching a reaction against the proposals for Confederation, appear to have had little or no connection with the political life of British Columbia.

The British anti-confederationists were divisible into two classes, the Family-Company-Compact and the government officials. The members of the latter group seem to have opposed federation partly because they feared the introduction of responsible government and the termination of their appointments in British Columbia and partly because of their lack of sympathy with the leaders of the Confederation movement in the colony. Governor Seymour, as we shall see, was also an anti-confederationist. Although a weak man, he seems to have been determined to delay any movement towards Confederation as long as possible. His success may be judged from the fact that the government of British Columbia took no official action favouring federation during his régime. It should, however, be remembered that when Seymour died in 1869 the transfer of the Hudson's Bay territory to Canada was not yet complete.[53]

The confederationists were led by the group which has been described as Canadian, Amor de Cosmos, John Robson, J. F. Mc-Creight, Robert Beaven, and George A. Walkem, all of whom were destined to hold in turn the office of Prime Minister of British Columbia. The first move towards union with Canada occurred on March 8, 1867, when De Cosmos introduced a motion into the Legislative Council in reference to Confederation. The

53. Seymour, however, before his death had received word that negotiations for the transfer were complete. Cf. *British Colonist*, March 19, 1869, and Sir Joseph Pope, *Memoirs of The Right Honourable Sir John Alexander Macdonald* (London, 1894), II, 143-4.

Council went into committee of the whole to consider the motion, reported progress, and asked leave to sit again. This was done on March 18 when the following motion was unanimously passed by the Legislative Council: "Resolved, That this Council is of opinion that at this juncture of affairs in British North America, East of the Rocky Mountains, it is very desirable that His Excellency be respectfully requested to take such steps, without delay, as may be deemed by him best adapted to insure the admission of British Columbia on fair and equitable terms, this Council being confident that in advising this step they are expressing the views of the Colonists generally."[54]

Governor Seymour in his speech proroguing the Legislative Council on April 2, 1867, announced his intention of communicating with the Secretary of State and the Governors of Canada and the Hudson's Bay Company regarding Confederation. But Seymour was at heart opposed to federation and delayed sending the message to Downing Street. He did not communicate with Lord Monck, Governor-General of Canada. It is very possible that he did write to the Hudson's Bay Company.[55] In his long-delayed despatch of September 24, 1867, with which he transmitted the resolution of March 18, Seymour stated that it was the wish of the people of the colony and his own "for a fusion or intimate connection with the Eastern Confederation," but he left the details to the British government. One sentence in the despatch suggested the possible continuation of colonial status under Canadian control, i.e. that British Columbia would become a territory rather than a province of Canada. "Merely to join the Confederation on the condition of sending delegates to Ottawa, and receiving a Governor from the Canadian Ministry would not satisfy the popular desire."[56] The Duke of Buckingham and Chandos replied in November stating that the question of Confederation would have to wait until the Hudson's Bay territory had been taken over by the Dominion.

54. *Journals of the Legislative Council of British Columbia*, 4th Session, 1867 (New Westminster, 1867), 40, 50. The Governor's reply is given on page 56.

55. On this subject see F. W. Howay, "The Attitude of Governor Seymour towards Confederation," *Royal Society of Canada Transactions*, XIV, sec. II, 35, 48.

56. Public Archives of Canada, Seymour to the Duke of Buckingham and Chandos, September 24, 1867, Separate.

The citizens of Victoria were becoming restless at the delay and on January 28, 1868, held a public meeting at which a lengthy memorial was drawn up in favour of federation. A copy of this memorial was sent to Ottawa where it was favourably received by the Canadian government, which recommended that the Governor-General communicate with the Secretary of State for the Colonies, requesting him to "instruct Governor Seymour to take such steps as may be deemed proper to move the Legislative Council of British Columbia to further action in terms of the Imperial Act."[57]

At the opening of the 1868 session of the Legislative Council Seymour made an evasive reference to Confederation and claimed that the resolution of the previous session was the "expression of a disheartened community longing for change of any kind." The majority of the members of the Council was now definitely opposed to federation. But the minority found its position greatly strengthened when the Dominion Cabinet announced its policy in the following telegram: "The Canadian Government desires union with British Columbia and has opened communication with the Imperial Government on the subject of the Resolutions and suggests immediate action by your Legislature and the passage of an address to Her Majesty regarding union with Canada. Keep us informed of progress."[58] But the official members of the Legislative Council would not pass the necessary resolution even though they were urged by Amor de Cosmos, who was now heavily backed by public opinion. Instead they went on record as follows: "That this Council, while confirming their vote of the last session in favour of the general principle of the desirability of the union of this Colony with the Dominion of Canada to accomplish the consolidation of British interests and institutions in North America, are still without sufficient information and experience of the practical working of confederation in the North American Provinces

57. *Papers on the Union of British Columbia with the Dominion of Canada* (British Parliamentary Papers, 1868-9, 6, hereafter cited as *Confederation Papers*. The British North America Act, sec. 146, as we have seen, provided for the admission of British Columbia on receipt of addresses from the Parliament of Canada and the Legislature of British Columbia. The memorial of the citizens of Victoria is given on pages 6-7. See also *Sessional Papers of Canada*, 31 Vict., 1868, no. 59.

58. *British Colonist*, March 27, 1868. The telegram to H. E. Seelye of the *British Colonist* from the Hon. S. L. Tilley was dated March 25; cf. R. E. Gosnell, *Year Book of British Columbia, 1897* (Victoria, 1897), 51.

to admit of their defining the terms on which such a union would be advantageous to the local interests of British Columbia."[59] Governor Seymour concurred in this resolution. The forces of reaction were momentarily triumphant.

The reply of the federationists was the formation on May 21, 1868, of a Confederation League under the presidency of James Trimble, Mayor of Victoria. Prominent on the executive were Amor de Cosmos, Dr. I. W. Powell, J. F. McCreight, and Robert Beaven. The object of the League was "To effect Confederation as speedily as possible, and secure representative institutions for the colony, and thus get rid of the present one-man government, with its huge staff of overpaid and do-nothing officials."[60] Branches of the League were soon organized in New Westminster, Hope, Yale, and Lytton.

Confederationist sentiment was strong in Cariboo. On July 1, 1868, a large open-air meeting was held at Barkerville. Dr. R. W. W. Carrall and J. Spencer Thompson spoke in favour of union with Canada and resolutions were passed condemning the conduct of the government of British Columbia and stating that the people of the colony "should at once adopt some organized and systematic mode of obtaining immediate admission into the Dominion of Canada." J. S. Thompson argued that by Confederation alone the colony could get out of debt, that as part of the Dominion "the now despised colony of British Columbia" would be "the last link in the chain of independent provinces, uniting the Atlantic to the Pacific under one name—one Dominion—sheltered by the spreading folds of the glorious British banner."[61] There could be no question of the almost unanimous feeling of the colonists in favour of union with Canada, but the Governor and the official members of the Legislative Council were preventing the wishes of the people being carried into effect.

On September 14, 1868, at Yale on Fraser River was held the Yale Convention. The anti-confederationists of Victoria, led by Dr. J. S. Helmcken, went to some pains to cast ridicule upon this unofficial gathering of their political opponents, but it is evident

59. *Confederation Papers*, 13. De Cosmos's address praying for the admission of British Columbia into federation is given on pages 14-15.

60. Begg, *History of British Columbia*, 379.

61. *Ibid.*

today that this meeting was one of the important events in the story of Confederation. Thirty-six delegates including three members of the Legislative Council were present at Yale. They represented all portions of the colony and were unanimous for Confederation. De Cosmos as chairman of a special committee presented a lengthy report setting forth the case for Confederation and explaining that the Convention had been called by the Confederation League and "by the authority of the people of British Columbia." The government of the colony was shown not to exist "by the free and just consent of the governed" and was denounced as a despotism under Governor Seymour. Terms of union were discussed.[62]

When he transmitted an account of the Yale Convention, Governor Seymour took pains to send also clippings from the *British Colonist* stating that the Convention had not represented the views of certain leading citizens of Victoria, who were, as it happened, either office holders, annexationists, or believers in the continuance of the Crown colony.[63] At the opening of the new session of the Council in December, 1868, the Governor, as usual, tried to dodge the issues of Confederation and responsible government. The Council on February 17, 1869, passed the following resolution by a vote of eleven to five: "That this Council, impressed with the conviction that under existing circumstances the Confederation of this Colony with the Dominion of Canada would be undesirable, even if practicable, urge Her Majesty's Government not to take any decisive steps toward the present consummation of such union."[64]

This resolution marks the high water-mark of the anti-Confederation movement in British Columbia. The official members were making full use of their majority in the Council to thwart the expressed wishes of the people of the colony. It would seem that, in the main, they were acting from selfish motives, but it should be remembered that they had no guarantee as yet that after Confederation any provision would be made for them. They rallied to the support of Seymour who seems to have been definitely playing

62. The report is given in full in *Confederation Papers*, 17-26.

63. *Ibid.*, 16-28. Seymour's speech at the opening of the Legislative Council, December 17, 1868, is to be found in the *Journals of the Legislative Council of British Columbia*, 6th Session, 1869, 2-5.

64. *Journals*, 1869, 43.

into their hands. But it should not be forgotten that the "Crown colony point of view" had many supporters in Victoria, that Canada was far away, that the intervening territory had not yet been taken over, and that the demand for responsible government was coupled with that for Confederation.

The death of Seymour in June, 1869, as we have seen, changed the whole situation. Canada took a definite stand. The cession to the Dominion of the Hudson's Bay territory and the appointment of Governor Musgrave prepared the way for the victory of the confederationists. Musgrave played his cards well. He gave assurances to the officials that in the event of Confederation the magistrates would receive county court judgeships under the Dominion government "totally independent and without the control of the Provincial Government."[65] The Executive Councillors were promised pensions, or if they stayed in the British Colonial Service and vacancies were available, transfers to other posts. By such means the opposition of the official members was broken down.

When the Legislative Council met on February 15, 1870, the changed attitude of the officials became apparent. Governor Musgrave was careful to distinguish between the two issues of Confederation and of responsible government. The first he favoured but not the second. In the speech from the throne read at the opening of the Legislative Council Musgrave clearly expressed his opinion regarding responsible government: "I have had experience of several forms of Colonial Government, and I have no hesitation in stating my opinion that the form commonly called 'Responsible Government' would not be found at present suited to a community so young and so constituted as this. It is not known in any of the neighbouring States or Territories. Experience has shown that the system is expensive in its results, and its operation is not successful except in more advanced communities, with population of more homogeneous character than ours."[66] He thus avoided what might have been a serious cleavage in the Council. The more progressive

65. Public Archives of Canada, Musgrave to Granville, no. 29, October 30, 1869.
66. *Journals of the Legislative Council of British Columbia*, 1870, 4. For a fuller discussion of the problem of responsible government see W. N. Sage, "From Colony to Province: The Introduction of Responsible Government in British Columbia," *British Columbia Historical Quarterly*, III, 1-14.

members wished for responsible government, the more conservative opposed it. The Confederation debate began on March 9, and the officials supported Confederation. The opposition now came from the popularly elected members from Victoria and Nanaimo led by Dr. Helmcken. The gist of Helmcken's argument is contained in the following paragraphs:

No union between this Colony and Canada can permanently exist, unless it be to the material and pecuniary advantage of this Colony to remain in the union. The sum of the interests of the inhabitants is the interest of the Colony. The people of this Colony have, generally speaking, no love for Canada; they care, as a rule, little or nothing about the creation of another Empire, Kingdom, or Republic; they have but little sentimentality, and care little about the distinctions between the form of Government of Canada and the United States.

Therefore no union on account of love need be looked for. The only bond of union outside of force—and force the Dominion has not—will be the material advantage of the country and the pecuniary benefit of the inhabitants. Love for Canada has to be acquired by the prosperity of the country, and from our children.[67]

These were prophetic words. Helmcken was voicing the real feelings of the Crown-colony group. The subsequent relations between British Columbia and the Dominion, the quarrels over the building of the railway, the struggle for "Better Terms," the freight rates agitations and even the secessionist cry which has been raised when it was felt that British Columbia had not profited as she should from joining Confederation are sufficient commentary on Helmcken's realistic, though somewhat cynical attitude in 1870. But at the time Confederation was in the ascendant. In spite of the supporters of the Crown-colony position, British Columbia could not remain isolated. The British government was now throwing all its weight on the side of Confederation. Annexation was merely a will-of-the-wisp. All that remained was to settle the terms of union with Canada.

Terms were fully discussed in the Confederation debate and resolutions passed setting forth the demands of British Columbia. A delegation of three, Messrs. Trutch, Helmcken, and Carrall, was appointed to proceed to Ottawa to discuss terms of union with the Dominion government. Governor Musgrave stated that he picked

67. *Confederation Debate*, 1870, 13.

these men as representing the various interests in the colony. After meeting with the British Columbia delegates the Dominion government finally agreed to the terms with some alterations and additions.[68] Canada assumed the debts of British Columbia, agreed to pay a subsidy to the new province, also to provide for necessary services including the salaries of the Lieutenant-Governor and the judges, the maintenance of posts, telegraphs, customs, fisheries, the militia, lighthouses, quarantine, marine hospitals, the penitentiary, and the geological survey. Suitable pensions were provided for officials who would lose by the entrance of the colony into the Dominion. The Canadian tariff was to be adopted when railway connection was provided, but the new province could adopt the Canadian tariff at once if it so desired. Steamship communication with San Francisco and Olympia, for the conveyance of mails, was to be continued.

The most important clause provided for the construction of a transcontinental railway to join British Columbia with Eastern Canada. The new province undertook to provide a land grant by conveying to the Dominion, in trust, a tract twenty miles wide on either side of the railway. Executive authority and the Legislative Council of British Columbia were to remain as they were at the time of the union, subject to the provisions of the British North America Act, but it was understood that the Governor of British Columbia intended to alter the existing constitution of the Legislature so as to make the majority of the members elective. It was also understood that the Dominion government would "consent to the introduction of Responsible Government when desired by the inhabitants of British Columbia."[69] In accordance with these proposals Governor Musgrave altered the constitution and called for a new election. The new Legislative Council, the majority now being elective, met in January, 1871, and passed the terms of union. On July 20, 1871, British Columbia officially entered the Dominion of Canada.

68. The full text of the terms as accepted by the Committee of the Privy Council for Canada is given in the *Journals of the Legislative Council of British Columbia*, 1871, 4-6.

69. H. E. Seelye of the *British Colonist* had gone as an unofficial delegate to Ottawa to secure responsible government. Cf. Sir Charles Tupper, *Recollections of Sixty Years* (London, 1914), 127-8.

With the creation of the new province the colonial period of British Columbian history ends and the Canadian period begins. Up till now it has hardly been possible to speak accurately of Canadian-American relations upon the Pacific slope. But the inter-relations of Great Britain, the United States, Canada, and British Columbia, especially during the critical period 1866-71, were so close that no discussion of the relations between the Dominion and the Republic on this coast since 1871 would be intelligible without a fairly full discussion of what went before. But the direction of future development had been determined and forces were set to work which were to integrate British Columbia into the Confederation of British North America in the same way as the Pacific Coast states were integrated into the American system. The possible drift towards a unified economy on the Pacific Coast received a death blow. The policies which were to bring prosperity or adversity were those framed at Washington and at Ottawa; the political battles were to be fought within two separate nations; and in neither nation was the Pacific seaboard to be a dominantly influential element. In Canada economic integration began with the construction of the Canadian Pacific Railway and proceeded to gather momentum until the opening of the Panama Canal was to produce a radical reorientation of the trade relations of British Columbia. And British Columbia was to remain part of a world-wide empire.

CHAPTER IX

THE SAN JUAN BOUNDARY

1845-1872

THE treaty signed at Washington on June 15, 1846, defining the international boundary west of the Rocky Mountains, was unfortunately not free from ambiguity.[1] As the treaty had been drafted at the British Foreign Office and accepted by the United States without textual change,[2] the ambiguity must be attributed rather to ignorance of the geography of the region or to carelessness in wording than to a basic difference of view. The text of article 1 has been set out in chapter VI.[3] The crucial phrase was: "The line of boundary between the territories of the United States and those of Her Britannic Majesty shall be continued westward along the said forty-ninth parallel of north latitude to the middle of the channel which separates the continent from Vancouver's Island; and thence southerly through the middle of the said channel, and of Fuca's straits to the Pacific Ocean."

No difficulty arose in determining the centre of the Strait of Georgia at the 49th parallel, and the centre of the Straits of Juan de Fuca; but between these points there were three possible channels: Haro Strait to the west of the Haro Archipelago, commonly called the San Juan group; Rosario Strait to the east; and an intermediate passage by San Juan Channel and Middle Channel which divides the islands. The location of the boundary involved the sovereignty over the islands, which comprised eight of some size and numerous smaller ones, in all about 170 square miles. If the importance of these islands had been almost entirely overlooked when the treaty of 1846 was concluded, it came to be grossly

1. Throughout this chapter great use has been made of an unpublished manuscript which Dr. Hunter Miller generously placed in the hands of the editor. This work when it appears in volume VIII of *Treaties and Other International Acts of the United States of America* will constitute the most authoritative account of the San Juan boundary dispute.

2. *Treaties and Other International Acts of the United States of America*, V, 6-9, 69-82.

3. *Supra*, 128.

exaggerated when the boundary dispute focussed attention upon them.

The largest island in the group, San Juan Island, was formally claimed by the agents of the Hudson's Bay Company in July, 1845, and the Company established a salmon-curing plant there in 1850.[4] In November, 1853, the Company established a sheep farm on the island, partly as a defensive measure against American claims. As was anticipated the response of the United States took the form of a claim by the Collector of Customs. Meanwhile diplomatic correspondence between London and Washington made it clear that Great Britain and the United States each considered San Juan Island part of its territory and intended to perform normal acts of administration there. In 1855 the sheriff of Whatcom County, in the course of his fourth attempt to collect taxes from the Hudson's Bay Company, seized and removed thirty-four breeding rams, "before the British residents could muster for the protection of their property."[5] The "residents" were, of course, the staff of the Hudson's Bay Company. For this seizure a claim was presented by Great Britain to the United States on behalf of the Company on July 27, 1855.

An exchange of notes between the American Secretary of State, W. L. Marcy, and the British Chargé d'Affaires, John F. Crampton, effected an understanding by which both parties were to abstain from all acts likely to provoke conflict. "The title ought to be settled before either party should attempt to exclude the other by force or exercise complete and exclusive sovereign rights within the fairly disputed limits."[6] This understanding was recognized as the continuing policy of the United States, but appears at times to have been overlooked by Great Britain.

In 1856 a Boundary Commission was appointed to locate the boundary from the Rocky Mountains to the Pacific Ocean. It con-

4. Letter of James Douglas to Sir William Molesworth, December 13, 1855, in the Archives of British Columbia.

5. Douglas to Grey, May 18, 1855, *ibid*.

6. Marcy to Isaac I. Stevens, Governor of Washington Territory, July 14, 1855, Department of State 44, Domestic Letters 201 f., of which an excerpt was transmitted to Crampton on July 17, Department of State 7, Notes to Great Britain 485 f., and acknowledged by Crampton on July 18, Department of State 32, Notes from the British Legation.

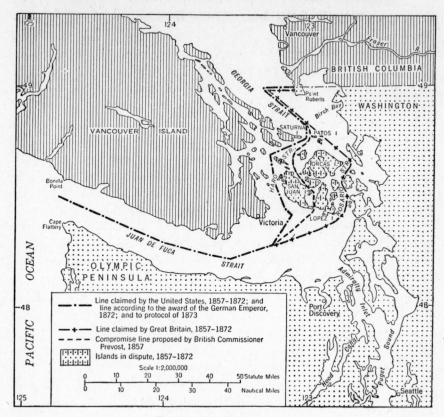

THE SAN JUAN BOUNDARY

sisted of Archibald Campbell for the United States and (as regards the water boundary) Captain James C. Prevost, R.N., for Great Britain. Prevost's instructions from Lord Clarendon were that Rosario Strait appeared "so clearly and exactly in accordance with the terms of the treaty that it may be hoped you will have no difficulty in inducing the American commissioner to acquiesce in it"; but he was given "liberty to adopt any other intermediate channel which you may discover on which the United States commissioner and yourself may agree as substantially in accordance with the description of the treaty."[7]

The Commissioners could not agree on the water boundary.[8]

7. December 20, 1856. See Senate Executive Document no. 29, 40th Congress, 2nd Session, Serial 1316, 103 ff.

8. Correspondence summarized in J. B. Moore, *International Adjudications* (New York, 1929-36), I, 219-22.

Prevost, with the full approval of the British government, vainly offered a compromise by which all the channels between the continent and Vancouver Island were to be regarded as one channel. This would have given the United States all the larger islands except San Juan, to which Prevost attached enormous importance:

San Juan is a large and beautiful island with a large extent of open prairie land; but were it barren and rocky and intrinsically worthless, it is of the utmost value to Great Britain commanding as it does the channel of communication between Vancouver's Island and British Columbia. . . . In my opinion, it matters not if all the other islands between San Juan and the Continent pass to the United States, but San Juan is invaluable to our possessions; it is clearly ours both in right and equity, and to yield it to the United States would be to depreciate our contiguous territory to an extent that someday might prove fatal to Her Majesty's possessions in this quarter of the globe.[9]

In the meantime the Hudson's Bay Company's establishment on San Juan Island had prospered, and since 1855 no attempt had been made to collect taxes although these were regularly assessed each year. Until some squatters came in 1858 and 1859 there were very few Americans on the island. The British government, acting on a suggestion from Douglas, asked the United States to discountenance any settlement by Americans pending a definitive agreement as to sovereignty over the island.[10] This request ignored the understanding of 1855 which would have precluded further British as well as American occupation. By silence it assented to American settlement on the other islands between Haro and Rosario straits.

Before an answer to this request was received a collision had actually occurred. On June 15, 1859, an American, Lyman A. Cutler, shot a pig belonging to the Hudson's Bay Company. Heated words passed; there was a wide difference of opinion as to the value of the pig; it is possible that there was a threat to take Cutler to Victoria for trial. On July 23 Douglas appointed John Fitzroy de

9. Foreign Office Memorandum, 28, July 23, 1859, in the Archives of British Columbia.

10. Lyons to Cass, May 12, 1859, Senate Executive Document no. 29, 40th Congress, 2nd Session, Serial 1316, 218.

Courcy a Justice of the Peace and a stipendiary magistrate for the District of San Juan, and wrote to Captain Prevost requesting that the new magistrate should be conveyed to the island in the corvette *Satellite*. This was done on July 27. Earlier on that day an American force of sixty men, commanded by Captain G. E. Pickett, landed on the island.

Pickett had been despatched by Brigadier-General William S. Harney who since October 24, 1858, had been in command of the Department of Oregon, with headquarters at Fort Vancouver. Harney's view was that there would be little British emigration to British Columbia and that Vancouver Island "as important to the Pacific States as Cuba is to those on the Atlantic" would eventually be yielded to the United States.[11] San Juan, he considered, offered the best location for a naval station on the Pacific Coast.[12] The reason which he gave for sending Pickett to San Juan was a threat to arrest Cutler alleged to have been made by Mr. Dallas, the Chief Factor of the Hudson's Bay Company, who (it was stated) had been conveyed to the island "in the British sloop-of-war, Satellite."[13] Pickett's orders were to protect the inhabitants of the island against the northern Indians and to afford protection to American citizens in their rights as such.[14]

On July 29 Henry R. Crosbie, a magistrate of Whatcom County, came to San Juan on a temporary visit but, finding an English official claiming to be the civil authority on the island, decided to remain as the American civil authority.[15] His relations with de Courcy were amicable.

When Douglas heard of Captain Pickett's landing he at once asked Captain Michael de Courcy,[16] senior naval officer at Victoria, to despatch a powerful vessel of war to prevent the landing of

11. Report to General Scott, July 19, 1859, quoted in Senate Executive Document no. 2, 36th Congress, 1st Session, Serial 1024, 107 ff.

12. *Ibid*.

13. *Ibid*. Mr. Dallas came on the *Beaver*, a steamer of the Hudson's Bay Company. It is not established that he made the alleged threat.

14. *Ibid*.

15. Report of H. R. Crosbie, House Executive Document no. 77, 36th Congress, 1st Session, Serial 1056, 5.

16. Cousin of John Fitzroy de Courcy, the magistrate.

further armed parties.[17] The *Tribune*, Captain Geoffrey Phipps Hornby, was sent the same day, with the Attorney-General of British Columbia, George Hunter Cary. When Cary wrote to Douglas that the American forces were more powerful than had been reported and that there was a strong probability of resistance,[18] Douglas suggested to Captain de Courcy that a second vessel should be sent to the island. He did not, however, insist in the face of a protest against the employment of armed force against the troops of the United States, and withdrew his orders that Captain Hornby should prevent further landings or the erection of fortifications. He also instructed Magistrate de Courcy not to issue any process against the United States troops at San Juan.

The official conversations between Magistrate de Courcy and Captain Pickett, between him and the Whatcom County magistrate, and between Captain Prevost of the Boundary Commission and Captain Pickett appear to have been correct and even friendly in tone.

The next move of Douglas was to instruct Captain Hornby, who had succeeded Captain de Courcy as senior naval officer, to effect a joint military occupation of San Juan, each country to withdraw its civil magistrate. Pickett refused to consent to this and asked that action be delayed till the two governments had been consulted; and Hornby decided that it would be unwise to use his superior force to accomplish his purpose. His reasons were weighty: To land a force would be to follow the bad example set by the United States of occupying territory about which proceedings were pending; it would condone any subsequent reinforcement by the Americans; superior strength made it dignified to be forbearing; and in the event of a serious dispute Lord Palmerston would be almost certain to give up the island.[19] But to Douglas, Captain Hornby's sagacity was irritating. When Admiral Baynes returned to Esquimalt on August 5, he strongly approved the course taken by Captain Hornby and strongly disapproved the action which

17. Douglas to Sir Edward Bulwer Lytton, August 1, 1859, in the Archives of British Columbia. See W. N. Sage, *Sir James Douglas and British Columbia* (Toronto, 1930), 266-7.

18. Foreign Office Print, 67 f., in the Archives of British Columbia.

19. Hornby to Douglas, August 4, 1859 (Private), in the Archives of British Columbia.

had been suggested by Douglas. He ordered Captain Hornby to avoid all interference with the American force.[20]

At Washington, the reports from General Harney led to much diplomatic activity and President Buchanan decided to send Lieutenant-General Winfield Scott to Washington Territory. He was told in his instructions that Governor Stevens had been instructed in accordance with the understanding of 1855 that the title to the island should be settled before either party attempted to exclude the other by force; that much was left to his discretion; that the President's main object was to preserve the peace and prevent collision between the British and American authorities on the island until the question of title could be adjusted by the two governments; and that it would be desirable to provide during the intervening period for a joint occupation of the island.[21]

On his arrival at the coast General Scott wrote to Douglas proposing joint military occupation. Although this had been Douglas's own idea a few weeks earlier, he replied suggesting withdrawal of the armed forces of both countries and joint civil occupation. An alternative suggestion, made orally, was for unilateral reduction of the American forces followed by an invitation to land British forces if that were thought desirable. The outcome was an understanding for joint military-naval occupation with very limited forces.

Instructions from London directed Douglas to effect a joint military occupation and a detachment of marines was landed on March 21, 1860. Shortly afterwards General Harney sent Captain Pickett back to San Juan to replace Captain Hunt, against whom there had been a complaint for "stopping trade" (i.e., liquor selling). Pickett was directed by Harney to acknowledge and respect the authority of the Territory of Washington. General Scott, writing to the Secretary of War,[22] said: "If this does not lead to a collision of arms, it will again be due to the forbearance of the British authorities; for I found both Brigadier General Harney

20. A. W. Shiels, *San Juan Islands* (Juneau, Alaska, 1938), 58.

21. Senate Executive Document no. 29, 40th Congress, 2nd Session, Serial 1316, 160 ff.

22. *Ibid.*, Serial 1316, May 14, 1860, 212 f.; quoted in William Fitzwilliam, Viscount Milton, *A History of the San Juan Water Boundary Question* (London, 1869), 354.

and Captain Pickett proud of their *conquest* of the island, and quite jealous of any interference therewith on the part of higher authority." The instructions were the theme of a remonstrance by the British Ambassador in Washington.[23] The response of the administration was to "regret and disavow" General Harney's order. General Harney was recalled from his command.[24] Captain Pickett remained in command on San Juan Island until the summer of 1861, on friendly terms with his British "opposite number."

Negotiations proceeded for a final settlement of the status of the islands. The American government expressed in June, 1860, its willingness "to receive and fairly consider any proposal which the British government might be disposed to make for a mutually acceptable adjustment."[25] The British government offered to submit the water boundary to arbitration, the arbiter to have power "if the precise line cannot be ascertained" to chart "a line which will furnish an equitable solution of the difficulty."[26] This proposal was never answered. A resolution approving such an arrangement was reported from the Committee on Foreign Relations of the Senate on February 27, five days before the 36th Congress ended. In the next Congress the Committee reported advising that the arbitrator should not have power to establish any line other than that provided by the treaty. But consideration of this resolution of Senator Sumner was postponed and not resumed.

Joint military occupation was therefore continued during the American Civil War. It involved serious difficulties because the American military officers felt bound to prevent the exercise of American civil authority and so incurred serious personal liabilities. It also led to American protests to Washington against their action and in 1869 a treaty was signed providing for arbitration on the lines suggested by Great Britain in 1860. This treaty was not acted on by the Senate.

In 1871 the question of the northwest water boundary came

23. June 6, 1860, Department of State Notes from the British Legation. See Serial 1316, 256 f.

24. Serial 1316, 213.

25. Cass to Lyons, June 25, 1860, Serial 1316, 262.

26. *Ibid.*, 264 f.

before the Joint High Commission.[27] The compromise proposed by Great Britain was again offered and declined. By Articles 34-42 of the Treaty of Washington of May 8, 1871, the controversy was referred to the German Emperor, who was to decide which of the two claims (respectively to Haro Strait and Rosario Strait) "is most in accordance with the true interpretation of the Treaty of June 15, 1846." On October 21, 1872, the German Emperor decided in favour of the claim of the United States that the boundary should run through Haro Strait.[28] The joint occupation of San Juan ended on November 25, 1872, by the withdrawal of the detachment of Royal Marines.

From the standpoint of British-American relations on the Pacific Coast of North America the history of the San Juan boundary is full of significance.[29] The dispute occurred in a period when the two nations were still land-hungry and defence-conscious. The islands, it is true, were of little importance for colonization and there was ample room elsewhere. In relation to the military technique of the day San Juan Island had a real value, although it is amusing to find that an island, which was not considered worthy of specific mention in the treaty of 1846, should be described, a decade later, as of vital strategic importance. The opinion of the British Admiralty that freedom of navigation was what mattered most may well have been the sanest estimate of the situation.

The period was also one of relatively slow communication, so that the men on the spot had to act without frequent consultation with their superiors. This difficulty was of particular importance in the case of Great Britain, and was intensified by the fact that it was the Colonial Office which communicated with Governor Douglas, and the Foreign Office which communicated with the government of the United States. It is easy to see the conflict in

27. Moore, *International Adjudications*, I, 224 f., and L. B. Shippee, *Canadian-American Relations, 1849-1874* (New Haven, 1939).

28. See Moore, *International Adjudications*, I, 227 ff., and P. E. Corbett, *The Settlement of Canadian-American Disputes* (New Haven and Toronto, 1937), 17 ff.

29. It is dealt with in two other volumes in this series. Corbett, *Settlement of Canadian-American Disputes*, 17 ff., discusses briefly the method of settlement and the weight of the arguments; Shippee, *Canadian-American Relations, passim*, relates the controversy to the general diplomatic situation as between Great Britain and the United States and brings out the attitude of Canadian opinion both before and after the entry of British Columbia into Confederation.

both nations between those who felt keenly that they could not take the responsibility of relinquishing the slightest part of the national heritage entrusted to their care, and those who took broader and saner views of the national interests.

It was not very realistic to insist on interpreting strictly the words of a treaty which had obviously not been based on as close a survey of the topography as its interpreters had at their command, and to rely on the treaty as if it had been carefully drafted to deal with islands which it had not, at the time, been thought worthwhile to mention in it. But, though it might have been sounder to give wider powers to the arbitrator, there is not the slightest ground for assuming that to have done so would have affected the ultimate decision. There were moments when a negotiated compromise might have been possible; but negotiated compromises can be attacked, at the moment by politicians and later by historians, and involve responsibilities which judicial settlement makes it possible to disclaim.

CHAPTER X

RAILWAY BUILDING IN BRITISH COLUMBIA
1871-1915

DURING the period of the fur trade, of the gold rush, and of early settlement, the problem of transportation was relatively simple in the sense that the choice of method was limited. The routes of access by sea, by way of Cape Horn or the Cape of Good Hope, both involved a voyage approximately half way round the world. In the middle years of the nineteenth century it was possible to come northward by ship from Panama, and when the Union Pacific Railroad was completed in 1869 it was possible to cross the United States overland and to take ship from San Francisco to Victoria. In the fur-trading days the overland journey had been by the canoe route from Montreal to the Red River and then across the plains to Edmonton. The Columbia River, reached by way of the Athabaska River and Athabaska Pass, brought the traveller to Fort Vancouver. In 1862, as we have seen, the Over-landers came to Cariboo by the Yellowhead Pass. Another party followed the North Thompson to Kamloops. Some of the gold seekers from the south came by the Okanagan River and Okanagan Lake, while others entered the Kootenay country; but the majority came by sea from California to Victoria and then crossed the Gulf of Georgia and proceeded up the Fraser River to the diggings.

To understand the policies which were pursued to provide for a transportation system within British Columbia, we must form an idea of the immense difficulties encountered by the early road builders and by the railway engineers—difficulties which have remained serious in the second period of road construction that followed the introduction of the automobile. The stern facts of geography made movement from east to west extremely difficult. West of the great barrier of the Rockies is the Rocky Mountain Trench, in which three rivers, the Columbia, the Kootenay, and the Fraser take their rise. The Trench is a gigantic "fault" and the rivers make "big bends" in order to avoid the Selkirk massif. The general direction of these rivers is north and south, although both

228

the Columbia and the Fraser ultimately flow westward to the sea. The Kootenay flows south from its source, but swings around its big bend to flow north to Kootenay Lake, out of which it flows west to join the Columbia at Castlegar.

The difficulties inherent in the nature of the terrain were increased by the fact that the political boundary, which had been adjusted in 1846 to gratify the desire of the United States for a good sea port in the Northwest, had taken no account of the problem of selecting routes for transcontinental roads or railways. The Columbia River Valley was placed under two flags and the old fur-trading route followed by the Hudson's Bay Company's brigades up the Columbia from Fort Vancouver to its big bend, across Athabaska Pass to Jasper House, and by way of the Athabaska to Fort Assiniboine, was broken by the international boundary.

Finally there was the question of expense. Mountain roads and mountain railways are alike costly to build. The pioneer settlers on a new frontier have slender resources. In spirit they may be willing enough to gamble on the potential wealth of the country and pledge their credit in constructing the facilities for developing it, but the flesh is weak and recourse must be had to the ambition of some parent community, or to the hope of speculative profit of some outside investors, or to both these auxiliaries. When they do provide the money, they decide how it is to be spent and we shall find that the railway map of the main lines in British Columbia has been drawn by outside interests. It is only occasionally that the rapid development of a local industry will itself provide the funds necessary for the initial investment in roads.

During the gold rush Governor Douglas began the construction of the Cariboo Road, nearly four hundred miles long, from Yale at the head of navigation, to Barkerville, the so-called "capital" of Cariboo. The mining excitement in the Kootenay and Big Bend districts in the years 1864 to 1866 led to the construction of the first west-to-east trail across the Colony of British Columbia. The Hope-Princeton trail leading from the Fraser, across the Cascade Mountains into the Similkameen, was commenced by Edgar Dewdney and Walter Moberly in 1860. In the autumn of 1864 Governor Seymour sent out an expedition under J. J. Jenkins to find a trail from Hope to the Kootenay country. Jenkins followed the Dewdney Trail to Princeton and "located a line by way of Princeton, Similkameen, Osoyoos Lake, Rock Creek, and Kettle River to the Columbia River near the mouth of Kootenay River and thence down St. Mary's River."[1] Governor Seymour determined to construct a trail from the terminus of the Dewdney Trail of 1860 to the "metropolis of Kootenay," Wild Horse Creek. In 1865 Edgar Dewdney undertook the contract and completed the work by the middle of September of that year at a cost of approximately $74,000. Although the route was by no means identical with that followed half a century later by the Kettle Valley Railway and the Canadian Pacific line in the Kootenays, its general direction was the same. The attempt to connect the coast with the Kootenays failed because it was found impossible to compete with the Americans who could enter the Kootenay region by the natural north and south lines.[2]

The early period of road building came to an end in British Columbia when the Canadian government offered to construct a transcontinental railway instead of the waggon road demanded by the colony. Explorations for the waggon road had already been made and Governor Douglas, "the king of roads," had proposed its construction to the British government in 1863. He claimed at a later date that he "would have carried through to Red River settlement in 18 months." He had "everything ready to make a beginning, a large body of Engineers, tools, labourers, the means of transport and all other appliances requisite for the great enterprise."[3]

The railway builders, in search of a route across the continent, had to look for passes through the mountain ranges which would

1. E. O. S. Scholefield and F. W. Howay, *British Columbia from the Earliest Times to the Present* (Vancouver, 1914), II, 233; see also 94, 96.

2. On this subject, which will be more fully discussed in chapter XI, compare W. J. Trimble, *The Mining Advance into the Inland Empire* (Madison, 1914), 58. "Hope, the nearest village on the Fraser, by the round-about trail that was followed, was over five hundred miles distant, and part of the trail, that from Fort Shephard [*sic*] to Wild Horse Creek, was so bad that, in 1864, one of the Hudson's Bay Company trains was fourteen days in making the trip from that post and lost six horses in doing so."

3. Letter of Sir James Douglas to his son James W. Douglas, May 22, 1868, in the Archives of British Columbia. Cf. W. N. Sage, *Sir James Douglas and British Columbia* (Toronto, 1930), 338.

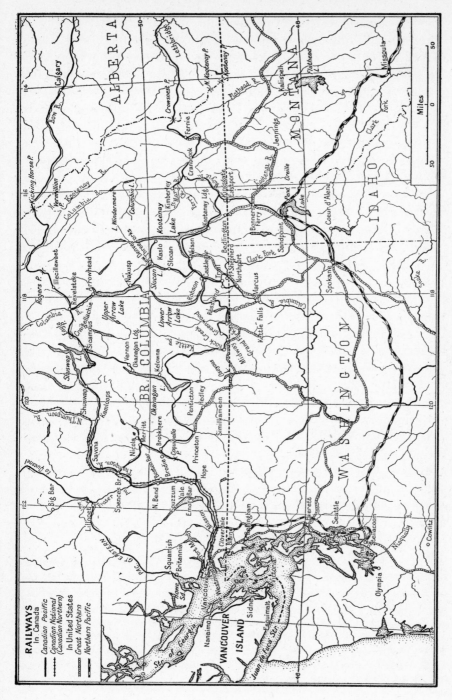

RAILWAYS IN BRITISH COLUMBIA

avoid the necessity of following the rivers in their roundabout courses. It was no light task. Captain Palliser in his report to the British government in 1863 argued against the building of a railway "from Canada across the continent to the Pacific exclusively through British territory." "The time has for ever gone by," he stated, "for effecting such an object, and the unfortunate choice of an astronomical boundary line has completely isolated the central American possessions of Great Britain from Canada in the east, and also almost debarred them from any eligible access from the Pacific coast on the west."[4]

Captain Palliser was looking at the problem from the point of view of the prairies, "the central American possessions of Great Britain." Walter Moberly, who was appointed Assistant Surveyor-General of British Columbia in 1864 and placed in charge of explorations in the Columbia River Valley, conceived the plan of a railway across British Columbia. In 1865 he found the Eagle Pass in the Gold Range and in 1866 one of his assistants, Albert Perry, explored the western slopes of the Selkirks leading to Rogers Pass, through which at a later date the main line of the Canadian Pacific was constructed. Moberly thus records the results of his investigations: "At the completion of the Columbia River explorations at the end of the year 1866, I was fully convinced that a remarkably good line for a railway, considering the rugged nature of the country, could be obtained from Burrard Inlet via the Eagle Pass, the valley of the Columbia River and the Howse Pass through the Rocky Mountains to the Prairie country."[5]

Moberly's plan was to explore the possibilities for the construction of a line of railway in the Columbia River Valley from the site of the present town of Revelstoke, the point at which the trail across Eagle Pass reached the Columbia, around the big bend to the mouth of Blaeberry Creek, then up that creek to Howse Pass. Thus the difficult crossing of the Selkirks would be avoided and a much lighter grade across the Rockies would be obtained than by way of Kicking Horse Pass. Branch lines could be constructed to the north through the valley of the Canoe River and to the south by

4. Great Britain, *Parliamentary Papers*, 1863 (3164), 16 ff., quoted in L. J. Burpee, *Sandford Fleming* (London, 1915), 109.

5. Walter Moberly, *Early History of Canadian Pacific Railway* (Vancouver, Art, Historical and Scientific Association, n.d.), 6.

way of Upper Columbia lakes and the Kootenay River to connect
with the American railways which would ultimately be built to
Spokane Falls.

The next year, 1867, Moberly visited the western states in order
to examine at first hand the progress of the Union and Central
Pacific Railroads. By the end of that year, the Union Pacific
officials stated, railhead would be 537 miles west of the Missouri,
or 20 miles beyond Cheyenne. The Central Pacific was building
eastward across California and had reached the Sierras.[6] The
"last spike" was driven at Promontory Point, near Ogden, Utah,
on May 10, 1869. But what interested Moberly most was the
projected Northern Pacific Railroad which had been incorporated
by the United States Congress on July 2, 1864, to construct a line
from Lake Superior to Puget Sound, with a branch to Portland,
Oregon. Speaking of the four years, 1867-71, which he spent in the
United States, Moberly remarked: "I wished to ascertain the
probable effect the building of this latter railway would have in
drawing away Canadian trade into American channels, in order
that my proposed Canadian railway should be prepared to meet
such an emergency by branch lines properly located for that
purpose."[7]

In 1871 Moberly changed his plans and decided that the railway
could run through the Kicking Horse and across the Selkirk Range
by the valley of the Illecillewaet. He purchased supplies on the
American side at New Fort Colville and established a depot near
the mouth of Blaeberry Creek. He still purposed surveys around
the "Big Bend" and over Howse Pass, but now these were to be
alternative to the Kicking Horse and Selkirk route.[8]

The location of the line in British Columbia would, of course,
be determined by the pass chosen through the main chain of the
Rockies and by the terminal on the Pacific. The "battle for the
terminals" belongs to a later date but the question of the passes
was raised in 1869 by Alfred Waddington in his paper "On the
Geography and Mountain Passes of British Columbia in Connection with an Overland Route." In this paper Waddington listed

6. E. B. Oberholzer, *A History of the United States since the Civil War* (New York,
1926), I, 326, 330.

7. Moberly, *Canadian Pacific Railway*, 6.

8. Walter Moberly, *The Rocks and Rivers of British Columbia* (London, 1885), 66.

eight passes across the Rockies and pronounced in favour of the Yellowhead Pass and the Bute Inlet route.[9]

It is impossible to retell here in detail the heroic story of the construction of the Canadian Pacific Railway.[10] Nor can the long wranglings between British Columbia and the Dominion over the fulfilment of the terms of union be discussed at length.[11] But it is essential that the "railway clause" of the federation agreement should be given in full.

The Government of the Dominion undertake to secure the commencement simultaneously, within two years from the date of the Union, of the construction of a Railway from the Pacific towards the Rocky Mountains, and from such point as may be selected, east of the Rocky Mountains, towards the Pacific, to connect the seaboard of British Columbia with the railway system of Canada; and further, to secure the completion of such Railway within ten years from the date of the Union.

And the Government of British Columbia agree to convey to the Dominion Government, in trust, to be appropriated in such manner as the Dominion Government may deem advisable in the furtherance of the

9. Waddington in this paper and in his pamphlet *Sketch of the Proposed Line of Overland Railroad through British North America* (Ottawa, 1871), influenced Canadian opinion in favour of the projected transcontinental. In 1869 "The Canadian Pacific Railway" applied for a charter from the Dominion government to construct a road from Minnesota across the prairies to the Yellowhead Pass at a cost of £20,000,000 (H. A. Innis, *A History of the Canadian Pacific Railway*, London, 1923, 20, n. 9).

The eight passes listed by Waddington are as follows:

Name of Pass	Location	Latitude	Longitude	Altitude
1. Yellowhead	Athabaska to Upper Fraser	52.54	118.33	3,760
2. Howse	Red Deer to Upper Columbia	51.57	117.07	6,347
3. Kicking Horse	Bow to Upper Columbia	51.16	116.32	5,420
4. Vermillion	South Saskatchewan to Kootanie	51.06	116.15	4,947
5. Kananaskis	Bow to Kootanie	50.45	115.31	5,985
6. Crow's Nest	Crow River to Kootanie	49.38	114.48	5,985
7. British Kootanie	Railway River to Kootanie	49.27	114.57	5,960
8. Red Stone Creek or Boundary	Waterton River to Kootanie (partly in U.S.A.)	49.06	114.14	6,030

construction of the said Railway, a similar extent of public lands along the line of Railway, throughout its entire length in British Columbia, not to exceed, however, Twenty (20) Miles on each side of the said line, as may be appropriated for the same purpose by the Dominion Government from the public lands in the North-West Territories and the Province of Manitoba. Provided, that the quantity of lands which may be held under preemption right or by Crown grant within the limits of the tract of land in British Columbia to be so conveyed to the Dominion Government shall be made good to the Dominion from contiguous public lands; and provided, further, that until the commencement within two years, as aforesaid, from the date of the Union, of the construction of the said Railway, the Government of British Columbia shall not sell or alienate any further portions of the public lands of British Columbia in any other way than under right of preemption, requiring actual residence of the preemptor on the land claimed by him. In consideration of the land to be so conveyed in aid of the construction of the said Railway, the Dominion Government agree to pay to British Columbia, from the date of the Union, the sum of $100,000 per annum, in half-yearly payments in advance.[12]

British Columbians have, perhaps, tended too often to consider that the railway clause was placed in the terms of union at the instance of the British Columbian delegates who were sent to Ottawa in 1870. This is not the case. The Pacific Coast delegates had been instructed to ask for a waggon road and it was the Canadian government which substituted a railway for the road.[13]

10. See Innis, *Canadian Pacific Railway*, and G. P. deT. Glazebrook, *A History of Transportation in Canada* (Toronto and New Haven, 1938).

11. On this subject compare F. W. Howay, *British Columbia, the Making of a Province* (Toronto, 1928), 189-216; Scholefield and Howay, *British Columbia*, II, 341-416; E. O. S. Scholefield and R. E. Gosnell, *British Columbia, Sixty Years of Progress* (Vancouver and Victoria, 1913), part II, cci-x; H. J. Johns, "British Columbia's Campaign for Better Terms, 1871-1907," M.A. Thesis, 1935, in University of British Columbia Library; also *British Columbia in the Canadian Confederation: Submission Presented to the Royal Commission on Dominion-Provincial Relations* (Victoria, 1938). *Parliamentary Debates*, Canada, 1871-1885, set forth in detail the political reactions in the Dominion as a whole.

12. Article 11, Order in Council respecting the Province of British Columbia, in *Statutes of Canada*, 1872, lxxxviii, quoted in Innis, *Canadian Pacific Railway*, 295, and in Scholefield and Howay, *British Columbia*, II, 696-7.

13. The government of British Columbia in 1938 emphasized that the railway clause was added in Ottawa: "The British Columbia delegation which visited Ottawa to discuss the question of Confederation requested that British Columbia be connected with Fort Garry by a wagon-road.   Instead of a wagon-road the Province

Sir John A. Macdonald favoured a railway from Canada to the Pacific Coast.[14] When the British Columbia delegates arrived in Ottawa, Sir John A. Macdonald was very seriously ill, but the terms of union were discussed with Sir George Etienne Cartier and other members of the Dominion Cabinet. As a result of these conferences the railway clause was inserted. Macdonald and his Cabinet favoured the railway as a *national* project and were prepared if necessary to undertake heavy financial obligations and to make generous promises to British Columbia.

In the debates in the Canadian Parliament on the terms of union the Liberals, then in opposition, made it clear that although, on the whole, they approved of the admission of British Columbia to federation they were opposed to the railway clause.[15] Sir Alexander Tilloch Galt was highly critical of the clause and offered an amendment which failed to carry.[16] The building of the Canadian Pacific Railway thus became a sort of political football and when after the Pacific Scandal Sir John A. Macdonald resigned and Alexander Mackenzie and the Liberals came into power there was a definite attempt on the part of the Dominion government to modify the

was promised the construction of the Pacific railroad. It has often been said that the construction of this railroad was a concession to British Columbia and was in the nature of a grant. However, the national and imperial character of the road was obvious and it is now generally admitted that it should not be looked upon in any sense as a charge to British Columbia on its entry into Confederation" (*British Columbia in the Canadian Confederation*, 10).

14. Cf. Sir John A. Macdonald to C. J. Brydges, Ottawa, January 28, 1870: "One of the first things to be done is to show unmistakably our resolve to build the Pacific Railway" (Sir Joseph Pope, *Memoirs of the Right Honourable Sir John Alexander Macdonald*, Ottawa, 1894, II, 162).

15. Cf. *Parliamentary Debates*, Canada, 1st Parliament, 4th Session (Ottawa, 1871). The Hon. Alexander Mackenzie definitely favoured the union of British Columbia with Canada but strenuously opposed the railway. In the Senate, the Hon. Luc Lettelier de St. Just thus spoke his mind fully: "It was gratifying certainly to many persons to see the Dominion enlarged in area and increasing in influence, but it must not be forgotten at the same time that Canada was to defray not only the expenses of the local Government of British Columbia, but was to bind herself, according to the contemplated arrangement, to build a railway to the Pacific. . . . The people of British Columbia might be very loyal people—very anxious to unite with Canada; but he could not understand why they should not be willing to join their fortunes with the Dominion except at such an enormous price" (*ibid.*, 34).

16. *Ibid.*, 763-4.

railway clause. Mackenzie had a strong case, but the Walkem government in British Columbia stood on the Carnarvon Terms.[17]

The railway clause was not a one-sided bargain, although for years many in Eastern Canada considered it to be so. British Columbia gave a land grant, the Dominion government paid her for it[18] and undertook the construction of the railway. The railway was a national undertaking, essential to the building up of the Dominion from sea to sea. It was also to be a link in an imperial chain, a vital part of the "all red route" which was to bind together the various portions of the far-flung Empire. The United States Ambassador in London informed the Foreign Secretary that the United States would not regard its completion with favour.[19] The construction of the railway was, in short, an act of high policy. Without the railway, British Columbia could never really be an integral portion of the Dominion. But, even if British Columbia had not entered Confederation, the Dominion would have had, sooner or later, to build a railway across the prairies and in all probability a connecting link north of Lake Superior. The entrance of British Columbia into Confederation could not safely have been postponed. It forced the Dominion to undertake the gigantic railway venture before the people of Western Canada were convinced of its necessity, or indeed of its practicability.

There was, for a time, a real danger that the promise to build

17. Cf. J. A. Maxwell, "Lord Dufferin and Difficulties with British Columbia," *Canadian Historical Review*, XII, 364-89.

18. In its brief (Exhibit 180, *Brief of Argument*, 10 ff.) presented to the Royal Commission on Dominion-Provincial Relations, the government of British Columbia treated the annuity of $100,000 a year paid for these lands as a means of meeting the financial demands of British Columbia, without using the device of a fictitious population of 120,000 for calculating federal subsidies. "The unreality of the original relation between this payment and the conveyance of land must be kept in mind." In the course of argument the province abandoned this contention and elected to treat the annual grant as a *bona fide* purchase price for the land, while agreeing that it was only through finding a purchaser for this asset that British Columbia could afford to enter Confederation. The Dominion, it was said, might not have been willing to buy the land had this been the entire transaction.

19. Allan Nevins, *Hamilton Fish* (New York, 1936), 421. Motley appears to have had no authority for making this protest. On the history of railroading both sides of the Canadian-American border and the rivalries described in the following pages, see also another volume in this series, W. J. Wilgus, *The Railway Interrelations of the United States and Canada* (New Haven, 1937).

the railway would not be honoured. British Columbia was determined to insist on its implementation. "Carnarvon Terms or Separation" became a political cry. The secession resolution was fortunately "lost" at Ottawa until the election of 1878, which returned Sir John A. Macdonald to power, made it clear that the terms would be carried out. If Sir John A. Macdonald's government had not succeeded the Liberals in 1878 it is more than probable that British Columbia would have severed its connections with the Dominion of Canada. This would have been a fatal step for British Columbia, but it would also have cut off Canada from her "window on the Pacific." No doubt the insistence of British Columbia that the railway must be built was a most important factor in the situation but the Canadian Pacific Railway was a *national* and not a provincial issue. Until it was completed not only British Columbia, but also Manitoba and the North West Territories had no real connecting link across Canadian territory with the eastern provinces. To be sure the white population of the Canadian West was very small in comparison with that of the older provinces, but Canada needed the vast territory west of the Great Lakes. It was to her what the Trans-Mississippi West was to the United States.

The preliminary surveys for the Canadian Pacific Railway were commenced almost as soon as British Columbia entered the Dominion. Sandford Fleming issued his first report in 1872, his second in 1874. Various routes were surveyed and a long discussion took place as to the location of the terminal. In the end the "battle for the terminals" became a contest between Vancouver Island and the lower mainland. The Fraser Valley route was chosen and the terminal was placed at Port Moody on Burrard Inlet. At first the Yellowhead Pass was favoured but in 1882 the line was located over the Kicking Horse Pass. The inhabitants of Vancouver Island wished to have the island railway from Esquimalt, a suburb of Victoria, to Nanaimo, the coal city, included in the transcontinental scheme and the government of British Columbia attempted, unsuccessfully, to induce the Dominion government to build "the island section of the Canadian Pacific Railway." But the story of the building of the Esquimalt and Nanaimo Railway must be told separately since it was destined never to be part of the main line of the Canadian Pacific.

In the late autumn of 1879 the Dominion government called for tenders for the construction of the line from Emory's Bar on Fraser River to Savona's Ferry on Thompson River, a distance of 128 miles. This stretch of rail would connect the navigable waters of the lower Fraser with inland lakes and rivers. The government asked for tenders for four sections varying from $28\frac{1}{2}$ to $40\frac{1}{2}$ miles. In the end the Onderdonk syndicate constructed the whole of the line from Port Moody on Burrard Inlet to beyond Savona.[20] Andrew Onderdonk was a brilliant young American engineer who had been very successful in certain contracts in California and was backed by D. O. Mills, a multi-millionaire of San Francisco. Onderdonk brought with him as engineer and adviser, E. G. Tilton, but many of his assistants were born in Eastern Canada or in the British Isles.

The date fixed for the completion of the contracts on the section from Emory's Bar to Savona's Ferry was June 30, 1885. The general offices of the syndicate were placed at Yale, where powder and acid works, construction and repair shops of all kinds were also established. Yale in construction days was a busy, cosmopolitan place. In 1882 and 1883 between Emory's Bar and Lytton approximately 2,500 white and 6,500 Chinese were employed. The Chinese population of British Columbia in 1879 had been about 6,000 and it is evident that many of these Orientals were employed by Onderdonk before others were imported. Construction was rushed and by February, 1883, the rails had passed North Bend. The Cariboo Road was destroyed from Yale to the Suspension Bridge at Spuzzum. At the beginning of January, 1885, the line was complete from Emory's Bar to Savona's Ferry and had been extended a little beyond Sicamous on Shuswap Lake. From Savona to Sicamous the line had been more easily located because it was readily accessible to the water. By June 30, 1885,

20. According to the *Canadian Pacific Railway Annual Report*, 1880, 318, 322, 324, Onderdonk obtained three contracts from the government, nos. 60, 62, 63, for $2,727,300, $2,056,950, and $1,746,150, respectively. H. J. Cambie, who was associated with Andrew Onderdonk in this enterprise states that the contract for the first section from Emory's Bar to Boston Bar, twenty-nine miles, was awarded to A. P. Macdonald from Middlesex County, Ontario, but that Onderdonk bought him out (Scholefield and Gosnell, *British Columbia*, part II, 103). Onderdonk bought out Ryan, Goodwin and Company. The contract from Port Moody to Emory's Bar, eighty-five miles, for $2,680,000, was awarded to the Onderdonk syndicate in 1882 (*Sessional Papers of Canada*, 1882, no. 48).

the date when the original Onderdonk contracts were to be completed, the rails stretched from Port Moody to Shuswap Lake and beyond. Onderdonk had completed all his contracts before the date set for the fulfilment of his original contracts.

While the Onderdonk syndicate was building east the Canadian Pacific Railway was hurriedly laying its rails across the continent. The road was completed on November 7, 1885, five and a half years before the agreed date, May 1, 1891.

The Canadian Pacific Railway was, from the start, a Canadian institution. Its close connection with the Dominion government is clear evidence of this. The President and Vice-President, George Stephen and Duncan McIntyre, were Canadians. George Stephen was also President of the Bank of Montreal and Richard B. Angus its General Manager. Donald A. Smith, afterwards Lord Strathcona, although not a director, was a large shareholder in the Canadian Pacific. The well-known hostility which existed between Sir John A. Macdonald and Donald A. Smith accounts for the omission of the latter from the Board of Directors of the new railway. J. J. C. Abbott, afterwards Prime Minister of Canada, was the counsel for the railway.

But United States influences were prominent. Chief among these must be reckoned James Jerome Hill, a Canadian by birth, an American by adoption, and by nature a railroad promoter and "empire builder." With the assistance of Donald A. Smith, George Stephen, and Norman W. Kittson, James J. Hill had taken over the St. Paul and Pacific, later the St. Paul, Minneapolis and Manitoba. From these small beginnings Hill was to build up the Great Northern Railway. Hill entered into the Canadian Pacific scheme with the anticipation that the line around the North Shore of Lake Superior would not be constructed for some time, if at all. When other counsels prevailed, Hill withdrew from the company in 1883 and sold his stock. After that James J. Hill was to be counted among the opponents of the road. The Great Northern was to become one of the chief rivals of the Canadian Pacific, especially in southern British Columbia.

The construction of the Lake Superior section was strongly urged by the American-born General Manager of the Canadian Pacific, William Cornelius Van Horne. A native of Chelsea, Will County, Illinois, Van Horne had had considerable railroad experience before he received an invitation from President George Stephen to join the staff of the Canadian Pacific. By one of the little ironies of history it happened that it was James J. Hill who first suggested Van Horne to Stephen. Van Horne was to become one of Hill's most aggressive rivals. There is a story that when Hill became convinced that Van Horne intended to build the Lake Superior section and that nothing would turn him from his purpose the great American railway magnate exclaimed: "Van, if you build that Lake Superior section I'll get even with you if I have to go to hell and shovel coal."

Van Horne became the driving force of construction days. The rails were laid across the prairie with feverish speed. Donald Grant and the "front train" have become part of the epic of Western Canada. The dynamic General Manager sought the shortest route across the plains and through the mountains. Major A. B. Rogers, another American, located the route through the Selkirks and discovered, or more probably rediscovered, Rogers Pass.

The route through the Kicking Horse was found to be feasible, and in 1883 Sandford Fleming, no longer chief engineer for the Canadian Pacific Railway, made his way through from Kicking Horse to Kamloops. The "scenic route through the Rockies" was preferred to the more round-about and less spectacular, but on the whole more practical, route by the Yellowhead Pass. It is very possible that fear of American competition had something to do with the adoption of the more southerly route. Events were to prove that even the Kicking Horse was too far north to link the mineral-bearing Kootenays with the remainder of Canada.

The gap between east and west was finally closed when the last spike was driven by Donald A. Smith at Craigellachie in Eagle Pass, British Columbia, on November 7, 1885. It was a simple ceremony in contrast to the lavish celebration which accompanied the driving of the last spike of the Northern Pacific in 1883, and the last spike of the C.P.R. was an ordinary iron spike. Van Horne's speech was the briefest on record: "All that I can say is that the work has been well done in every way." The conductor of the special train shouted "All aboard for the Pacific" and in a few moments the train rolled on its way to Port Moody. It was an historic event, the significance of which was not lost upon the little band of onlookers. Federation was now complete. British Columbia was, at long last, an integral part of the Dominion of Canada. Craigellachie had stood fast.

In his life of James J. Hill, Joseph Gilpin Pyle, after telling of the ceremony at Craigellachie, contrasts the policies and objectives of the Canadian Pacific and the Great Northern as follows.

Eight years more were to elapse before the St. Paul, Minneapolis and Manitoba, by that time become the Great Northern, was to reach its objective point on Puget Sound. But the first (i.e., the Canadian Pacific), was a government enterprise, concentrating on a single through line, whose purpose was primarily political, and whose value in developing the intermediate country was to be realized only slowly through the next twenty-five years. The second built up the country as it grew, occupied strategically the whole region through which it passed and which it expected to serve, following its supreme purpose as a prime factor in the industrial development of the American Northwest. The Canadian Pacific in 1885 was still a mere charcoal sketch in outline. When the Great Northern Company was formed in 1890, the system, although many important details remained to be filled in, was in plan and theory a finished work. The two present a sharp contrast of methods and ideals.[21]

One can hardly expect an unbiased opinion from the "authorized" biographer of "Jim" Hill, but there is something in his statement that "the Canadian Pacific in 1885 was still a mere charcoal sketch in outline." The main objective, the linking of east and west in Canada, was accomplished by the completion of the main line. Settlement had to catch up with the main line before any extensive series of branch lines could be attempted.

In British Columbia, however, there were two lines which had to be constructed as soon as possible. These were the extension of the main line from Port Moody to Vancouver, and the Esquimalt and Nanaimo Railway on Vancouver Island. The first of these may be disposed of in a few sentences.

By the time the first regular passenger train which had left Montreal on June 28, 1886, arrived at Port Moody five days and seventeen hours later, it was evident that the "statutory terminus" would have to yield to the real terminus. Port Moody is not favourably located to become a large terminal city. Vancouver, or as it was then termed, Granville, offered greater opportunities. The

21. J. G. Pyle, *The Life of James J. Hill* (New York, 1936), I, 326.

government of British Columbia in February, 1885, offered to the railway company a free grant of six thousand acres of land and all the unalienated lots in Granville if the railway was built to the new terminus. The company was willing, but legal objections were raised. At length it was officially decided that the extension was to be considered as a branch. Technically the main line still ends at Port Moody, but it matters little. Granville in anticipation of the arrival of the railway grew rapidly and in April, 1886, was incorporated as the City of Vancouver. The infant city was burned down on June 13 of the same year, but arose triumphant from its ashes. In May, 1887, the first Canadian Pacific Railway train steamed into Vancouver.[22]

The attempts of the government of British Columbia to have the island railway included in the main line of the Canadian Pacific have already been mentioned. In the final settlement, the province agreed to grant to the Dominion of Canada an area of 1,900,000 acres on Vancouver Island.[23] The Dominion used this land and provided a grant of $750,000 as a subsidy for the construction and operation of the Esquimalt and Nanaimo Railway. At the same time the Dominion promised to take over, complete, and operate the graving dock at Esquimalt, and to repay the province $182,000 which had already been expended by the province, and in addition a sum of $250,000.

The building of the Esquimalt and Nanaimo Railway was undertaken by Robert Dunsmuir, the "coal king" of Vancouver Island and four American colleagues, Collis P. Huntingdon, Mark Hopkins, Leland Stanford, and Charles Crocker, of the Southern

22. Since much confusion has occurred because Vancouver, British Columbia, is on the mainland and not on Vancouver Island, and also because there is a City of Vancouver, Washington, built on the site of the well-known Hudson's Bay company's post, Fort Vancouver, a word should be added as to how the so-called "City of Imperial Destiny" obtained its name. The intention was to call the new terminus Van Horne. But the General Manager of the railway modestly refused the honour and suggested that the city be called after Captain George Vancouver who in 1792 had visited and named Burrard Inlet. Vancouver was not the first white man to sight what is now Vancouver. That honour belongs to the Spaniards, but the early publication of Vancouver's *Voyage* first gave wide publicity to his achievements and it is only in recent years that the Spanish explorations have become widely known. The citizens of Vancouver are proud of the name given to their city.

23. *Sessional Papers of Canada*, 1884, no. 15.

Pacific and Central Pacific Railways, the "Big Four" or "Pacific Quartet." According to R. E. Gosnell the Marquis of Lorne, who as Governor-General visited British Columbia in 1882, persuaded Robert Dunsmuir to undertake the construction of the island railway. Dunsmuir had come to Vancouver Island in 1851 to mine coal for the Hudson's Bay Company and had later successfully formed and operated his own company. He had for years marketed his coal in San Francisco and was well known on the Pacific Coast as a shrewd financier. At no time did his Scottish sagacity show itself to more advantage than in the terms which he made with his American associates. Although the railway, the land grant with its coal rights, and the Dunsmuir collieries were held in common by Dunsmuir and the "Big Four," Dunsmuir possessed the right to nominate a majority of the directors and so controlled the financial policy of the organization.

The Esquimalt and Nanaimo Company was from the first a close corporation. It sold no debentures or bonds, but financed its construction from the Dominion subsidy and from the sums provided by Dunsmuir and his partners. The railway had to depend on its local traffic but for years did not pay. It was not until James Dunsmuir, son of Robert Dunsmuir, his successor as President of the coal company and later also President of the railway, established a ferry between Vancouver and the coal mines at Ladysmith that the railway company's books showed a balance on the right side.[24]

The financial connection with the United States not unnaturally caused comment in British Columbia. It was feared that, for business reasons, Robert Dunsmuir was on the point of advocating annexation to the United States. A violently worded resolution was passed in the provincial Legislature praying the Lieutenant-Governor to suspend him from membership and providing for the appointment of a Select Committee to investigate into the charges made against him by the Hon. T. B. Humphreys.[25] Humphreys

24. Scholefield and Gosnell, *British Columbia*, part II, 118.
25. The text of Humphrey's original resolution indicates the temper of local politics at the time. It reads:
    "February 20, 1888.
    "The Hon. Mr. *Humphreys* moved, seconded by Mr. *Semlin*,—
    "Whereas it is alleged that the Hon. *Robert Dunsmuir*, President of the Executive

failed to appear and the Committee, unable to make an investigation, was discharged. Such evidence as exists exonerates Dunsmuir from the charge of disloyalty. He is reported to have said that, while commercial union with the United States would be of advantage to him primarily, he could not advocate it, fearing the ultimate outcome would be annexation.[26]

Robert Dunsmuir died in 1889 bequeathing his many interests to his sons, Alexander and James. Alexander became President of the railway and Manager of the selling agency for the mines in San Francisco. James took over the coal company, but after Alexander's death in 1900 inherited the family interests *in toto*. In the autumn of 1902 he bought out the four San Francisco share-

Council and Member of the Legislative Assembly, commonly called *Robert Dunsmuir*, owner of coal mines, steamships and President of the Esquimalt and Nanaimo Railway Company, did, at divers times and places, in the presence of credible witnesses, *openly* express his desire to annex Vancouver Island to the United States of America.

"And whereas it hath been alleged that the said *Robert Dunsmuir* did use similar disloyal, open and advised speaking at *Portland, Oregon*, United States of America, and such open, advised, and disloyal speaking was printed and published in the Portland Daily News, 23rd December, 1887, and read as follows:

"'Mr. R. *Dunsmuir* of *Victoria* who came to *Portland* last Friday to attend the railroad celebration, is still in the city. Yesterday his two sons, one from *Wellington*, B.C. and the other from *San Francisco*, came here to confer with him in regard to their coal business in *San Francisco*, and an extension of the *Esquimalt* and Nanaimo Railroad to reach the Dunsmuir's new coal mines, eighty miles beyond *Nanaimo*. Mr. Dunsmuir regrets that the price of coal has been forced up so high in *San Francisco*, and one object of his conference with his sons, who manage that end of the business is to effect a reduction. Besides his coal and railroad and steam and sailing vessels, Mr. *Dunsmuir* owns a large area of timber lands on *Vancouver Island*. The day before he came to *Portland* he sold the timber on 50,000 [*sic*] acres to a Michigan lumberman for $250,000. The magnitude and value of his various enterprises, as well as the ability of their management, places Mr. *Dunsmuir* in the first rank among the business men on this coast. *The only regret we have heard him express respecting his situation is that Vancouver Island is not part of the United States. It would be to his pecuniary advantage if this were the case, for during the first eleven months of this year he paid $210,000 in duties on his coal in San Francisco. But apart from this private consideration, he is rightly of opinion that it would be better for British Columbia if it belonged to the United States of America*, since its natural commercial interests are with this country.'

"And whereas, such open and advised speaking is disloyal to the Queen, a violation of allegiance and oath of office sworn and subscribed by the said *Robert Duns-*

holders, paying them $1,500,000 for their half interest in the railway and the Comox coal mines.[27]

Earlier in this year the Canadian Northern Railway made an attempt to buy up the Esquimalt and Nanaimo Railway. At this time Mackenzie and Mann, the owners of that railway, were negotiating with the government of British Columbia for assistance in building a line to the coast. The route suggested was by way of the Yellowhead Pass, Quesnel, and Bute Inlet. The Esquimalt and Nanaimo Railway would give access to Victoria but it would be necessary to extend it to the north of the island. James Dunsmuir, however, was not prepared to dispose of the railway to Mackenzie and Mann. In 1905 he sold out to the Canadian Pacific for approximately $3,000,000.[28] The last spike of the island railway had been driven near Shawnigan Lake on August 13, 1886, by Sir John A. Macdonald. Nearly thirty years later the Canadian Pacific secured its "island section." But Mackenzie and Mann were still interested in Vancouver Island. In 1910 they bought up the Dunsmuir collieries, the coal rights in the Esquimalt and Nanaimo Railway belt, "and all business in connection therewith" for $11,000,000.

The story of the E. & N., to give it its popular title, is interesting as an example of British Columbian railway history. American financial interests were fully awake early to the advisability of putting capital into the Canadian railroad. In this case, however, financial and executive control remained in Canadian hands.

muir as President of the *Executive Council* and Member of the Legislative Assembly; be it, therefore,

"Resolved, That an humble Address be presented to His Honour the Lieutenant-Governor, praying that His Honour may be pleased to transmit the foregoing Resolution to His Excellency the Governor-General of Canada, humbly entreating His Excellency to nominate and appoint a 'Royal Commission of Inquiry' to take evidence and examine witnesses touching the alleged open and advised speaking of the said *Robert Dunsmuir*" (*Journals of the Legislative Assembly of British Columbia*, 1888, 24 ff. and ci).

26. Letter to J. C. McLagan, *ibid.*, cii.

27. This is the figure mentioned by Dunsmuir in his statement in the Victoria *Daily Colonist* for June 19, 1910. Gosnell (Scholefield and Gosnell, *British Columbia*, part II, 122) states that Dunsmuir paid the Pacific Improvement Company, the name adopted by the "Big Four" in this venture, "$3,000,000 and became sole owner of the railway, land, collieries, shipping fleet, and the business in its entirety."

28. Cf. *C.P.R. Annual Report*, 1905, 7, where the terms are given in full.

The Dunsmuirs were skilful negotiators and James Dunsmuir became the sole owner. Threatened by the competition of another Canadian line, the Canadian Pacific purchased the Esquimalt and Nanaimo, extended and developed it. The rise of motor transport has since seriously affected the island railway, but the through freight conveyed from Vancouver by the Nanaimo car ferry, flying the house flag of the Canadian Pacific, is a daily witness to the wisdom of the purchase of the "island section."

We must next discuss the development of railways in the south-eastern region of British Columbia. The main line of the Canadian Pacific had been located too far to the north to serve the mining district in the Kootenays which for many years remained more accessible from the United States than from Canada.

In no portion of British Columbia has geography so influenced railway development as in the Kootenay. The district has been described as "an isosceles triangle with its base on the 49th parallel (United States boundary) and its summit at the head of the Big Bend."[29] The mountains spread out towards the base of the triangle and the natural means of communication are with the United States. Three distinct regions of the Kootenays are, in the main, shut off from one another by mountain ranges or swift water. The first of these consists of the western portion of the Columbia, flowing south from the "Big Bend" down through the Arrow Lakes to its confluence with the Kootenay at Castlegar. The second is the Kootenay Lake region, a "pocket" with its body in Canada and its mouth opening into the United States, "an inner horseshoe with a crack upon its west side," a trough by which the Kootenay finds its way out to the Columbia. The third section, the eastern valley of the Columbia, is separated from the western valley by the Selkirks and by unnavigable stretches of water, and could only be reached from the Kootenay Lake region by a difficult overland trail. The great mining district of the Kootenays was an integral portion of the "Inland Empire," tributary to Spokane. The railway history of this region was, as we shall see, a struggle between American interests and the Canadian Pacific Railway.

The completion of the Northern Pacific Railway in 1883 first brought the Kootenays in touch with a railway. Up till then all

29. Report on the Kootenay country by Gilbert Malcolm Sproat, in *Sessional Papers of British Columbia*, 1884, 310.

goods had been freighted in by pack train from long distances. One pack route was from Missoula, Montana, through Tobacco Plains and up the east of the Kootenay River to Wild Horse Creek. Another, and more favoured, route was from Walla Walla to Sand Point on Lake Pend d'Oreille in Idaho, and thence up the Moyie Valley to either Joseph's Prairie or Wild Horse Creek. The coming of the Northern Pacific to Sand Point made this route still more attractive.

Gilbert Malcolm Sproat on behalf of the government of British Columbia visited Kootenay and prepared a report on conditions there. He appreciated the necessity for opening up communication with the Canadian Pacific Railway and noted the effects of the coming of the Northern Pacific.

Nothing is more needful now, to the development of Kootenay, than suitable means of communication down the whole eastern valley from the Canadian Pacific Railway to the boundary at the 49th parallel. . . . The approach of the Northern Pacific Railway to the district has somewhat tended to cheaper transport, but the Canadian Pacific Railway will make the most important change in this respect and in the direction of trade. The district will be mainly supplied direct from the east. Our seaboard cities will have to make a considerable effort to secure a share of the Kootenay trade.[30]

Sproat was a true prophet when he wrote that the British Columbia coast cities would have to make an effort to obtain a portion of the trade of the Kootenays and that the district would be mainly supplied direct from the east. He was wrong when he thought that the Canadian Pacific Railway would get any large share of the Kootenay trade. The competition of the American lines and especially of the Great Northern was too severe.[31]

30. *Ibid.*

31. How severe it was in the middle and late 1890's may be gathered from the following extract from the Boundary Creek *Times* of February 27, 1897:

"That the C.P.R. is anxious to secure the Boundary Creek trade is, of course, obvious. It is just as clear that unless a branch line is built from Penticton to Boundary, the bulk of the freight consigned to local storekeepers will be shipped via Marcus, over the American roads. The people of Boundary are patriotic Canadians only as far as they can afford to be; and if they find that American transportation is cheaper than Canadian, they will invariably choose the former, despite sentiment."

And from the same paper on February 13, 1897:

"Mr. G. G. Dixon, general agent for the Great Northern R.R., with headquarters

There was an important difference in policy between the Great Northern and the Canadian Pacific. James J. Hill had made it his policy to build "feeders" north from his main line toward the international boundary. A glance at any Great Northern map will show this. All across the prairies and into the mountains these tentacles spread north or northwest. In a few places they cross the border into Canada. In southern British Columbia they reach Fernie, Nelson, Grand Forks, Midway, and Princeton. All these British Columbia "feeders" join the main line of the Great Northern and "drain" towards Spokane.

The branch lines of the Canadian Pacific in southern British Columbia may now be divided into two classes, those which by rail, lake, and river connect up with the main line to the north, and those which now form part of the southern route from Medicine Hat by way of Crowsnest Pass, Fernie, Cranbrook, Kootenay Landing, Nelson, Grand Forks, Midway, Penticton, Princeton, and Hope to the main line to Vancouver. The few remaining lines in southern British Columbia are now tributary to the Crowsnest-Kettle Valley route. The historical importance consists in the fact that the American roads were first in the field. The Canadian Pacific bought up several of the more important of these roads and connected them with the Crowsnest and finally by the Kettle Valley route through the Coquihalla Pass provided a direct route to the coast. But this did not become an all-rail route until well on into the third decade of the twentieth century.

at Spokane, visited the district this last week and was interviewed by a representative of the Times

"'Yes,' he said, 'I believe you will have two railroads this year. From what I can learn the Spokane and Northern will be extended from Northport, and very probably Mr. Heinze will build his line.'

"'That would mean that all the freight for this district would be shipped over American roads, would it not—unless of course a section of the proposed road connecting Boundary with Vancouver is built at the same time from Penticton?'— 'Yes, undoubtedly; goods would not be shipped over the C.P.R. and transferred to wagons, when they could be brought the entire distance by rail. Even now, I imagine, we have the lion's share of the transportation business of this district.'

"'And why is that? Are not the rates uniform over the competing roads?'—'Our service is faster, as we have fewer transfers to make. Our line of steamboats carry goods in bond from Victoria to Seattle and thence they are shipped direct to Marcus. Whereas the C.P.R. are obliged to transfer at Vancouver, Okanagan Landing, and Penticton. With Grand Forks in particular we do a good business.'"

It will now be necessary to trace in greater detail the history of some of these competing roads in southern British Columbia, especially in the Kootenay and boundary countries. They are the Columbia and Kootenay, the Columbia and Western, British Columbia Southern, Vancouver, Victoria and Eastern Navigation and Railway Company, and the Nelson and Fort Sheppard Railway.

The Columbia and Kootenay Railway and Transportation Company was incorporated by an Act of the Legislature of British Columbia in 1883. Section 10 of the act provided: "The company shall lay out, construct, acquire, build, equip, maintain, and work a continuous line of Railway from the outlet of Kootenay Lake through the Selkirk range of mountains to a point on the Columbia River as near as practicable to the junction of the Kootenay with the Columbia River in British Columbia; and such Railway shall be built either upon the broad or narrow gauge and be known as the Columbia and Kootenay Railway."[32] The company was also empowered "to acquire, build, equip, maintain and navigate a line of steamers suitable for passenger and freight traffic" upon the Columbia River. The act provided that the government of British Columbia should set apart and reserve tracts of land six miles wide along the proposed railway line and also on Kootenay River or Lake, commencing fifteen miles from the international boundary.[33]

This act of the Legislature was disallowed by the federal government. The reason advanced was that the citizens of Victoria, at a public meeting held on April 28, 1883, had protested against the passage of the bill on the grounds that it would give the company the control of the trade of the most valuable portions of the province, that it was unfair to the Canadian Pacific Railway, that it would establish a "mischievous monopoly," and above all, that it would "convey to three Americans 750,000 acres of the best land in the Province free of taxes."[34] It is interesting in this connection that the "monopoly clause" of the charter of the Canadian Pacific

32. *Statutes of British Columbia*, 1883, p. 97.

33. In 1884 the distance from the international boundary was changed to twenty-one miles (*ibid.*, 1884, c. 24).

34. *Sessional Papers of British Columbia*, 1884, Papers relating to the disallowance of certain acts of the Legislature of British Columbia.

Railway was not invoked in this case as it had been in Manitoba. The appeal was to national sentiment and took the form of an attack upon an alleged American monopoly.

But the Columbia and Kootenay did not give up. The company kept on petitioning the Legislature and acts of incorporation were duly passed. Up to 1888 the American interests were still predominant. Then came a transition year in which three Vancouver residents petitioned, quite possibly for the Americans. In 1890 the petitioners were headed by Harry Abbott of the Canadian Pacific Railway. On August 22, 1890, the Canadian Pacific Railway secured control of the Columbia and Kootenay by a 999 years' lease. A railway line, twenty-six miles long, was built from Nelson to Robson, connecting Kootenay Lake with the Columbia River and Arrow Lakes. Six years later the directors of the Canadian Pacific Railway purchased the property of the Columbia and Kootenay Navigation Company for $280,000, thus obtaining full control of this river and lake traffic.[35] When the act of 1890 came up for review in Ottawa, the Minister of Justice, Sir John S. D. Thompson, reported in favour of the company on the ground that its objects were not provincial but international. He cited the fact that the Parliament of Canada at its previous session had declared the railway was a "work for the general advantage of Canada."[36]

The Columbia and Western Railway is a conspicuous example of a railway projected by a financier who was unable, or unwilling, to invest his own capital in the project, but hoped by means of the security, which a land grant and subsidy would ensure, to attract others to invest their money in a scheme which would bring him large returns. Frederick Augustus Heinze was born in Brooklyn, December 5, 1869. His father was German, apparently of mixed Lutheran and Jewish descent, and his mother a Connecticut Yankee with a strain of Irish blood. He was educated at the Brooklyn Polytechnic Institute, the Columbia School of Mines, and in Germany. At the age of twenty, he went to Butte, Montana, where he made his fortune in copper. In 1895 he bought the Minnie Healy mine, the richest copper vein in Butte, and decided to

35. *C.P.R. Annual Report*, 1896, 9.

36. *Sessional Papers of British Columbia*, 1891, Papers relating to acts passed by the Legislature of the Province of British Columbia, Session 1890. The federal act cited is 53 Vict., c. 87.

invade the Kootenay region. He secured a contract to treat 75,000 tons of ore from Red Mountain and to do so built the first smelter at Trail which he connected with the mines by a narrow-gauge railway. From this small enterprise has sprung the Consolidated Mining and Smelting Company in which the Canadian Pacific Railway is now heavily interested. The City of Trail also dates from this venture of Heinze.

Heinze wished to open up communication to the west of the Columbia and also in the Rossland-Trail district. The great days of Rossland were beginning and the boundary country was beginning to attract attention. There was a golden opportunity for the railway promoter and Heinze seized it. He visited Victoria, where his dinner parties at the Driard Hotel attracted attention, and there made valuable political allies. Lieutenant-Governor Edgar Dewdney became one of the directors of the Columbia and Western Railway. Heinze hoped to be able to interest British capital in his project, but his mission to London was unsuccessful. In the spring of 1897 he mortgaged property owned by his brother and himself in Butte, Montana, for $1,500,000. This led to a report in the Spokane papers that the road from Robson to Midway would be built as soon as the weather became settled.[37]

But the subsidy-hunting Heinze was in no hurry to build the road. It was quite possible that he might be able to obtain grants from both Victoria and Ottawa. There was, unfortunately for Heinze, a competitor to the Columbia and Western in the field. This was the Vancouver, Victoria and Eastern Navigation and Railway Company, commonly known as the V.V. & E. The promoters of this scheme attempted to secure its incorporation by federal statute, but the brief session of 1896 came to an end before the necessary legislation was passed. Norman McLean, one of the promoters, visited Ottawa but to no avail. At first there was opposition in Victoria to the V.V. & E. Dr. Milne of that city objected to the charter on the grounds that it would interfere with the Burrard Inlet and Fraser Valley Railway scheme, another project of the period. But Dr. Milne became heavily interested in the V.V. & E. and brought pressure to bear at Ottawa on its behalf. The V. V. & E. was backed by British capital. Heinze was

37. Boundary Creek *Times*, March 27, 1897, quoting the Spokane *Chronicle*.

also in Ottawa at this time seeking aid for his Columbia and Western.

The federal Minister of Railways, A. G. Blair, was prepared to grant the usual bonus of $3,200 a mile, and was reported to favour the doubling of this subsidy for the building of certain portions of the line where the engineering difficulties were exceptionally great. The Canadian Pacific Railway was naturally interested in the proposed lines, but for the time being did not declare its policy. Reports were circulated in the boundary country that William Mackenzie and Donald Mann of Toronto, the "fathers" of the Canadian Northern Railway were becoming interested in the Vancouver, Victoria and Eastern.

The Columbia and Western in 1897 built a line from Trail to Rossland, twelve miles, and from Trail to Robson where connections were made with the Columbia and Kootenay. The Rossland *Miner* in its issue for September 23, 1897, commented favourably on the new road as follows: "During its short existence the Columbia and Western has manifested remarkable enterprise. Without it Rossland would have been at the complete mercy of that great philanthropist and promoter of Canadian industries [?] Mr. D. C. Corbin." The last spike of the Trail-Robson line was driven on September 27, 1897.

In 1898 the Columbia and Western was formally leased by the Canadian Pacific Railway. Construction of the line from Robson to Midway in the boundary country commenced at once. The charter of the Columbia and Western empowered the company to build a line from Midway to Penticton, where access was available to the C.P.R. steamers on Okanagan Lake and by the Shuswap and Okanagan, a leased line of the Canadian Pacific, to the main line at Sicamous Junction. But this section was not built by the Columbia and Western. The Kettle Valley Railway, incorporated in 1901, began construction from Midway to Princeton in 1910. The line was completed in 1912 and leased to the Canadian Pacific Railway in 1913. Extension to the coast was rendered difficult by the fact that the Vancouver, Victoria and Eastern Railway and Navigation Company possessed the charter to build from Hope to Princeton. These rights had been acquired by the Great Northern Railway. The Great Northern, however, was not anxious to build this section and at length a compromise was arrived at whereby both Canadian Pacific and Great Northern obtained running rights over the section from Princeton to Brookmere (now Brodie), a distance of about thirty-eight miles. The Canadian Pacific then built two connecting links, one from Brookmere to Merritt, thirty miles, completed by 1915, the other from Brookmere to Hope and across the Fraser to Petain (Odlum) on the main line. This last link of the Canadian Pacific with the Kootenays was complete in 1916. But by that time the great days of the Kootenay were past.

The British Columbia Southern was another railway which eventually became part of the Canadian Pacific system. This line now forms that portion of the Crowsnest route from the Great Divide in Crowsnest Pass to Kootenay Landing. The original name of the line was the Crow's Nest and Kootenay Lake Railway Company and as such it was incorporated by the Legislature of British Columbia in 1888. Its promoters were residents of Wolf Creek in the Kootenay district. In 1891 the company was rein-corporated as the British Columbia Southern. D. C. Corbin of the Spokane Falls and Northern Railway had become interested in a possible railway from Crowsnest to the coast, and there was some talk in 1890 of his acquiring the Crow's Nest and Kootenay. The provincial government favoured Corbin's project but nothing came of it.[38]

In the middle 1890's the competition of the American roads became so severe that the Canadian Pacific Railway decided to strengthen its hold on the Kootenay country. The rich deposits of the Slocan were being opened up and both the Canadian Pacific and the Great Northern constructed lines to connect with the lake and river routes. The former built the Nakusp and Slocan between 1893 and 1895 to draw the trade to the Columbia River. The Kaslo and Slocan, the feeder of the Great Northern, completed in 1895, was designed to take the ore out by Kootenay Lake. The Columbia and Kootenay built a branch line from Slocan Junction to Slocan City. This provided the Canadian Pacific with another entrance to the Slocan.

In the *Annual Report* of the Canadian Pacific Railway for 1896, Sir William Van Horne thus expressed his opinion as to the necessity for a more energetic policy in the Kootenays:

38. The correspondence on this subject is to be found in *Sessional Papers of British Columbia*, 1890, 395-9.

The Company has been at a great disadvantage in reaching the traffic of the mining districts of Southern British Columbia in having to depend upon steamboat connections controlled by other parties. The rapid growth of the traffic, the high rates exacted, and the inadequate service performed, led your Directors recently to negotiate for the purchase of the entire property of the Columbia and Kootenay Navigation Company, consisting of seven steamboats, ten barges, mechanical shops, office buildings, warehouses, etc., and to put under contract for immediate construction three additional steamers for service on the Arrow and Slocan Lakes. You will be asked to approve the expenditure of $280,000 for the boats purchased and under contract, and for a tug-boat and barges that will probably be required.

In the event of the establishment of direct rail connections with the mining districts, both from the east and the west, this steamboat property will still have ample occupation, for the extraordinary system of navigable waters in Southern British Columbia will afford for many years to come the most feasible means of connection with many of the most important mining sections.

But even with these important additions to its facilities for handling the traffic of the mining districts, your Company will continue at a disadvantage in competing with the American lines (which have already reached Nelson, Rossland, and other important centres in these districts) until it shall have direct railway connections of its own. Until then the greater part of the mining traffic will be beyond its reach, and will continue to be, as at present, carried by the American lines southward.

Your Directors are strongly of the opinion that any delay in securing your interests in that direction will be extremely dangerous,—that unless your Company occupies the ground others will, the demand for shipping and travelling facilities being most urgent. The Directors feel that they cannot too strongly urge the immediate construction of a line from Lethbridge to a connection with your Columbia and Kootenay Railway at Nelson, a distance of 325 miles, and anticipating your approval they have already taken steps towards commencement of the work on the opening of spring.[39]

The Canadian Pacific bought the line from Dunmore Junction to Lethbridge from the Alberta Railway and Irrigation Company in 1897 and at once commenced the construction of the line from Lethbridge to Crowsnest Pass. They leased the British Columbia Southern in 1898. The line from Crowsnest to Kootenay Landing was built during 1897 and 1898. The whole line was open for traffic

39. *C.P.R. Annual Report*, 1896, 9-10.

in 1898. The great Canadian railway company had at length obtained direct access to the Kootenays from the east. The water gap between Kootenay Landing and Nelson was finally closed in 1932.

The American railway builders in the meantime had not been idle. James J. Hill was busily engaged in extending the St. Paul, Minneapolis and Manitoba to the Pacific Coast. The Great Northern Railway was organized in 1889 and on January 31, 1890, it took over the St. Paul, Minneapolis and Manitoba on a 999 year lease. Active work on the Pacific extension commenced in 1890 and the last spike was in place by January 5, 1893.

The first branch of the Great Northern in British Columbia was the New Westminster Southern. This line was originally incorporated in 1883 by a syndicate headed by the Hon. Hugh Nelson, but nothing definite was accomplished. In 1887 after James J. Hill had become interested in the project a start was made. The road was constructed between 1888 and 1891 from New Westminster to the international boundary at Blaine. There it joined the line of the Fairhaven and Southern Railroad.

In the Kootenays the Nelson and Fort Sheppard linked up in a similar way with the Spokane and Northern at Northport. The Nelson and Fort Sheppard was incorporated in 1891 and when finally built in 1895 afforded direct access to Nelson from Spokane. Its promoters were all residents of British Columbia.

The Spokane Falls and Northern, now a part of the Great Northern Railway, was the work of Daniel Chase Corbin of Spokane. Corbin was one of the builders of the "Inland Empire" and his influence extended into the Kootenay and boundary countries. Born at Newport, New Hampshire, in 1832, he had surveyed lands in Iowa and Nebraska, operated waggon trains from the Missouri via Denver to Salt Lake City in the early 1860's, engaged in a banking business in Helena, Montana, and had been between 1876 and 1882 associated with his brother Austin Corbin in the financing and management of the Manhattan Beach Railway. When the Northern Pacific Railway was approaching completion in 1883 Corbin came west again, this time to the Coeur d'Alène country. He constructed a concentrating plant and then organized the Coeur d'Alène Railroad and Navigation Company, operating steamers on Lake Coeur d'Alène and constructing a railway connecting the mining camp with the head of navigation. The railway was completed in 1887 and Corbin sold it to the Northern Pacific a year later. In 1889 he moved to Spokane. "He grasped the importance of the site as a strategic center for the transportation and distributing developments, based on the great agricultural, mineral, and timber resources of the Inland Empire."[40] In that year he began the construction of the Spokane Falls and Northern Railway through Colville to Northport on the Columbia River. In order to secure access to the important mining camp of Rossland, Corbin in 1897 built the Red Mountain Railway, a branch of the Spokane Falls and Northern, from Northport to Rossland. In 1899 he sold out to the Great Northern.

During the early years of the twentieth century, the Great Northern continued to drain the Kootenay and boundary countries. Its branch lines north from Spokane tapped the best portions of these regions. Spokane was the natural centre of the whole "Inland Empire," on both sides of the international boundary. The British Columbia coast cities could not hope to compete, and even after the completion of the Crowsnest line the pull was still to the south. Winnipeg was too far away and Calgary was herself being drawn into the Spokane orbit. A good example of the activities of the Great Northern may be found in its extension in 1905 to Grand Forks, British Columbia. The Granby Company commenced operating its smelter at Grand Forks in August, 1900. Ore had to be brought thirty miles from the mine to the smelter. The Canadian Pacific had a monopoly of this hauling and charged the Granby Company one dollar a ton. When the Great Northern came in it was ready to cut the price to twenty-five cents a ton. After some negotiation between the three companies the price was fixed at twenty-five cents a ton, the Great Northern to get two-thirds of the business and the Canadian Pacific one-third. This ratio was adopted for all ore shipments by the Granby Company whether to the smelter or not. It so happened that the Granby Company, the Nichols Copper Company, the chief purchaser of the Granby products, and the Great Northern Railway had interlocking directorates. The Great Northern also controlled the Crows Nest Coal

40. *Dictionary of American Biography*, IV, 437.

Company which provided the smelter with coke. Thus all coke was hauled to Grand Forks by the Great Northern.[41]

For a time it seemed probable that the Great Northern might build through to the coast on Canadian territory. This would have been a rather doubtful policy on the part of James J. Hill, but colour was given to the rumour by the taking up by the Great Northern of the old charter rights of the Vancouver, Victoria and Eastern Railway and Navigation Company. But as we have already seen the Great Northern did not avail itself of this opportunity. The line from Oreville to Princeton gave her sufficient access to the Similkameen.

In the *Canadian Magazine* for 1907 there is to be found an interesting article entitled "Greenwood, B.C., An Eldorado" from which the following sentences regarding the plans of James J. Hill are taken:

James J. Hill today has many miles of his own railroad in British Columbia, running daily trains from Spokane and Northport to Rossland, and from Portland, Tacoma and Seattle to Vancouver, where a few weeks ago he acquired an extensive site on Burrard Inlet. . . . Upon this site, which almost adjoins that of the C.P.R., Great Northern steel will in a few months, meet Great Northern keel in an extensive terminal and wharf.

In Vancouver this is regarded as the first important step towards an alliance with the G.T.P. in Hill's onward march from Oregon and Washington to Uncle Sam's Alaska. But the C.P.R. is closely watching every movement of its rival, and in addition to running daily trains to Seattle in alliance with the Northern Pacific is extending its lines in British Columbia north and south.

The reference to Great Northern steel meeting Great Northern keel recalls the venture entered into by James J. Hill in 1900 when he formed the Great Northern Steamship Company to engage in trans-Pacific trade. The *Minnesota* was launched in 1903 and the *Dakota* the following year. But American shipping regulations at that time militated against the growth of the line and James J. Hill sought other fields. Possibly he may at one time have considered an alliance with the Grand Trunk Pacific (the G.T.P. referred to above), but he never threatened seriously the supremacy of the Canadian Pacific on Vancouver's waterfront.

41. The late Mr. W. B. Bishop of Vancouver, former Superintendent of the Granby Company's smelter at Grand Forks, contributed this information.

In the second and third decades of this century the Great Northern began to abandon some of its less paying lines in British Columbia. The mines in the boundary country were playing out and the Kootenays, including the Slocan, were not as rich as they used to be. The Kaslo-Slocan line, the Victoria-Sidney line on Vancouver Island, and the Red Mountain Railway all ceased operation. They were no longer profitable to the Great Northern.

Not all of the branches of the Canadian Pacific Railway in British Columbia have yet been mentioned, e.g. the Revelstoke-Arrowhead branch, opened in 1896 to replace the steamers of the Columbia and Kootenay Navigation Company on the Columbia River. This branch gave access to the Arrow Lakes from the main line at Revelstoke. It was a parallel to the earlier Shuswap and Okanagan, built in 1892 and leased by the Canadian Pacific Railway, by which communication was opened with Vernon and Lake Okanagan. The Canadian Pacific did its best to draw traffic to its main line. In the end it was left in practical possession of most of southern British Columbia. But it never could undo the hard facts of geography.

In spite of the efforts of the Canadian Pacific Railway the trade of the Kootenays and the boundary country remained in American hands until after the turn of the century. The American and not the Canadian lines received most of the business of the miners and merchants. Supplies from Spokane were fresher and cheaper than those from more distant Canadian cities. Ores were usually shipped to American smelters, until smelters were erected on the Canadian side, often by American capital. It was not until the Trail smelter which, since its purchase from Heinze, had been in the possession of the Canadian Pacific Railway, passed under the control of the Consolidated Mining and Smelting Company of Canada in 1906 that Canadian capital began to become dominant in Kootenay. The movement from American to British capital commenced in the late 1890's but as late as 1896 the trade was 90 per cent American. In November of that year the Nelson *Miner* bitterly complained: "While Canada dilly-dallies about providing a main line of the Canadian Pacific through the Crows's Nest Pass into the Kootenay, Americans own and operate at great profit, three railways." Such was the railway situation in southern British Columbia in the palmy days of the Kootenay mines. The period of bitter rivalry between

Canadian and United States railways in that region lasted from 1898 to 1906. Subsequently agreements were made between them fixing the proportion of the shipments of ore and bullion to go by each line.

The railway development of southern British Columbia has been dealt with in some detail because of the close inter-relation of United States and Canadian interests. For the sake of completeness this chapter must include a brief account of railway development in central British Columbia. It came early in the twentieth century as a result of the rapid settlement of the Canadian prairies. The facilities of the Canadian Pacific Railway and of the lines constructed by Mackenzie and Mann, known as the Canadian Northern Railway, were inadequate to handle the traffic. In 1902 both the Grand Trunk and the Canadian Northern Railways applied to the Dominion for assistance in building transcontinental lines. In a spirit of optimism the Dominion acceded to both requests, and did not even persist in the attempt to induce them to plan lines so as to avoid wasteful duplication.

The negotiations with the Grand Trunk interests resulted in four acts.[42] These provided for a railway, the National Transcontinental, to be built from Winnipeg to Moncton by the Canadian government and leased to the Grand Trunk for fifty years, and for a railway to be built by the Grand Trunk Pacific Railway from Winnipeg to the Pacific Coast, at Port Simpson or some other port. The Grand Trunk hoped that by opening up a route to the Pacific two hundred miles shorter than those of competing lines it might be in a position to secure a good share of the Oriental trade; and the colonization of central British Columbia was also an objective.

The Rockies were to be crossed by the Yellowhead Pass leading to the head-waters of the Fraser River. From Prince George, where the Fraser River turns southwards, the railway was to follow its tributaries, the Nechako and Endako Rivers northwest to Decker Lake where the Bulkley Mountains can be crossed by a short pass to the head-waters of the Bulkley River. This river flows northwest to the Skeena which flows southwest through the Coast Range to

42. *Statutes of Canada*, 1903, c. 71 and c. 122; 1904, c. 24 and c. 80. For a more detailed account see J. A. Lower, "The Construction of the Grand Trunk Pacific Railway in British Columbia," *British Columbia Historical Quarterly*, IV, 163.

the Pacific Ocean.[43] This route had the advantage of passing through land suitable for colonization. Construction of the so-called "mountain section" of 840 miles, 710 of which were in British Columbia, was completed on April 5, 1914. Kaien Island was chosen as the coast terminal which, as the result of a competition, was named Prince Rupert. The 180 miles from Hazelton to Prince Rupert was both difficult and costly to construct. The Skeena River drops a thousand feet in 120 miles. The last 60 miles are tidal and the railway for this distance is cut through almost solid rock. The regular passenger service did not begin until after the outbreak of the Great War.

The Grand Trunk Pacific Branch Lines Company, incorporated in 1906, chartered two lines in British Columbia, which it did not ultimately construct. One of these would have connected the main line with Dawson, in the Yukon. The other would have provided a route to Vancouver. This latter line was begun by the Pacific Great Eastern Railway, chartered by the government of British Columbia in 1912. The securities of the company were guaranteed by the provincial government up to $35,000 (and later $42,000) per mile. The government had to take over construction itself in 1918 and the railway was never completed. Work was abandoned in 1918 when the line extended 348 miles from Squamish at the head of Howe Sound to Quesnel, 80 miles south of Prince George.[44] The original company had an agreement with the Grand Trunk Pacific that traffic for Vancouver should be routed by its line. When the Dominion was compelled to take over both the Grand Trunk Pacific and the Canadian Northern this expectation became valueless as traffic was routed by the latter line. The Pacific Great Eastern, in which the provincial government estimates that it has invested $78 million, has thus become a serious burden to the taxpayers.[45]

The Canadian Northern Railway was a venture of the celebrated railway promoters, Mackenzie and Mann, whose abortive negotia-

43. Lower, "Construction of the Grand Trunk."

44. *Ibid.* For a detailed account of the Pacific Great Eastern Railway, see R. E. M. Yerburgh, "The Pacific Great Eastern Railway" (1928), and Netta Harvey, "History and Finances of the Pacific Great Eastern Railway" (1935), MSS in University of British Columbia Library.

45. See *infra*, 384.

tions with the government of British Columbia for a railway which would have crossed the straits to Vancouver Island have already been mentioned. In their varied careers they had built many railways and projected many more. At one time they had concluded arrangements with Sir Clifford Sifton for the construction of a line from the Stikine to Teslin Lake, which with the help of river steamers would have given access to Dawson by an all-Canadian route. But the bill to incorporate this railway was never enacted, for opposition developed when it was found that government assistance was to take the form of 3,750,000 acres of mineral land in the Klondike—more than four times the area which had been prospected at Dawson.[46] It was a sign of a changing outlook that the assistance given for the transcontinental project took the form of bond guarantees by the Dominion[47] and by the western provinces. There was no substantial equity investment. The British Columbia portion of the line, at first known as the Canadian Northern Pacific Railway, crossed the Rocky Mountains by the Yellowhead Pass. It then followed the Fraser River to New Westminster and Vancouver. It was opened for traffic from coast to coast in 1915.

During the Great War no small part of the Canadian financial problem was concerned with the two new transcontinental railways. Their only economic justification could have been the continuation of the period of prosperity and rapid colonization, which might have built up the unproductive territory through which they passed. With the war construction costs rose and the railways were quite unable to borrow abroad. The Railroad Inquiry Commission of 1916 recommended that the government should take over the railways and assume their liabilities. This it did to the great relief of the provinces which would have faced serious liabilities as guarantors had the railways gone into bankruptcy. With the financial problems of the Canadian National Railway system we are not concerned here. We have, however, endeavoured to explain how British Columbia came to be crossed by three transcontinental railways and how the province came to invest in a peculiarly expensive railway venture of its own.

46. A railway from| Skagway, Alaska, to White Horse, Y.T., was ultimately built by other interests. It will be described in the chapter on the Klondike.

47. *Statutes of Canada*, 1911-12, c. 6.

From what has been said in this chapter it will be clear that the railway map of British Columbia can be explained historically but cannot be justified as evidence of money spent so as to produce the best results in transportation. The map is the resultant of a curious interplay of forces of which the political ambitions of nation-builders and the profit-motive of investors have been the chief. But both political and business motives have been effective at various levels. The boom conditions which result from vigorous railway construction financed by capital raised outside the province have often been the aim of those able to influence political decisions, and shippers have often pressed for facilities without consideration for the eventual fortunes of the railways. Expensive as the result has been it is only in respect of the Pacific Great Eastern Railway that any heavy burden has fallen on British Columbia taxpayers as such. And one of the results of the federal system of government has been that probably no one in public life has felt any great personal responsibility for the wastage that has occurred.

CHAPTER XI

THE AMERICAN MINING ADVANCE INTO SOUTHERN BRITISH COLUMBIA

1864-1910

IN a sense the history of mining on the Pacific Coast began not in California but in the Spanish mining ventures in Mexico and Peru. The silver mines of Zacatecas and Durango were early counterparts of later mining advances in western North America. For centuries the Spaniards were seeking *Otero Mexico, Otero Peru.* But it was the discovery of gold by Marshall at Sutter's Mill in 1848 and the world-renowned gold rush of 1849 which first directed general attention to the mineral wealth of the Pacific slope.

From California the search for gold spread north to British Columbia. In an earlier chapter we have seen the important part which the gold rush on the Fraser River in 1858 played in the development of the Colony of British Columbia. In later chapters we shall have to describe the rushes further north: to the golden Cariboo in the early sixties; to Omineca, the Stikine, Cassiar, and finally to the Klondike and Atlin, along the "Trail of '98."

While the earlier of these developments were taking place, the mountainous regions from California to Colorado were being prospected and mined. The mining movement in the Kootenays and the boundary country in British Columbia was based on the development of the "Inland Empire" of Montana and Idaho. William J. Trimble in his *Mining Advance into the Inland Empire* has called attention to the eastward moving frontier, the mining frontier which spread from California eastward and northward over the western states and into British Columbia: "American population, which had advanced westward up to 1840 in comparatively gradual and connected movements, in the decade 1840-1850 leaped to the Willamette and the Sacramento; now it was recoiling eastward and in this recoil was meeting the old frontier, which was still advancing westward. In this beginning of the fusion of frontiers there was an interesting commingling of men reared in the East and men habituated to Californian ideas and usages."[1] This mining advance was, as Trimble has shown, based on a single industry. "Whether north or south of the Line, in British Columbia, Idaho or Montana, men talked of mines, struggled for mines, and founded their laws and industries on mines. Other forms of industry were subsidiary to mining."[2]

In what sense, then, was mining in southern British Columbia a northward thrust of the "Inland Empire"? The vast majority of the prospectors and miners came from the United States. This was true in the case of the early gold rushes and nowhere more evident than in the Wild Horse and Big Bend excitements of the 1860's. The whole mining movement in the Kootenays and the boundary country during the last two decades of the nineteenth and the first decade of the twentieth century originated south of the international boundary and came north as claim after claim was staked. Practically all of the early capital was American, although British and Canadian capital came in during the later nineties. The discussion of railway problems in the preceding chapter showed that the natural lines of communication in the Kootenay and boundary mining districts were from the south and that the isolation of these districts from the British Columbian coast cities was permanent. Vancouver was never really alive to the needs of southeastern British Columbia. Victoria, although perhaps kept more aware of conditions in these out-lying regions by the periodic meetings of the Legislature and the annual publication of the report of the Minister of Mines, never displayed more than a languid interest.

Spokane, the capital of the "Inland Empire," was the natural metropolis of the Kootenays and the boundary country. Nelson, Rossland, Trail, New Denver, Slocan City, Sandon, Kaslo, Grand Forks, Phoenix, Greenwood, Princeton, Cranbrook, and Fernie were all tributary to Spokane. None of these mining towns ever grew to a sufficient size to dream of rivalling the big American city. One has merely to walk the main streets of Spokane or to gaze at the rather garish glories of the Davenport Hotel to realize what the "Inland Empire" has meant to that city. To be sure Spokane

1. W. J. Trimble, *The Mining Advance into the Inland Empire* (Madison, 1914), 11. Trimble gives a detailed account of the early mines in Idaho, Montana, Eastern Washington, and Oregon.

2. *Ibid.*, 11-12.

has never been entirely dependent upon mining, but many of the big buildings in Spokane date from the days of the mining boom, and her greatest periods of growth coincided to a remarkable degree with the highest points of production in the Coeur d'Alène, Kootenay, and boundary camps.

The movement across the international boundary between 1864 and 1866 was part of the northward movement of placer mining which began with the gold rush to Fraser River in 1858. It was almost entirely American and, as it links up closely with mining development in Idaho, Montana, and Washington, it may be considered part of the northward thrust of the "Inland Empire."

The centre of the 1864 rush was Wild Horse Creek which flows into the Kootenay River about fifty miles north of the international boundary. In the autumn of 1863 James Manning from Colville, Washington Territory, had brought out gold which he had received from a Kootenay Indian. The next spring Manning took a party to Wild Horse Creek. News of the new diggings spread fast and by June there were approximately five hundred miners in the vicinity. A boom town, Fisherville, soon made its appearance on Wild Horse Creek, a typical mining camp containing three restaurants, a brewery, several saloons with their usual appendages, and some stores. The inhabitants of Colville were sufficiently interested to construct a trail through to the new gold field, practically all of it through British territory.

The mines extended about four and a half miles along Wild Horse Creek. They were shallow diggings, gold being found from four to ten feet beneath the surface on the bed rock, which was a blue slate, soft and easily worked. Five hundred claims were staked and the total population of Wild Horse at the height of the boom was about a thousand. The largest nugget found on the creek weighed 37 ounces and was valued at $666. It was the largest yet found in the colony.

Governor Seymour of British Columbia first read of the new discoveries of gold in an American newspaper. When news of Wild Horse reached New Westminster, J. C. Haynes was appointed Gold Commissioner for the Kootenay mines, but on reaching the mines he found that the miners had already organized and had issued a code of mining laws. Haynes had, however, no difficulty in enforcing his authority. The Provincial Secretary, Arthur N.

Birch, a young Englishman of good family, was so much impressed by Haynes's reports that he determined to visit Kootenay. He found Haynes guarding some 75 pounds of gold, valued in the neighbourhood of $15,000, which, through lack of any safer receptacle, he had placed in an old portmanteau. Haynes did not winter in Kootenay and in the spring of 1865 Peter O'Reilly, who had been previously stationed in Cariboo, was sent to Wild Horse to look after the "wild boys." O'Reilly did well in Kootenay, but by the time he reached Wild Horse the rush was over and the "boys" were off to Big Bend.

The colonial government made attempts to open up communication with Kootenay. Edgar Dewdney constructed an additional portion of the trail which he had built from Hope to the Similkameen. F. J. Barnard in 1865 sent in an express to Big Bend and R. T. Smith and W. H. Ladner took in the first cargo of colonial goods. There was more chance for colonial competition in Big Bend than there could ever be at Wild Horse. Wild Horse was too close to the border and the Dewdney Trail was impracticable. But a real attempt was made to capture the trade of Big Bend from the Americans. Judge Howay has reproduced a dodger published in Victoria by the Board of Trade which sets forth the advantages of travelling via Victoria, Yale, Kamloops, over the new government trail to the Columbia River and by boat to Gold Creek, Big Bend.[3]

Both Wild Horse and Big Bend were typical placer camps—a sudden rush, good returns for the moment, and then rapid decline. Wild Horse depopulated the Boise mines in Idaho and Big Bend depopulated Wild Horse. Of the two Big Bend was the more disappointing. By September, 1866, the exodus had become general and Big Bend was denounced as the "Big Bilk." Mining continued on Wild Horse, a few patient miners, mainly Chinese, kept working over the old claims, but the first Kootenay rush was over.

The importance of this rush is that it was American, through and through, except for the administration of justice and the gold export tax. This unpopular tax the American miners steadily evaded. Even Peter O'Reilly thought that the tax was unwise and

3. E. O. S. Scholefield and F. W. Howay, *British Columbia from the Earliest Times to the Present* (Vancouver, 1914), II, facing 239.

ought to be repealed. The attempts of the colonial government and the coast merchants to obtain access to the Kootenay diggings only bring into higher relief the inexorability of the geographic factor.

During the 1870's Kootenay was peacefully slumbering. Some placer mining continued but few new discoveries were made and the population dwindled. According to the figures given in the *Sessional Papers of British Columbia* in 1874 there were 35 voters in all of Kootenay. In 1877 the number had risen to 47. The next year it had declined to 29, but in 1879 there was a slight recovery, the number of voters being 33. None the less Kootenay still had representation in the provincial Legislature! In January, 1873, however, A. W. Vowell was relieved of his position as stipendiary magistrate in Kootenay, the government of British Columbia having decided to curtail expenses by abolishing the office.

In 1879 the government agent in Kootenay, William Fernie, wrote to the Minister of Mines as follows:

I am sorry to be unable to report any improvement in the prospects of the mines in this section of British Columbia. There has been very little prospecting done this year and nothing new found. The old claims being worked have paid generally as well as in former years. There are quantities of what are called small diggings in this vicinity, but the present high prices of provisions prevent their being worked until men can live cheaper. There is no doubt that this portion of the country will support a much more numerous population than is here at present when its resources are properly developed.[4]

During the late seventies British Columbians were more exercised over the construction of the Canadian Pacific Railway than they

4. *Sessional Papers of British Columbia*, 1880, 240. In the report of the Minister of Mines for 1878, the following statistics for Kootenay occur (*ibid.*, 1879, 369):

	Wild Horse Creek	Perry Creek
Number of claims worked	16	4
Number employed		
Whites	13	2
Chinese	32	16
Rates of wages		
Whites	$4.00	$4.00
Chinese	$3.50	$3.50
Estimated yield	$20,650.00	$4,750.00
Value per ounce	$18.00	$18.00

were over possible mining development in such a remote portion of the province.

With the decline of placer mining attention turned towards quartz mining. In 1871 an attempt was made near Hope, British Columbia, but it came to nothing. Five years later there was a miniature boom in quartz mining in Cariboo but the high cost of transporting machinery, coupled with high wages and living costs, resulted in failure. It remained for Kootenay to initiate the real revival of mining in British Columbia.

In 1882 Robert Evan Sproule with two companions set out from Bonner's Ferry, Idaho, and descended Kootenay River to Kootenay Lake. While making their way along the eastern shore of the lake they noted a large stain on the face of a cliff. On examination this proved to be a remarkably wide ledge of silver-bearing galena. Thus was discovered the well-known Blue Bell mine.[5] Sproule naturally wished to register his claim, but to do so it was necessary for him to travel 240 miles to Wild Horse and to return within 72 hours. Such were the mining regulations of the province regarding placer mining and at this time they were being applied to lode mining as well. It was clearly impossible for Sproule to comply with the regulations, but he seems to have started off to record his claim none the less. It so happened that another prospector, Thomas Hamil, was in this district operating in the interests of Captain Ainsworth of the Columbia and Kootenay Railroad. Hamil had evidently heard of the Blue Bell, since he had taken the precaution of bringing the Gold Commissioner from Wild Horse with him. After Sproule had been gone the legal 72 hours, Hamil staked the claim and the Gold Commissioner recorded it. Sproule was incensed and went to law. Finally he recovered the Blue Bell but the sheriff intervened and seized the claim to pay the court costs. This was more than Sproule could bear. He waylaid Hamil and murdered him. After a long legal battle Sproule was convicted and executed. Possibly an Idaho or a Montana jury

5. A. G. Harvey in his article, "David Douglas in British Columbia," *British Columbia Historical Quarterly*, IV, 235-6, has disposed of the oft-told story that David Douglas discovered the Blue Bell Mine in 1825. Old stories die hard, and this particular one is no exception to the rule. There is no mention in Douglas's journals of any such discovery.

might have viewed the case more leniently, but Sproule had committed his crime on British soil.

After the deaths of Hamil and Sproule interest in the Blue Bell waned. It was long considered to possess a very large ore body of such low grade that it would not be profitable to develop it. At length, about the year 1887, an American company, under the management of Dr. W. A. Hendryx, began operations at the Blue Bell but, although Hendryx held the property for a number of years, the Blue Bell was never a great financial success.

In 1884 Gilbert Malcolm Sproat's report on Kootenay was published in the British Columbia *Sessional Papers*, an indication that some interest was being taken in that mining district. Messrs. Ainsworth and Company in that year sent in Captain Brown, "a well-known mineralogist and assayer of San Francisco," to test the ore on the ledge at the Blue Bell claim. He spoke favourably of the locality.[6]

By the end of 1884 Kootenay Lake was attracting considerable attention. A. W. Vowell writing to the Minister of Mines under date of December 23, 1884, states that "many old Californians, familiar with Leadville and other valuable quartz mines of notoriety, who have visited Kootenay Lake during the past season, have predicted for those mines a brilliant future." Vowell was of opinion that there would be a hundred men "actually engaged in quartz mining at Kootenay Lake next season, besides a great many miners prospecting." His recommendation was that "an officer be provided for that place as well as a record office and lock-up."[7]

The "find" that really made Kootenay was that of silver and copper by the Hall Brothers in 1886 on Toad Mountain, five miles from Nelson, from which developed the Silver King mine. The following extracts from a letter written by C. H. Montgomery, storekeeper of Colville, Washington Territory, under the date of December 6, 1887, tell of the riches of the new field:

Those mines were discovered late in the autumn of 1886 by Winslow, Hall and Co. Nothing was done until spring of 1887, after the discovery

6. *Sessional Papers of British Columbia*, 1884, 260, A. S. Farwell to the Chief Commissioner of Lands and Works. Farwell writes: "No work of any consequence has been done on this ledge during the past season, all the claimants to the ground having been engaged in law suits before the Gold Commissioner."

7. *Ibid.*, 1885, 424.

had become known. I outfitted two men who went to the mines with about ten others, and all made locations, working them during the summer, I myself went there in September last, to look at the mines and see what my men were doing. I found about thirty men in camp, and more coming every day . . . the mines the best ever discovered on the Pacific Coast . . . ledges there running from ten to thirty feet in width, and all looking well.

Mr. Cobaugh, who went in there with his assay office with Messrs. Hall & Co., made assays from the rock of the different ledges as high as 1,600 ounces in silver. The average assay of ore at the time I was there ran a little over $300, and without a doubt this will be one of the best camps in British Columbia.

At the time I left this camp, the last of September, there were about thirty claims, located, and men working on about eighteen of them. Experts were coming in from all parts of the country examining the mines. I am informed there have been about twenty-five more locations since I left.

Montana and country south, as well as our own, are all excitement now over these mines, and there is no doubt but that as early as they can get there in the spring there will be 1,000 or 1,500 men in that camp. The only drawback now is an outlet.

The easy way to go to this camp now is by Northern Pacific Railway (Kootenay Station), 40 miles land travel to Bonner's Ferry, from which excellent water navigation, down Kootenay River and through Big Kootenay Lake to the western outlet, six or seven miles from the mines.[8]

It is typical of the period that it was from this American source that the government of British Columbia quoted when giving out information relative to the new mining camp in Kootenay! In its origin this rush was almost entirely American.

On the west arm of Kootenay Lake a new town came into being. Henry Anderson, the mining recorder, in 1887 named it Salisbury, but Gilbert Malcolm Sproat, the Gold Commissioner, who held the first sale of town lots in October, 1888, called it Stanley. The Post Office authorities settled the dispute by bestowing on the new settlement the name of Nelson, after the Hon. Hugh Nelson, who was then Lieutenant-Governor of British Columbia. The following description of the town is from the pen of Judge Howay:

For the first two years of its existence Nelson was merely a collection of rough log-huts, roofed with dirt, shakes, or canvas. Denny & Devine opened the first general store in a cabin on the site of the present Provincial Gaol,

8. *Ibid.*, 1888, 261.

but they soon disposed of the business to Lemon & Hume. Nelson's first hotel was a commodious and airy tent; its proprietor, John F. Ward, soon replaced it with a log house. James A. Gilker was, in 1889, appointed as Nelson's first postmaster, the mails being brought in weekly, down the Columbia and across to the new town. Early in 1892, the Columbia and Kootenay Railroad connecting Nelson and Robson gave access to the steamers operating on the Columbia River. With these increased transportation facilities, population poured in; business blocks and stately private residences soon arose where the pioneers' log-huts had stood; railway lines began to converge toward the spot, and Nelson entered upon an era of prosperity as the real centre of Kootenay. By the end of 1893, it boasted eight hundred inhabitants and looked peaceful and prosperous. In 1895 the Nelson & Fort Sheppard Railway gave access to the entire American system.[9]

The Silver King became one of the paying mines of Kootenay and it was one of the first to be absorbed by British interests. By 1897 the Hall Mines Company, Limited, of London, England, owned eighteen claims in the Nelson mining division. Of these the original four, the Silver King, Kootenay Bonanza, American Flag, and Kooh-i-noor were on Toad Mountain. Sir Joseph Trutch, former Lieutenant-Governor of British Columbia, was chairman of this company. The Canadian headquarters were at Nelson, where the company established a smelter for the treatment of the Toad Mountain ores. The Silver King ore was conveyed to the smelter by a wire-rope aerial tramway, four and a half miles long. By the end of 1896 nearly 30,000 tons of ore from the Silver King had been treated at the smelter. For the next three or four years the average tonnage was between 30,000 and 40,000, but as the depth became greater the quality of the ore slowly deteriorated. In 1900 only 20,500 tons were produced and after that production steadily declined.

From Kootenay Lake prospectors set out in all directions. Some of them followed the old Dewdney Trail. In the vicinity of Trail Creek near the international boundary some of the richest claims in British Columbia were discovered. The first claim in this region was located in 1889 by Joseph Bourgeois and recorded in 1890 under the title of the Lily May by J. Bordeau. Bourgeois in 1890

9. Scholefield and Howay, *British Columbia*, II, 471.

located the Centre Star and the War Eagle and his partner
J. Morris staked the Virginia and the Idaho. Bourgeois and Morris
discovered the Le Roi, the most famous of these Red Mountain
mines, but they could not file on any more than one claim on the
same vein. E. S. Topping by paying the expenses of recording
became the owner of the Le Roi.[10]

In November 1890 Topping met two Spokane attorneys, George
Foster and Colonel William Redpath, at Colville, and offered to
sell them a half interest in the claim for $30,000. They became
interested and associated with them a leading mining authority,
Oliver Durant. Durant came to Red Mountain, examined the
claim, sampled the ore which assayed as high as $60 a ton in gold,
and visited the other claims in the vicinity. He was satisfied that
here was a great mining camp. Leaving E. J. Kellie in charge of
the sinking of a shaft from which samples were to be sent every
week all winter, Durant returned to the United States. In the
spring of 1891 ten tons of pure sulphide ore from the bottom of
the 35-foot shaft were packed out to the Columbia River and forwarded to the Colorado Smelting Works at Butte, Montana. The
ore tested out at $84.40 a ton, three ounces of silver, five and
twenty-one hundredths per cent copper, and about four ounces of
gold. Topping's terms then were accepted in a modified form and a
controlling interest purchased for $30,000. Later the partners
bought out Topping's remaining interest for $11,000 and the Le Roi
Gold Mining Company was formed. Durant remained in charge of
the work for about a year and then sold out to his colleagues.

10. E. S. Topping was born in the State of New York in 1844. Little is known
of his early life except that before he came west he was a sailor for eleven years.
In the West he was a railroad builder, trapper, miner, fisherman, constable, and
author. He was a member of Cook's expedition against the Sioux in 1876 and acted
as a newspaper correspondent during the campaign. After prospecting for some
years in the Yellowstone, "before there was a settler anywhere," he was in 1883
employed by Hubert Howe Bancroft to collect material. But Topping seems to have
made use of his own material under the title of *The Chronicles of the Yellowstone*
(St. Paul, 1883).

Topping's subsequent career is thus recorded in the Trail Creek *News* for
October 23, 1896 (republished in the Nelson *Daily News*, April 29, 1932).

"After four years of prospecting worthless ground, he went to Nelson where
an accident laid him up for some months and almost exhausted his small savings.
As soon as he could get about again he started fishing, and managed to make about

Communication with the outside world was a problem at first, but through the efforts of Durant a trail and later a road were built from Northport up Sheep Creek to the diggings. Captain Fitzstubbs, Gold Commissioner for West Kootenay, gave orders for the construction from the Columbia up Trail Creek and in the winter of 1893-4 the Le Roi was able to ship out ore by sleighs over the Trail Creek road. With the construction of the Red Mountain Railway in 1897 all problems of communication were finally solved.

Frederick Augustus Heinze and Daniel Chase Corbin, whose activities in connection with railway construction have been noted in the preceding chapter, now became interested in the Red Mountain, or Rossland, area. Heinze, who as one of his multifarious activities, was head of a smelter in Butte, Montana, sent in two men to investigate the possibilities of establishing a smelter. After much negotiation with the Le Roi Company he entered into an agreement to smelt their ore. With a grant from the provincial government and a federal bonus of one dollar per ton for all ore smelted, Heinze built the Trail smelter, now the property of the Consolidated Mining and Smelting Company of Canada. D. C. Corbin, in the meantime, constructed his line from Northport to Nelson and the branch into Rossland previously referred to, the

$100 per month with the use of one hand in managing his boats and nets. Then he took charge of a store and was appointed recorder and constable, and was in fact, the government of West Kootenay.

"In 1890, when the famous sulphide ore was discovered he had samples assayed and it was his advice that the two discoveries [sic] who had been discouraged at the poor showings, continued their work and as a result five claims were staked out and the Le Roi claim at Rossland was given to Mr. Topping for having the whole five recorded. Report of the later assays soon spread and very soon the district was filled with prospective prospectors.

"Mr. Topping staked out 320 acres of land where Trail now stands. He and another gentleman started a hotel which was conducted for several years.

"Trail was surveyed in 1891, the year in which Mr. Topping became a Canadian citizen, and several Victoria men made profitable investments in the town."

According to this account Topping bonded the Le Roi for $30,000 "but being dissatisfied with the management he sold out all interest in the mine for $11,000." In 1895 as an inducement to F. A. Heinze to build the Trail Smelter, Topping deeded to Heinze forty acres of land on the hill and one-third interest in the main parts of Trail.

so-called Red Mountain Railway. Work on the Trail smelter was commenced in October, 1895; the first furnace was fired up in February, 1896; and by 1897 five furnaces were in operation.[11]

Up to February 1, 1898, the Le Roi, which produced gold and copper, had paid $725,000 in dividends. In that year it was sold for $4,000,000 to a British syndicate in which Lord Dufferin, a former Governor-General of Canada, was interested. Profits from the Le Roi in 1904 were over $400,000 (£80,000).

One of the best-known of the British Columbia mining districts was the Slocan where silver, lead, and zinc were found, metals which were all much higher in price than they are today. Situated between Kootenay Lake on the east and the Arrow Lakes on the west and cut off from both by the mountains, the Slocan district and Slocan Lake were but little known. In his annual report for the year ending December 31, 1893, the Hon. James Baker, Minister of Mines, included a "comprehensive and accurate description of the Slocan country" from a report written for the Nelson *Tribune* by "that well-known and practical miner, Randall H. Kemp," from which the following is taken:

It appears almost incredible, even to those well informed on the subject, that it is scarcely two and a half years since the first mineral discoveries were made in that portion of the Selkirk range lying between Kootenay and Slocan Lakes, now locally known as the Slocan District. Previous to the summer of 1891, when rich ore was first found, a few prospectors had pushed their way up Kaslo River as far as Bear and Fish Lakes, and one or two small parties had reached Slocan Lake by way of Slocan River, but neither were rewarded by finding mineral.

In August, 1891, Andrew Jardine returned to Ainsworth from the Blue Ridge Mountains, thirteen miles westerly from the present city of Kaslo, with a quantity of high-grade silver-lead ore. On the value being ascertained, which was quite flattering, a stampede for the neighborhood of the new find was a natural result. Prospectors swarmed the hills, and many fairly good discoveries were made. Early in September, the late John L. Seaton and Eli Carpenter, having penetrated farther westward than the others, found themselves within sight of Slocan Lake. Disputing on which course to take to return, they divided their outfit, Seaton starting to return to Kootenay Lake by way of Kaslo River and Carpenter *via* Slocan Lake and River. In retracing his steps, Seaton discovered the croppings of the Payne

11. *Year Book of British Columbia*, 1897, 362.

mine. While engaged in staking the claim he was overtaken by Carpenter, who had changed his mind regarding the route out. The Payne was staked jointly by them on September 9th, and was the first location made in the justly famed Slocan District. Returns from the ore they took back to Ainsworth caused the wildest quartz mining excitement ever known in British Columbia. The season was well advanced, and snow was falling on the higher ranges, yet 140 claims were located and recorded by January 1st, many of which have since become famous as producing mines. In October S. S. Bailey, representing capital, visited the district, and purchased the Payne, Maid of Erin, Mountain Chief, and Two Jacks claims, the transfer being the first made in the district.[12]

The chief problem which beset the prospectors was how to find suitable trails into the Slocan. The inhabitants of Nelson took the lead in opening up a trail to Slocan Lake. In 1892 a route was opened up from Kaslo to Bear Lake and on to Sandon and New Denver, and a rough trail from Nakusp to the head of Slocan Lake. Dr. E. C. Arthur, who in 1890 left Ontario to become a Canadian Pacific Railway surgeon on construction work in the Kootenay and has been for many years a resident of Nelson, has thus described the difficulties encountered in getting into the Slocan:

A section of the country more inaccessible than that was, would be difficult to find. From the Kootenay lake side men struggled up the rough brush-grown banks 20 miles or more before they reached the mineralized area. From Nelson the Slocan river was the route chiefly used, although various prospectors essayed to reach the Mecca of their dreams by going up the valleys of the Sproule, Six-Mile and Kokanee creeks. Thence on [sic] 12 or 15 miles of open lakes had to be traversed in small boats, canoes, or rafts to the mouth of Carpenter Creek where New Denver now is. Another eight miles through trackless wilderness, over rocks and logs, through thick brush, brought them to the present site of Sandon.

In company with Messrs. Wilson and Alfred Hill, the writer left Nelson on October 28 and were 15 days making the trip to the head of Slocan lake and back to Nelson in an old birch bark canoe. Incidentally there were only three of the 15 days in which rain did not fall sometime in the 24 hours.

On the return of our party to Nelson, a public meeting was called and money was subscribed to open a trail from Ward's Pool to the foot of Slocan Lake. The Hill brothers were in charge of the work, and by the middle of December a passable trail was opened to where Slocan City now stands.

12. *Sessional Papers of British Columbia*, 1894, II, Report of the Minister of Mines, 1052.

This was extensively used during that winter and to a less extent for about two years.[13]

The chief productive lead, silver, zinc[14] mines of the Slocan in the early days were the Payne, the Slocan Star, the Whitewater, the Reco, and the Noble Five. The Payne was the first discovered but until 1897 was surpassed in production by the Slocan Star. More than 50,000 tons of ore were shipped from the Payne, valued at approximately $4,000,000. Between 1897 and 1904 it paid $1,438,000 in dividends. The Slocan Star was the bonanza mine of the region. At the depth of 100 feet the vein was 50 feet between the walls, every particle of which—apart from the first class ore—could be concentrated with profit. The Slocan Star consisted of four original claims located in October, 1891, the Slocan Star, the Slocan King, the Jennie, and the Silversmith. In 1894 the Byron N. White Company, organized under the laws of Wisconsin with a capitalization of $500,000, was the owner. Presumably this greatly exceeded the actual investment, but by 1896 the mine had paid $300,000 in dividends. Up to July 1, 1904, it had shipped 32,453 tons of ore and paid dividends amounting to $525,000. The Reco group, consisting of the Ruecau, Texas, New Denver, Ephriam, and Clifton claims, was noteworthy because it depended very little on outside capital but was financed by the production of the mines. The Whitewater and the Noble Five were also well-known mines.

The Payne was 7,100 feet above sea level and the Slocan Star 5,000 feet. The ore was transported by waggon roads, aerial or other tramways, or by "rawhide trails." On these trails, a load of fifteen sacks of ore wrapped in a raw cowhide was drawn by horses down the mountain sides over the snow. Each horse hauled a cowhide containing from 1,500 to 2,000 pounds of ore and from one to four horses were in charge of a driver, depending on the state of the trail. It was an original, but apparently a highly successful, method of transportation. When the railways were built into the Slocan in the middle nineties transportation problems were lightened, but the "rawhide trails" remained in use at least as late as 1898.

13. Nelson *Daily News*, April 29, 1932.

14. Zinc, although higher in price then than now, was not considered so important on account of difficulty in smelting.

In East Kootenay placer gold mining still continued on Wild Horse Creek, Perry Creek, and Moyie River. The yield in 1892 was $29,700. But quartz mining was much more profitable than placer, and prospectors were busily engaged in searching for ledges similar to those found in West Kootenay. Joseph Bourgeois, who had located some of the richest claims on Red Mountain, in June, 1892, found an immense body of steel galena on Mark Creek, about twenty miles west of Fort Steele. The North Star, "the representative mine of East Kootenay," which was the result of this discovery, furnishes an early instance of eastern Canadian capital taking over a Kootenay mine. In July, 1893, it was acquired by Donald D. Mann, later Sir Donald Mann of the Canadian Northern Railway, and the North Star Mining Company, Limited, of Montreal was formed, with Mann as president, H. S. Holt, the late Sir Herbert S. Holt, as secretary, and N. W. Curran, Fort Steele, as business manager.

The most famous of the East Kootenay mines, the Sullivan at Kimberley, was discovered in 1892. The Sullivan is now probably the largest lead and zinc mine in the world and is the largest producing silver mine in Canada. But its early history gave no indication of its subsequent fame. The discovery of the North Star had led in the summer of 1892 to a rush to East Kootenay. Among the miners who left the Coeur d'Alène region in Idaho were Pat Sullivan and John Cleaves. At Fort Steele they were joined by Ed. Smith who knew that part of the country. James Cronin, also from the Coeur d'Alène, met the trio and formed a working agreement with them. On reaching the North Star the trio found all adjacent claims taken up, and so they crossed Mark Creek and prospected the opposite mountainside. Their search was rewarded when they came upon outcroppings of what is now the Sullivan mine. The three miners staked three claims, one for each of them, and a fourth for Cronin. Cronin did not see his claim till 1893, and as he was then interested in the St. Eugene mine at Moyie he abandoned the claim staked by Sullivan and his partners.

The Sullivan claims were eventually worked by the Sullivan Group Mining Company of Spokane in which the Guggenheims were interested. When systematic development began in 1900, after the Canadian Pacific Railway had built a branch line from Cranbrook to Kimberley, about two miles from the Sullivan outcroppings, the ore samples ran about 40 per cent lead and about 15 ounces of silver to the ton. In 1902 a smelter and power plant were built at Marysville five miles below Kimberley on Mark Creek. By 1905 the North Star was worked out and the Sullivan took its place as a large silver-lead mine. In that year the Sullivan's yield was 11,500,000 pounds of lead or 20 per cent of the total lead production of the Province of British Columbia. But the ore was very hard to treat and the first attempts at separating the lead and zinc were unsuccessful. Late in 1907, as the original ore bodies were being rapidly depleted and no new deposits seemed to be available, the mine and the smelter closed down. The Crow's Nest Coal Company had even obtained judgment and made a seizure on account of an unpaid coal bill.

Two years later a reorganization took place under the title of the Fort Steele Mining and Smelting Company. As this new company was controlled by the Federal Mining and Smelting Company, the Guggenheims once more had an interest in the mine. But Consolidated Smelters of Trail were now anxious to obtain control. In December, 1909, they took a lease and bond on the Federal Mining and Smelting Company's interest in the Fort Steele Mining and Smelting Company and in the following year they took over the mines. In 1915, at the Trail smelter, a successful process was developed for the recovery of the zinc and in 1917 the first flotation experiments were made at Trail. A method was eventually found for the treatment of the highly complex Sullivan ores. The first concentrator was built at Kimberley in 1922 and since then the Sullivan has really come into its own.

The St. Eugene mine at Moyie was the next great lead-silver "find." Father Coccola, O.M.I., of the St. Eugene Mission, after scolding his Indians for their laziness and poverty, had held up to them the example of the white prospectors. Stung by the father's remarks one Pierre, or Pielle as the natives pronounce it, went out to the hills and found pure galena and brought a sample back to the priest. Father Coccola, obtaining a miner's licence, followed Pierre and with his friend James Cronin staked the claim. From his share of the mine Father Coccola built a church at the St. Eugene Mission. The St. Eugene became the greatest producing lead mine in British Columbia and in 1905 its output was 900,000 ounces of silver and 36,500,000 pounds of lead. It, also, came into the hands of the Consolidated Mining and Smelting Company of Canada.[15]

The ore from East Kootenay was, at first, conveyed by trail or road to Fort Steele and thence down the Kootenay River to Jennings Landing, Montana, to be shipped by the Great Northern to the smelter at Great Falls, Montana. But the Kootenay was navigable only for a few months in the year—in spring and autumn the channel was blocked by sand bars. A mass meeting of the citizens of Fort Steele called upon the Dominion government to improve the navigation on the Kootenay, "it being an impossibility to ship ore up the river to connect with the Canadian Pacific Railway at Golden." The petitioners pointed out that the natural route to the smelters from the Kootenay was down the river to the Great Northern Railway and that the American government intended to improve the river on their side of the line.[16] But the authorities at Ottawa were slow in taking action and the inhabitants of Fort Steele grumbled impatiently: "To the south we have an unlimited market, but we are unable to take advantage of this, on account of the Government persisting in refusing to improve the river, so giving us several months more of navigation, for the paltry reason that it also benefits the United States. . . . Why should this country be retarded and kept back by Government 'in order not to benefit the States?' . . . We have all that is requisite to make a rich and prosperous mining camp. But for want of means of transport all this vast mineral wealth is idle."[17] Such was the protest not only of Fort Steele but of the Kootenays and, in fact, of all southeastern British Columbia. The Crowsnest line was built, but the pull to the south remained. Kootenay was politically part of British Columbia. Geographically and economic-

15. For information concerning these East Kootenay mines, compare *Sessional Papers of British Columbia*, 1894-1908, Reports of the Minister of Mines; *Year Book of British Columbia*, 1897, 369-76; Scholefield and Howay, *British Columbia*, II, 477-8; B. F. Townley, *Mine-Finders* (Toronto, 1936), 186-97; Sylvia L. Thrupp, "A History of the Cranbrook Region of East Kootenay," MS in University of British Columbia Library. Information was also supplied to the writer by Professors J. M. Turnbull and H. V. Warren of the University of British Columbia.

16. Thrupp, "Cranbrook Region," 68, quoting the Fort Steele *Prospector*, November 9, 1895.

17. Fort Steele *Prospector*, November 23, 1895.

ally it was largely tributary to the "Inland Empire," although eastern Canadian capital was gradually becoming more interested.

It is impossible to state accurately the relative proportion of American, Canadian, and British capital invested in the camps of Kootenay. The statistics published in the *Sessional Papers of British Columbia* do not differentiate between American, Canadian, and British investments. Often the head office of the company is some guide, but in most instances the companies are listed as having British Columbia addresses. Many of the Kootenay mines were local affairs and in nearly every case the big companies had British Columbia headquarters. Such evidence as there is indicates that in the early nineties American capital so predominated as to exclude British and Canadian almost entirely. There were some exceptions, notably that of the Silver King, which were controlled by British capital from an early date. In the later nineties, however, British and Canadian capital began to come into Kootenay in fairly large quantities. The dividing line is about 1897 or 1898, by which time the Americans had reaped quite a rich harvest.

A few examples may suffice. The War Eagle at Rossland, a gold-copper mine, was discovered in July, 1890, by Joseph Bourgeois and Joe Morris. Morris sank a shaft on the War Eagle property, but found the ore too low in grade to be worth transporting to an American smelter. In the autumn of 1894 he bonded the claim to Patsy Clark of Spokane for $17,000. Clark went to Butte, Montana, to sell shares in the new company, but had no success. He then returned to Spokane where he disposed of his shares at six and a half cents. A change in the location of the tunnel resulted in the disclosure of a large ore body. Within a few months the War Eagle declared a dividend of $27,000. American capitalists now began to make enquiries and a San Francisco syndicate sent in two mining experts to look over the field. At this juncture D. C. Corbin took a hand on behalf of some London interests, who sent over two representatives to investigate. This was in 1896. The report was favourable and as a result two London financiers journeyed to British Columbia on behalf of the British-Rossland-War Eagle Gold Mining Company, which had been recently formed with a capital of $2,000,000. The British company now endeavoured to obtain control, but the property did not formally change hands.

Canadian money was now beginning to flow westward and Toronto financiers were looking round for investments in Kootenay mines. J. B. Hastings, mining property expert for Gooderham and Blackstock, sent back a favourable report on War Eagle. A rumour reached Rossland that the War Eagle had been sold to the Canadian company for $850,000. The remainder of the story is thus told in the Rossland *Miner* of August 29, 1897:

Matters drifted along until January 20, when a special meeting of shareholders of the company was called in Spokane to consider pending offers for the property. These were as follows: the Gooderham-Blackstock syndicate offered $700,000 cash for the mine as it then stood, without assets or credits of any kind. F. E. Henage, for an English syndicate, $900,000 to include all credits and cash, $200,000 cash, balance in forty days. F. E. Burbridge $900,000, to include all credits and cash, $25,000 cash, half in sixty days and the balance in ninety days, together with ten per cent. of the stock in the new company.

On a vote taken the Gooderham-Blackstock offer was accepted. . . . The new company took formal possession of the mine on January 22. John B. Hastings, then consulting engineer for the purchasers, was appointed manager and has held that position up to date. The War Eagle Consolidated company, owning the War Eagle and Crown Point group in the Trail Creek district, and the Richmond group in the Slocan, was then floated, with a capital of $2,000,000, George Gooderham being the first president and T. G. (Blackstock) vice-president.

. . . the purchasers being well-known Canadians and keen buyers, additional interest in Rossland was created in Toronto and the east generally.[18]

The Josie mine, one of the important Rossland claims, was sold in October, 1897, to the Hon. Charles H. Mackintosh, a South African mine owner, who was representing the British American Corporation. Many of the smaller mines were consolidated under the corporation. The largest consolidation to take place was in 1906 when the Consolidated Mining and Smelting Company of Canada, Limited, was incorporated. It included the St. Eugene lead-silver mine at Moyie, the War Eagle and Centre Star at Rossland, both gold-copper mines, and the assets of the Canadian Smelting Company which had been formed at Trail in 1898. In 1909 the Consolidated purchased the Sullivan mine at Kimberley.

18. Rossland *Miner*, August 29, 1897, quoted in Isabel Bescoby, "Some Social Aspects of the American Mining Advance into Cariboo and Kootenay," MS in University of British Columbia Library.

At first the ore from the Kootenay mines went to American smelters, to Tacoma, Helena, or Butte. The early smelters in Kootenay were erected by American companies which imported equipment and even coal from the United States. A large American company built a smelter in Revelstoke in 1891, but it was not large enough to compete seriously with the existing American plants. The Pilot Bay Smelting Company was incorporated in 1894, with E. W. Herrick of Minneapolis as President and R. P. Rithet of Victoria as Vice-President. Most of the capital came from New Haven, Connecticut, and from Minneapolis. The Hall Brothers smelter at Nelson was the first to be built by British capital. The Trail smelter, established in 1895, was by 1897 the largest in Canada, with a capacity of smelting 530 tons a day. Once again Canadian and British capital supplanted American, and the Trail smelter, today said to be the largest non-ferrous smelter in the British Empire, became in 1898 the property of the Canadian Pacific Railway. In 1907 it was transferred to its present owners, the Consolidated Mining and Smelting Company of Canada.

The Americans were first at the mines, as they had been first in railway construction. In both types of enterprise Canadian and British capital arrived after the speculative profits had been made. In many cases control passed into Canadian hands but American influences remained strong.

The boundary country is separated from the Kootenays by the Gold Range. At first it was designated as the "Boundary Creek portion of the Kettle River Mining Division of Yale" and included a territory of about 150 square miles, drained by Boundary Creek, which flows into the Kettle River at Midway near the international boundary. But the term was soon applied to the mining area west of Kootenay, adjacent to the State of Washington, and east of the Similkameen district. In 1906, when the boundary was the best producing mineral area in the province, the Boundary District comprised the Greenwood, Grand Forks, and Osoyoos Mining Divisions. The following paragraph on the topography of the boundary country is taken from the *Year Book of British Columbia* for 1897:

The topography of the district, while it affords a considerable diversity, is not very different to that of the great interior plateau of British Columbia. Whilst mountainous, its highest points seldom exceed 5,500 feet in altitude above the sea, and the greater number of its well-rounded mountains do not exceed 5,000 feet—Kettle River, at the mouth of Boundary Creek, being about 1,800 feet above sea level. The ruggedness and nakedness of many parts of Kootenay are not at all in evidence, for these rounded hills are splendidly forested to their very summits, with a great variety of coniferous trees. The eastern, southern, and western slopes are open and afford a prolific growth of bunch-grass, and along the valleys are many ranches which are specially adapted to diversified farming with the aid of irrigation.[19]

In May, 1891, prospectors from the Kootenays located the Mother Lode three miles west of the site of Greenwood. Two rich copper claims, Old Ironsides and Knob Hill, discovered near Phoenix in July of that year, later became the Granby mine. Some small shipments of ore were made in 1893 and 1894 from claims near Greenwood. The ore was taken out by pack train to Marcus, Washington, where it was conveyed to the smelter by the Spokane Falls and Northern Railway. But the ore body was so great that it could not be fully developed until better railway facilities were provided.[20]

By 1900 the boundary copper mines were becoming important. The chief camps were Deadwood, Greenwood—also known as Phoenix—Summit, Wellington, and Central, or White's. The Mother Lode was the producing mine in the Deadwood Camp, but the Morrison gave good promise. The Mother Lode installed a steam power plant in 1898, and by 1901 there were seven such plants in the camp. Greenwood Camp was the leader in ore shipments. The chief properties in this camp in 1901 were the Miner-Graves group, including Old Ironsides, Knob Hill, Victoria, and Grey Eagle; the Dominion Copper Company's group, the Brooklyn, Stemwinder, Idaho, and Rawhide; and the Snowshoe and the Gold Drop. The Miner-Graves group were later taken over by the Granby Consolidated Mining, Smelting and Power Company, an American organization which, by 1906, was the largest mining company in the province. The Snowshoe and Gold Drop were run by separate companies. Summit Camp, eight miles from Greenwood, was second in production in 1901, but Deadwood was

19. *Year Book of British Columbia*, 1897, 366.
20. See chap. x.

running it close. The leading mine in the Summit Camp was the B.C., "which is considered to be one of the most promising mines in the Boundary Country."[21] The Wellington and Central Camps were not so productive in 1901 as they had been previously. Other camps included in the boundary country were on the west fork of the Kettle River, on the north fork, and on the main portion of the river above Rock Creek.

From the first it was evident that, on account of the heavy ore bodies, smelters would have to be established in the boundary country. The Granby Company constructed a smelter at Grand Forks in 1900. In August its first furnace was "blown in" and in October its second. The British Columbia Copper Company commenced operating its smelter at Greenwood in February, 1901. By April 30 of that year the Granby Company had smelted 136,443 tons of ore and the British Columbia Copper Company 24,857 tons.[22]

The boundary country mines produced, in the main, low-grade copper ore. Their success, therefore, depended upon low mining and smelting costs and upon the price of copper, which, fortunately, was high during the greatest period of the boundary mines. Transportation was a problem but, as related in the previous chapter, the Granby Company was able to profit by the construction of the Great Northern branch line into Grand Forks. For the year ending December 31, 1906, the Granby Consolidated Mining, Smelting and Power Company paid a dividend of 12 per cent amounting in all to $1,753,000.[23] The total output of ore for the six and a half years from 1900 to 1906 from the mines of the boundary country amounted to 4,609,042 tons. Of this the Granby mines contributed nearly three-quarters, or more than 3,000,000 tons, all this ore coming from the Phoenix camp. The British Columbia Copper Company's Mother Lode produced about

21. *Year Book of British Columbia*, 1897-1901, 336. Most of the information contained in the above paragraph comes from this source. Gosnell in 1901 brought the 1897 *Year Book* up to date by the addition of new material. A comparison of the sections on the boundary country in the two editions is a clear indication of the development which took place in this district between 1897 and 1901.

22. *Ibid.*, 340.

23. *Sessional Papers of British Columbia*, 1907, H 155. Report of W. G. McMynn, Gold Commissioner for the Greenwood Mining Division, in Report of the Minister of Mines.

830,000 tons; the Dominion Copper Company's holdings, 380,000 tons; and the remaining 450,000 tons were from the B.C., the Snowshoe, and other smaller mines. Approximately 136,000,000 pounds of copper were produced. The value of the ore, including gold and silver, is placed by McMynn at over $30,000,000. Since the chief companies operating at this period in the boundary were American, this portion of the southern British Columbian mining region was, in very truth, a northward thrust of the "Inland Empire."

The Consolidated Mining and Smelting Company of Canada, however, obtained a foothold in the boundary country by taking a lease of the Snowshoe from the Snowshoe Gold and Copper Mines, Limited. The Hall Mining and Smelting Company, Limited, also became interested in the Summit Camp, although the British Columbia Copper Company, too, had extensive holdings. During the year 1906 the Summit mines shipped 2,079 tons to the British Columbia Copper Company, 1,025 tons to the Granby Company, and 8,060 tons to the Hall Company. The value of the ore was $53,229, or $4.77 per ton.[24]

Although the price of copper had fallen from 20 cents in 1907 to 13 cents in 1910, the value of the product of the boundary mines for that year was close to $6,000,000. Approximate tonnage figures for 1910 were: Granby Company, 1,050,000 tons; British Columbia Copper Company, 450,000 tons; and the Consolidated Mining and Smelting, 150,000 tons. The Granby mines then had an output capacity of 4,000 tons a day and the British Columbia Copper Company's mines nearly 2,000 tons.

The Granby smelter had eight blast furnaces with a total capacity of 4,000 to 4,500 tons a day and its copper converters could produce about 36,000,000 pounds of blister copper a year. The smelter was the largest copper smelter in the British Empire and ranked second to the Washoe works at Anaconda, Montana. The British Columbia Copper Company's three blast furnaces could treat 2,600 tons of ore a day, and averaged between 2,400 and 2,500 tons. The West Kootenay Power and Light Company installed a local generating plant at Cascade Falls, Kettle River,

24. *Ibid.*, H162, Report of R. S. Almond, Gold Commissioner for the Grand Forks Mining Division.

Boundary District. Its main stations, however, were at Bonnington Falls, near Nelson. Thus the mines and smelters of the boundary country were furnished with hydro-electric power.

During the war years the price of copper rose from 10 cents to 30 cents or more, but the boundary mines began to give out. Phoenix became exhausted and the Granby Company looked for new fields for development. They finally settled on Anyox in the Portland Canal District in northern British Columbia and, when the Grand Forks smelter was closed, a new plant opened there. By 1920 the boundary country had ceased to be an important mining region.[25]

West of the boundary camps were Camp McKinney and the Fairview and Central Camps. Camp McKinney was situated between the Okanagan and Kettle Rivers, fifty-six miles east of Penticton. It was discovered in 1894 but not really developed until the finding of the Cariboo vein in 1897. It continued operation until 1904. Another mining camp in this region was Camp Hedley on the north side of the Similkameen River. Its leading mine was the Nickel Plate which, in 1908, produced 44,068 tons of ore. It was owned by the Yale Mining Company of Hedley and controlled by the Daly Estate of Montana and New York, and was listed as a gold producer. Although these mines did not actually belong to the boundary country they were all located in the Yale District.

Taking it all in all, the boundary country owed its development to American capital and American enterprise. The Granby and the British Columbia Copper Companies, which controlled the chief mines and operated the smelters, were American. Railways from the south tapped the boundary country and effectively competed with the Canadian Pacific. As in the Kootenays Spokane was a magnet, drawing to the south. The coast cities simply could not compete. The following extract taken from the *Boundary Creek*

25. For information regarding the boundary country about 1910, cf. *Year Book of British Columbia*, 1911, 182, 186. Later statistics may be found in the reports of the Minister of Mines in the *Sessional Papers of British Columbia*. A convenient summary of mining statistics for British Columbia down to 1929 may be found in *British Columbia Manual*, 1930, published by the Provincial Bureau of Information, Victoria, 110-24.

Times for May 15, 1897, when the country was just being opened up, puts the case extremely well:

The Spokane Falls and Northern Railway Company, as represented by Mr. Corbin, have not long delayed in taking steps to neutralize—we might say nullify—the efforts put forward by the C.P.R., feebly enough it must be confessed, to secure the bulk of the Boundary Creek trade. As intimated elsewhere, the S.F. & N. have made arrangements for the shipment of goods via Marcus direct to consignees here at a fixed rate, reducing thereby the cost of freighting over this route from 2c. per pound (the present charge) to 1¼c. Furthermore, the American railroad agrees to assume all responsibility for goods until they have passed through the customs. We have here a capital opportunity of contrasting American with Canadian enterprise. The C.P.R. had last winter every chance to seize the opportunity when it occurred. As they failed to do so they must abide by the consequences of the grasping, penny-wise, pound foolish policy which they have adopted with regard to this matter. So far as the people of the district are personally concerned, Mr. Corbin's move is hailed with every indication of satisfaction. Its immediate results decrease the cost of carriage from railroad termini; but beyond this it is exceedingly probable that its influence will be farther reaching and eminently more important, for it will demonstrate to the C.P.R. in an unmistakable manner that one course, and one course only, is open, if the trade with this valuable section is not to be irrevocably lost to the company,—and that is the imperative necessity for the construction of a branch line south from Penticton at once.

The boundary country had to wait years for the construction of the "branch line south from Penticton." In the meantime the American railroads and their satellites, including the Vancouver, Victoria and Eastern, captured what trade there was. Geography had much to do with it, but American initiative and enterprise had even more.

Enough has already been brought forward to show that Kootenay was almost, if not constantly, under American influences. But was it "Americanized"? This is a very difficult question—one which cannot be answered statistically. Geographically the Kootenay and the neighbouring boundary country were cut off from the British Columbia coast. But the Kootenay stretches far north into British Columbia. Its northern portion is crossed by the main line of the Canadian Pacific Railway. The boundary country is merely the southern part of the great plateau which occupies so much of the

interior of British Columbia. It might have been linked up with the
rest of the plateau country long before it was.

It will be recalled that in colonial days Governor Seymour once
described British Columbia as a "road with a gold mine at one end
and a city in a neighbouring colony at the other."[25a] The gold mine,
of course, was Cariboo, the city Victoria. The trouble with the
Kootenays and the boundary country always was that the road was
lacking. It is idle to dwell upon "might have been's," but if
Governor Douglas's project of 1863 had gone through, and it had
proved practicable to construct a road through southern British
Columbia, across the Rockies by a southern pass to link up with a
road built west from Red River, how different might the fate of
Kootenay have been! Or, if the Canadian Pacific had been built
through the Crowsnest Pass, or failing that, if the Crowsnest
branch had been built earlier and continued through to the coast,
then Kootenay might have been linked up with the rest of the
province in a way it has never been. Even then the natural route
would have been from north to south and not from east to west.
Kootenay was isolated from the rest of British Columbia. It was
not isolated from Spokane. Was Kootenay, then, American rather
than Canadian? Was it ever British Columbian? Is it perhaps
more correct to say that Kootenay felt the effects of the American
mining invasion more directly than any other portion of British
Columbia and in that sense had a more Americanized tone?

The Kootenays and the boundary country were essentially mining regions and as such possessed certain definite characteristics.
There was the usual inrush of prospectors, followed later by the
experienced promoters and capitalists who knew the risks and were
adept at the development of mining claims. These promoters as a
rule lived in Spokane, but they were able to interest New York
capitalists in their successful ventures.

There was no essential difference between mining methods on
either side of the international boundary. Placer mining, as we have
seen, originated in California and spread northward and eastward.
Lode mining spread out from Nevada where the Comstock Lode
had become an almost legendary producer of wealth. Canadians
followed American mining methods, making whatever adaptations
the localities required. At first there was more American than
Canadian capital invested because Spokane was close and Montreal

25a. *Supra*, 180.

and Toronto almost as far away as New York. With the rise of the Rossland mines in the middle 1890's Canadians became interested in the mines of southern British Columbia. But the source of the capital invested made little or no difference to mining methods.

The chief differentiation between British Columbia mining conditions and those in the neighbouring states of the American Union seems to have been a result of the character of government. W. J. Trimble has pointed this out in his *Mining Advance into the Inland Empire*, but it should be remembered that he is describing British Columbia during the colonial period before 1871, when the Governor ruled with the assistance of a Legislative Council. The introduction of responsible government in 1871-2 gave to British Columbians as full rights of self-government as were enjoyed by the citizens of Washington, Oregon, Idaho, and Montana. But Trimble's analysis is important and will bear quotation:

A marked feature of the life in the Kootenai was the submission of the miners to the lawful authorities. Here were a thousand or so rough miners, all collected from the American territories at the time when Montana was going through vigilante throes; government was represented by a lone magistrate with two or three constables unsupported by any possibility of aid from the Fraser; and the district was close to the boundary line, a condition permitting easy escape for transgressors. And yet the testimony of the British officials is unanimous as to the orderliness of the miners.

Reviewing . . . the prominent features of the different governmental forms applied under the British and under the American auspices in the mining advance, we see, on the one hand government largely in the hands of an efficient executive, who made laws and organized administration on summary methods; on the other, representative government, under hampering conditions, working tardily and painfully towards order, and meeting local or occasional reinforcement. Under the former society was from the first under control, and there was a tendency to restrain the individuals for the benefit of society—a restraint at times verging to over-repression; under the latter individualism was feebly controlled from above, but had to generate within itself forces of order, and it tended to undue license hurtful to society. The American system developed a country the more swiftly, the British more safely. Under both systems strong men labored courageously and well to adjust forms of order to unorganized society.[26]

26. Trimble, *Mining Advance*, 58-9, 246-7. On the character of the colonial government in British Columbia and the introduction of responsible government,

The real difference is that there was less local self-government in British Columbia than in Idaho, Montana, and Washington. The province was divided into federal electoral districts and into "ridings" or local electoral districts for the provincial House. There were no counties nor townships as in the United States and the eastern Canadian provinces, but there was a provision for the creation of municipalities, urban or rural, whenever the population in any locality was sufficiently great. In 1897 there were thirty-one such municipalities in British Columbia of which five, Rossland, Nelson, Kaslo, Grand Forks, and Greenwood, were in the Kootenay and boundary countries. Eleven of these municipalities were urban, the balance being classed as rural. All of the mining municipalities are listed as urban.[27] Municipalities, urban or rural, possessed powers of local self-government. Until such municipalities were created administration was in the hands of provincial officials. In the mining areas the provincial official was usually the Gold Commissioner, who also possessed magisterial powers. Although miners' meetings did in a few instances occur in British Columbia they were never a regular procedure as in American mining camps. On occasion American miners coming into an unorganized district, in which there was as yet no representative of the government of British Columbia, held a meeting and drew up regulations which remained in force until the authorized official arrived.

Trimble rather over-emphasizes the efficiency of the British Columbian governments. In comparison with the weak administrations which all too often controlled the American states and territories during the hectic days of the mining rushes, the colonial Governors, and after federation the provincial Cabinets, were no doubt strong. None the less Governor Frederick Seymour, during whose weak rule the first rush to Kootenay occurred, was notorious for his inefficiency, and several of the early provincial administrations cannot be classed as vigorous. What British Columbia did

see Scholefield and Howay, *British Columbia;* W. N. Sage, "Early Days of Representative Government in British Columbia," *Canadian Historical Review,* III, 143-80, "From Colony to Province: The Introduction of Responsible Government into British Columbia," *British Columbia Historical Quarterly,* III, 1-14, "John Foster McCreight, the First Premier of British Columbia," *Royal Society of Canada Transactions,* XXXIV, sec. II, 173-85.

27. *Year Book of British Columbia,* 1897, 143.

possess was a tradition of law and order which had come down from colonial days when that great trio, Governor Sir James Douglas, Colonel Richard Clement Moody, and Judge Begbie, demonstrated that British justice and British traditions would be upheld. Much praise is due to the local magistrates and Gold Commissioners who performed their tasks fearlessly and efficiently. It would be hard to find a finer body of men than these early pioneers of law and order in British Columbia. The same miners who in Montana or Idaho might have been prominent vigilantes, in British Columbia unhesitatingly obeyed the law. The reason was the same in both cases. The miners became vigilantes only when other recognized methods of law enforcement had not yet been inaugurated or had broken down. To be sure, as Trimble has shown, the American miners preferred vigilante hangings to state executions.[28] In British Columbia the traditions of Douglas and Begbie remained, but probably the essential difference was that the American gold seekers in Kootenay, as in Cariboo, came in expecting that law and order would be enforced and were not disappointed.

An interesting contrast of political conditions north and south of the international boundary in 1866 may be culled from the pages of the Victoria *British Colonist*. In October of that year an election for a member for Kootenay in the British Columbia Legislative Council was held. The issues were the union of the colonies of Vancouver Island and British Columbia and the problem of road tolls. Candidates were nominated and speeches made. The *Colonist* reported that "the Kootenay election will probably go to R. J. Smith who believes in Union and the abolition of road tolls." The election passed off quietly and Kootenay was duly represented at New Westminster. The previous July a territorial convention had met at Boise, Idaho Territory, to select a delegate to Congress. The following account from the Portland *Oregonian* was quoted in the *Colonist* for July 4, 1866:

28. Trimble, *Mining Advance*, 175, quoting the Rev. A. M. Hough, "Establishment of our Mission in Montana: Notes from My Diary" (MS in Montana Historical Library, at Helena, Montana): "One of the things I could never understand, was that in communities where the population was ready to rise *en masse* and hang men guilty of great crimes or sustain an organized Vigilance Committee in doing it, a legal conviction and execution will not be sustained."

The "harmonious Democracy" of Idaho, had a pretty general row in their Territorial Convention at Boise on the 18th—a sort of knock-down-drag-out arrangement. The row finally culminated in a shooting spree, in which most of the coppery magnates took a lively interest, Burmester and D. W. Douthett, took shares in it, and the latter, in a playful mood, fired a revolver point blank at Street, the editor of the WORLD, who was only saved from a trip to the next world, by the intervention of a pocket book in his vest pocket. Street at the same time gave vent to his hilarity and good feeling by firing a shot at our D. Wm., which, however, overshot the mark and lodged in the ceiling. The row went on pleasantly and gaily for some time, but at last accounts, all was quiet on the border.

Holdbrook was nominated a delegate to Congress.

It is easy to over-emphasize this "law and order" aspect of British Columbia mining, but, after all, it was important. If Kootenay were really a northward extension of the American mineral frontier in the fullest sense, then "frontier" conditions as they existed in the neighbouring American territory should have been reproduced on British soil. The fact is they were not in Cariboo, Kootenay, or later in the Klondike. Economically the mining frontier moved north in the 1860's and to a great extent in the 1880's, 1890's, and 1900's, but its legal, administrative, and political aspects did not appear in Canada. The "westward movement" in British North America is never quite the same as it is in the United States.

Was later Kootenay "Americanized"? In the sense that the majority of its inhabitants seems to have come from the United States it was. But these Americans were "anxious to conform to the laws of the country."[29] They were usually prepared to become good "Kootenayans," and even good British Columbians and good Canadians. But sentimentally they were, naturally, attached to their old homes. Excursions to Spokane, and even Chicago, were well patronized. Excursions to the British Columbian coast cities seem to have been conspicuous by their absence. "Goodwill visits" from Spokane were quite common. Until the Kootenays were well served by professional men of their own, Spokane doctors and lawyers were called in.

The feelings of the American inhabitants of Kootenay were well expressed in 1898 when Lord Aberdeen, Governor-General of

29. *Sessional Papers of British Columbia*, 1888, 271.

Canada, visited Rossland. On that occasion General Charles S. Warren replied to the toast to "Our American Cousins" at a banquet given in honour of His Excellency. The General spoke, in part, as follows:

I congratulate you, Sir, upon your administration as Governor-General of Canada. You are respected and loved as well by Americans as by your own subjects. Any time the American citizen comes across the line, he expects to obey your laws, feeling that your interests are ours and ours are yours. Your Excellency, your American cousin is a part of the history of this country. As you saw sailing down the Arrow Lakes last night, the hundred camp fires, reaching from the lake shore to the timber line, it is safe to say that those fires were built by your American cousins. They blazed the trail for you to follow—they are responsible for the Kootenays— they are responsible also for the Klondike. They do not build many railroads in this country, they simply blaze the way for you to do so. The winter or the summer storm has no terror for your American cousins. Wherever you find him in this broad land, you find an enterprising, progressive, law-abiding citizen, proud of you, proud of your institutions, and proud of the greatest and noblest queen the world has ever known, but prouder still of the land that gave them birth.[30]

Stripped of its rhetoric, and allowing for the usual extravagances of an after-dinner speaker, this statement may be accepted as indicative of a fairly large section of Kootenay opinion at the time of the Spanish-American War.

Unfortunately it has not been possible to arrive at any definite conclusion as to the number of Americans in Kootenay during its greatest period. Until 1911 the Census of Canada combined Kootenay statistics under the general head of Yale and Cariboo. According to the Census of 1901 out of a total British Columbian population of 178,657 only 17,164 were American-born. Of these 9,156 lived in the federal electoral riding of Yale and Cariboo. In 1901 the population of Kootenay was just over 30,000. In 1911 it had reached 50,000 and ten years later had declined slightly.[31]

But whatever the actual percentage of American-born in the population it is evident that Kootenay was constantly under

30. *Rossland Board of Trade Report* (Toronto, 1898), 13, quoted in Bescoby, "American Mining Advance."

31. The figures for 1901 are from the *Census of Canada*, 1901, I, 416, 418. The figures for Kootenay are based on the *Year Book of British Columbia*, 1911-1914, 404, and *British Columbia Manual*, 1930, 69.

United States influence. American capital, as we have seen, was with few exceptions responsible for the opening up of the Kootenay and boundary mines and for the construction of the smelters. The American tariff of 1897 which raised the import duty on lead ores was as much responsible for the growth of the Trail smelter as was the increasing pro-Canadian and pro-British sentiment in the Kootenays which would favour smelting the ore at home. Even after British and Canadian capital began to come to Kootenay at least 90 per cent of the trade was American.[32]

The only Canadian provinces which at that period could have invested capital in mining were far away. They were interested to some extent, but, as has been shown, Spokane was the magnet which drew Kootenay and the boundary country. As a result some Kootenayans felt that Canada was neglecting them. The editor of the Rossland *Miner* unburdened himself on May 4, 1895, as follows:

The absolute indifference of Canadians generally and eastern Canadians in particular to the mining development of their own great country is enough to make a citizen of West Kootenay weary and tired. If the capital in Montreal, Toronto, Ottawa and other eastern cities that is annually used for gambling on Wall Street, New York, or on the wheat exchange, Chicago, Illinois, or on the mining exchange, Denver, Colorado, were put into development work throughout the great mineral zone in British Columbia, which is as great or greater than any mineral bearing area in the United States, not only would we see more rapid development of the country, but we would see immense fortunes made by our own countrymen. We would also see some point in the east become one of the world's great trading centres for the refined product of Canadian mines. Canada would become a great exporter of the precious metals and Canadian commerce in every branch would feel the stimulus. But no, our precious metals now being mined in bulk must filter through the markets of the United States into the commerce of the world, bringing prosperity it is true to the loyal Canadians of West Kootenay, but in their ultimate and far-reaching effects doing no more for Canada than if the 49th parallel ran north instead of south of West Kootenay. Trail Creek is now producing $4,000 a day in solid gold. During 1895 it will export $2,000,000 worth of the precious metal or 5 per cent of the whole output of the United States. . . . Trail Creek is now greater than Cariboo in its palmiest days and more permanent, but British

32. Nelson *Miner*, November 14, 1896.

Columbian ears are so stuffed with the traditions of Cariboo that the noise of the present day movement disturbs them no more than it would the lotus eaters of Alfred Tennyson.

The editor of the *Miner* was probably giving vent to feelings which had some justification. The Rossland *Miner* no doubt had but little circulation in Eastern Canada, but the editor's diatribe may have produced a feeling of self-satisfaction in Spokane. The gibe about Cariboo is worth a moment's attention. It comes very close to the truth. Cariboo is a tradition in British Columbia, especially in the coast cities, and Kootenay was far away from Vancouver and Victoria. Just as Vancouver was to lose out to Seattle in the gold rush to the Yukon, so Spokane had outdistanced all competitors. The Cariboo road through the Fraser canyons had been partially destroyed by the building of the Canadian Pacific, and the work of destruction was to be completed by the construction of the Canadian Northern Pacific, but the old road had a reality, whereas the old Dewdney Trail by 1910 was hardly even a memory.

Socially Kootenay was a strange amalgam of American, Canadian, and British customs and traditions. At first the American naturally predominated, but as the population became more stable and the towns grew, British and Canadian elements became more prominent. As a wise British Columbian mining man, who had been in Kootenay in the late 1890's, once remarked to the writer: "The boom was American; when it died down the Canadian elements came into their own." As late as 1900 the national holidays of both Canada and the United States were celebrated in Kootenay, but the fourth of July was the big day. It is reported that one postmaster in Kootenay kept his office open on Dominion Day, July 1, but closed it on the "Glorious Fourth." On the other hand, at a time when pro-Boer sentiment was widespread in the United States, the Canadians and Americans in Rossland combined in 1900 to celebrate the relief of Mafeking.

A word should be added about Rossland, "the Johannesburg of British Columbia." When the claims were being staked, a certain Ross Thompson who was hunting and prospecting had a log cabin on Red Mountain. "Ross's Land" was the name ironically applied to Thompson's cabin. The name stuck, and when the inevitable town grew up near the mines it was named Rossland.[33] Rossland in 1894 contained four log houses; in 1896 it possessed a population of 4,000; in 1901 its population was well over 6,000 and it was one of the best known mining camps in North America. But its hey-day was passing. In 1911 its population was under 3,000.[34]

Rossland in its early days was a rather typical mining camp. It represented the peak of the boom and therefore attracted the Americans. For a brief period it ran "wide open" and Sourdough Alley rivalled the Klondike City of the worst days in Dawson. But Rossland obtained municipal government in 1897 and promptly cleaned house.

The churches and schools were essentially a Canadian influence. Perhaps it might be suggested that the Anglican Church was even more a British than a Canadian influence, but that is perhaps drawing the distinction rather fine. The Methodists and the Presbyterians came into Nelson in 1891. St. Paul's Presbyterian Church was dedicated in 1892; the Methodist church was built in 1894; the Salvation Army hall in 1896; and the Anglican and Baptist churches date from 1898. In 1898 Father Ferland was in charge of the Catholic church. The Methodist church in Rossland, which was built in 1895, was also used as a public school until the Department of Education in Victoria could have a proper building erected, and opened in July, 1896. But the school population of Rossland was growing so fast that another school had to be opened soon after. In the main street a memorial still attests the gratitude of the Rosslanders to the most famous padre of the Kootenays,

33. Such seems to be the generally accepted account of the origin of Rossland; cf. Scholefield and Howay, *British Columbia*, II, 474. B. F. Townley, in *Mine-Finders*, 202, tells the following story: "In 1891, capitalising the rush to the camp, Ross Thompson, a miner at the Centre Star, found an easier occupation selling town lots at thirty dollars each on a claim he staked on the present site of Rossland, naming the town 'Thompson' after himself. By the spring of 1893 a financial panic sweeping the country temporarily wrecked the fortunes of the camp and the boom waned as quickly as it had started. With the dropping of the War Eagle development, the townsite was facetiously dubbed 'Ross's Land,' its sole residents being Thompson and his mistress, living in a log cabin and ekeing out an existence from the unguarded supplies of the Centre Star mine."

34. Population statistics from the censuses of Canada to be found in the *Canada Year Book*, 1940, 100, give the following figures for Rossland: *1901*, 6,156; *1911*, 2,826; *1921*, 2,097; *1931*, 2,848.

the Rev. H. Irwin, "Father Pat," of Rossland, a real "sky pilot," well suited to a mining community.

One institution in Rossland should be mentioned, the Rossland Club. In its hey-day it was equal to any club in Canada, at least such is the claim of old Rosslanders, and even in its decline it was impressive. Its bar was one of the most patronized institutions in Rossland. Into the bar counter some jovial soul had hammered a dime. Many a man has tried to scoop that dime with his change, only to be greeted with shouts of laughter from the bystanders. The club outlived the great days of Rossland and lingered on, a mute memorial of a vanished past. It was burnt down a few years ago, but has now been rebuilt and is again flourishing.

To sum up, Kootenay was probably more American than the rest of British Columbia, but it did possess Canadian and British Columbian attributes. In company with the boundary country, it was isolated from the rest of the province, constituting, before all else, a mining region whose characteristics were determined by the nature of the industry. American capital, American men, and American energy made Kootenay in the first place, and although British and Canadian capital finally displaced American and the leading economic institutions of Kootenay are nearly all Canadian-controlled today, the country still bears the stamp of its origin. The pull to the south has never been overcome. Probably most Kootenayans would not wish it to be overcome. But Kootenay is now a part of British Columbia. It has its own local loyalty, of course, and has developed its own institutions but it is more closely linked up with the rest of Canada than it was in the early days. The northward thrust of the "Inland Empire" rapidly crossed into Kootenay and the boundary country and then later receded, leaving not a rearguard but a durable influence conducive to the perpetuation of friendly and even intimate relations.

CHAPTER XII

LUMBER AND FISH

1860-1913

THE two products most generally associated with British Columbia
are perhaps the Douglas Fir and the Sockeye Salmon. The cedar
and the hemlock and the halibut, though commercially important,
are less famous. From the time when the Indians were the sole
inhabitants of the country to the present, the products of the forest
and the fishery have been basic in the economic life; and from a
very early period of trade and settlement the prosperity of those
who exploited them has depended not merely on the techniques of
the day and the availability of suitable capital and labour but also
on access to foreign markets. A sketch of the economic history of
British Columbia which omitted to trace the growth of these two
staple industries would be incomplete indeed, and although the
lumber industry has been amply treated in another volume in the
present series[1] and the Pacific Coast fisheries in another recent
work,[2] it is necessary to give a brief account of both industries here.

To the Indians lumber and salmon were vital necessities. "The
material culture of the coastal tribes hinged on the shoals of salmon
that annually ascended the creeks and rivers, and on the abundant
stands of free grained cedar trees; for the salmon provided them
with an assured food supply throughout the year and the cedar
furnished timber for dwellings, canoes and household utensils, and
bark for clothing and mats."[3]

I. LUMBER

The coast Indians of British Columbia differed from all other
tribes in Canada in their use of plank houses. "The cedar trees
that furnished so much of their dress, furnished also beams and

1. W. A. Carrothers, "Forest Industries of British Columbia," in A. R. M.
Lower, *The North American Assault on the Canadian Forest* (Toronto and New
Haven, 1938); for the period prior to 1914, see also A. C. Flumerfelt, "Forest
Resources," in *Canada and Its Provinces* (Toronto, 1914), XXII, 487 ff.

2. H. E. Gregory and Kathleen Barnes, *North Pacific Fisheries* (New York,
1939); for British Columbian fisheries prior to 1914, see D. N. McIntyre, "The
Fisheries," in *Canada and Its Provinces* (Toronto, 1914), XXII, 445 ff.

3. Diamond Jenness, *The Indians of Canada* (Ottawa, 1934), 327.

planks of solid timber, from which the Salish tribes around the straits of Georgia and Juan de Fuca, and the Nootkas on the west coast of Vancouver Island, built oblong dwellings of amazing size, several hundred feet long in some cases by fifty or sixty feet wide."[4] "The most remarkable feature about all these West Coast houses was the extraordinary labour and patience required to fell and dress the trees, carve the posts, and split off and dress the planks, with no other tools than adzes and chisels of stone or shell, and wedges of wood or antler."[5]

The explorers used the wealth of the forest for other purposes and replenished their vessels with masts and spars.[6] "In 1786, James Strange of the East India Company writes from Nootka 'there is no doubt that the timber with which this coast is covered (and which in its size and fine grain is nowhere to be excelled) would compose a valuable addition to our trading, as this article carries a very advanced price in China and is always in demand there, especially such as is fit for masts and spars.'"[7] In 1788 Captain John Meares carried a deck load of spars to China.[8]

As the overland fur trade developed sawn timber was used in the construction of trading posts. We can only guess as to the practice of the Spaniards at Nootka, but we are told that "the first step in building any Hudson's Bay fort was always the construction of a saw-pit which was operated by two men."[9] "A staging was built, sufficiently high for a person to walk under, and a log, two sides of which had been flattened with a broad-axe, was lashed to this. Boards were sawn from the log by two men, one on top of the staging and the other underneath [i.e., in the "pit"], who operated a long saw with handles at both ends."[10]

It was the famous Dr. McLoughlin who erected the first sawmill

4. *Ibid.*, 93. A full description of the dwellings is given.

5. *Ibid.*, 95.

6. Carrothers, "Forest Industries," 254.

7. *Ibid.*

8. *Ibid.*

9. H. C. Copeland, "Some Historical Highlights on the British Columbia Timber Industry," *Western Lumberman*, Vancouver, August, 1922, cited by Carrothers, "Forest Industries."

10. W. K. Lamb, "Early Lumbering on Vancouver Island," *British Columbia Historical Quarterly*, II (January, 1938), 40, n. 30.

on the coast at Fort Vancouver in 1827-8.[11] It did more than supply local needs and in 1829 a cargo of deals was shipped to Hawaii. On the construction of the Hudson's Bay Company's fort at Victoria, a mill was set up there in 1848. Its operations were precarious. Its machinery, and for that matter the millwright, could only be replaced from England, and the mill stream ran dry in summer.[12] But it, too, worked for export, as well as for home consumption, and cut deals for San Francisco.

A steam sawmill, of which no trace was left beyond a heap of sawdust, was erected at Albert Head, near Victoria, in 1853-4. In 1860 a relatively large sawmill was constructed at Port Alberni. In the first five years of operation its output amounted to approximately 35 million board feet. It was well located, in proximity to big timber, at a point easy of access by sea but from which workmen could not desert by land. It was able to compete with Puget Sound mills on their own ground, but many of its markets were far afield in China, Australia, New Zealand, the Sandwich Islands, and South America[13] and its customers included the governments of France, Spain, and Sardinia.[14] But, while ships were being loaded for the export trade, there was sometimes a shortage of lumber in the colony for local construction and importation from Puget Sound might be needed.[15]

On the mainland a demand for lumber accompanied the settlement which followed the collapse of the gold rush. A mill was built at Fort Yale in 1858 and by 1859 there was also a mill at Fort Langley. The first sawmill on Burrard Inlet came into operation in 1863. Its principal market was at Victoria. It was not until the mill had changed hands that a successful export trade was built up. On the south shore on the inlet the well-known Hastings Mill was established in 1865 by Captain Stamp, who had previously operated at Port Alberni, and who had ample capital at his command. It is worthy of notice that the sales in the San Francisco

11. Carrothers, "Forest Industries," 254.

12. *Ibid.*, 255.

13. W. K. Lamb, "Early Lumbering on Vancouver Island, part II," *British Columbia Historical Quarterly*, II (April, 1938), 106. This article contains a detailed account of this and other early enterprises.

14. Carrothers, "Forest Industries," 256.

15. *Ibid.*, 259.

market were made in competition with Puget Sound mills and in the face of a tariff of 30 per cent *ad valorem*. The industry was depressed from 1865 to 1867 but revived in 1868, when exports quadrupled. There was a further increase in 1869 and a slump in 1870. On the whole little expansion occurred before 1880. Throughout the period foreign markets were widely scattered and in addition to the United Kingdom and the United States included Australia, South and Central America, and China.[16]

A transformation of the industry came with the construction of the transcontinental railway which began in 1880. Lumber, equivalent perhaps to the previous annual output, was needed for construction operations and when the railway was completed a new market was opened on the prairies. In the period from 1884 to 1894 the capacity and the cut of the British Columbia mills more than doubled. By 1900 they doubled again, although rough lumber and lumber sawn on not more than one side and shingles were admitted free of duty from the United States.[17] The amount of timber cut in British Columbia has been estimated as follows by the Forest Branch of the provincial Department of Lands:

	Million f.b.m.
1848-70	250
1871-80	350
1881-90	550
1891-1900	1,327
1901-10	4,754
Total 1848-1910	7,231

The great expansion of the industry was to come later.[18]

On the technical side lumbering in British Columbia had to contend with difficulties which had not been encountered elsewhere on the continent. The logs, in the coast area, were of immense size and weight. Even at the present day, when much of the best timber has been logged off, a single log may weigh as much as 21 tons. Then, too, the terrain is extremely rough, while as a result of the heavy rainfall soft ground may be encountered.

16. *Ibid.*, 260-7.

17. Corresponding concessions were made in the United States market to Canadian finished lumber, but owing to freight charges these tariff concessions were not of much value to British Columbia.

18. Carrothers, "Forest Industries," 270.

These two conditions, large, heavy logs and rough country, have been the principal factors in the demand for logging equipment of great power. The early lumbermen of the Pacific coast found forests which extended to the water's edge. The stages in the development of mechanized logging coincide first with the cutting of the fringe along the shore, then with the cutting of successive strips of timber, each a little further from tidewater, higher in elevation, and rougher in surface. The first trees were felled towards the water, and jackscrews and wedges were used to roll the logs into the inlet. But such methods, known as "hand logging" were almost impossible beyond a strip along the shore of two or three hundred feet. Oxen were introduced as the next step; and one, two and eventually twelve yoke of oxen were used to haul a string of several logs, chained or dogged one behind the other, along a "skidroad" to the water. Exploitation continued and the "skidroad" increased in length and cost of operation. Soon a small railroad was being used to haul cars of logs from the center of woods operations to the "log-dump" at tidewater. Oxen and horses were still used, but were confined to "yarding" the logs to a rollway by the side of the railroad.[19]

The limitations which these difficulties imposed on the earlier enterprises are well illustrated from the history of the Alberni mill. Its founders complained that "there is no wood in the district to supply the wants of a large mill" and regretted that they had not invested their capital on Puget Sound. In 1864 the manager wrote to the Colonial Secretary:

It requires a large tract of land anywhere to furnish 20 million feet of logs every year for the use of a Mill, but especially in a country so totally unsuitable for large Sawmills as this Island, owing to the broken character of the country and the Smallness and Shallowness of the Streams. At Alberni there are roads from 6 to 8 miles in length for the purpose of transporting hay and bulky articles to the logging camps; a water course of two miles long, dams, piers and abutments constructed at a great cost to raise a lake and river and at any time if the mill can exist much longer, we may have to make a railway to convey logs for many miles.

He went on to describe the Alberni sawmill as "the largest and probably the only industrial enterprise of the kind" that would ever exist on Vancouver Island.[20] Modern technique has, of course, refuted this pessimism.

19. *Ibid.*, 246 f.
20. Extracts quoted in Lamb, "Early Lumbering."

Booms of logs had to be towed to the sawmills. At first whale-boats rowed by men were used, and later tugboats. For land haulage the draught animals were replaced by donkey engines, and by the nineties the use of the steam donkey engines was general.

In the sawmills also the equipment used had to be adapted to the size of the logs.

The conversion of a log into lumber involves three main operations: first, the sawing of boards or cants from the sides of the log; then the edging or squaring the edges of these boards or cants and ripping them into narrower pieces; and third, the trimming of the ends of the lumber after passing through the edger. The size and weight of the Pacific coast logs have made special demands on the equipment for the first two of these operations. The "trimmers" found in the Pacific coast mills do not differ greatly in design or strength from those found in the eastern mills; but carriages and log-deck machinery of exceptional ruggedness and power are necessary to handle the large Douglas fir, hemlock and spruce logs sent to British Columbia mills. Pacific coast-type edgers are much heavier, larger, and of greater strength than those used in other lumbering regions of Canada or the United States.

The methods and manufacturing equipment of the first of the larger mills did not differ greatly from those found in some of the older mills in operation a few years ago. Circular head-saws were used, a rope drive supplied the power to the set works on the carriage, and logs were dogged on the carriage by hand, men being stationed for that purpose. A chain and overhead gear were used to turn the logs on the carriage. Bandsaws, though developed comparatively early, were late in coming into general use on the Pacific coast. It was not always easy to find men expert in hammering and fitting bandsaws to suit Pacific-coast conditions, and the loss of lumber due to the extra width of the circular saw tooth, compared with that of a bandsaw, was not as great a consideration as it is at the present time.

Since 1900 changes have been in the nature of refinements of present methods and equipment rather than development of new ones.[21]

In a general way it can be said that the use of specialized and expensive equipment—for it was uneconomic to use heavy machinery for the lighter work—combined with the need for marketing organization to lead to the establishment of large-scale production units.

Shingles are a sufficiently important product to deserve separate

21. Carrothers, "Forest Industries," 250-1.

mention.[22] As roofing material they are the natural refinement of the shakes used by the Indians of the Pacific Coast. The abundance of straight-grained cedar on the Pacific Coast and its exhaustion in other parts of the continent have, in recent years, concentrated the production of shingles in the Province of British Columbia and the State of Washington. Since 1921 the output of British Columbia has been about 80 per cent of the total Canadian output and in some years it has exceeded the combined output of Washington, Oregon, and California. During the period under review in this chapter the production of shingles steadily increased. There were five shingle mills in British Columbia in 1881 and nine in 1891.[23] In the next eighteen years the percentage of the Canadian shingles produced in British Columbia rose from about 1/10 of 1 per cent to 50 per cent. Much of this was for the United States market. In 1890 the United States duty on cedar shingles was 30 cents per thousand.[24] The duty was removed in 1894, restored in 1897, raised to 50 cents per thousand in 1909, and abolished in 1913.[25] Sometimes the production of cedar shingles appears to vary in disregard of the laws of supply and demand. This is because an area may be logged off primarily to obtain Douglas fir, but the cedar trees in the area must be utilized at the same time. It follows that cedar shingles may occasionally be priced on the "sales realization" principle that applies to joint products.

In the early days when the timber resources of the province seemed unlimited timber lands were acquired, like all other lands, by purchase and grant from the Crown. Indeed any attempt to reserve economic rent for social purposes would have run directly counter to the ambitions which had led the settlers to the West Coast. A series of timber regulations was passed by the Legislative Council of Vancouver Island in 1853. Under these regulations a duty of tenpence per load of 50 cubic feet[26] was imposed upon all timber cut on the public lands, and it was provided that "no person, not being a subject of Her Majesty the Queen and a

22. For a fuller discussion see *ibid.*, from which source this account is taken.

23. These are census figures for mills employing more than five men.

24. Other shingles are often more lightly taxed.

25. The control of imports by quota in recent years is discussed in the final chapter.

26. Approximately 33⅓ cents per 1,000 board feet.

resident of Vancouver's Island, shall cut timber on the public lands under a penalty not exceeding £20." In reporting to the Colonial Secretary, Governor Douglas explained that the purpose of this legislation was "altogether protective" and that it was designed to prevent waste and destruction of timber and to throw as much as possible of the timber trade into the hands of the actual colonists.[27]

In 1888 a royalty of 50 cents per 1,000 board feet was reserved on all timber cut upon lands *thereafter* granted.[28] The act which established this royalty also provided for the granting of special licences to cut timber on Crown lands. The licence was for a year only and the area covered was limited to 1,000 acres. No person could hold more than one licence and licences were not transferable. The fee was $50 and the royalty of 50 cents per 1,000 board feet cut was the same as on lands granted by the Crown. On Crown lands other than timber limits timber could be cut by the holder of a hand-logger's licence, for which the annual fee was $10.[29]

Timber leases of unpre-empted lands of any extent, permitting the cutting of spars, timber, and lumber, had been authorized by the Land Ordinance of 1870. These leases were granted only to persons actually engaged in lumbering and conditions might be made for the erection of a sawmill of suitable size. The act of 1888 made this condition obligatory, and a lessee had to erect a sawmill capable of cutting at least 1,000 board feet per day of twelve hours for each 400 acres included in the lease. Leases were limited to thirty years, a rent of 10 cents per acre was charged, and the same royalty was imposed as on other timber lands.[30] In 1891 a deposit of 10 cents per acre was required on all timber leases. In 1892 the term of the lease was limited to twenty-one years and it was enacted that the leases should be offered to public competition.[31]

An important step was taken in 1896 when further purchases of Crown grants of timber lands were prohibited. Timber lands were

27. Lamb, "Early Lumbering" (January, 1938), 50 f.

28. Carrothers, "Forest Industries," 233, citing *Statutes of British Columbia,* 1888, c. 16, s. 21.

29. *Ibid.,* 233 f.

30. *Ibid.,* 233.

31. *Ibid.,* 234, citing *Statutes of British Columbia,* 1891, c. 15, s. 10, and 1892, c. 25, s. 6.

defined for this purpose as comprising all lands west of the Cascade
Range carrying 8,000 board feet to the acre, and all lands east of
the Cascades carrying 5,000 board feet to the acre.[32] At the time
of enactment land grants in aid of railway construction constituted
the chief alienation of timber which the province had made. Of
these two deserve mention. Both had been made prior to the act.
The first was the Dominion Railway Belt conveyed to the Dominion
under the terms of entry into Confederation. It contained 17,100
square miles of which 10,313 are estimated to have been timber
lands; and it was supplemented by 5,470 square miles in the Peace
River Valley estimated to contain 3,779 square miles of timber
land. In 1930 the Dominion returned to the province all the land
comprised in these grants which the Dominion had not alienated.
The second large grant had been made in 1884 in aid of the building
of the Esquimalt and Nanaimo Railway on Vancouver Island.
It comprised 3,000 square miles, and 780 square miles of mature
timber were still held by the railway in 1935.[33]

After the act of 1896 timber rights could be acquired from the
province only by lease, or by the 1,000-acre special licence, or by
hand logger's licence. Leases were made renewable in 1901. The
area covered by a special licence was reduced to 640 acres but the
same man might hold two licences at the same time. The fee was
raised to $100 and the grant or renewal of licences was made at the
discretion of the Chief Commissioner of Lands and Works.[34] The
act of 1901 provided for the forfeiture of any timber cut from
provincial lands which was not manufactured within the confines
of the Province of British Columbia.

In 1905 it was provided that no further leases should be granted.
All future sales of timber were to be by special licence. At the
same time the licence was given some of the features of the lease.
All licences in force, or applied for, were made transferable and
renewable for a period of sixteen years at the fees then paid. New
licences were to be transferable and renewable for twenty-one years.
Within three years more than 14,000 licences were issued. It was
obvious that the timber on the huge area for which licences had
been issued could not be cut, with advantage to the province,

32. *Ibid.*, 234, citing *Statutes of British Columbia*, 1896, c. 28, s. 12.
33. *Ibid.*, 235.
34. *Ibid.*, 235 f., citing *Statutes of British Columbia*, 1930, c. 30, s. 7.

within a period of twenty-one years and the government by Order-in-Council, dated December 24, 1907, reserved all unalienated timber in the province. Two years later a Royal Commission on Timber and Forestry in British Columbia was appointed.[35] On the presentation of an interim report in 1910, the privileges of licencees were extended indefinitely. The final recommendations of the Commission were embodied in the Forest Act of 1912.[36]

This rapid survey of forestry legislation has brought us down to the age of conservation, when an obvious threat of grossly uneconomic depletion focused attention on the need for restraint in the pursuit of immediate gain. The groping for plans on which a permanent economy could be based, which was to characterize a later period, will be discussed elsewhere. For our present purposes the Forest Act of 1912 which established a fund to meet the cost of precautions against the destruction of forests by fire and provided for the creation of forest reserves not available for sale and settlement marks the end of the openly predatory era in forestry.[37] It remains to consider here how far the lumber industry contributed to the establishment of a provincial economy in the last half of the nineteenth century.

We have seen that from the outset lumber did more than provide, as it had done for the Indians, the raw material for local construction and that a precocious export trade in spars brought British Columbia into contact with markets as distant as those whose urgent demand had exterminated the sea-otter. And before the period of rapid exploitation, which was to follow the completion of the Panama Canal, the export of timber to the prairies, largely from areas east of the Cascades, was one of the mainstays of provincial trade. But it is reasonable to push our enquiry somewhat further and ask what sort of society had been built up on the basis of this trade and to examine how the men who were occupied with political self-determination in the very infancy of the colony faced the parallel problem of determining their economic development.

To some extent the very character of the forestry legislation will help us in answering these queries. The self-assertion of the pioneer

35. For an account of this Commission and its work, see Flumerfelt, "Forest Resources," 496 ff.

36. Carrothers, "Forest Industries," 237.

37. *Statutes of British Columbia*, 1912, c. 17, s. 11.

settler is to be seen in the privileges of the hand-logger, privileges which were denied to Orientals and, rather more curiously, to North American Indians. The insistence that licencees must erect suitable sawmills shows anxiety that the development of the country should not be impeded by holding timber limits speculatively and has a distinct relationship to the doctrine of single-taxes which was to have its effect on municipal taxation. The same tendency is seen in the termination of the policy of leases, and of Crown grants of timber lands. The limiting factor in this as in other provincial industries was the scarcity of suitable labour, and we find rather an attempt to exclude Asiatic labour than an effort to raise the working conditions of the European or American immigrants, who were believed to be adequately protected by the prevalent rates of wages. For it was not only labour which had to be attracted but capital as well: and the province had to represent itself as a region in which high profits could be made. The plain circumstances of the case made this line of development natural enough. Yet it was not entirely spontaneous, but was influenced, perhaps even dominated, by the experience and the policy of communities in somewhat parallel circumstances, whose growth was envied or whose mistakes were cited as examples to be avoided.

Fifty years ago no one formulated the problems of the lumber industry in the terms which might be employed today. But the problem was no simpler because its ramifications were not always expressly stated. British Columbia was producing for foreign markets as well as for home consumption one of the basic raw materials of the construction industry. The demand was variable; more than one grade of lumber was inevitably produced at the same time; the markets were highly competitive and were affected in many cases by tariff barriers as well as by transportation costs. Even if the governments of those days had been gifted with almost incredible foresight, it would have been no easy thing to regulate such an industry on lines beneficial to the general economy and fair alike to the labourers and to the investors who were attracted to the province. It is no wonder that the problem of conservation was neglected or postponed and that the power of beautiful scenery and well-kept forests to attract foreign visitors was not foreseen. Not foresight, so much as the even rarer quality of sympathetic imagination, would have been needed to look on beautiful scenery as of direct value to the inhabitants of the land. Sympathetic imagination on such a matter could not have been expected from the politician of pioneer days.[38] He was ready, as a matter of common sense, to trade the scenery for wealth just as the Indians, who were assumed to have been insensible to its beauties, were considered to have traded it for blankets and firewater. As for posterity its education was in the hands of the pioneering generation and appreciation of the beauties of nature found no place on the curriculum which they devised. And today the problem is approached indirectly as a matter of business in order to cater to the incomprehensible tastes of tourists who in their hours of leisure may demand scenery as well as blankets and firewater.

II. FISH

If the forests were important in providing the material for their dwellings, fisheries provided the staple food of the coast Indians, at least in summer,[39] and conditioned their whole lives. Relatively speaking, from the standpoint of the Indians, food was plentiful in British Columbia and the population was denser than in most parts of Canada.[40] What we should be tempted to call today a higher standard of living was reflected in cultural achievement and the assured food supply. "The only Indians, indeed, who excelled in either sculpture or painting were the natives on the Pacific coast where both these arts attained an unexpected brilliance."[41]

The fishing industry followed a course not dissimilar in essentials to that of the lumber industry. In both cases the raw material was almost embarrassingly plentiful. In both cases the unusual conditions presented peculiar technical difficulties; for the unusual size of the British Columbia trees and the uneven character of

38. As late as the 1920's the writer has seen an electoral placard erected in the forest itself urging the electors to vote for men who would remove all this and build homes.

39. Jenness, *Indians of Canada*, 47 f. On the mainland the Indians hunted moose and other animals during the winter; on Vancouver Island they relied on halibut, cod, and shellfish from March to August, on salmon, taken at the heads of fiords, for their winter food.

40. *Ibid.*, 52.

41. *Ibid.*, 209.

the terrain delayed the development of the lumber industry much as the difficulty of preserving salmon for transport to distant markets delayed the development of the fisheries. In both cases the initial difficulties led to the adoption of small operating units which were later found entirely unsatisfactory so that the whole set-up of the industry had to be replanned in the light of local experience. In both cases the earliest efforts at governmental control were concerned with the endeavour to protect the interests of the labour employed while offering no excessive deterrent to the investment of outside capital. And in both cases the menace of depletion at length necessitated a programme of conservation.

The early fur traders and the early settlers preserved salmon by salting, and barrels of salted salmon figured among the earliest exports. The early records of the trade in fish show attempts to find markets for barrels of salted salmon. The market had to be one in which the product could be sold with a wide margin of profit; and there were many complaints about the quality of the salting. However, the Hudson's Bay Company did sell its fish in London and in Hawaii before it had moved its headquarters from the Columbia, and it must have seemed as if the cheapness of the salmon in British Columbia would ensure a regular and profitable trade.[42] It is, of course, the salmon cannery which furnishes the great output of today, but as late as 1867 the process of preserving salmon in hermetically sealed tins was still in the stage of experiment and demonstration. In October of that year the product of James Symes received special mention from the directors of the Agricultural Exhibition at New Westminster.[43]

The first recognized salmon cannery of British Columbia was built in 1870 at Annieville, some three miles below New Westminster, by Alexander Loggie, Alexander Ewen, James Wise, and David Hennessy. It was operated in conjunction with a saltery.[44] Two other canneries were established on the Fraser River within the next few years and in 1877 Marshall M. English, who came

42. By the courtesy of W. K. Lamb, Librarian of the University of British Columbia, the author has had access to excerpts from unpublished documents.

43. Gordon Strong, "The Salmon Canning Industry in British Columbia, 1934," MS in University of British Columbia Library.

44. *Ibid.*

from the southern states, erected a plant opposite New Westminster. By 1882 the annual pack on the Fraser River amounted
to about 250,000 cases of four dozen one-pound cans.[45]

In 1883 a floating cannery, "Spratt's Ark" appeared, built in
Vancouver and operated by Joseph Spratt, who retired two years
later. By 1891 combinations made their appearance with the
Anglo-British Columbia Packing Company, founded by Henry
Bell-Irving. "As a group the early packers [on the Pacific Coast]
were far from successful in the making of profits or even in maintaining solvency. From 1878 to the beginning of the World War
the number of failures of canneries and salteries was extraordinary.
The history of this period of 36 years is replete with stories of bank-
ruptcies of companies, destruction of plants, frequent abandonment
of canneries, and removal to new locations. Many sales of going
concerns and plants were recorded."[46]

The reasons for these combinations, which had their counterpart
in other industries about the same time, are to be found in the
multitude of small canneries, the introduction of the fish trap in
the United States, the improved processes for preserving fish,
technical devices such as the automatic cleaner introduced in 1903
known as the "Iron Chink," soldering machines and the can-
making machine, and the accessibility of new markets by rail and
water. In these ways the economies of large-scale production
appeared at a time when markets were expanding and the raw
material was abundant. And yet these very conditions were fatal
to the fortunes of many of the smaller enterprises. "The shores of
Alaska, British Columbia, Washington and Oregon soon were
strewn with the wreckage of concerns that rushed into the little-
understood operations of fishing, packing and marketing canned
salmon. . . . No other fishery in the world in the 1890's, it was
said, equalled the salmon fishery for scope of techniques."[47] Low
prices resulted in distress selling by the weaker producers which in
turn reduced the prices. In 1901 the British Columbia Packers
Association was formed including twenty-nine out of the forty-
eight plants on the Fraser River and twelve of those in northern

45. *Ibid.*
46. Gregory and Barnes, *North Pacific Fisheries*, 90.
47. *Ibid.*, 91.

British Columbia.[48] Its formation was part of a movement common to the United States branch of the industry.[49]

The techniques of the industry must obviously depend on the habits of the salmon.

The first salmon to return [from the open sea] in the year is the Spring species,[50] which makes its appearance in the rivers and streams around the first of June and continues till well on in August. Following the Spring Salmon comes the Sockeye,[51] the king of them all for canning purposes. It arrives about the first of July in schools and continues until the first half of September. Cohoe[52] begin to appear in numbers about the first of August and the run continues until the latter part of September. The last two weeks in August witness the arrival of the Pinks,[53] the most prolific of all the five species. The Chum[54] is the latest running of all the salmons, fishing for this species being in full swing about the first of October and continuing until the latter part of November.[55]

All five varieties are canned, but only in recent years have extensive markets been found for Pinks and Chums. "The Sockeye run in all the mainland rivers of British Columbia, in some of the rivers of the west coast of Vancouver Island and in the Nimkish River, near the head of the east coast of the island. . . . It frequents the northern waters of Puget Sound and the Fraser River in greater numbers than any other region, at least it did until the landslide [on the Fraser] of 1913."[56] They normally mature in their fourth year. "As the Sockeyes attempt to get to the headwaters of the river to spawn, they are in prime condition at the mouth of the river where they start on their long journey with ample reserves of nourishment."[57]

"In British Columbia, practically the entire quantity of salmon

48. *Ibid.*, 95.

49. *Ibid.*, 92 ff., for an account of combinations in the United States.

50. *Chinook*, on the Columbia, sometimes known as *King*, sometimes as *Tyee*.

51. *Blueback*, on the Columbia, *Alaska Red* in Alaska.

52. *Silver* on the Columbia, *Silverside* in Alaska.

53. Or *Humpback*.

54. Or *Dog*.

55. Strong, "Salmon Canning Industry," 27. The varieties are discussed in Gregory and Barnes, *North Pacific Fisheries*, 11 ff.

56. *Ibid.*, 28.

57. Strong, "Salmon Canning Industry," 36.

for commercial purposes is taken with the gill net, purse and drag seines, trolling and traps."[58] The traps are greatly disliked by fishermen as a labour-saving device likely, if used extensively, to diminish the volume of employment. Their use in British Columbia began experimentally in the 1880's, but they were not much used before 1900 and were never used extensively. In the years following the World War they were reduced as a means of spreading work among the fishermen.[59] In Alaska and the State of Washington the history of traps has been somewhat different. Traps were used experimentally in the 1880's. But "the introduction of fish traps in Alaska and the State of Washington in the 1890's and 1900's furnished the first important impetus to the growth of the salmon canning industry. For many years the investment of capital paralleled the rate of trap installations. Salmon traps have constituted a strategic factor in enlarging and stabilizing supply, although their efficiency has necessitated regulation in the interest of conservation. Being expensive as well as efficient, they have fostered a concentration of control over fish supplies. To a lesser extent they have also furnished a storage facility."[60] In British Columbia it has been contended that the costs of the industry have been enhanced by the necessity of providing establishments which can deal with the peak requirements.[61]

The freezing of salmon, which is relatively more important today in Canada than in the United States, began in the late 1880's in California and on the Columbia River and spread to Alaska and British Columbia in 1902. The output of frozen salmon has expanded greatly since 1913.[62] The process of freezing is also used for the halibut. Halibut fishing had begun as early as 1885, when schooners from Puget Sound operated off Cape Flattery. It developed rapidly with the introduction of cold storage for export. The production of the Pacific Coast rose from 6,877,640 pounds in 1899 to 21,706,000 in 1909. In the later year about half was taken by ships operating from Canadian ports, and some of the

58. *Ibid.*, 40.

59. Gregory and Barnes, *North Pacific Fisheries*, 23. At one time as many as twenty traps were in use at Sooke, but now there are only five.

60. *Ibid.*, 21. The use of traps was abolished by initiative in Washington in 1934.

61. *Ibid.*, 23.

62. *Ibid.*, 34.

American ships operated in Canadian waters.[63] However, the rate of production was kept up only by enlarging the area of operations as the more accessible grounds were fished out. The halibut fisheries are of peculiar interest because it seems possible that the Pacific Coast fishery, which by 1920 was in imminent danger of the permanent depletion that has overtaken halibut fisheries elsewhere, may be rehabilitated through international action. This question, however, falls within the age of planning and conservation and will be discussed in a later chapter.

In the pioneering age, with which we are concerned in this chapter, one of the most important aspects of the fishing industries is to be found in the type of permanent population attracted to the country. The work is seasonal and occupies from three to six months. There is a danger of a shortage of fish in any year and also a danger of permanent shortage if conservation methods are not followed. As the number of men engaged in fishing increases the catch per man will decline. The shore workers are also seasonally employed. They must be recruited, transported to their cannery, and provided with living quarters there. A very high proportion of non-white labour is employed. It cannot be said that the full implications of this labour situation were understood in the period under discussion. What was obvious was the conflict of interest between the operators who required cheap labour to make their enterprises profitable and the employees who were anxious to restrict the use of labour-saving devices such as traps, and to protect themselves against competitors willing to accept lower wages or lower prices for their fish.

As fish were sold in foreign markets, the demand for protection was one which came from labour and was opposed by employers. In 1892 a regulation was made limiting licences to resident British subjects. The salmon canners, who relied to some extent on migratory fishermen from the United States, disliked the regulation and it was frequently evaded. To make it more effective, registration was required in 1899. The canners and their agents complained bitterly that the number of boats would be cut down from 6,000 to 2,500 by stopping fishermen from coming from Oregon and California.[64]

63. McIntyre, "Fisheries," 469.
64. *Ibid.*, 452 f.

But the competition of a foreign race may be even more annoying than the competition of citizens of the United States. Japanese fishermen entered the field in the early years of the present century and by 1911 about half the men employed in gill netting were estimated to be Japanese.[65] The Japanese could of course receive licences only if they were naturalized, but at this time naturalization in Canada did not deprive them of Japanese nationality which they resumed on returning to Japan.[66] Popularly they were considered aliens. In 1912 special inducements were offered to white fishermen by extending to them privileges not enjoyed by Japanese or even by North American Indians.[67] The policy of progressive reduction and ultimate elimination of licences held by those who were not white or Indian came a decade later.

Both in the case of conservation and in that of labour pioneer communities were slow to learn the need for foresight and planning. Some salmon hatcheries were in operation in the 1880's, but this method of maintaining the supply of fish was later found by experiment to be uneconomical. The scientific conservation of a later age had to await the advance of knowledge and the creation of an atmosphere in which international action was possible. But it can hardly be said, even today, that the problem of social security has been squarely faced in relation to a seasonal occupation exposed to economic hazards both from failure of supplies and failure of markets. In the period under review it was left to take care of itself.

65. *Ibid.*, 459. One thousand out of nineteen hundred in northern British Columbia, a figure believed to be typical of conditions elsewhere.

66. Canadian Naturalization Act, *Revised Statutes of Canada*, 1906, c. 77, s. 24: "An alien to whom a certificate of naturalization is granted shall, within Canada, be entitled to all political and other rights, powers and privileges, and be subject to all obligations to which a natural born British subject is entitled or subject within Canada. . . ." The wording seems to have been chosen in the belief that s. 16 of the Imperial Naturalization Act of 1870 operated to restrict the powers conferred on the Parliament of Canada by the British North America Act of 1867. See W. H. P. Clement, *The Law of the Canadian Constitution* (Toronto, 1916), 179 ff.

67. McIntyre, "Fisheries," 459.

CHAPTER XIII

THE FUR-SEALS: DEPLETION AND CONSERVATION
1867-1912

THE history of the Pacific Coast of North America illustrates the changes in economic life which took place as the need for conserving sources of wealth forced itself upon the attention of governments. Scientific measures for conservation require careful planning based on careful research; they require the existence of a strong and energetic government ready to participate in the control of economic life; and they frequently require, in order to be efficacious, the honest co-operation of two or even of several nations. Before the era of scientific conservation we are likely to find lip-service paid to the idea and to find conservation itself used as a pretext for advancing national claims in a spirit which is still that of the predatory era. Not only is the Bering Sea fur-seal arbitration of 1893 "one of the *causes célèbres* of Canadian-American history,"[1] but it is an important landmark in the progress of scientific conservation with due regard for the various interests involved. It did not, indeed, mark the end of predatory exploitation, which was to flare up in the Klondike gold rush, nor of embittered international controversies which were to reach a climax in the Alaska boundary dispute, while sealing itself did not come under thoroughgoing international control until 1912.

In the days of the early maritime fur trade the fur-seal, as a source of wealth had been overshadowed by the sea-otter. The British and American fur traders hunted fur-seals on Staten Island and on many of the islands off the western coast of South America which were close to the track of their vessels,[2] and it was mainly the ease with which thousands of seal-skins could be obtained that recommended these animals to their attention. In Edmund Fanning's *Voyages*[3] there is an illustration showing that

1. It is treated as such in the volume in this series by P. E. Corbett, *The Settlement of Canadian-American Disputes* (New Haven and Toronto, 1937), 41 ff.
2. *Supra*, chap. I.
3. New York, 1833.

the vessel merely lay off and on, while the sailors went ashore and clubbed the fur-seals to death. But seal-skins were then worth only 50 cents or a dollar each, while a sea-otter skin brought from $20 to $30.

Similarly, the Russians from 1766 onward hunted the fur-seal on the Aleutian Islands. As the sea-otter approached extinction, more effort was made to secure seal-skins. Slowly they rose in value; but all the hunting was done on land. Most of the ships sold by the Americans to the Russians in the early 1800's were paid for in seal-skins, and the discharged crews were paid in the same currency. The extent to which this trade grew may be inferred from the fact that in 1813 the American ship *Atahualpa* delivered to the letter-of-marque schooner *Tamaahmaah* some 46,000 seal-skins for transport to China. The decrease in sea-otters caused the Americans to look further afield for fur-seal. From 1803 to 1812 numerous American vessels made contracts with Baranoff, the head of the Russian American Company, whereby for a share of the catch he supplied them with Aleuts and their baidarkas for otter and seal hunting off the coast of California. Here was the earliest form of pelagic sealing: an Aleut with his spear and baidarka.

The American vessels from Boston so engrossed the trade of Russian America and cut into the returns of the Russian American Company that national jealousy was aroused. This bore fruit when in September, 1821, Alexander I issued a ukase forbidding any foreign vessel to approach within one hundred Italian miles of the coast between Bering Strait and 51° north latitude. The American ship *Pearl* in the autumn of 1822 had just begun to trade at Sitka, and had bartered goods valued at $680 for 373 seal-skins (showing their value to have risen to almost $2 apiece) when the Russians ordered her off the coast.[4]

Both Great Britain and the United States immediately challenged this preposterous claim on the part of Russia. John Quincy Adams, the Secretary of State of the United States, demanded for its citizens the right of prosecuting their lawful commerce, and protested against "an interdiction manifestly incompatible with their rights." In a subsequent letter he stated: "The United States

4. Fur Seal Arbitration, IV, *Appendix to British Case* (Washington, 1895), 403.

can admit no part of these Russian claims; their right of navigation and of fishing is perfect, and has been in constant exercise from the earliest times, after the peace of 1783, throughout the whole extent of the Southern Ocean, subject only to the ordinary exceptions and exclusions of the territorial jurisdictions."[5] Later the United States Minister used the following language: "The existence of territorial rights to the distance of 100 miles from the coast, and the prohibition of approaching to the same distance from these coasts, and from those of all intervening islands, are innovations on the law of nations, and measures unexampled."[6] In the end the dispute was settled by the treaties of 1824 and 1825 between Russia on the one hand and the United States and Great Britain respectively, on the other. By them the southern boundary of Russian America was fixed at 54° 40', and the wide claim of jurisdiction over the high seas abandoned.

Matters then went along peaceably, save for some minor disputes. In 1867 the United States purchased Russian America. That cession embraced "all the territory and dominion now possessed by his said Majesty on the continent of America and in the adjacent islands." The boundaries were set out in detail; the western, the only one concerned in this dispute, may be summarized as beginning at a certain point in Bering Strait, and extending thence northerly without limitation, and from the same point in a southwesterly direction through Bering Strait and Bering Sea, passing midway between the Island of St. Lawrence and the Asiatic shore and midway between Attou Island and Copper Island, "so as to include in the territory conveyed the whole of the Aleutian Islands east of the 193rd meridian."[7]

In July, 1788, John Meares, coasting along between the Columbia River and Vancouver Island, had noticed "seals without number."[8] Doubtless these were a part of the seal herd in its annual migration to the rookeries on the Pribilof and other islands of Bering Sea. From an area of about ten million square miles of ocean these animals, following their instinct, converge towards that sea.

5. Z. A. Lash, "The Behring Sea Question," *Canadian Magazine*, I, 291.
6. *Ibid.*, 292.
7. The treaty of cession may be found in many books, e.g., Fur Seal Arbitration, II, *Appendix to the Case of the United States* (Washington, 1895), 43 ff.
8. John Meares, *Voyages* . . . (London, 1790), 172.

Though they are spoken of as a "herd" they do not congregate, but travel northward in twos and threes, widely scattered, but following the same general direction. In their travels the herd passes near the coast of Vancouver Island. While their skins were comparatively valueless the fur-seals attracted but little attention, and nothing was known of their habits. After the purchase of Alaska, an American schooner, *Pioneer*, ventured to the Pribilof Islands and secured a remunerative catch. But a few months later the United States government granted to Hutchinson, Kohl, and Company, who subsequently transferred their rights to the Alaska Commercial Company, the exclusive privilege of killing seals on those islands. In this monopoly lies the germ of the Bering Sea, or fur-seal, dispute; for it closed the land sealing and left but the pelagic, out of which the trouble arose.

In 1866 the first attempt at sealing on the open sea was made by Hugh Mackay, in the schooner *Ino*, of Victoria. For some years pelagic sealing was merely ancillary to a general trading with the Indians along the ocean coast of Vancouver Island. The animals, swimming along or lying asleep on the water thirty or forty miles off the coast, were easily killed by the Indian hunters from the canoes. The industry developed and soon became an end in itself; and the spear gave place to the rifle, which was displaced by the shotgun. Sealing schooners increased in numbers—all armed with the most modern guns. It was claimed, and doubtless with truth, that many of the seals killed on the high seas were lost. The percentage that sank is not known, the supporters of pelagic sealing claiming that the loss was negligible, and the opponents claiming that it was enormous. In 1882 the Victoria sealing fleet numbered fourteen; but by 1891 it had grown to fifty schooners. The annual catch of a sealer was frequently as large as two thousand skins. In 1892 it was estimated that the capital invested in the Victoria sealing fleet was about $780,000.[9]

The British were not alone in this pelagic sealing. American vessels from Puget Sound found the widely scattered, northward-moving herd off the mouth of the Columbia River and hung upon its flanks, picking off a seal at every opportunity. Farther northward the British from Victoria caught up with the pennipeds and

9. Fur Seal Arbitration, VIII, *Counter Case of Great Britain* (Washington, 1895), 264; *ibid.*, III, 499.

joined in the chase. Male and female, old and young, fell under the guns of the hunters. No discrimination was exercised. At first the cruises were comparatively short, but as the sealers became better acquainted with the movements of the animals they reached out to greater distances. San Francisco and other American ports entered the chase. Though the Bering Sea trouble was an international dispute regarding the conduct of the United States in seizing, confiscating, and otherwise interfering with the sealing schooners from Victoria, it must be remembered that, side by side with them, were the American vessels from Puget Sound and San Francisco.

The pursuit of the herd led at last to Bering Sea, a body of water of enormous extent: from east to west 1,100 miles, and from north to south 800 miles. The hunters had, at last, tracked the seals over countless miles of ocean to their breeding grounds, principally the islands St. Paul and St. George of the Pribilof group. The first sealing vessel to enter Bering Sea and engage in pelagic sealing was the American schooner *City of San Diego*, in 1883. In the next year the British schooner *Mary Ellen*, of Victoria, followed her. Each year the number of schooners in Bering Sea increased, pursuing and depleting the seal herd. The business was very profitable. The Victoria fleet employed more than five hundred Indian hunters and more than two hundred canoes. The building, repairing, and outfitting of the vessels brought wealth to that city and gave employment to a large number of men; the returns increased its trade. And Victoria was very proud of her fleet.

Between 1868 and 1873, Congress had enacted a series of statutes extending the laws of the United States on customs, commerce, and navigation to the area ceded by Russia. They prohibited any person from killing fur-seals within the territory and its waters except under lease or permit from the Secretary of the Treasury. No firearms were to be used or any means employed in the industry tending to drive the seals from their habitual breeding grounds. In 1870 the Secretary of the Treasury leased to the Alaska Commercial Company for twenty years the privilege of killing 100,000 seals annually on the islands of St. Paul and St. George.[10]

The effect of Canadian competition was felt by the Alaska Com-

10. This paragraph is adapted from Corbett, *Settlement of Canadian-American Disputes*, 41.

mercial Company, in smaller catches and reduced prices. The monopoly of the company would become valueless if the sealing schooners were permitted to intercept the herd not only when scattered far and wide over the ocean, but also when converged into the vicinity of their breeding grounds. In the interests of the public and for the conservation of a source of wealth, it was certainly desirable to prevent the indiscriminate slaughter, with the consequent loss and possible extinction of the seal herds, by some regulations for their protection in their transit to, and especially in the vicinity of, their breeding grounds.

But, instead of any attempt to arrange an international agreement to conserve the penuipeds, the United States government, in 1886, to protect the interests of the monopoly-holding company, entered upon a course of illegal, high-handed conduct, altogether opposed to the traditions of that nation. The revenue cutter *Corwin* was sent to Bering Sea with orders to seize all vessels found sealing in those waters, British and American alike. In that sea, a part of the high seas, the *Corwin* swooped down on three Canadian sealing schooners, sixty miles or more from the nearest land, took possession of them, and towed them to Alaska for trial upon the charge of killing fur-bearing animals in contravention of the laws of the United States. "This act was the beginning of one of the most disgraceful and unjust policies to which the United States has ever been a party."[11] The three vessels were taken to Oonalaska, stripped of their supplies, seal-skins, and rigging, and left on the beach to await developments. Their owner saw them there a year later. The captains and mates were tried at Sitka for killing fur-bearing animals and fined $500 and $300 respectively, and each was sentenced, moreover, to one month's imprisonment. On learning of these seizures the other Victoria sealers in Bering Sea hurried away, which was doubtless what they were expected to do. In the following year six American and six British sealing schooners fell a prey to the revenue vessel *Richard Rush.*[12] And so, year by year, the seizures continued, until some twenty sealers had been seized and a number more ordered out of Bering Sea.

11. Lewis and Dryden, *Marine History of the Pacific Northwest* (Portland, Oregon, 1895), 428.

12. For details, see Fur Seal Arbitration, IV, *Case of Great Britain* (Washington, 1895), 133 ff.

On the trial of the captains and mates in Sitka, Judge Dawson thus laid down the law: "All the waters within the boundary set forth in this treaty of cession to the western end of the Aleutian Archipelago and the chain of islands are to be considered as comprised within the waters of Alaska, and all penalties prescribed by law against the killing of fur-bearing animals must therefore attach against any violation of law within the limits before described." If this does not mean that in his view that part of the Pacific Ocean known as Bering Sea is *mare clausum*, it is perilously near that interpretation. Whatever may be said of it as regards American vessels, it is plain that it was absolutely unmaintainable as to British vessels. The following quotation, also taken from the volume already cited, an American publication, may be given in this connection:

A Bering Sea seizure was made sixty-five years before this, at which time the virtuous roar of indignation had come from American throats. The vessel was the American whaler *Bounty*, seized by the Russians in 1821. The United States Government protested and made a winning contest on the ground that Russia had no jurisdiction beyond the three-mile limit. The *Bounty* was accordingly released and an indemnity paid her owners. This decision regarding the limit was accepted as satisfactory by all nations concerned, and naturally enough the claim of the United States to rights which she had once refused to concede to the former owner of the disputed territory was declared unreasonable and invalid. When the enormity of the outrage that had been perpetrated in the name of the law was realized in the councils of state, the United States receded from the position it had taken and ordered the release of the *Onward*, *Caroline*, and *Thornton*, but, before this decision was arrived at, the schooners had been rotting on the beach in Alaska for two years. The natural supposition would be that this Government, after thus acknowledging a wrong, would hasten to recompense the sufferers. Such was not the case. The men who had been confined in the squalid prisons, as well as those who were deprived of their means of livelihood for months, as yet have received not even an apology.[13]

The British government immediately protested against the seizures of 1886 and those of subsequent years down to and including the year 1889. The usual long-spun, diplomatic correspondence commenced and continued, becoming a trifle acrid. "Nor was

13. Lewis and Dryden, *Marine History*, 430. The date of the American protest was 1822. See Lash, "Behring Sea Question," 292.

international friendship increased by the imperious tones of Lord Salisbury, or the crude and prejudiced bluntness of Secretary Blaine."[14] John W. Foster states that the seizures by the United States revenue cutters were never authorized, that "the subject was never considered by the Secretary of the Treasury, the Secretary of State, the Attorney-General, or the President," and that they were brought about through the influence of the Alaska Commercial Company, which had in Washington "an agent more distinguished as a lobbyist than learned as a lawyer." This seems strange in the circumstances and in view of the fact that the seizures were continued for four seasons, 1886, 1887, 1888, 1889, and that even thereafter the sealers were warned to leave Bering Sea. But he goes on to say that "the legal proceedings were instituted without instructions or knowledge of the Attorney-General," that in truth the brief was prepared by the Alaska Commercial Company's agent and sent to the company's representative at Sitka, who passed it on to the District Attorney, and that it formed the basis of the judge's decision; that when the Attorney-General learned of the suits at Sitka "he sent a telegram ordering their dismissal and the release of the vessels, but as it was not confirmed (as is usual) by letter, it was treated as spurious and not observed."[15] However this may be, the continued seizures and condemnations, the arrest and imprisonment of peaceable captains and mates merely pursuing their vocations, the ordering of vessels out of Bering Sea, aroused a feeling in Canada, and, especially in British Columbia, that was decidedly hostile.

Meanwhile, as early as 1887 Mr. Bayard, American Secretary of State, had opened negotiations with Great Britain, France, Russia, and Japan for an arrangement to protect the Bering seal fisheries, and proposed a closed season between April 15 and November 1. Lord Salisbury, British Foreign Secretary, was disposed to agree until his hand was stayed by a protest from the Canadian government,[16] which was in possession of sufficient data, mostly from American official sources, to make it doubtful if the restrictive measures were necessary.[17] Their main effect, it was

14. H. L. Keenleyside, *Canada and the United States* (New York, 1929), 246.
15. J. W. Foster, *Diplomatic Memoirs* (London, 1910), II, 26 f.
16. Corbett, *Settlement of Canadian-American Disputes*, 42.
17. *Ibid.*, 43.

suggested, would be to enhance the value of the American land fisheries.

By an agreement dated December 18, 1891, each government was to appoint two commissioners to investigate all facts bearing on seal life in Bering Sea and to suggest measures for its preservation.[18] The Canadian government concurred and one of the two British commissioners was a Canadian, Professor George M. Dawson, of the Canadian Geological Survey. Pending arbitration sealing both in Bering Sea and on the islands had been stopped and, in spite of the protests of the commercial interests, this *modus vivendi* was renewed in 1892.[19]

The correspondence between the United States and Great Britain disclosed widely divergent and irreconcilable claims. The United States contended that it had dominion and legislative jurisdiction over the portion (about two-thirds) of Bering Sea lying within the boundaries set forth in the cession from Russia; that it had a property in the seal herds frequenting the islands of that sea, and the right to protect that property by search, seizure, and confiscation of vessels of other nations infringing it; that it had the right to protect the seals in the ocean as *domestic animals* only temporarily out of its possession, and with the same powers of search, seizure, and condemnation; and that, in any event, rules and regulations should be framed in its interests, preventing other nations from taking the animals. Great Britain claimed that Bering Sea was a part of the Pacific Ocean and free to all the world; that the seals were wild animals (*ferae naturae*), and any right of property in them must be confined to the three-mile limit; that Bering Sea, being a part of the high seas, the vessels of her subjects therein could, in the absence of agreement, only be interfered with for piracy; and that any regulations established should have a just and equitable regard to all the interests affected.

In the opinion of John W. Foster, the agent of the United States, the claim of jurisdiction over Bering Sea was not maintainable; but he thought that the United States had more solid ground in the contention that it had such a property in the Pribilof seal herd and interest in the industry as entitled it to preserve the herd from destruction, by force if necessary. He discussed the various courses

18. *Ibid.*, 44.
19. *Ibid.*

that were open to President Harrison: to abandon the claim of jurisdiction beyond the three-mile limit, recede from the position taken, and pay the damages; to turn a deaf ear to the British complaints and continue the policy of seizing any British vessel engaged in pelagic sealing in Bering Sea; or, lastly, to submit the whole question to arbitration.[20]

By a treaty, dated February 29, 1892, the two countries agreed to submit five questions arising out of, or involved in, the dispute to the decision of seven arbitrators: two to be nominated by the United States; two by Great Britain; and one each by the President of France, the King of Italy, and the King of Sweden and Norway. The arbitrators were to "be jurists of distinguished reputation in their respective countries," and, if possible, all were to be acquainted with the English language.[21] The United States appointed Mr. Justice John M. Harlan and Senator John T. Morgan; Great Britain named Lord Hannen and Sir John S. D. Thompson; France, Baron de Courcel; Italy, the Marquis Emilio Visconti; and Sweden and Norway, Mr. Gregers Gram.

The five questions were:

What exclusive jurisdiction in the sea now known as the Behring's Sea, and what exclusive rights in the seal fisheries therein, did Russia assert and exercise prior and up to the time of the cession of Alaska to the United States?

How far were these claims of jurisdiction as to the seal fisheries recognized and conceded by Great Britain?

Was the body of water now known as the Behring's Sea included in the phrase "Pacific Ocean" as used in the Treaty of 1825 between Great Britain and Russia; and what rights, if any, in the Behring's Sea, were held and exclusively exercised by Russia after said Treaty?

Did not all the rights of Russia as to jurisdiction and as to the seal fisheries in Behring's Sea, east of the water boundary, in the Treaty between the United States and Russia of the 30th March, 1867, pass unimpaired to the United States under that Treaty?

Has the United States any right, and if so, what right, of protection or property in the fur-seals frequenting the islands of the United States in Behring's Sea when such seals are found outside the ordinary 3-mile limit?

20. Foster, *Diplomatic Memoirs*, II, 29.
21. *Treaties with the United States affecting Canada* (Ottawa, 1915), 93 ff.

The Tribunal sat in Paris from March to August, 1892, and heard lengthy arguments on both sides. Upon the questions submitted it unanimously declared that Bering Sea was a part of the Pacific Ocean, and that the United States succeeded to all the rights of Russia. But upon the other questions the majority, Lord Hannen, Sir John S. D. Thompson, Baron de Courcel, Marquis Visconti, and Mr. Gregers Gram, found that Russia had exercised no exclusive jurisdiction beyond the three-mile limit; that Great Britain had not recognized or conceded any claim of Russia beyond that limit; that no exclusive jurisdiction or rights were exercised by Russia after 1825 outside of that limit; and that the United States had no rights in the seals when they were beyond that limit.[22]

These findings were against the contention of the United States and the seventh article of the Arbitration Treaty had provided that, in such an event, the arbitrators should frame regulations to govern the seal fisheries outside the jurisdictional limits of the respective governments. They accordingly, by a majority of four to three, prohibited sealing within a zone of sixty miles around the Pribilof Islands and forbade any sealing between May 1 and July 31, in Bering Sea or the Pacific Ocean north of 35° north latitude and east of 180° longitude. They also specified the weapons and vessels to be used and the records to be kept.

This regulation of pelagic sealing while no restrictions were placed on the operations of the Alaska Commercial Company on the Pribilof Islands aroused criticism in Canada. The inclusion of the right to make such regulations resulted, in the words of the Ottawa *Citizen*, in giving Canada the shell and handing the kernel over to the United States. But it was justified in the imperial House of Commons, not "on the ground of absolute right or justice, but on the ground that it is a friendly act towards a friendly power."[23] Mr. Phelps, who had been of the United States counsel in the arbitration, said: "The stringent regulations propounded in restriction of pelagic sealing will amount, in my judgment, to a substantial prohibition of it and give the United States all the fruits they would have obtained by a decree in favour of the claim of

22. The award is given in full, together with the dissenting opinions of the American arbitrators in Fur Seal Arbitration, I, *Proceedings of the Tribunal of Arbitration* (Washington, 1895), 75 ff.

23. *Hansard*, June 1, 1891, 1402.

right."[24] Theodore Roosevelt, then Police Commissioner of New York City, took a totally opposite view which is of interest because of his conduct of the negotiations concerning the Alaska boundary. In an article dealing with the subject he wrote: "The one failure of President Harrison's Administration in foreign affairs was in the Bering Sea case. . . . We ought never to have agreed to an arbitration. . . . It is not a page of American diplomacy upon which we can look back with pride; but it offers a most hopeful lesson. It should teach us to beware, beyond all others, of peace-at-any-price men. It should teach us to be extremely cautious about entering into any arbitration."[25] If John W. Foster is right in saying that President Harrison had only the three possible courses, it would be interesting to surmise which one of them Roosevelt would have chosen. Foster, while claiming that the United States only suffered "a technical defeat," states that for a time "international arbitration was unpopular" in that country, yet concludes: "But the better and prevailing judgment of our country is that the course pursued by President Harrison in this matter was the correct one. It was far better that we should submit our rights and interests in the seal-herd to the arbitrament of an impartial tribunal than risk the horrors of a war between the two kindred peoples."[26]

The actions of the United States having been declared illegal by the finding of the Tribunal, the question of the damages remained to be settled. The British claims aggregated $542,169.26 with interest. In August, 1894, the American government offered $425,000 in full settlement. This was accepted. Congress refused to pass the appropriation. One ground urged was that if the Victoria sealers were to be compensated the owners of American vessels should be treated in a similar manner. The dispute drifted along for two years more. In February, 1896, the long-standing claims were referred to a Judicial Tribunal. Twenty-three claims, aggregating $1,289,008, were considered and settled at $473,151.26. The sale of the seized vessels had produced $83,073.72. After considerable delay the awarded damages were paid by the United States.

24. *The Empire*, August 17, 1892.
25. Foster, *Diplomatic Memoirs*, II, 30.
26. *Ibid.*, 49 f.

The regulations made by the Tribunal were accepted and amplified by the two governments. They were for five years. But there still remained open the westerly portion of Bering Sea. British sealers resorted to that part, while Russian and Japanese vessels, not being included in the award, frequented the other section. The Canadian government refused or neglected to take any action (as the United States government had done) to prevent its people from engaging in this pelagic sealing. This caused great dissatisfaction in the United States. Matters drifted along for more than ten years, but in 1911 Great Britain and the United States reached an agreement to prohibit all pelagic sealing in the Pacific Ocean north of 35° north latitude and east of the 180th meridian and, as the United States would then alone be able to carry on the industry, it was provided that one-fifth of the catch was to be assigned to Canada.[27] In July, 1912, an agreement was made by Russia, Japan, Great Britain, and the United States, whereby pelagic sealing was forbidden north of 35° north latitude. All hunting of seals was to be on land. The United States was to give to Canada 15 per cent of its catch and 15 per cent to Japan; Russia to give 15 per cent of its catch to Canada and 15 per cent to Japan; and Japan to give 10 per cent of its catch to Canada, 10 per cent to Russia, and 10 per cent to the United States. These complicated arrangements were made at a time when the national and international recognition of the need for conservation had made substantial progress and may be regarded as falling well outside the predatory era.[28]

27. *Infra*, 378.
28. Corbett, *Settlement of Canadian-American Disputes*, 48.

CHAPTER XIV

THE KLONDIKE: THE GOLD RUSH AND AFTER

1896-1903

In an earlier chapter the progressive exploration of the mineral wealth of the Pacific slope has been described. The great mining advance, which had started in California, penetrated northward as far as southern British Columbia where permanent communities were built up in the Kootenays. It remains to deal with the discovery of gold in Cariboo, Omineca, and Cassiar, before passing on to the great rush to the Klondike, which will be treated in some detail because it was the last flare-up of the economy of the predatory age and brought Canadians and Americans together under frontier conditions long after both countries had settled down to an organized transcontinental economy.

The Fraser River gold rush, which has been the theme of an earlier chapter, was followed in the 1860's by the discovery of gold in Cariboo. Prospectors entered by way of the Fraser River. Governor James Douglas planned and directed the building of the Cariboo waggon road which led from Yale, the head of navigation on the Fraser, to Barkerville on Williams Creek, the so-called capital of Cariboo. Millions of dollars worth of gold was transported by this route, the "Appian Way" of British Columbia in the middle 1860's, twenty million dollars worth from Williams Creek alone. But the gold accessible to the techniques of that day was soon exhausted and the rush ended when Barkerville was destroyed by fire in September, 1868.

Meanwhile gold strikes were reported in several parts of the colony. Rock Creek, in the boundary country, west of the Okanagan and east of the Kootenays, had its brief flurry. At Leech River on Vancouver Island, gold was found in sufficient quantities to lead to a short gold rush. In the Kootenays, Wild Horse Creek was a centre of excitement in 1864 when it attracted some two thousand miners. Two years later Wild Horse had been abandoned and the prospectors had moved on to the Big Bend of the Columbia River.

North of Cariboo gold strikes occurred on the Stikine River in 1861. The miners penetrated into the mountain fastnesses and

Glenora became the centre of a new gold rush.[1] Access was not easy. The voyage to the Stikine, which is some nine hundred miles from Victoria, took at least three weeks by sailing ship and the S.S. *Labouchere* by 1862 was making the trip regularly in two weeks. When the diggings had to be reached by canoe the journey lasted a further week or ten days, but later small river steamers covered the distance in two days. The mining season was short as operations on the bars of the river were possible only between July and October. In the face of these difficulties there were never more than five hundred miners on the Stikine. When hopes were high the district was, for a brief period, organized as a separate unit under the governorship of James Douglas. But after 1863 little was heard of the Stikine.

Gold was also found on Peace River and in Omineca, a district which takes its name from a tributary of the Peace. From 1862 to 1872 this region contained productive mining camps of which the chief were on the Peace River itself and on Vital, Germansen, and Manson Creeks. Access to the Omineca field, where the richest claims were found, was either by way of Peace River or from the coast up the Skeena River. The end came suddenly, as was the case with many rushes. In 1871 there were a thousand miners in Omineca; in August of the next year, six hundred; in September, two hundred and fifty, of whom, according to the Victoria *Colonist*, only a few were "making grub."

At this time a new field of activity was found in Cassiar, in the Liard River basin in the far north of British Columbia. This district was productive from 1872 to 1880 and the operations there form a connecting link between the gold rushes of British Columbia and those of the Yukon and Alaska. The operations, like those on the Stikine, were highly seasonal. For instance, in June, 1874, there were fourteen hundred miners in Cassiar; in October the number had fallen to less than a hundred.

It is quite impossible to make an estimate of the part played by Americans in these minor gold rushes in British Columbia. The miners were a transient, cosmopolitan population and they pushed

1. For a full account of these northern gold rushes see A. S. Trueman, "Placer Gold Mining in Northern British Columbia, 1860 to 1880," M.A. Thesis in the University of British Columbia Library.

their explorations northwards from California with little more regard for political boundaries than the fur traders had displayed. In both cases the aim was to appropriate the products of nature in a way that in an individualistic era seemed little different from the exercise of the natural rights of man. This is an ideology that must be kept in mind in discussing the Klondike.

The Klondike gold rush had its background in the development of gold mining in Alaska. Although in 1869 some of the miners from the Stikine went north to Alaska and, in 1877, some mining was done on Baranoff Island near Sitka, serious gold mining did not begin until 1881 when John Treadwell bought the Paris claim on Douglas Island from Pierre Erussard, "French Pete," for $5 and thereby laid the foundation of the well-known Treadwell mines. Three years earlier, John Muir had explored southeast Alaska for the United States government and had reported that the area would rival California. In 1880, when a prospecting party under Joseph Juneau, a French Canadian, and Richard T. Harris, an American, returned from Gold Creek with 800 pounds of ore, a rush from Sitka began. The town which sprang up at the diggings was named Harrisburg, but in 1881 a miners' meeting changed the name to Juneau.

In 1883 gold was first found on the Yukon River in United States territory by a party under Edward Schleffelin, following up the despatch to St. Michael of two nuggets of gold which had been given to George Holt by a Tanana River Indian three years earlier.[2] In 1886 Franklin and Henry Madison found coarse gold on bed rock on Fortymile Creek near the international boundary. By 1895 Fortymile was credited with an annual output of $300,000, and its population was put at six hundred. Until the discovery of the Klondike in 1896, Fortymile divided attention with Circle City, which had been founded in 1893 twelve miles above its later site.[3] It was on the upper waters of the Yukon that most gold was found. As early as 1868 we hear of minute specks of gold having been

2. See H. B. Goodrich, "History and Condition of the Yukon Gold District in 1897," in *18th Report of United States Geological Survey*, III, 111; William Ogilvie, *Early Days on the Yukon* (London, 1913), 105, 107; and Frederick Schwatka, *Along Alaska's Great River* (New York, 1885), 317.

3. Ogilvie, *Early days on the Yukon*, 113.

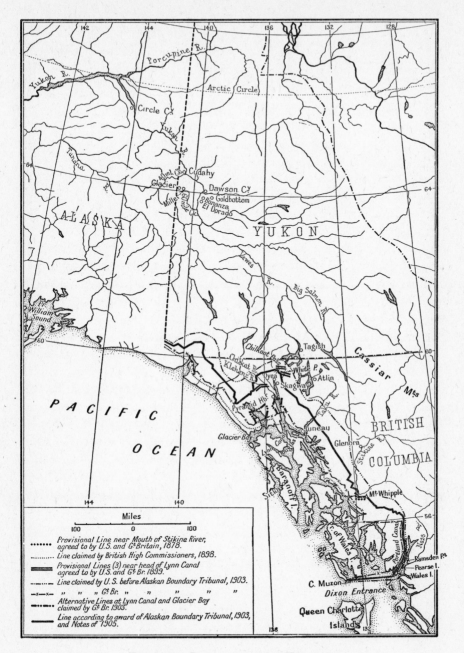

THE ALASKA BOUNDARY AND THE KLONDIKE

found there by the Hudson's Bay Company's men.[4] George Holt, who had sent out the first nuggets to St. Michael, made several trips to the Yukon in the 1870's and "brought back glowing accounts of coarse gold on the upper Lewes."[5] In 1880, twenty-five men under Edward Bean constituted the first prospecting party to enter the Yukon. With the help of Captain Beardslee, of the United States Navy, the Indians were persuaded to allow them to cross the mountains. The next year a party of four, under G. Langtry which descended the Lewes to the mouth of the Big Salmon and ascended the latter stream for some two hundred miles, discovered the first paying placers in the Yukon district. In 1882, the Chilkoot was again crossed, this time by twelve miners who wintered at Fort Reliance, the post of the Alaska Commercial Company. One of them, Joseph Ladue, led a party in 1883 to prospect Sixtymile and Fortymile creeks, but nothing of note was found at that time. Lieutenant Frederick Schwatka, who descended the Lewes and the Yukon to the sea in 1883, wrote, on returning to the United States: "From the D'Abbadie [the Big Salmon] almost to the very mouth of the great Yukon, a panful of 'dirt' taken with any discretion from almost any bar or bank, will when washed, give several 'colors' to use a miner's phrase."[6]

Gold prospecting on the Yukon and its tributaries continued until the rush to Fortymile Creek in 1886. In 1887, we are told that "the discovery and working of Franklin Gulch marks an advance from the primitive bar working to the gulch diggings, in which sluice boxes are used, and the current of the stream is made to perform most of the work."[7] In 1892 gold was found on Miller and Glacier creeks, both in British territory close to the boundary, and both tributaries of Sixtymile Creek. The North American Transportation and Trading Company founded Cudahy in 1892,

4. Frederick Whymper, *Travel and Adventure in the Territory of Alaska* (London, 1868), 227.

5. Goodrich, "Yukon Gold District," 108. See also G. M. Dawson, *Report of an Exploration in the Yukon District, N.W.T., and Adjacent Northern Portion of British Columbia, 1887* (Geological and Natural History Survey of Canada, Montreal, 1889), 179B. Holt was murdered by an Indian at Cook Inlet in 1885. The date of his reports is variously given as 1872, 1875, and 1878.

6. Schwatka, *Along Alaska's Great River*, 190.

7. Goodrich, "Yukon Gold District," 116. Goodrich places the yield of Fortymile much lower than Ogilvie's estimate and suggests $60,000.

three-quarters of a mile below the post of its rival at Fortymile.[8] Bonanza Creek was discovered in the summer of 1896 when Fortymile was at the height of its prosperity.

The Klondike was the name given to the whole mining area, which Americans at least usually believed to be in United States territory, because gold was found in the creeks of the Klondike River, a tributary of the Yukon. There has been endless controversy as to who did discover the Klondike. Of the two possible discoverers, Robert Henderson, a Nova Scotian, was probably in the region earlier than George Carmack, an American. But Carmack was probably the first to discover the rich claims on the Bonanza. It was news of his rich strike which led to the Klondike gold rush.[9]

8. M. H. E. Hayne, in *The Pioneers of the Klondyke* (London, 1897), 89, describes Fortymile's attractions: "There was abundant variety of all kinds, both of men and amusements. Several saloons were kept going day and night, and did a roaring trade. There was also a variety entertainment, started by an enterprising manager with a troop of music-hall girls from San Francisco. The entertainment was really excellent, especially the dancing of one or two of the girls."

9. F. W. Howay possesses a mass of correspondence on this subject, including a letter from William Ogilvie which states that Robert Henderson discovered gold on Indian River fully a year before Carmack was in the Klondike "in any way as a miner"; that Henderson discovered gold in the Klondike months before Carmack; and that it was through information and advice given him by Henderson that Carmack thought of visiting the Klondike creeks as a miner. Ogilvie adds, "For the above statements I have the personal narratives, given to me at the time by both Henderson and Carmack and the two Indians, Skookum Jim and Tagish Charlie, who were with Carmack at the time when they made the actual strike which led to the rush."

The following account, taken from *The Yukon Territory: Its History and Resources*, issued by direction of the Hon. W. J. Roche, Minister of the Interior (Ottawa, 1916) 11-12, seems fair and unbiased: "In 1894 Robert Henderson, of Nova Scotia, and a small party arrived in the territory. They prospected along the bars of the upper Yukon and rocked out $54.00 in fine gold at the mouth of the Pelly. When they reached the trading post at Ogilvie, Joe Ladue contributed the latest information respecting the strikes or discoveries which had been made. As a result of the information furnished by Ladue and after a short stay at Ogilvie, Henderson started for Indian river. He prospected along this stream to the mouth of what is now Quartz creek, up which he proceeded to the divide on Hunker. No large prospects were found, and Henderson returned to Ogilvie for provisions. During the following year Henderson prospected on various creeks in the Watershed of Indian river. After cleaning up about $600.00 for the season on Quartz creek he crossed the divide to Gold Bottom where he found a two cent prospect. During the summer

The first rush, that of prospectors from the Yukon district on both sides of the line, led to the staking out of the most valuable claims long before the second rush from the outside world started. But, even in the Yukon, it was some time before all the other camps had heard of the new diggings. It was not until bed rock was reached, twelve or fourteen feet down, that the real riches were revealed, for the coarse gold lies on or near bed rock. Arthur T. Walden states that he helped to bring the first word to Circle City in January, 1897.[10] The first letter to reach the "outside" was written by W. D. Jones on December 21, 1896, and published in Chicago, March 2, 1897. Eli Gage, son of the Secretary of the United States Treasury, was one of the first to bring out the news of the Klondike.[11]

of 1896 Henderson made a trip to Ladue's post at Ogilvie for supplies. The water in Indian river was low and he knew that it would be almost impossible to proceed up that stream. He came to the conclusion that Gold Bottom flowed into a tributary of the Yukon some distance below Ogilvie so he proceeded down the Yukon to its confluence with the Tron Deg, which is the Indian name for the Klondike, where he found George W. Carmack and two Indians named 'Skookum Jim' and 'Tagish Charlie,' who were fishing for salmon. In accordance with the usual custom Henderson announced the discovery he had made, and invited Carmack to stake on Gold Bottom. A short time afterwards Carmack and the two Indians proceeded to Gold Bottom and staked claims near to where Henderson and his party were working. Henderson states that he advised Carmack and the Indians to cross the divide and prospect in the gravels of what is now known as Bonanza creek. He asked Carmack to advise him, by sending back an Indian, if good prospects were discovered.

"As a result of this trip rich prospects were discovered on Discovery Claim, which Carmack staked as well as No. 1 below. 'Tagish Charlie' staked No. 2 below and 'Skookum Jim,' the other Indian, No. 1 above. Carmack and the Indians at once proceeded to Fortymile and filed their applications with the recorder for the district. Up to this time the majority of the miners in the territory had been working on Fortymile, but as soon as the discovery on Bonanza became known all the miners in the Fortymile district stampeded to the new strike and in a short time Bonanza creek was staked from end to end. Meantime, Henderson and his party were working on Gold Bottom, and did not hear of the new strike until all the creek had been staked. Extensive prospecting at once commenced at Bonanza, and in a few months was revealed the remarkable wealth contained in the gravels of Bonanza and Eldorado creeks." Carmack as discoverer was entitled to two claims.

An interesting newspaper controversy on the "discoverer of the Klondike" was carried on in the pages of the Vancouver *Star* from December, 1927, to April, 1928, commencing with a letter written on December 21, by Major Henry J. Woodside upholding Henderson, and concluding with a vigorous defence of Henderson by H. H. Cleugh of Vancouver on April 5. R. L. Reid, K.C., of Vancouver collected

The rush from "outside" may be said to have begun with the sailing of the *Mexico,* the first steamer to leave Seattle for Dyea after the news arrived. Many of her 402 passengers were citizens of Seattle, who had taken the gold fever. Propaganda may have played a part in spreading the disease,[12] but the return of the successful miners with their gold was more important. William J. Sloan, afterwards Provincial Secretary of British Columbia, with his partner returned to Nanaimo in July, 1897, with over $50,000 in gold. This fired Nanaimo and Vancouver, but Seattle was already aflame. "Seattle," runs the editorial of the Vancouver *News-Advertiser* of July 18, 1897, "has never witnessed anything like it before, and the hero of the hour is a man who a few months ago was the General Secretary of the Young Men's Christian Association, who has now come back with $65,000 in gold dust in his gripsack." But gold fever is a dangerous disease and even the newspaper adds a caution.[13] Official bulletins were issued by

these in his Yukon scrap-book, from which much of the above information has been taken. Dr. T. A. Rickard's account of the discovery is given in *Through the Yukon and Alaska* (San Francisco, 1909), 189 f.

10. *A Dog-Puncher on the Yukon* (Boston, 1928), 69.

11. He spent the winter in the Klondike as an official of the North American Transportation and Trading Company. He returned to the United States in the spring and published three articles in the Chicago *Record.*

12. E. B. Osborn writes scornfully in *Greater Canada: The Past, Present and Future of the Canadian North-West* (London, 1900), 3, ". . . every Western scribbler was hard at work inventing circumstantial lies, many of which were reproduced not only by the most respectable journals of the Eastern States and Eastern Canada, but also by those of the mother country. Possibly nine-tenths of these fictions originated in Seattle, and other sea-coast towns in the Pacific States, where nearly all the Alaskan miners buy their outfits and supplies, and the head offices of the transportation and trading companies with an Alaskan connection are generally to be found."

13. Vancouver *News Advertiser*, July 18, 1897. "But there will be many disappointments, and a large proportion of the eager argonauts will return home, broken in health and disappointed in their errand. It is well to warn those who may be inclined to throw up steady employment or reasonably good incomes that there is another side to the story.

"It is, however, of little avail to utter warnings in such cases as this. Gold is a magnet which incites men to brave every danger and to take tremendous risks, and the experience of the rushes to California, to Colorado, the Black Hills and other places, shows that when once started, the current will flow until its source is exhausted, or it is turned by the disappointment of the many against the success of the few."

Washington and Ottawa warning gold-seekers of the dangers that lay before them. Mr. Bliss, Secretary of the Interior, was more explicit than the Hon. Clifford Sifton, Canadian Minister of the Interior.[14] These warnings fell on deaf ears. A gold rush cannot be stopped. The fever must slowly burn itself out. The hundreds of dead pack horses in the Chilkoot and White Passes were mute witnesses to its virulence. And there were human victims too.

It is an ill wind that blows no one any good. Business boomed in Seattle, as a visitor from Vancouver noted:

It is the best thing which has happened for the prosperity of Seattle for some time. The hotels are full of people, stores are doing a rushing business, and everyone is on the jump.

It has been a Godsend to the transportation companies of the South. Old steamers which have been tied up for a number of years are being refitted and started towards the North. The Willamette, which started from San Francisco, an old collier with only sleeping quarters for the officers and crew, has been fitted up with bunks, and has a passenger list of 600.[15]

The head of the Alaska Commercial Company, who was in a position to see both sides of the question, issued a statement on July 26, 1897, warning the gold-seekers and blaming the propagandists:

I regard it as a crime for any transportation company to encourage men to go to the Yukon this fall. With the present and prospective rush, it will be impossible to get enough provisions through to supply the demand. The Seattle people who are booming the steamship lines may be sincere, but a heavy responsibility will rest on their shoulders should starvation and crime prevail in Dawson City next winter.

We have tried to give the facts to all applicants and discourage this wild rush of clerks, professional men and women who are unused to any

14. As quoted by A. C. Harris, *Alaska and the Klondike Gold Fields* (Cincinnati, 1897), 70, the statement of Mr. Bliss included the following: "In view of information received at this department that 3,000 persons with 2,000 tons of baggage and freight are now waiting at the entrance to White Pass, in Alaska, for an opportunity to cross the mountains to Yukon River, and that many more are preparing to join them, I deem it proper to call the attention of all who contemplate making that trip to the exposure, privation, suffering, and even danger incident thereto at this advanced period of the season, even if they should succeed in crossing the mountains."

15. Vancouver *News-Advertiser*, August 11, 1897.

hardships, and whose chances of getting out of the country will be very slender, even though they should make money. . . .

But on the Yukon, if a man can't get work as a miner, he must leave the country or starve. If it is winter he cannot get out, and so, should the food supply run low, hundreds will perish miserably. Hence, I repeat it is a crime to encourage this rush, which can only end in disaster for three-quarters of the new arrivals.[16]

It has been estimated that between 200,000 and 300,000 persons started for the Klondike and that of these nearly 50,000 "reached the interior of Alaska and Canada." The cost per person "ranged from $500 to $10,000."[17] The vast majority came from the United States.[18] In July, 1898, about three-quarters of the population were Americans. Of 3,000 gold-seekers at Unalaska in June, 1898, "perhaps two-thirds were from the United States, largely from the Pacific coast. Of the remaining third, a goodly proportion were Swedes."[19]

The choice of route by which to reach the Klondike was fraught with difficulty. Canadians wished for an all-Canadian route and some of the routes proposed were fantastic. In Ogilvie's *Klondike Official Guide*, we are told that the James and Hudson's Bay route "leaves the Canadian Pacific at Mattawa, about 200 miles up the Ottawa River from Ottawa City."[20] The same publication lists

16. C. F. Stanbury, *Klondike* (New York, 1897), 35 f.

17. H. W. Clark, *History of Alaska* (New York, 1930), 103.

18. Osborn, *Greater Canada*, 7, estimates that "110,000 persons (of whom at least two-thirds came from the Western States and about one-sixth from Canada) journeyed to the Pacific Coast in the year ending May, 1898; of which number less than 60,000 made any serious attempt to reach their destination. Of those who made the attempt, hardly a third got through."

19. Jeremiah Lynch, *Three Years in the Klondike* (London, 1904), 3. The special correspondent of *Harper's Weekly*, who had wintered in Dawson, in 1897, wrote of the Swedes: "There are many Swedes in Klondike,—a fact attributed largely to the Treadwell Mine at Juneau having brought them there to work, and there they got the grub-stake which brought them to the Yukon. They are a hard-headed lot, men accustomed to cold and hard, "bone" labor, patient, and satisfied with small returns in the absence of better" (Tappan Adney, *The Klondike Stampede*, New York, 1900, 267).

20. (Toronto, 1898), 122. Its subsequent course is elaborated in detail. "Thence up the Ottawa River to Lake Temiscamingue, some 36 miles and up that lake 70 miles to its head. From the head of Lake Temiscamingue to James Bay, a distance of nearly 500 miles, a route once much travelled by the Hudson's Bay Company's

four other Canadian routes.[21] Osborn is scornful of the motives of their advocates.[22] The most popular routes were the long sea voyage round by Bering Strait to St. Michael and up the Yukon to Dawson, and the trails from Dyea and Skagway over the Chilkoot and White Passes. Of these the second was most often chosen. Both Dyea and Skagway became mushroom towns and, when a railway was built over White Pass, Skagway became the permanent settlement.

The trail over the passes was, perhaps, not difficult for a mountaineer, but it was a terrible and often a fatal test for the inexperienced. "At times," writes an observer, "the trail is full of men, with sore backs and feet, lying on the snow in utter despair. Many even weep from disappointment."[23] If they persisted it was because, to borrow a phrase from the poet Service, "They're all

employees." Omitting the lengthy directions for getting from Lake Temiscamingue to Moose Factory on James Bay, we proceed thus: "We now have a distance of nearly 900 miles across Hudson Bay, which is only open about half the year; thence up Chesterfield Inlet and Baker's Lake, a distance of about 200 miles; thence over an unknown and barren country, between 300 and 400 miles to the end of Great Slave Lake, which is frozen from early in December until very late in June, the ice attaining a thickness of from four to six feet. This lake is about 350 miles in length, and in some places as much as 40 miles in width, so that the wind sweeping down it or up it lengthwise gets up quite a rough sea. This route might be amended and made more of an all-water route by making Montreal or other seaport the point of departure and going round by the Atlantic Ocean and Hudson Straits, and thence across Hudson Bay to Chesterfield Inlet, and from there on as above." From Great Slave Lake we descend the Mackenzie, cross overland to the Porcupine, descend that river to the Yukon, and ascend the Yukon to the Klondike.

21. Edmonton route, Cariboo and Cassiar route, Stikine route and Taku route. The two last crossed the panhandle of Alaska.

22. Osborn, *Greater Canada*, 5 f. "The world-wide attack of Klondikitis, which occurred two winters ago, was not, however, altogether a result of journalistic enterprise. To begin with, everybody in Canada or the States who had a spade or a pound of tea in stock, made up his mind to sell it to one or other of the prospectors going up last spring; and those storekeepers who found themselves located in such out-of-the-way North-Western towns as Prince Albert, Edmonton, and Ashcroft, sent the hat round to collect funds for advertising that one of the nine or ten 'Canadian routes' which passed through their particular street. Though some of these routes are practicable enough, and may be justly called 'poor man's trails,' owing to the abundance of fish and game in the country through which they pass, their great length is against them; for the best of them (such as those which take in the Mackenzie or the Liard rivers) cannot be traversed in less than a summer."

23. W. M. Stanley, *A Mile of Gold* (Chicago, 1898), 25.

millionaires in their minds."[24] The worst hardships resulted from inexperience. This has been forcibly expressed by Dr. Rickard: "The crowd that crossed the passes during the excitement of 1898 were 'mushers' not mountaineers; they were gold-hunters from the cities, not prospectors; they were 'cheechakos' of the greenest kind. Hence their troubles."[25] And the hardships lost nothing in the telling by "scribes who snatched an ephemeral fame by misinforming a credulous public."[26]

Of the two passes the Chilkoot offered the shorter route, twenty-three miles as opposed to thirty-five. At first it was favoured but, after a fatal accident in which sixty-three persons perished, the White Pass was more used. Arthur T. Walden, who crossed the Chilkoot in the spring of 1896, has described his journey. It took his party twenty-three days to go twenty-three miles. From Dyea the trail led across the flats and up the Dyea River. Suddenly a canyon or rift opened up in the mountain wall which shut in the river. Walden continues:

The rift was sheer rock and was from fifteen to fifty feet wide, and a hundred or more feet high, with a few trees clinging to it; the grade through it was steep, over a series of waterfalls. The stream had frozen while the water was at high level, after which it had dropped, taking the thinner parts of the ice with it, so that we had to go around holes on a narrow ledge of ice where the raging torrent was twenty or thirty feet below us. In some places pole bridges had to be made, almost like ladders; in others there was only a narrow rim to crawl around on. The later the season the harder the travelling, as the ice was giving way. It was so thick before the thaw that a band of horses had been taken over it, but at this time only dogs and men could do the work. From one hundred to one hundred and fifty pounds was all that a man could handle alone, with help over the bad places.

The canyon then opened out into a round valley called "Sheep Camp." This was the headquarters of the mountain sheep hunters who camped here in the last timber of this side of the range. The valley is like a basin, surrounded by high rocky mountains impossible to climb, with a sharp notch in the rim. This notch is the notorious Chilkoot Pass. From Sheep Camp to the foot of the pass was five miles of steep grade. A horse weighing a thousand pounds was barely able to haul a load of three hundred pounds

24. Robert W. Service, *The Trail of '98* (Toronto, 1928), 63.
25. Rickard, *Through the Yukon and Alaska*, 142.
26. *Ibid.*

on a narrow Yukon sled, with two men to help him. The snow was very deep, but it was so hard that it would bear the horses up. . . .

When the foot of the pass was reached, everything had to be packed on men's backs for the last twelve hundred and fifty feet. The grade was so steep that a man standing in the footholds cut in the hard snow could touch the wall in front of him without losing his balance.

Horses were fastened in a rope sling and led up the trail on a long rope, with a hundred men or more to each horse, until losing their footing they were hauled up to the summit lying on their sides. They were then led through the sharp cut, blindfolded, backed over the edge, and slid down the other slope on their backs to Crater Lake, some four hundred feet below.[27]

The trail through the White Pass, which was cut by the British Yukon Company during the summer of 1897, was less dangerous. The company over-optimistically announced that Lake Tagish might be reached from Skagway in two days. But even when the summit had been reached the dangers were not at an end. Some built boats at Lake Linderman; others constructed them at Lake Bennett. They all had to face the White Horse Rapids and not all were fortunate enough to reach Dawson.

In the Klondike the mining was chiefly in and near the creeks and there were few camps, such as flourished in the Kootenays. In addition to the creek claims, which were naturally the first to be worked, there were hill claims, mainly in glacial gravel three or four hundred feet above the creek bottoms, and bench claims, on what were evidently the remains of former creek beds. There were also some "intermediate claims" or hybrid claims, "not necessarily in regular bench gravels, but casually deposited in crannies of bedrock near the surface, just under the moss, or in slide material, or in gravels lodged on quite steep hillsides."[28] The hill claims, often extremely rich,[29] were easily worked at first but became more difficult as depth increased. The benches occur where the hillsides slope gently. At Bonanza, for instance, three earlier creek levels can be traced. Sluices cannot, of course, be used

27. Walden, *Dog-Puncher on the Yukon*, 5 ff.

28. A. N. C. Treadgold, *Report on the Goldfields of the Klondike* (Toronto, 1899), 25.

29. On French Hill, two rockers and four men took out 144 ounces of gold in seven hours; on Skookum Hill two men and one rocker took out 114 ounces in twenty hours.

for hill and bench claims, and water for the rockers must be carried from the creeks below. The country in which these low hilltops and wide shallow valleys are to be found closely resembles the Siberian valleys. Of the creeks Bonanza was the first to be staked, and one of its "pups" or side creeks, the Eldorado, became the richest creek in the Klondike.[30]

The placer mining methods developed from the practices elsewhere. A pan was used to obtain "colour," that is to test for gold. Then a rocker was used to wash the gravel from the gold.[31] From the rocker developed the "Long Tom," a rough trough from ten to twelve feet long, narrow at the upper end and widening out at the lower. It is set on an incline and has an iron plate on the bottom, so perforated that gold will drop through in the washing process. After the "Long Tom" came the sluice-box, a trough twelve feet long and a foot wide. The bottom has riffles, or long narrow slips of wood, placed on it. These allow the gravel to pass over them but retain the black sand which contains the gold. When the box is in operation it is placed on a grade, the head being five or six inches higher than the foot, and is submerged to a depth of about four inches. When most of the water is turned off and the riffles taken out, more gravel and sand are washed away. The miner then shuts off the water and pans the residue, or even uses quicksilver to collect the small flakes of "flour gold." Hydraulic mining involves turning a powerful stream of water on a gold-bearing bank and washing it into a long flume or ground sluice.

30. Adney, *Klondike Stampede*, 321 ff.

31. Ernest Ingersoll, *Gold Fields of the Klondike* (Englewood Publishing Company, 1897), 127 f., describes a rocker: "It is a box on rockers, about four feet long, two feet wide, and several inches in depth, with the upper end elevated so that the water will pass through freely. A hopper, or riddle box, with perforated sheet-iron bottom occupies the upper half. Under this is an apron of cloth or sheet-iron, sloping downward toward the upper end. Two cleats are nailed across the bottom, one in the middle and one at the lower end. The riddle box being filled with auriferous dirt from the bank, the miner rocks the cradle, pouring in water meanwhile to dissolve the mass. The latter is carried through the perforations upon the apron and thence down over the bottom of the 'rocker' to the lower end and out into the stream. The gold, being heavy, is lodged behind the cleats or 'riffles,' and there the miner gathers them and repeats the operation. The finer particles of gold are often lodged on the apron, and this is frequently washed in a bucket and the metal taken from the bottom."

Some peculiar difficulties were encountered in the Yukon and were met by new techniques. Bed-rock was from fifteen to forty feet underground and the summer thaw penetrated only a few feet. A primitive method of thawing the ground, known as burning, was invented by Fred Hutchinson in 1887 and made it possible to work in winter as well as in summer. It consisted in lighting a fire on the ground, digging out the unfrozen earth, and lighting another fire in the hole. When bed-rock was reached it was necessary to tunnel or "drift" to find the gold. This process required two men, and at least thirty cords of wood were needed for a winter's work. In 1898 a better method was discovered by C. J. Berry, who noticed that the exhaust from his steam engine had thawed a hole in the "muck." Dr. Rickard tells the story thus: "Berry noticed this and picked up the exhaust pipe, which was a rubber hose. On applying it to the frozen ground he found that it could thaw the muck so as to penetrate for the full length of the hose within a few minutes. This excited the men who happened to be watching the experiment. All of them began at once to devise a scheme for doing this work effectively. A rifle barrel was chosen, then a small hole was bored into one side so as to admit the steam. Thus the steam-point was invented."[32] Dredging was first attempted as early as 1898 but, on account of expense, it was not freely used in the Yukon until the Klondike had long ceased to be a poor man's diggings.[33]

If the Klondike did not produce mining camps, such as flourished in the more southerly districts, it did produce a local metropolis. In 1896 Joe Ladue picked out the Dawson townsite and on September 1 commenced building the first house. Within six months there were over five hundred houses, stores, hotels, restaurants, saloons, and other places of amusement, or worse, in the new "city." Ladue held 178 acres and the government the remaining 22.[34] By July, 1897, the population was estimated at five thousand and a real estate boom carried the price of building lots to $800 and even $8,000.

But it must be borne in mind that all prices were high. Com-

32. Rickard, *Through the Yukon and Alaska*, 215. For a description of burning and drifting see Adney, *Klondike Stampede*, 241 ff.

33. Cf. Ogilvie, *Early Days on the Yukon*, 233 ff.

34. Joseph Ladue, *Klondyke Facts* (New York, 1897), 152.

modity prices had risen very sharply with the rush. Ogilvie thought
the price level in the Klondike moderate in 1896.[35] During the
winter of 1897-8 supplies were short. Flour sold on the street from
$75 to $120 a sack of 50 pounds. "Dogs were almost any price a
man asked, $300 being paid for good native dogs. A common
Yukon sleigh, worth $7 'outside' was $40; a 'basket' sleigh, $75.
Fur robes, without which it was said no one could reach Dyea,
were from $200 to $300 each."[36] Even after the "Dawson famine"
was over, Superintendent Primrose pointed out that one dollar in
Eastern Canada was equivalent to five in the Yukon.[37] Ogilvie
mentions $450 as a fair "grub stake" in the Yukon, while the same
stake could be bought in Edmonton for $200 "or may be less."[38]
What was true of prices was true of wages which might amount to
$15 or $20 per day.[39] All mining supplies were expensive.[40] A

35. Department of the Interior, *Information respecting the Yukon District from
the Reports of William Ogilvie* (Ottawa, 1897), 50. "I would bring in nothing in
quantity but bacon, on which I might save a dollar or two a hundred, it being sold
here from $30 to $35 per hundred."

36. Adney, *Klondike Stampede*, 182.

37. *Sessional Papers of Canada*, no. 15, 63 Vict., A 1900, North-West Mounted
Police Report, Part II, Appendix B, 53.

38. W. Ogilvie, *The Klondike Official Guide* (Toronto, 1898), 138 f.

39. Adney, *Klondike Stampede*, 467 f., cites:

"Ordinary miners, $1 to $1.50 an hour.

Foremen in mines, $15 and upward per day of ten hours.

Ordinary labor other than mining, $1 per hour.

Tin-smiths, $1.50 an hour; skilled wood-workers, $17 per day of ten hours;
    tailors' workmen, $1.50 an hour.

Bartenders, $15 per day; book-keepers, $17.50 per day; faro-dealers, $20 per
    day; musicians, $17.50 to $20 per day.

Typewriters, 50 cents per folio.

Services of man and two-horse team, $10 per hour; drivers $300 per month
    and board.

Typesetters, $1.50 per hour, or $2 per thousand ems.

Cooks in restaurants, $100 per week and board; men waiters, $50 per week and
    board; women waiters, $100 per month and board.

Barbers, 65 per cent. of receipts of chair, $15 to $40 per day."

40. Alexander McDonald in support of the miners' petition to Ottawa in 1897
cites prices and costs as follows:

"That the cost of lumber undressed averaged 40 cents a board foot on the
claims.

"That, as an average, 100 sluice-boxes are used on every claim worked as warehouse, which would have cost $4,500 in the middle west, cost $93,000 in Dawson. W. B. Haskell tells us that "it is difficult for an economical man to get around in 'society' for less than fifty dollars a day. I heard of people who spent five hundred dollars a day just in killing time while waiting for the steamer to go out with their gold."[41]

In a hastily built town, fire is a constant danger. After one fire, suspected of being of incendiary origin, subscriptions were collected to buy fire-engines and equipment. A second great fire broke out in October, 1898, while the engines were being held awaiting full payment. They were unpacked during the conflagration and paid for later. And a volunteer fire brigade was organized.

In the winter of 1896-7 there was a food shortage in Dawson and in the following year there seemed to be danger of a famine. The proximate cause was the seizure of supplies by miners at Circle City, so that the last boats before the "freeze-up" brought little food. There was undoubtedly real suffering but the reports which reached the outside world were exaggerated. The United States government organized a reindeer relief party, which, however, did not reach Haines Mission near Skagway until April 15, 1898, and progressed less than eighty miles by September when of the original 558 animals only 140 remained.

summer diggings, with dimensions as follows: Length, 12 feet; at top, 10 by 11 inches; at bottom, 10 by 13 inches; the 10 in each instance representing depth.

"That 72 sets of block riffles per claim are used during the summer season, as claims are worked at present in said district, and these cost an average of $5 a set.

"That the cost of sluice-boxes, riffles not included, average of $5 a set.

"That the cost of setting a line of sluice-boxes, and keeping said lines set during the summer, averages $2,000.

"That the cost of building a rough dam sufficient for the ordinary working of the average 500-foot claim in said district is about $1,200. I think it an average ditch.

"That the cost of handling the dirt 'summer working,' from the ground-sluicing to the clean-up, averages (labor bills) $5 a cubic yard on the entire quantity moved.

"That the cost of pumping for drainage of summer pits 400 feet long by 30 feet wide averages $72 per twenty-four hours.

"That wheelbarrows cost $25 apiece; shovels, $3.50 apiece, mattocks, $5 apiece; blacksmiths' portable forges, about $200 apiece; average-weight grindstones about $35 apiece; hammers 60 cents a pound; saws, $5.50 apiece; nails, 40 cents a pound; rope, 50 cents a pound; gold-scales of average capacity, $50 a pair; quicksilver, $1.25 a pound; black powder, $1.25 a pound; fuse, 2½ cents a foot."

41. *Two Years in the Klondike* (Hartford, 1898), 372.

A matter-of-fact account of the dangers of the situation is given by Superintendent Constantine in his report dated "Fort Herchmer, Dawson, N.W.T., 18th January, 1898":

The present system of contracting for supplies with the companies here has not proved satisfactory. For the past two years we have not been able to secure sufficient food for full rations, especially is this the case this year. We have only enough to barely last until the 1st of June on short rations, and a considerable amount of our supplies had to be purchased outside of the contracting company. . . .

The outlook for the coming summer is most serious, as no quantity of food can possibly arrive here until nearly the end of July, and even then it is improbable, as food will be so scarce at the mining camps at Minook Creek, Fort Yukon and Circle City that the steamers will be held up and unloaded at these points. Word has been received from Capt. Ray of the U.S. army, who is in charge at Fort Yukon, explaining the seriousness of affairs there. He was compelled to take over the company's stores and issue out rations. At Circle City food is scarcer than it is here. Mr. Healy, manager of the N.A.T. & T. Co. here, who received the letter from Capt. Ray, admits that it is doubtful whether the boats will reach here with much cargo on their first trip from St. Michael. This means we cannot reasonably hope for much relief from the outside until the latter part of August. New Companies with new boats on the river can hardly relieve the situation, as it is proven that boats cannot be built at St. Michael and arrive here with a cargo the same year. By the time the boats are completed the river is so low at the Yukon flats that even did they get through it could only be with a light cargo.

Relief can only come to us down the river, and it is necessary that the government should take immediate action and ship supplies in over the summit, which must be freighted over the ice to the foot of Lake Labarge, scows built there and the provisions brought down by the first water, so that we may receive them not later than the 1st June, when our present stock will be entirely exhausted.

For a time last fall it looked very much as if at least half of our men would have to be sent out. Inspector Harper brought no provisions. This further reduced the rations, especially in bacon and flour. At the lower post for some time ¾ lb. of flour and 4 oz. of bacon per man per day was all that could be allowed. The arrival of several rafts of beef relieved the strain. I purchased 6,812 lbs. of beef at from $1 to $1.50 per lb.

The companies at present trading here do not care about having the police contracts, as the prices they get from the miners are two or three times what the Government pays, consequently there is grumbling all round. The companies because they say they are losing money, the miners because the police seem to get so much, and the police because they do not get more. The only way I can see out of the difficulty is for the Government to ship in their own supplies and be independent of all outside parties. The quality of the provisions supplied has been good.[42]

An epidemic of malarial-typhoid fever attributed to the lack of a system of sewage disposal led to an ill-conceived attempt by Canadian doctors to exclude their American colleagues from practising.[43]

Dawson was not without religious influences. The Rev. William H. Judge, S.J., who came from Fortymile, was the first Catholic priest to arrive. He built the first church in 1897. And the first hospital in Dawson was opened by the Catholic Church in the same year. Bishop Bompas, the great Anglican "Apostle of the North," was in the Yukon when the rush began, but his long Indian experience did not fit him for work among the miners.[44] His colleague, the Rev. R. J. Bowen, built the first Anglican Church. The first Methodist missionaries in the Klondike were the Rev. James Turner and the Rev. A. E. Hetherington.[45] The Presbyterians were represented by the Rev. John and the Rev. George Pringle. The latter, another "Lion of the North," spent eleven years on the outlying Klondike creeks.

In 1898 three newspapers were started in Dawson. Two, the *Yukon Midnight Sun* and the *Klondike Miner*, were weeklies. The *Klondike Nugget*, the best known of the three, was a semi-weekly.

42. *Sessional Papers of Canada*, no. 15, 61 Vict., A 1898, North-West Mounted Police Report, App. LL, 308 f.

43. Adney, *Klondike Stampede*, 430, recounts the incident: "At this juncture, when the amount of sickness had become a matter for general alarm, the Canadian doctors, who were greatly outnumbered by American, began prosecutions against the latter, and several of the highest standing, but who had come unprovided with licenses to practise in Canada, were haled before the magistrate, jailed and fined. While Americans should have expected this, it was admitted by most persons that a more unfortunate moment for the prosecutions could hardly have been chosen. The American physicians continued practising, however, without signs or asking fees. In all there were about seventy physicians in the camp, only a few of whom, however, found lucrative practice."

44. See H. A. Cody, *An Apostle of the North* (New York, 1908), 253 ff.

45. They found the cost of church building almost prohibitive, but the government donated a lot on which a tent was erected. See *Western Methodist Recorder* (Victoria, 1901), 11.

The price of a single copy was 50 cents and an annual subscription cost $16. The issue of July 8 enables us to chronicle the arrival of the first milk cow.[46]

Dawson matured rapidly. Jeremiah Lynch, who had been there during the winter of 1898, noted a great change a year later, and described conditions as follows:

> Dawson was full of men and women. To promenade Front Street on the river-front was like walking for a block or two in the Strand. The street was sewered, macadamized, and side-walked. Shops with full stocks and plate-glass windows occupied the east side. The west side consisted of wharves fronting the river. Scores of handsome women sauntered up and down dressed in most appropriate costumes. But one could see from their overbright eyes and carmine cheeks that they had been late overnights. The number of modest and refined women was still scanty. Wives and daughters were coming slowly. Homes had to be provided, and the future of the husband fairly well assured, before he dared to send for his family. Besides, people outside had such odd notions, both of Klondikers and the way they lived, that it took love and persuasion combined to induce women to come to the Far North. These imaginary terrors were ultimately dispelled, and the next year Dawson supported two schools and three churches.[47]

On American territory, Skagway, the port of disembarkation for the Yukon, had an equally rapid growth and an even more sinister reputation. When the first steamer arrived on July 26, 1897, there was one log building and a tent on the site. In less than a month there were two thousand inhabitants. On August 12, a public meeting set up a town government. By the time the town was a hundred days old, its hotels and lodging houses could accommodate eighteen hundred guests, and a hotel to take four hundred more was under construction. Electric light was being introduced and a water supply was being brought in by flume.

---

46.   "THIRTY DOLLARS A GALLON."

"The first milk cow ever in Dawson arrived on Wednesday. She is not very well pleased with her surroundings and did not give much milk, but that first milking brought in just $30 in Klondike dust. She will be treated to the best that Dawson affords—flour and packing-case hay—and is expected to do better as the days grow shorter. One hundred dollars a milking is not too much to expect of her, as she comes of good family. . . " (quoted by Adney, *Klondike Stampede*, 430 f.).

47. Lynch, *Three Years in the Klondike*, 166.

To cap it all, a jail had been built, but "Soapy" Smith, the famous racketeer of the seaport, did not occupy it.

We must now leave the bright lights of the cities and turn to the question of the maintenance of law and order among the miners. The Canadian government, acting on the advice of William Ogilvie,[48] made no attempt to exercise police powers in the Yukon until 1894 when Captain Constantine and Sergeant Brown of the North West Mounted Police were sent to take formal possession of Fortymile and to collect customs. The next year, Constantine, who had returned for the winter, took out a party of twenty. In spite of the arrival of the police, lynchings were not unknown.[49] There were miners' meetings to deal with civil disputes as late as 1896. They annoyed Joe Ladue, who spoke of them as follows: "The miners on the Yukon are shrewd, experienced men, and sometimes they are tricky. I do not like the kind of government they set up for themselves, except in the very first stages. It is all by miners' meetings [sic]. They begin by being fair, but after a while cliques are formed, which run things to suit the men who are in them, or, what is just as bad they turn the sessions into fun. Nobody can get justice from a miners' meeting when women

48. The following account of Ogilvie's conversation with A. M. Burgess, Deputy Minister of the Interior, is taken from Ogilvie, *Early Days in the Yukon*, 142 ff. "I told him that our mining regulations, as far as known, were unfavourably commented on in comparison with those of the United States where each mining community elected its own recorders, regulated the size of its claims, and did nearly everything else the majority of the miners thought wise, so long as they did not clash with the general mining law of the United States. I advised him that while Forty-mile seemed to possess the essentials for a pretty stable camp, most of the diggings on it were on the American side of the boundary, that at the time there were not freighting facilities enough to support more than one small camp, and that until such time as there were more and better means of transport it would be unwise in us to interfere with the affairs of the region, for the reason that most of the miners, while of foreign origin, were American citizens, or had declared their intention to become so, many even of Canadian birth and education having done so, for the advantage it gave them in the region, no alien being allowed to stake and record claims in the American territory of Alaska, while Canada allowed any one to stake and secure title. I informed him that about sixty thousand dollars' worth of goods, local value, entered the territory from American ports every season, but that to collect customs on them would likely endanger prospecting in our country. Generally, my advice was that, as the country was in a very unsettled state, and our mining laws, so far as known, unsatisfactory to the miners, even of our own nationality, any attempt to take charge of affairs on our side of the line would

are on one side."[50] The reports of the Mounted Police give a picture of the life as the police found it:

Although the majority of the population are honest people, hard-working and anxious to make money to enable them to start in life elsewhere, there are at the present time at many points in the Yukon Territory, but particularly in Dawson, a very large number of desperate characters. Many of them have committed murders, "held up" trains, stage coaches, and committed burglary and theft in the United States.

These men are at present giving us very little trouble, but as times are getting hard in the town of Dawson, work difficult to obtain and the clean up still distant, when gold will be plentiful, I expect that some serious crimes may be committed if immediate action is not taken.

I have therefore given orders that such characters might be arrested immediately and brought before a magistrate for examination. The patrols are directed to seek out any on the creeks or in the different mining camps.

When I arrived here in September, I took action which received earnest support, setting detectives to work to obtain the names and modes of life of such characters as those to whom I refer. Many were arrested and fined, and steps were taken with such satisfactory results as to make this large mining camp tolerable for respectable people; particular [sic] the wives and families of those who have settled down in the country.[51]

The police were not puritans, although they did on one occasion fine a man for fishing on Sunday. The "miners' delights" of Dawson were allowed to go on without censure, but they were regulated. Policemen had a habit of lounging around the dance-halls, apparently not taking any notice of anything. But towards morning, if anything began to get rough, the police would be there to intervene. They also saw to it that the gambling-halls were "orderly, well-conducted and on the square."

There was a limit to what the police and the magistrates could

hinder prospecting by driving most of the prospectors to the American side, and they would stay there till something very rich was discovered in Canada, and that the chance of this would be put back by our action, if we entered with authority then."

49. W. B. Haskell tells of fifty lashes being inflicted for the theft of a bag of sugar near the White Horse Rapids in 1896; and of a thief, who had stolen flour and bacon, being shot by six vigilantes in August, 1897 (*Two Years in the Klondike*, 131 f. and 472 f.).

50. Interview recorded by Lincoln Steffens, "Life in the Klondike Gold Fields," *McClure's Magazine*, September, 1897, 964 f.

51. *Sessional Papers of Canada*, 62 Vict., no. 15, N.W.M.P., A. 1899, III, 29.

do and in 1897 Major J. M. Walsh was appointed Commissioner. Accompanied by a party of officials, he reached his winter quarters in the Yukon in November.[52] In the following year the Canadian Parliament passed the Yukon Territory Act to establish a form of civil government in the Yukon. It set up a Legislative Council to consist of the Commissioner and six persons to be appointed by the Governor-General in Council. The Territorial Court was established as a Supreme Court of Record with civil and criminal jurisdiction. William Ogilvie became Commissioner in 1898.[53] On July 27 the Dominion Cabinet announced its policy towards the Yukon. Customs duties were to be collected; a royalty of from 10 to 20 per cent was to be collected on gold; alternate claims were to be reserved for the government; a monthly mail service was to be established; and the mining regulations which limited claims to 100 feet were to be enforced.

This policy aroused opposition. A mass meeting of miners named a committee to go to Ottawa to protest. Before they arrived some concessions were made. The royalty was fixed at 10 per cent; the exemption was raised to $2,500; creek claims were extended to 250 feet; adjoining beach claims might be 250 feet wide and 1,000 feet deep; other claims were to be 250 feet square; and free miners' licences were to cost $10.

In August, 1898, a committee appointed by a mass meeting drew up a petition to Sir Wilfrid Laurier, Prime Minister of Canada, complaining about the Gold Commissioner's office and about other officials. One paragraph runs:

The gold commissioner's office is practically closed—and has been for a considerable time—to the miner who has not the means or desire to bribe the clerks in order to obtain knowledge of the records which ought to be public. It is an undisputed fact that those with money obtain easy access, concessions and valuable information. The gold commissioner allowed the clerks to work overtime for those who were willing to pay them for so doing. This naturally led to many evils which have developed into a scandal, and the system is a great detriment to the camp. Wholesale

52. The sole survivor of this party which contained several men of note is the Hon. T. D. Pattullo, former Prime Minister of British Columbia, who has advocated the union of Yukon territory with that province.

53. The territory was given a member in the Canadian House of Commons by 2 Edw. VII, 37, and the Legislative Council was made elective by 7-8 Edw. VII, 76.

information with regard to unrecorded ground is conveyed to certain individuals outside the office who obtain men to stake and record the ground in consideration of an interest in the same, thereby defrauding the miner who cannot obtain correct information by legitimate means.[54]

In October, 1898, William Ogilvie was appointed to investigate these charges, but the terms of his commission limited him to events prior to the signing of the petition. Thus limited, the enquiry was abortive, although some of the officials in the Gold Commissioner's office were convicted of bribery.

On the whole civil government seems to have been successful, and no complaint was ever made of the Mounted Police. The Territory of Alaska was less fortunate in preserving law and order. The bad characters who had been ejected from Dawson congregated at Circle City where, to their disgust, they found fewer opportunities and fewer pleasures.[55] The miners' meetings which decided disputed claims were not above suspicion. "A body of miners," we are told in a Canadian North West Mounted Police report, "will get together and resolute and declare a creek open for relocation without any justification, and in some cases there is a very small percentage of property owners present at these meetings."[56] Nor did the Canadian police think highly of the work of their American colleagues in Skagway:

The town of Skagway [wrote Superintendent Steele], at this time, and for some months later was little better than a hell upon earth. The desperado commonly called "Soapy Smith" and a numerous gang of ruffians ran the town. Murder and robbery were daily occurrences, hundreds came there with plenty of money and the next morning had not sufficient to buy a meal, having been robbed or cheated out of their money. Men were seen frequently exchanging shots in the streets. On one occasion half a dozen in the vicinity, and around the North-west Mounted Police Offices, were firing upon one another, bullets passing through the buildings. There was a United States deputy marshal at Skagway at this time for the purpose of maintaining law and order, but no protection was expected from him.[57]

54. *Sessional Papers of Canada*, no. 87, 62 Vict., A 1899, 2.

55. See Lynch, *Three Years in the Klondike*, 237.

56. *Sessional Papers of Canada*, no. 15, A 1899, III, 78.

57. *Ibid.*, 4. Gang rule in Skagway terminated with the death of "Soapy" Smith in a gun fight, July 8, 1898.

A great improvement in Alaskan administration took place with the appointment of Judge Wickersham in 1902 to succeed Judge Arthur H. Noyes, who with his assistant Alexander McKenzie had been removed to California for trial.

We must next examine how the two adjacent communities treated each other in matters of daily intercourse. In some matters Americans were better treated in Canada than were Canadians in the United States. Under United States law only citizens and persons who had declared their intention of becoming citizens could take up and hold mining claims. In the Yukon no discrimination was made against Americans. If this difference in treatment did not give rise to more ill-feeling than it did, the reason seems to have been that the Canadian claims were more attractive than the Alaskan.

The two leading trading companies in the Yukon were American, for the Hudson's Bay Company, which had explored the region as early as 1843 and established fur-trading posts from 1847 onwards, withdrew after 1889 when their post at Fort Yukon was found to be on the American side of the boundary. The Alaskan Commercial Company had been formed in 1868 to buy out the Russian-American Company. Its great rival was the North American Transportation and Trading Company, founded in 1892 by a group of Chicago capitalists. Both these companies built warehouses in Dawson when it became the centre of the Yukon trade.

From the beginning of the Klondike gold rush, Canadians had trouble with the American customs authorities at Skagway. Bonded goods might in principle pass through and it was recognized that tents and blankets were the ordinary equipment of the traveller. But $30 a head was demanded for horses. Adney describes the situation as he found it:

Here is a strip of territory, a few miles in width, which must be crossed before Canadian territory can again be reached. There are no facilities for the transit of goods in bond. Not one in twenty of those here would willingly stop. The privilege of bonding goods through the territory is elsewhere extended by both governments; but here is a trail three weeks old and no facilities for transit. The only means of transfer is the miner himself and his horse's back. The miner's word is the only bond. Even to lead the horse across empty, the horse and the man must eat, and the man must carry on his own back the oats for his horse, as well as his own food, according to the rules of Mr. Jones, United States deputy collector for the sub-port of Dyea. There is nothing to do but step up to the custom-house, look pleasant, and pay the $30 a head on our stock.[58]

The Legislature of British Columbia on May 4, 1897, passed a resolution praying the Lieutenant-Governor to urge the Dominion government to arrive at some arrangement with the United States to facilitate the transit of goods through Alaskan territory.[59] The United States government eventually set up the Port of Dyea and later included Skagway within this port.

A long correspondence took place between Ottawa and Washington about the entry of goods by way of St. Michael. Canada claimed, under Article xvi of the Treaty of Washington of 1871, that British subjects had equal rights with United States citizens to navigate the Yukon.[60] The United States regulations required shipment via a port in the State of Washington, with a bond that the goods would be exported within a given time. If the goods were held up at St. Michael, they should remain in a warehouse at the wharf under customs supervision. An extension of time would be allowed if an obstruction occurred. But there was no bonded warehouse at St. Michael in the autumn of 1897.[61]

On the Dyea-Skagway route a system of convoys was introduced for goods in transit which could not be conveniently bonded. This system was subject to serious abuse and it was often cheaper to pay the United States customs duties. It is described in a report of the Mounted Police:

The class of people who went in this year [1898], as a general rule, were not legitimate miners, and it was astonishing the number of men who were (thanks to Soapy Smith, and the convoy system, established by the American officials at Skagway), practically without money when they reached the Summit. The convoy system was this; every Canadian, or in

58. Adney, *Klondike Stampede*, 50 f.

59. *Journals of the Legislature of British Columbia*, 1897, 148.

60. *Sessional Papers of Canada*, no. 79, 62 Vict., A 1899, 9. The clause reads: "The navigation of the Rivers Yukon, Porcupine, and Stikine, ascending and descending from, to and into the sea, shall for ever remain free and open for the purposes of commerce to the subjects of Her Britannic Majesty and to the citizens of the United States, subject to any laws and regulations of either country within its own territory, not inconsistent with such privilege of free navigation."

61. *Ibid.*, 8.

fact any one who purchased their goods in Canada, had to employ a convoy at the rate of $6 per day and $3 a day subsistence, this making a total of $9 per day for convoy; thus, when a man with a small outfit, hauling his own stuff from Skagway to the Summit, reached the latter, the expense of the convoy (for on an average it would take him two weeks to get all his stuff there) cost him as much, if not more, than the total duty would have amounted to on the said goods, if they had been purchased in Seattle or San Francisco. The convoys in some cases attempted to get right through to Lake Bennett, but acting under orders from Superintendent Steele, I gave them to understand they would not be permitted to pass the Summit. In one instance a convoy threatened to hold a party's goods at the ford on the Skagway side of the Summit, if the said party refused to pay him in advance for the time he, (the convoy), calculated it would take him to go to Bennett from the Summit, this the owner of the goods did in order to have them released.[62]

Of course Americans who entered the Yukon had to meet the demands of the Canadian customs. A customs post was established at Tagish in September, 1897. The officer in charge seems to have been fairly accommodating. He told Adney: "I ask them if they have dutiable goods; I take their statement, or they offer me their bills. I do not look into a miner's boat. I try to judge each case, and I recognize that few have any surplus cash when they reach here. In such cases I have taken a day or two's labor whip-sawing, or something in lieu of cash, holding the same in trust until the duties are forwarded. I ask full duty on tobacco. I have taken flour at $20 a sack—trail price."[63] There were, however, complaints, one of which may serve to show the temper of the age:

During 1896-97 the Canadian Government allowed free entry of miners' blankets, personal clothing in use, cooking utensils in use, and 190 pounds of food for each person, charging duty on the excess.

This has been superseded by levying duty upon everything the miner possesses except the clothes on his back. This applies to articles bought not only in the United States, but England or anywhere outside of Canada.

As miners going in are not as a rule overstocked with funds, some heroic measures on their part may be anticipated sooner or later for which the Government and people of the United States will be compelled to find a solution, if the rush continues and population increases. . . .

62. *Ibid.*, no. 15, 62 Vict., 1889, III, 112.
63. Adney, *Klondike Stampede*, 136.

This may force the irrepressible conflict between British occupation and United States manifest destiny on the Pacific shores of the North American continent so emphatically upheld by Senator Charles Sumner of Massachusetts, and William H. Seward of New York, and many other statesmen great and small.[64]

An amicable arrangement was ultimately reached. The Hon. Clifford Sifton, Canadian Minister of the Interior, visited the Klondike in 1897. On his return he was besieged with requests from merchants in Victoria and Vancouver that Canada should retaliate against United States customs exactions. The United States War Department was, at the time, asking for permission to send $200,000 of provisions through Canadian territory for the relief of Americans in Alaska without paying duty. Sifton went to Washington and secured an agreement under which Canadian goods were to be allowed passage through Dyea and Skagway "without such inspection fees being charged as would virtually prohibit the transmission of Canadian goods without payment of duty."[65]

The customs issue became involved with the Alaskan boundary dispute which will be discussed in the next chapter. The Canadian posts were at the summits of the passes. The Americans claimed that the boundary lay at Lake Bennett, thirty-five miles from Dyea, and insisted on their convoys being retained to that point. The Canadians "politely but firmly" turned the convoys back.[66] On May 15 the United States stopped the convoys and placed customs officers at each summit.

Another phase of the relations of Americans and Canadians appeared in the competition of the American and Canadian coast cities. From the time that the first gold ships, the *Excelsior* of the Alaska Commercial Company, and the *Portland* of the North American Transportation and Trading Company, arrived at Seattle in June, 1897, the cities of Puget Sound were determined to capture the trade with the new gold fields. Seattle became the San Francisco of the new rush. The Chamber of Commerce opposed bonding facilities at Dyea and Skagway. The *Post-Intelligencer* denounced

64. D. R. Keim, *Our Alaskan Wonderland* (Washington, 1898), 349 f. This book was dedicated to W. H. Seward.

65. J. W. Dafoe, *Clifford Sifton in Relation to His Times* (Toronto, 1931), 161.

66. *Sessional Papers of Canada*, no. 15, 62 Vict., A 1899, III, 47.

the Canadian customs duties.[67] When the Canadian customs regulations were revised, the American ports got an increased trade and Seattle easily outdistanced Tacoma, Portland, and San Francisco. The Canadian ports were not backward in setting forth their advantages. The Board of Trade in Victoria explained in a circular:

The Yukon gold fields are wholly in Canada. Outfits purchased in the United States are subject to duty, which is rigorously exacted by customs officers and Mounted Police at the passes entering Canadian territory. A number of miners from the United States going north today were turned back, because unable to pay the duties, and had to dispose of their outfits at a loss.

Supplies of all kinds can be purchased in Victoria as cheaply as anywhere from the most experienced outfitters in America, and they will not be subject to duty or any unnecessary delay by customs officials. Steamers will ply frequently between Victoria and Dyea and Skagway Bay as long as the travel demands. The Secretary of the Board of Trade will give applicants by mail all needed information.[68]

Vancouver merchants were insistent in demanding a line of steamers from Vancouver to Dyea.

The regular steamship services to the north during the season of 1897 were those of the Pacific Coast Steamship Company and the Canadian Pacific Navigation Company. The former was American, the latter Canadian. In addition numerous "special ships" were employed.[69] There was a boom in shipping and in

67. The following sentences are quoted in the Vancouver *News-Advertiser* of August 3, 1897: "As a means of compelling prospectors to purchase rusty and old-fashioned outfits at the Provincial stores, the order is issued that every blessed thing a foreigner takes with him shall be subjected to a Canadian duty. . . . The whole thing is ridiculous and will be announced as an arbitrary attempt to bolster up local interests by the most sorely pinched monarchy in the universe. . . .

"The Canadian Government has already announced that it proposes to gobble 70 per cent. of the wealth discovered and developed by American grit and enterprise, and a halt might just as well be called now as at any other time. . . .

"The Government at Washington should be apprised immediately of the gross exactions now being practised by the Canadian officials and such retaliatory measures demanded as will bring this eleventh hour robbery to an end."

68. Quoted in the Vancouver *News-Advertiser*, July 30, 1897.

69. Ernest Ingersoll describes one of these, the Willamette, in *Golden Alaska, a Complete Account to Date of the Yukon Valley* (Chicago and New York, 1897), 10: "a collier, which was cleaned out in a few hours, and turned into an extemporized

ship-building. In 1897 two ocean steamers came to St. Michael, in 1898 more than twenty. In 1897 they were met by five river steamers which supplied Dawson. Adney tells us that in 1898, "forty-seven river steamers, some of them twice the tonnage of the largest previously on the river, and equalling in equipment and passenger accommodation the best Ohio and Mississippi river packets, were either on the stocks in Seattle or in sections on the decks of the steamers for putting together at Dutch Harbor and St. Michael, or were already at St. Michael and within the Yukon, awaiting the breaking-up of the river." Canadian competition grew slowly and on the whole the American lines maintained their supremacy. The river steamers were almost all American.

When the White Pass and Yukon Railroad came to be built, it was an international affair and three charters were required for its construction. The Pacific and Arctic Railway and Navigation Company built the Alaskan section from Skagway to the summit. The British Columbia Yukon Railway operated the section in British Columbia. And the British Yukon Mining, Trading and Transportation Company constructed the line as far as White Horse. The original intention to bring the line to Dawson was never carried out. In summer the river steamers went down from White Horse to Dawson. The building of this railway revolutionized transportation in the Yukon, as it was able to compete with the river route from St. Michael, and the use of the railway made it possible for Canadian goods to displace American in the import trade of the Klondike. At one time practically all the imports were of American origin. Eventually from 75 to 80 per cent were Canadian.[70]

The age of individual operations came to an end in the Yukon, partly because the dredges were able to displace hand labour. H. H. Rowatt describes how, during the earlier years of the twentieth century, the Yukon Gold Company, controlled by the

passenger-boat. The whole 'tween decks space was fitted with rough bunks, wonderfully close together, for 'first-class' passengers; while away down in the hold second-class arrangements were made which the mind shudders to contemplate. Yet this slave-ship sort of a chance was eagerly taken, and such space as was left was crowded with animals and goods."

70. For a full account of the railway and its effects on the Yukon, see H. A. Innis, *Settlement and the Mining Frontier* (Toronto, 1936).

Guggenheim interests, became dominant in the Klondike, by buying up claims:

The Yukon Gold Company entered the Klondike district at a time when the camp was rapidly approaching the last stage and when the individual operations had almost come to a close, and they have given it a new life. They have purchased, practically at the price asked, nearly all the creek, bench and hill claims on Bonanza and Eldorado creeks, and a large number of Hunker and Bear. Nearly all of the creek claims were worked out, so far as the operations of the individual miner are concerned, and in many instances the company paid liberal sums for bench and hill claims which were of no commercial value whatever to any miner of limited means, owing to the fact that they were beyond the reach of any ordinary water supply.[71]

Thus American capital came into control and although the Yukon is politically part of Canada it has been drawn commercially into the American orbit.

The era of individual exploitation of natural wealth in its easily appropriated forms was coming to an end and the subsequent history of mining in British Columbia belongs to a different period in which the more colourful scenes of the mining camps do not appear. Gold and base metals have been found in the Portland Canal, Bridge River, and Howe Sound districts of British Columbia.

The Portland Canal mines form a link with the Klondike. Their history begins with a claim staked and abandoned by Lieutenant Mosier of the United States Navy in 1896. Three years later it was restaked by John Flewin of Port Simpson. The greatest gold mine of the district is now the Premier, near the international boundary, twelve miles north of Stewart, British Columbia. Its early history was one of disappointment to the discoverers and promoters, but success came after 1916. Since 1919 the mine, which was acquired by American and Canadian interests combined in the Premier Gold Mining Company, has produced gold bullion worth more than $37,000,000 and has paid more than $17,500,000 in dividends. The Surf Inlet gold mine on Princess Royal Island paid out $1,500,000 in dividends between 1917 and 1926. The leading copper mine, the Hidden Creek, which has been owned

71. *Report with respect to the Yukon Territory, 1907* (Ottawa, 1908), 9-10. See also Innis, *Settlement and the Mining Frontier*, 237 ff.

since 1901 by the Granby Consolidated Mining, Smelting and Power Company, is said to have been the second largest producer of copper on the Pacific Coast.[72]

The record of the Premier mine has been challenged in recent years by those of Bralorne and Pioneer, the leading gold mines in the Bridge River area, near Lillooet, British Columbia. Although gold-bearing quartz had been found in this area as early as 1864, it was not until the late 1890's that any serious prospecting took place. In 1897 William Young staked the Lorne, now Bralorne, and Atwell found the Pioneer. As usual development was very slow. Pioneer did not come into its own until the late 1920's and Bralorne until the 1930's.

Copper pyrites was found at the entrance to Howe Sound in 1865 and an unsuccessful attempt to work it was made. The development of this region, however, begins in 1898 when Oliver Furry, a trapper, staked a claim on the mountains on the eastern shore of Howe Sound. This is now a portion of the well-known Britannia mine. Furry sold his interest to Leo Boscowitz of Victoria, who in turn sold a seven-tenths interest to an American syndicate headed by Howard Walters of Libby, Montana. The present Britannia Mining and Smelting Company was formed in 1908 by Grant B. Schley and associates, New York bankers. The Britannia is now the largest copper-producing mine in Canada.

Mining need not be a crudely predatory enterprise, such as a gold rush. But depletion is always in the background. Gold mines seem to run a definite course: a long period of quiescence, a sudden flare-up of production, and then, after a few years, the mine is worked out. The cycle of the base metal mines is longer, but the mineral supplies of the Pacific Coast are not inexhaustible. Improvements in metallurgy may prolong a mine's life for a time, but nothing can be done when the ore supply fails. In the early days of placer gold a poor man *might* make a fortune. Today both gold and base metal mining is usually in the hands of large companies. Much American capital is still invested in the mines of British Columbia and the Yukon, but there are also many Canadian investors. In a later chapter we shall see the consequences of this situation: the anxiety of a province faced with the prospect of

72. B. F. Townley, *Mine-Finders* (Toronto, 1936), 179.

depletion; and the wish to employ fiscal devices by which the investor in other jurisdictions can be made to pay a share of developmental and social service costs. Before coming to these developments, that belong to the age of long-range planning, we must turn to examine the Alaska boundary controversy, which was intimately bound up with the Klondike gold rush and which was itself, in temper as in substance, characteristic of the era of predatory exploitation—an era happily doomed to extinction.

CHAPTER XV

THE ALASKA BOUNDARY

1824-1903

In discussing the Oregon Question it was pointed out that by the treaties of 1824 and 1825 the southern boundary of Russian America was set at 54° 40′. The first of these treaties was with the United States and contained an agreement that the United States would make no settlement north of that line, and that Russia would make none to the southward of it. The Treaty of 1825, which gave rise to the Alaska boundary dispute, was made between Russia and Great Britain. Its second article provided that the subjects of either nation were not to land at any place in the possession of the other without the permission of the officer there in charge. The fifth article provided that British subjects should make no settlement in Russian territory, and that the Russians should make no settlement south of 54° 40′. The sixth gave the British the free navigation of the rivers; the seventh gave them for ten years free access to inland seas, gulfs, havens, and creeks on the coast. But the important articles, out of which the dispute arose, were Articles III and IV.

ARTICLE III

The line of demarcation between the possessions of the high contracting parties, upon the coast of the continent, and the islands of America to the North-west, shall be drawn in the manner following:

Commencing from the southernmost point of the island called *Prince of Wales* Island, which point lies in the parallel of 54 degrees 40 minutes, north latitude, and between the 131st and the 133rd degree of west longitude (Meridian of Greenwich), the said line shall ascend to the north along the channel called *Portland Channel*, as far as the point of the continent where it strikes the 56th degree of north latitude; from this last-mentioned point, the line of demarcation shall follow the summit of the mountains situated parallel to the coast, as far as the point of intersection of the 141st degree of west longitude (of the same meridian); and, finally, from the said point of intersection, the said meridian line of the 141st degree, in its prolongation as far as the Frozen Ocean, shall form the limit between the Russian and British Possessions on the continent of America to the North-west.

ARTICLE IV

With reference to the line of demarcation laid down in the preceding article it is understood:

First. That the island called *Prince of Wales* Island shall belong wholly to Russia.

Second. That whenever the summit of the mountains which extend in a direction parallel to the coast, from the 56th degree of north latitude to the point of intersection of the 141st degree of west longitude, shall prove to be at the distance of more than 10 marine leagues from the ocean, the limit between the British Possessions and the line of coast which is to belong to Russia, as above mentioned, shall be formed by a line parallel to the windings of the coast, and which shall never exceed the distance of 10 marine leagues therefrom.[1]

The first trouble occurred in 1834, when an expedition of the Hudson's Bay Company, attempting to navigate the Stikine River for the purpose of founding a trading post in British territory, was forcibly prevented by the Russians who took the position that the Russian American Company had already established Fort St. Dionysius on that river and that Article II of the treaty in spirit justified their action. The Hudson's Bay Company, of course, claimed damages, which were estimated at more than £22,150. After diplomatic correspondence and discussions between the two companies, the claim for damages was settled by the grant, in 1840, of a lease of the mainland coast from 54° 40′ to Cape Spencer on Cross Sound.[2] This lease was renewed from time to time and was in existence when, in 1867, the United States purchased Russian America, which then became the Territory of Alaska.

The necessity for marking the boundary line laid down in the Treaty of 1825, was, in 1872, brought to the attention of the Dominion of Canada, by the first Legislative Assembly of British Columbia. The geographical difficulties were not then known or even suspected. Ultimately the request reached Washington and President Grant. In December, 1872, he brought up in a Message to Congress the desirability of undertaking a survey of the line,

1. Alaska Boundary Tribunal, II, *Appendix to the Case of the United States* (Washington, 1904), 14 f.

2. *Ibid.*, 267 ff., 277, 315; for the terms of lease, which was for ten years, see *Certain Correspondence of the Foreign Office and the Hudson's Bay Company* (Ottawa, 1899), part II, 35 ff.

pointing out that the region was then sparsely settled, but that if action were delayed until it was occupied the two nations might again be arrayed in antagonism. The United States had just received a favourable decision in the San Juan dispute. When they reported that the cost of surveying the whole boundary line was estimated at such a sum as made it impossible, the British suggested that it might be possible to mark merely the points at which the boundary crossed the rivers flowing into the Pacific Ocean. After much delay, even this working arrangement was refused as being also too expensive.

In the meantime gold had been discovered in the Cassiar district of northern British Columbia. The only practicable access to it was by way of the Stikine River, whose navigation had by the treaty with Russia in 1825 been made free to the British. But in 1871 the Treaty of Washington between Great Britain and the United States had limited the British right of navigation of that river to purposes of commerce. Why this was done is not known. In 1877 Edward Blake declared himself "unable to form a plausible conjecture."[3] Yet when in 1873 the British had attempted to exercise that right, the American customs officer at Wrangel, at the mouth of the Stikine, informed them that the American government had ordered that no foreign bottom should be allowed to carry freight through American territory on that river. It may be that he had not been notified of the treaty; but, if so, two years seems an unconscionable length of time. There was, probably, a desire to engross the trade of the British mines in Cassiar, just as Whatcom in 1858 had striven to secure the trade of the Fraser River mines. As the nearest British post was Fort Simpson, while the Americans had a good port at Wrangel, the British feared that the Americans would derive more advantages from these mines than themselves. However, upon representations made to the United States, the officer at Wrangel was instructed, in January, 1874, "to act in accordance with the provisions of the Treaty of Washington."[4]

As a counter move the Canadian authorities enforced the coasting

3. The Treaty of Washington, 1871, will be found in *Treaties with the United States affecting Canada* (Ottawa, 1915), 64 ff., at 77; Alaskan Boundary Tribunal, III, *Appendix to the British Case* (Washington, 1904), 279.

4. *Ibid.*, 240.

regulations prohibiting American ships from trading at two con-secutive Canadian ports unless they had, in the meantime, called at an American port. Considerable local friction arose. Again, in 1874, the Legislature of British Columbia pressed for the marking of the boundary. In June, 1875, the local American and Canadian cus-toms officers, without any instructions or authorization and without reporting their action, fixed upon a point on the Stikine River some two and a half miles below Buck's (a trading post occupied by a British trader, Choquette) as being where the boundary line crossed the Stikine.[5] The actuating motive was merely to enable them to work harmoniously together.

Cassiar could only be reached by the Stikine River. There was no approach by land. Six hundred miles of unbroken forest separated it from the nearest occupied parts of the province and from the nearest road—the Cariboo road. In September, 1876, a man named Peter Martin, who had been convicted in Cassiar and sentenced to imprisonment, had to be taken to the nearest jail, Victoria. For that purpose he was taken down the Stikine, a route that must pass through American territory. At a point about thirteen miles from its mouth, and on American soil, he, attempting to escape, severely assaulted one of his guards. This incident and the subsequent conviction for the assault became the subject of a lengthy diplomatic correspondence, which resulted in the criminal's securing his freedom from punishment for the original offence because of his being transported through United States territory and also from punishment for the assault because the locus of that crime was on American soil.[6]

Time and again the British government pressed the American government for action towards marking the boundary line. The reply was stereotyped: Congress could not be induced to grant the necessary funds, and it made no difference whether the request was for the survey of the whole line, or the marking of the line where it crossed the rivers or only where it crossed the Stikine. After striving in vain for five years to obtain the co-operation of the American government,[7] Canada resolved to send an able

5. *Ibid.*, 294.
6. *Ibid.*, 251 ff.
7. *Ibid.*, 254 ff., 271, 289, 310.

engineer, Joseph Hunter, to locate the point where the boundary line crossed the Stikine River.

And yet, while consistently refusing to do anything towards fixing the physical position of the boundary, the Secretary of the United States Treasury in July, 1876, instructed the collector of customs at Sitka that Buck's (which lay on the British side of the line fixed by the local British and American customs officers) would be treated as United States territory. Choquette, the British trader at Buck's, was accordingly notified that he must either remove his goods in the spring of 1877, or pay duty upon them to prevent seizure. Learning that Joseph Hunter was about to settle the line on the Stikine River, the American collector of customs permitted the order to be extended until August, 1877.[8] Dealing with this the Hon. Alexander Mackenzie, Prime Minister of Canada, wrote in November, 1876: "It is very remarkable that while the United States Government should have hitherto refused or neglected to take proper steps to define the boundary, they should now seek to establish it in this manner in accordance with their own views, without any reference to British authorities, who are equally interested in the just settlement of the international boundary."[9] This man, Choquette, had a very large business with the Indians who, preferring British goods, passed by the American traders at Sitka and Wrangel to deal with him and the Hudson's Bay Company. "It is the object of the American Custom House authorities," wrote Mr. Justice Gray, "to kill this trade, and force the Indians to deal in American goods at Wrangel and Sitka."[10] Mr. Hunter fixed upon a point some nineteen miles at a right angle from the coast, as the place where the boundary crossed the Stikine River. In March, 1878, the United States agreed to accept this as a conventional boundary line, not in any way affecting the treaty rights of either nation.[11]

As the importance of the Cassiar diggings diminished, the interest in the location of the boundary lessened. It lay dormant from 1878

8. Alaska Boundary Tribunal, IV, *Appendix to Counter Case of United States* (Washington, 1904), 69 ff.; *Appendix to the British Case*, 262, 293.

9. *Appendix to the British Case*, 256.

10. Letter, Mr. Justice Gray to the Hon. A. Mackenzie, October 16, 1877, in *ibid.*, 257.

11. *Ibid.*, 316 ff.

until about 1884. The difficulty of fitting the line described in the treaty to the geographical conditions then began to attract attention: the treaty spoke of the boundary as passing north to Portland Channel, but the direction from the point of commencement to Portland *Canal* is easterly; Portland Canal does not extend to 56° north latitude; it seemed possible that the mountains were not parallel to the coast; in that event what was meant by the "windings of the coast" from which the ten marine leagues were to be measured?

Bar mining on the upper Yukon was, in the early eighties, attracting some attention. The Chilcat and Chilcoot (or White) passes, at the head of Lynn Canal, were the principal routes to these diggings. In 1888 the difficulties of working out the words of the treaty upon the ground were informally discussed by Professor W. H. Dall representing the United States and Dr. George M. Dawson representing Canada. Both sought possession of the head of Lynn Canal, thereby controlling the trade routes to the Yukon bar diggings; and each interpreted the treaty to favour the contention of his country. They, however, agreed on one point: The sooner the matter was settled and decided the better for both countries. President Grant's words of 1872 were coming true.

Nevertheless nothing was done towards that end until the Convention of July 22, 1892, which was framed to ascertain the facts necessary to the permanent delimitation of the boundary. Under its provisions W. F. King, Chief Astronomer of Canada, and T. C. Mendenhall, Superintendent of the United States Coast and Geodetic Survey, closely reconnoitred the coast region from Portland Canal northward. This examination showed that there was no distinct range of mountains parallel to the coast, and that the country was "a sea of mountains." Already the great question was emerging: If there are no mountains that satisfy the words of the treaty, is the boundary to be drawn ten marine leagues from the heads of the inlets and thus shut British territory off completely from the ocean, or parallel to and ten marine leagues from the general trend of the coast and thus leave to the United States a disconnected line of coast? Considering the words of the two articles it seemed difficult to interpret the "windings of the coast" as meaning that the boundary should run down the long, narrow inlets; and yet it was just as difficult to interpret the words "line of coast" as meaning pieces of the coast separated by the mouths of those inlets. The following resolution, passed in 1895 by the House of Representatives of the State of Washington, gives their viewpoint—albeit a trifle over-forcibly:

Whereas England with her usual cupidity and avarice, and pursuant to her time-honored custom of attempting at all hazards, to get control of all newly developed sources of wealth, in whatever country situated, and to appropriate to her own benefit the present and prospective commerce of the seas, whether rightfully or otherwise, has asserted claims to harbours, bays and inlets, through which the greater portion of the commerce and trade of and with the territory of Alaska must be carried on, and which, of right, belongs to the United States;

And whereas the United States will be robbed and despoiled of the trade and commerce of a veritable empire, and suffer a diminution of the wealth with which nature has endowed said territory, if the claims and policy of Great Britain as aforesaid shall prevail;

Therefore be it resolved by the House of Representatives of the State of Washington, the Senate concurring, that our members of Congress be requested, and our Senators instructed, to use all honourable means, that the rightful claims of the United States relative to said harbours, bays and inlets, be scrupulously maintained, and that an unequivocal policy on the part of the United States government in relation thereto, be fully carried out.[12]

On this strongly-worded resolution it may be remarked that the region whose trade was sought was the Klondike in the Canadian Yukon and not the United States Territory of Alaska. The whole thing is strangely reminiscent of the attitude of Whatcom in the Fraser River rush of 1858.

But to return. In 1896 came the news of the discovery of rich gold-fields in the Klondike, Yukon Territory, Canada, with the consequent rushes of 1897 and 1898. The unsettled boundary line was a source of much inconvenience to Canadians and Canadian vessels, though, in fairness, it must be said that this was largely due to the lack of proper instructions to the American officers. As an example, on August 19, 1897, the Secretary of State for Canada

12. Quoted in Alexander Begg, "Review of Alaska Boundary Question," in *British Columbia Mining Record*, July, 1900, 258.

telegraphed the Treasury Department of the United States: "Freight and passengers for Yukon are going by White Pass, and the landing is at Skagway Bay, three miles south of Dyea, American vessels deposit freight and passengers at the bay, but privilege refused to Canadian vessels. Customs officers can as conveniently pass entries at Skagway as at Dyea. Will you please instruct officials by wire to extend privilege of landing at Skagway Bay to Canadian vessels as conceded to American vessels? Please wire me if instructions will be sent." The following day came the courteous reply: "On sixth instant, limits of port of Dyea were extended to include Skagway and deputy in charge instructed accordingly. This action gave Canadian vessels same rights as vessels of United States. Have again wired deputy, all vessels may enter at Skagway."[13]

A Joint High Commission in 1898-9 split upon the interpretation of the treaty; but out of the battle of words came clearly the crucial question: whether the treaty called for a boundary drawn around the heads of the inlets or parallel to the general trend of the coast. For the necessary dispatch of business a *modus vivendi* was arranged, in October, 1899, fixing a conventional boundary on the Dalton trail near Klehini River and on the Dyea and Skagway trails at the summit of the Chilcoot and White passes.[14] The Commission suggested that the Alaskan boundary and other questions submitted to it should be settled by an "arbitral board composed of three eminent jurists upon each side." Canadians were not then willing to accept this suggestion, nor were the Americans ready to accept the British proposals for a board with a neutral umpire.[15] On January 24, 1903, a Convention for the settlement of the long-standing dispute was signed at Washington. By it seven questions, covering the points already outlined, were to be submitted to a tribunal composed of "six impartial jurists of repute, who shall consider judicially the questions submitted to them, each of whom shall first subscribe an oath that he will impartially consider the arguments and evidence presented to the Tribunal, and will decide thereupon according to his true judgment." Three members were

13. Alaska Boundary Tribunal, *Appendix to the British Case*, 375.
14. *Ibid.*, 377 f.
15. P. C. Jessup, *Elihu Root* (New York, 1938), I, 389.

to be appointed by each nation; and the award was to be signed by a majority.[16]

President Roosevelt accepted this arrangement reluctantly as he insisted that the Canadians "did not have a leg to stand on."[17] He made it abundantly clear that he did not contemplate the possibility of any one of the three American "impartial jurists of repute" failing to decide in favour of the contentions of the United States.[18] But (although this was not widely known at the time) he did ask two justices of the Supreme Court of the United States to serve.[19] The eventual appointees were Senator Henry Cabot Lodge of Massachusetts, Senator George Turner of Washington, and Elihu Root, Secretary for War. Various reasons have been assigned for these appointments. John Hay wrote at the time of Lodge's "intimate relations with the President which make it almost impossible that the President should deny him anything which he has to give him, and he insisted on this appointment to the tribunal."[20] Lodge himself has said that several senators refused to vote for ratification of the treaty until they knew the names of the proposed arbitrators "because they could not agree to have any body on that tribunal who would yield on the American claim."[21] Elihu Root wrote at the time, that he was "drafted . . . impressed . . . shanghaied."[22] Nineteen years later he wrote that he "probably said he [Roosevelt] should have some person of judicial standing." Very moderate criticism of these appointments by Sir Wilfrid Laurier in the Canadian House of Commons[23] enraged Roosevelt who, on March 25, 1903, sent "confidential instructions" to his "three impartial jurists,"[24] explaining their duties as follows: "There is entire room for discussion and judicial and impartial agreement as to the exact boundary in any given

16. *Correspondence respecting the Alaska Boundary, presented to Parliament, January 1904*, 41 ff.

17. Jessup, *Elihu Root*, I, 390.

18. *Ibid.*

19. *Ibid.*, I, 393.

20. *Ibid.*, I, 393, citing Tyler Dennett, *John Hay* (New York, 1933), 538.

21. *Transactions of Massachusetts Historical Society*, April, 1925. The Senator's statement is reproduced in *Canadian Historical Review*, VI, 332 ff.

22. Letter to Taft, quoted in Jessup, *Elihu Root*, 392.

23. *Canada, House of Commons Debates*, 1903, I, cols. 40 ff.

24. Jessup, *Elihu Root*, 395.

locality. . . . In the principle involved there will of course be no compromise."[25]

The Canadian government proceeded with its preparations. At their request the British government appointed Lord Alverstone, Lord Chief Justice of England, Sir Louis Jetté, Lieutenant-Governor of Quebec, and Mr. Justice Armour of the Supreme Court of Canada. Before the sittings commenced Mr. Justice Armour died; in his stead Mr. A. B. Aylesworth, K.C., one of the leaders of the Canadian bar was appointed.

The Alaska Boundary Tribunal sat in London in September and October, 1903. Senator Lodge, in close touch with President Roosevelt, kept him fully advised of anything indicative of the views of the British members, especially those of Lord Alverstone.[26] It seems probable that the American Embassy did communicate to the British government the American decision that in the event of a disagreement on the main issue the United States would establish posts in the disputed territory.[27] But though Lord Alverstone may have known of this, it does not appear that it influenced his decision on the main issue. On October 20, 1903, the award of the majority of the members—Lord Alverstone, Senator Lodge, Senator Turner, and Secretary Root—settled the questions submitted, in favour of the Americans,[28] at least so far as the great question of the heads of the inlets was concerned. F. C. Wade, who was attached to the British Commission, thus summarized the two conflicting views and the award thereon:

The Canadian contention was that there were mountains parallel to the coast within the meaning of the Treaty, and that the tops of the mountains nearest the sea should be the line of demarcation. The United States contended that an unbroken chain of mountains exactly parallel to the coast was intended and that as no such chain existed (or ever did exist in the known world) the boundary line should everywhere be placed back ten marine leagues from the shore, including in the term "shore" the heads of all inlets, bays, etc. The Tribunal found the Canadian contention to be

25. *Ibid.*

26. James White, "Henry Cabot Lodge and the Alaska Boundary Award," *Canadian Historical Review*, VI, 332 ff., at 343.

27. Jessup, *Elihu Root*, I, 396.

28. See the award of the majority and the dissentient judgments in *Correspondence respecting the Alaska Boundary*, 49 ff.

correct as to the existence of mountains within the terms of the Treaty, but arbitrarily chose mountains not along its coast but at a great distance from it.

The mountains chosen served the same purpose as the ten marine league strip, for they shut Canada off just as effectually from the access to the ocean. Mr. Aylesworth put it thus: "Instead of taking the coast line of mountains, a line of mountains has been drawn far back from the coast, clearing completely all bays, inlets, and means of access to the sea, and giving the United States a complete land barrier between Canada and the sea from Portland Canal to Mount St. Elias."[29] The Tribunal also found that Portland Canal was the Portland Channel of the treaty. But in that connection a strange thing happened. At the mouth of Portland Canal lie four islands: Pearse, Wales, Sitklan, and Kannaghunut. The Americans had claimed that the proper line should pass to the southward of the four; the British had contended that the boundary should run to the northward of them. The majority of the Tribunal held that Pearse and Wales should belong to Great Britain; but that the other two, Sitklan and Kannaghunut, should be a part of the United States. This decision involved a last minute compromise on the part of Lord Alverstone. There is in existence a draft of Lord Alverstone's original judgment whereby he declared that all four islands belonged to Great Britain; but when the award was made he was found to have changed his views and, with the three American Commissioners, joined in declaring that Sitklan and Kannaghunut belonged to the United States.[30] A compromise is never quite logical, and this particular compromise was attacked "with rather compelling logic"[31] by the two Canadian members. Canadian public opinion accused "the Lord Chief Justice . . . of handing over the islands to satisfy the American members' anxiety for a diplomatic victory and to prevent them from rejecting the whole decision. Such a course, very justifiable at a pinch in any process of conciliation or diplomatic negotiation, was held to be

29. For this and the preceding quotation, see F. C. Wade, *Treaties affecting the North Pacific Coast* (Vancouver, 1914), 15.

30. Cf. Lord Alverstone's judgment in *Correspondence respecting the Alaska Boundary*, 52 f., with the draft given by Wade, *Treaties*, 16 ff.

31. P. E. Corbett, *The Settlement of Canadian-American Disputes* (New Haven and Toronto, 1937), 20.

totally out of keeping with the judicial nature of the Tribunal as it is explicitly described in the convention of reference."[32] And it is quite probable that this minor compromise has been important in keeping alive for a long time Canadian indignation over the selection of the "impartial jurists of repute."

The Alaska boundary settlement presents an irresistible temptation to the moralist. No party to it acted irreproachably and perhaps none with great astuteness. The Canadians wished to have a rather dubious claim settled by judicial process, partly in order to make it easier for a government to abandon a not very tenable position, partly in order to secure the chance of a good "break" which always accompanies litigation. Theodore Roosevelt was unwilling to submit to a neutral tribunal a dispute in which he was convinced that the United States was a hundred per cent right— and his unwillingness must be understood in relation to an era in which the relinquishment of territory was regarded very seriously. To go through the form of a judicial settlement while ensuring against any risk of an unfavourable decision can, given a certain shallowness of judgment, pass as statesmanship. The British government was anxious to dispose, on the best possible terms no doubt, of a cause of dispute; and did not give adequate consideration to the repercussion which pressure was likely to have on the attitude of Canada towards Great Britain.

The most hopeful thing which can be said with complete confidence is that an experiment was made on material which did not matter very much and that useful experience was gained by trial and error. The incident is not likely to repeat itself. The Canadian government, were it to live through with the knowledge of today the crisis of a generation ago, would understand that it was folly to ask the United States to settle a boundary dispute judicially without first preparing the way for the appeal by careful propaganda directed to education of the American people. The government of the United States in the same circumstances would understand that a tribunal open to suspicion may be a greater irritant than the use of downright force, and that if we are to have good international relations the strong and powerful must submit to minor persecutions by their weaker neighbours and, in par-

32. *Ibid.*, 21.

ticular, must be ready to accept the risks incidental to judicial processes, in order to avoid the suspicion of abusing their strength. Finally (even if we neglect the development in Dominion status which has occurred since 1903), the British government would be quick to see that Canada would have a better chance in a dispute with the United States if she could pose as a fellow American democracy, anxious to join with the United States in showing the Old World that things are better ordered in the western hemisphere.

It is possible to advance these conjectures with some confidence because the material issues at stake were not really very important. Canada lost nothing of great value and the United States gained nothing of great value. If today the United States is anxious for access by road to Alaska, Canada should have no difficulty in securing, as the price of her consent, access from the sea to northern British Columbia and the Yukon. And if the Northwest Coast of America is to be fortified against perils to which both nations are sensitive, possession of the islands off Prince Rupert may carry a burden rather than an advantage. The change which took place in Canada's international position was a change that was bound to occur in any case, and the forces set in motion by the Alaskan boundary award might have had some far more provocative source had it not occurred.

It is significant that when a decade later a cause of dispute of much greater material importance to Western Canada arose over the interpretation of the Hay-Pauncefote Treaty the forces in the United States in favour of an irreproachably honourable settlement won the day, although by no very wide margin.[33]

33. See *infra*, 377 f.

CHAPTER XVI

THE AGE OF THE GOOD NEIGHBOURS

THE history of British and American relations on the Northwest Coast of North America prior to 1867, and of Canadian and American relations during the latter part of the nineteenth century, has been concerned with the fortunes of various attempts to exploit the rich natural resources of the region and with the international disputes incidental to those attempts. Inevitably most of these disputes have concerned boundaries and have been settled by international treaty or by arbitral awards.[1] From the raids which all but exterminated the sea-otters at the beginning of the century to the Klondike gold rush at the end, the search for easily gotten wealth has been the dominant motive both in commercial and diplomatic activity, and the leading economic enterprises have been frankly predatory or depletive in character. With the turn of the century the change to maturer forms of economy, which had been slowly developing from the first days of permanent settlement, becomes more and more evident; and with this change in economic outlook comes a change in the character and tone of international relations. If the Klondike gold rush was the last flare-up of the predatory economy, the Alaska boundary dispute was the end of a period of territorial acquisition on the North American continent. Canada was perhaps fortunate, from the point of view of prestige, in not having to bear the full responsibility for international negotiations with her powerful neighbour, until the boundary disputes, in which every concession could be regarded as a surrender of territorial sovereignty, had been brought to a conclusion. Boundary disputes are very intractable things, especially when they affect the allegiance and the political future of a politically conscious population, as well as the material interests

1. The peace settlement of 1814; the Treaty of 1818; the Treaty of 1846; the San Juan arbitration; the Alaska boundary award.   For other boundary settlements see P. E. Corbett, *The Settlement of Canadian-American Disputes* (New Haven and Toronto, 1937), 7 ff.

of a potential pressure group. In such affairs legal claims and considerations of expediency may point in opposite directions, and at the same time the most bitter emotions can be easily excited. When a young country makes its debut in international diplomacy, it may find that democratic countries such as Great Britain or the United States make good sparring partners, but even they cannot always be trusted to pull their punches when territorial sovereignty is at issue.

In other matters it is easier to be reasonable. If we need confirmation for the opinion that a new attitude towards international relations was coming to be adopted on the North American continent we may point to the Boundary Waters Treaty signed and ratified in 1909.[2] By this treaty an International Joint Commission was set up with compulsory jurisdiction in questions of diversion, obstruction, or new uses affecting the natural level or flow; with the duty to investigate and report, at the request of either government, upon any question or difference involving the rights, obligations, or interests of either party along the common frontier; and with the duty to serve as an arbitral tribunal upon consent of both parties for the decision of any difference between them.[3] As was indicated above, we may also contrast the methods employed in the settlement of the Alaska boundary dispute[4] with those employed a decade later in dealing with the question of the Panama Canal tolls. To Western Canada this issue was probably more important than the settlement of the Alaska boundary, although its importance was not fully appreciated at the time. Briefly, the question which faced the American government was how to meet the British claim that the Hay-Pauncefote Treaty of 1901, by which Great Britain had assented to the treaty between the United States and Colombia, debarred the United States from exempting its own coastwise shipping from the tolls charged for

2. Negotiations began as early as 1894-5. See *ibid.*, 50 ff.

3. *Ibid.*, 51 ff., for a brief record of the activities of the Commission. See also R. A. MacKay, "The International Joint Commission between the United States and Canada," *American Journal of International Law*, XXII, 292; C. J. Chacko, *The International Joint Commission between the United States of America and the Dominion of Canada* (New York, 1932), and L. J. Burpee, *Good Neighbours* (Toronto, 1940).

4. *Ante*, chap. xv.

the use of the canal. It was impossible to refer this claim to arbitration because the requisite two-thirds majority could not have been obtained in the American Senate. It was, however, politically possible to obtain the simple congressional majorities necessary for the repeal of the discriminatory legislation, and this course was followed.[5] It is true that this conciliatory and honourable course was possible only because of the split in the Republican party which had enabled Woodrow Wilson to become President. But this split was itself a symptom of a changing world. The spirit of law represented by Root and Hay had come to dominate the cruder sense of the fitness of things which had guided Theodore Roosevelt, and it enabled Woodrow Wilson to secure some Republican support.

The subsequent international negotiations affecting relations on the Pacific Coast were not similar in tone to those leading up to the settlement of the Alaska boundary. They continued rather in the tradition of the agreement respecting the pelagic seals[6] and aimed at conserving sources of wealth instead of delimiting the right to deplete them. The first treaty signed by a minister accredited by Canada alone provided for the preservation of the halibut fisheries in the Pacific Ocean and in Bering Sea.[7] This agreement was long overdue; for, as has been indicated in an earlier chapter, the halibut of the Pacific Coast had been brought to the verge of extinction before the international co-operation which was necessary for the rehabilitation of the fisheries could be secured. The halibut treaty considered as a landmark in Canada's constitutional development may have been a sign of national maturity; considered as a sensible measure to conserve a source of national wealth it must be taken as evidence of how slowly pioneer democracies are to act in such matters. Further evidence on the same point can be adduced in relation to sockeye salmon. As early as 1892 a joint commission was appointed to investigate the protection of the Fraser River-Puget Sound sockeye salmon, but so complicated were the interests involved and so powerful the

5. See R. S. Baker, *Woodrow Wilson* (Garden City, New York, 1931), IV, 396 ff.; and P. C. Jessup, *Elihu Root* (New York, 1938), II, 262 ff.

6. *Supra*, chap. XIII.

7. Signed, March 2, 1923, ratified October 21, 1924; the Hon. Ernest Lapointe signed for Canada.

political influences that a treaty for this purpose did not become
effective until 1937.[8] It provided for the appointment of a commission of three Americans and three Canadians to investigate the
sockeye and, *after a delay of eight years*, to promulgate regulations.[9]
As these treaties indicate, although the transition from wasteful
exploitation to conservation has been gradual and not always
smooth it seems fair to say that today North America is no longer
in the era of a predatory economy but comprises two reasonable
neighbours making working arrangements with one another and
settling their minor controversies by judicial means.[10]

If, however, the economy of the first quarter of the twentieth
century was radically different from that of the nineteenth, no one
year can be designated as marking the date of the change. Well
before the end of the last century permanent settlement had taken
root; and the settlers, while not yet ashamed to call themselves
colonists or offended if others did so, were already regarding the
country in which they had settled as the home-land of their
children and as a source of permanent wealth. On the other hand,
survivals of the predatory psychology remained until well on in
the twentieth century. It can be illustrated by the attitude of the
Province of British Columbia towards the exploitation of its forest
resources. An official statement runs as follows:

Assuming the present [1938] average cut to continue, we are using capital
in our forest industries which is not being restored to the extent of 38.7
per cent. of the annual cut, and even assuming an increase in accessibility
and the use of less mature timber, we would still be using capital to the
extent of 21.3 per cent. annually . . . the forests accounting directly
for 10.34 per cent. of the income and 18.62 per cent. of the wealth [of
the province]. Part of the income from transportation and other services
would also have its source in our forests.[11]

The argument, reduced to its simplest terms, is that the income of
the people and their standard of living would be sharply diminished
if measures were taken to make the forests a source of permanent

8. See H. E. Gregory and Kathleen Barnes, *North Pacific Fisheries* (New York,
1939), 72 ff.

9. *Ibid.*

10. For examples see Corbett, *Settlement of Canadian-American Disputes*, 63 ff.

11. *Brief submitted by the Province of British Columbia to the Royal Commission on
Dominion-Provincial Relations* (Victoria, 1938), 43.

income on the highest possible level. People therefore prefer to practise what the law calls "waste," as the fur traders did in their generation.

The economies north and south of the international boundary were in some respects complementary. At one time coal was exported from British Columbia to California; at another oil was imported. Citrus fruits came north, holly was shipped south. In other respects the two economies were keen competitors, for each produced fruit and vegetables, lumber and fish, and each sought to protect its home market against the foreign competitor. Then, too, there were cases of temporary collaboration, in which the raw products of one country were processed in the other, as when copper ore was exported for smelting; and there were many instances in which Canadian industries were built up by American capital, American management, and American specialists.[12]

It would, however, be quite wrong to consider the Pacific slope as constituting in any sense a single economic area. The international boundary, agreed on in 1846, was a determining factor in its development. The mountain and coast region of each of the two great federations has been tied to the fortunes and the policies of the federation of which it is a member.

The whole of the Canadian territory lying between the Rocky Mountains and the Pacific Ocean is comprised in the Province of British Columbia, with the possible exception of the Yukon Territory, which it has been proposed to include within the borders of that province. Even without this addition, British Columbia is equal in area to the three coast states to the south taken together —Washington, Oregon, and California. The weight which the province can exercise in the determination of Canadian national policies has been roughly proportionate to its population,[13] and is therefore of the order of 1:15 or at most 1:12 in the House of Commons, according to variations in population. In the Senate the proportion is 1:16. Within the framework set by the national policies, the Province of British Columbia must perforce deal with the multitudinous affairs of a highly diversified economy and, in

12. For examples, see H. Marshall, F. A. Southard and K. W. Taylor, *Canadian-American Industry* (New Haven and Toronto, 1936).

13. British North America Act, sec. 51; and Order in Council admitting British Columbia, sec. 8; British North America Act, 1915, sec. 1, (1) (ii).

linking together settlements scattered throughout its "sea of mountains," with an almost intractable problem of transportation.

To the south of the boundary are the three coast states and the belt of mountain states that must be considered as the corresponding area. They contain about 11 per cent of the population of the United States—a somewhat larger proportion than British Columbia comprises in the Canadian Confederation. While their congressional representation of 43 out of 435 is a function of their population, and their weight in presidential elections (65 electors out of 531) not greatly in excess of their population ratio, their representation in the Senate is relatively high, namely 22 out of 96, or higher than 1:5.[14] The American mountain and coast region is, therefore, less likely to be prejudicially affected by federal policies than British Columbia by Canadian policies. Indeed, on occasion, federal policies have been framed decidedly to the advantage of the western states, as in the case of the purchase of silver above the world price. This vast region is not, like its Canadian counterpart, under a single government, but is divided into eleven states.

To a great extent the mountain and coast region of each federation has been tied to the fortunes of the nation of which it is part. It is true that at times the whole western slope of the continent has been influenced by developments peculiar to the region and distinguishing it sharply from the rest of the continent. This was to be expected when the mountains and the coast had all the characteristics of an economic frontier. For instance the tide of prosperity began to flow in the West in 1886, after a recession which had been felt on the entire coast, and "a returning prosperity, unprecedented even in a land of booms, acted like a magnet to draw coastal Americans into British Columbia and midland Canadians into the states from California northward."[15] At this early period there were no restrictions on migration, except as regards Chinese. The movement was checked by the severe depression of 1893.[16] From 1896 onwards, we find British Columbia feeling, in common with the rest of Canada, the economic impetus

14. See F. O. Darvall, *The American Political Scene* (London, 1939), 26 ff.

15. M. L. Hansen, *The Mingling of the Canadian and American Peoples* (New Haven and Toronto, 1940), 203.

16. *Ibid.*, 204.

which accompanied the settlement of the prairies—itself a belated
response to the developmental policies of the Canadian government
—and the growth of a national economy based on the export of
wheat.[17] The creation of such an economy had long been an aim
of Canadian statesmanship. Wheat could be grown on the Canadian
prairies and sold in Great Britain at prices which, in spite of the
cost of transportation, would have enabled the Canadian farmers
to obtain manufactured goods on highly favourable terms. It was
possible to develop a protected market for some Canadian manufactures from Ontario and Quebec without making prairie-farming
economically unattractive; and in order to secure this protected
market the people of the older provinces were willing to assist in
financing the high capital costs incidental to the rapid development
of a new agricultural area. These costs were particularly high
because of the severity of the climate and the geographical difficulty
of access. This difficulty, in turn, was accentuated by the determination to protect the national identity of Canada by building
the railways entirely on Canadian territory, that is north rather
than south of the Great Lakes.[18]

As the wheat boom developed, the centre of the stage lay east
of the Rocky Mountains, but the effects of the rising tide of settlement and investment were felt in British Columbia as well. The
population trebled in the twenty years following 1896,[19] and the
province entered on an era of prosperity with the appearance of a
market on the prairies for lumber and fruit. Not only was this
market accessible, but within it British Columbia enjoyed a distinct
advantage. There was, for instance, little protest from British
Columbia members at Ottawa when rough lumber and shingles
were allowed to enter Canada free of duty.[20] By 1910, "the Canadian prairies had become the most important, almost the only,
outside market for British Columbia lumber."[21] They took 70 per

17. *Report of the Royal Commission on Dominion-Provincial Relations* (Ottawa,
1940), I, 66 ff.
18. *Ibid.*
19. *Ibid.*, 77.
20. W. A. Carrothers, "Forest Industries of British Columbia," in A. R. M.
Lower, *The North American Assault on the Canadian Forest* (Toronto and New
Haven, 1938), 270.
21. *Ibid.*, 271.

cent of it and the expansion of the lumber industry was the heart
of provincial prosperity.[22] The prosperity was general and sustained. By 1913 the production of non-ferrous metals exceeded
$17,000,000 and the exports of canned salmon reached $6,600,000.[23]
Prosperity brought with it all the characteristic symptoms of
frontier booms: a high rate of investment of foreign capital, much
of it speculative; rapid settlement, much of it ill-planned and
doomed to bitter disappointments; buoyant optimism in developmental expenditures, particularly in subsidizing railways; a legacy
of fixed charges dangerous for an immature economy; towards the
end of the period the wild orgy of a land boom; and finally the
inevitable depression: In short a rake's progress which has yet to
find its Hogarth.

Yet there is a difference. A rake lives merely for the pleasures
of the hour. Beneath the vicissitudes of boom and depression lay
a sturdy faith in the future of the province and a resolve to provide
generously for the rising generation. If the cycle of prosperity,
over-capitalization of the future, deflation, and adversity has been
characteristic of North American frontier economies, not less
typical has been the belief of a pioneering generation that it was,
at the cost of perils and often of hardships and injustices, creating
a better future for its children. If, in our day, this belief has been
associated rather with the naïvetés of communistic experiments in
the U.S.S.R., we must not forget that it once flourished on North
American soil and sweetened the lot of many of those semi-heroic
figures cherished by the local antiquarian. For hopes, even if at
times fantastic, are inspiring, and those who think of themselves
as trustees for posterity have perhaps a more confident and less
self-critical outlook than those who school themselves to be trustees
for backward peoples as well. This era of high hopes seems to have
been a delightful one in which to live. To work and even to suffer
for a posterity of one's own race and cultural background seems to
have required rather less soul searching and, indeed, to have
aroused less mocking criticism, than equally heroic devotion to
what was earnestly believed to be the real interest of culturally
backward peoples. It is perhaps one of the more amusing ironies
of history that the relatively selfish land-hunger of the colonist

22. *Report of the Royal Commission on Dominion-Provincial Relations*, I, 77.
23. *Ibid.*

has received much less general condemnation than an imperialism in which selfish motives were to some extent at least diluted by altruism. To have destroyed the cultural life of the North American Indian, and to have initiated processes likely to exterminate his race, has by implication been treated as a venial offence in comparison with the economic exploitation associated with imperialism. If, in the sophisticated language in which international affairs are often discussed, it is more respectable to be a retired murderer than a retired burglar, the reason seems to be that the former may profess to be reformed without being embarrassed by the prospect of having to recall his victims to life, while the latter cannot flaunt his newly won virtue without having to make financial restitution.

However, on the North American continent this period of buoyant hopes came to an end largely as the result of events on another continent, perhaps, indeed, as an indirect result of the very imperialism with which it has just been contrasted. War broke out in 1914 and the pre-war international economy of which the wheat boom was part has never been restored.

If it had not been for the outbreak of war in 1914, the depression, which followed the wheat boom and the investment boom which accompanied it, might have done little more than impose a temporary halt on the advance of the economy of Western Canada. And much of the enterprise which has since been deplored by the taxpayers might have found its justification. In British Columbia the permanent legacy of the boom remained in the form of the debt incurred for the construction of the Pacific Great Eastern Railway and of the charges incurred for the provincial university. The railway, which lost its *raison d'être* when the absorption of the Grand Trunk Pacific and the Canadian Northern Railways in the Canadian National Railway system[24] removed the need for a link between Prince George and Vancouver, has not been completed to either of its proposed terminals. It leaves the coast at Squamish and ends at Quesnel. Modestly operated it sometimes meets its operating expenses, but contributes nothing towards the bond interest which the province, as guarantor of the bonds, must pay.[25] There are frequent proposals for prolonging the railway to give

24. *Supra*, chap. x.
25. The direct obligations exceed $15,000,000 and the guarantees $20,000,000. The province in 1938 put its total investment in the P.G.E. at $78,000,000.

access to the Peace River district; and the province has made
something of the "moral" obligation of the Dominion to take
over the railway and assume its debt, on the ground that the
Dominion stands in the shoes of the railway company whose
assets have come into its hands.[26]

The creation of a provincial university is a very important
symptom of an established economic life capable of maintaining
itself without excessive reliance on other areas; for the university
makes it possible to train young men and women locally for those
careers which require higher education and so avoids the need for
importing leaders and for sending large numbers of young people
to other parts of the country for training. In this way the university makes it possible for a province which is emerging from a
frontier economy to provide its fair share of the personnel in the
service of the federal government at Ottawa. Apart even from more
exalted aims there was, therefore, little doubt as to the need for a
provincial university. But the grandiose plans which were made
in all seriousness, and the grandiose valuation set on a land endowment that was to prove worthless, show, almost in caricature, the
outlook of the period of boom. A magnificent site was provided,
and magnificent buildings were projected. But for ten years the
university lived in temporary quarters and, twenty-five years
later, only two permanent buildings have been erected. The other
buildings are temporary structures somewhat out of keeping with
the site; and the very real achievements of its graduates must have
tempted the university to discard its not very intelligible Latin
motto, *Tuum est*, as being something of a mockery, and substituting
the prouder Greek: *o'υ τείχη ἀλλ' ἄνδρες πόλις ἐστίν*.[26a]

The immediate participation of Canada from the outset in the
War of 1914-18 serves to distinguish sharply the outlook of the
American and the Canadian communities on the Pacific Coast.
For various reasons British Columbia was as enthusiastic for active
participation as any part of Canada. One factor was the large and
comparatively recent immigration from the British Isles, and the
contacts which it had helped to maintain with other portions of

26. For this argument, which was not accepted by the Royal Commission on
Dominion-Provincial Relations (*Report*, II, 244), see Exhibit 180, *Brief of Argument
of Counsel for British Columbia*, 34 ff.

26a. Not walls, but men, make a city.

the British Empire. More subtle, but none the less real, was the fact that loyalty to the Empire, to King and country, could be expressed without arousing any consciousness of the persistent conflicts of interest which are never quite absent in a federal system. For the King, unlike an elected official against whom millions have voted and thousands have campaigned, is above parties and beyond political strife; while in a vague way a great international association, which is the true nature of the British Commonwealth of Nations, will for many transcend the idea of a mere national state. Pride in Canada's war effort was enhanced when a citizen of British Columbia, General Currie (later Sir Arthur Currie), was placed in command of the Canadian Corps. In British Columbia, as elsewhere in Canada, there were times in the early years of the war when people felt and expressed great bitterness over American neutrality and the phrases in which it was enshrined.[27] If resentment was followed by gratitude tempered by a little jealousy after the United States entered the war, it revived in no mild form when, as it appeared to Canadians, the United States shrank from adopting the League of Nations' undertakings which its President had encouraged others to adopt.[28] No doubt, from the American point of view, it would be more accurate to say that a substantial minority in the Senate saved the American people from being committed by the undertakings of the American President. But no foreign people whose executive is responsible to its parliament will ever understand how a nation comes to maintain a constitution that enables it to speak with two voices.[29] It would be out of place to pursue these controversies here, but if we are to understand the relations of the two peoples we must not bury them in the tactful phrases which embellish school-books. They illustrate a very important point: two communities which appear to third parties to be as alike as two peas

27. See H. L. Keenleyside, *Canada and the United States* (New York, 1929), 362 ff.; H. F. Angus (ed.), *Canada and Her Great Neighbor* (Toronto and New Haven, 1938), 443.

28. *Ibid.*

29. See Harold Nicolson, *Curzon: The Last Phase* (London, 1934), 141: "For a parliament to refuse ratification of a treaty properly contracted would have been condemned almost as a breach of faith and as highly damaging to the diplomatic credit of the country concerned."

may be acutely aware of the minor differences which distinguish them from each other; and the smaller community will be more acutely aware of these differences than the larger.

The period between the two great wars is not one in which it is easy to detach the local economic history of British Columbia from the economic history of Canada. From the days of the maritime fur trade the economy of the coast had been an export economy dependent on the prosperity of the great centres of world trade. But after the War of 1914-18 its fortunes came more and more under the influence of national policies which could easily be attacked as contrary to its immediate interests.[30] British Columbia, owing to the opening of the Panama Canal and to the low ocean freight rates which prevailed after the war,[31] developed a post-war economy which depended largely on export.[32] In the course of the next decade a very high level of prosperity was achieved. Prior to the Smoot-Hawley tariff which closed this market in 1930, the ability of British Columbia to compete in the lumber markets of the United States Atlantic seaboard depended on the use of the Panama Canal at toll rates no higher than those charged to intercoastal American shipping.[33] As a result of low freight rates costs of shipment to New York which were $27.30 per thousand feet in 1920 had fallen to $10.11 in 1929, and these rates must be related to a mill cost of about $22.50 per thousand feet.[34] The output of lumber was almost doubled during this period.[35]

Lumber was not the only source of prosperity. The production of non-ferrous metals was greatly increased with the help of new

30. *Brief submitted by the Province of British Columbia*, I, 273 ff.

31. *Report of the Royal Commission on Dominion-Provincial Relations*, I, 122.

32. See H. A. Innis, "Canada and the Panama Canal," which is appendix v of *The Canadian Economy and Its Problems*, ed. H. A. Innis and A. F. W. Plumptre (Toronto, 1934).

33. If British diplomacy did not succeed in obtaining concessions on the Alaska boundary in return for the Hay-Pauncefote Treaty, it did at least, thanks to Woodrow Wilson and to the sense of honour of one of the much abused "impartial jurists of repute," Elihu Root, secure for a decade a valuable market for British Columbian lumber.

34. *Report of the Royal Commission on Dominion-Provincial Relations*, I, 122. See W. A. Carrothers, "Forest Industries of British Columbia," 286.

35. *Report of the Royal Commission on Dominion-Provincial Relations*, I, 122.

processes.[36] The output of copper increased by more than 100 per cent, of silver by 200 per cent, of zinc by 300 per cent, and of lead by 1,000 per cent.[37] This increased production involved a greatly increased investment. The development of water-power per head was higher than in any other province,[38] and the volume of new construction in British Columbia was nearly equal to those of the three Prairie Provinces combined.[39] The per capita income in British Columbia rose to $600 in 1929, compared with $470 for Canada as a whole.[40] It was higher than that of any other province.

An important result of the economic activity of the twenties was to transform British Columbia from an area economically dependent on the rest of Canada to one which lived by export to foreign markets. British Columbia was still bound by Canadian policies, which came to be very irksome,[41] precisely because British Columbia's economic interests had become independent of those of Canada. Half the lumber, most of the fish, nearly all the minerals, and a large part of the apples were sold in foreign markets.[42] This transformation was accompanied by an increase in wealth, but it was due in part at least to transitory causes such as low ocean freight rates, and it made the economy of British Columbia peculiarly vulnerable to any falling off in foreign markets or any fall in world prices.

This is the most convenient point at which to notice that during the decade the port of Vancouver had become one of Canada's few metropolitan areas. The city had been incorporated in 1886, and superseded Port Moody as the terminus of the Canadian Pacific Railway. It enjoyed the advantage of an excellent harbour and shipping could avoid the inconvenience of passing the Second Narrows of Burrard Inlet to reach Port Moody. The first through train reached Vancouver on May 23, 1887,[43] and the railway became the vital force in the development of the port. The staples

36. *Ibid.*
37. *Ibid.*
38. *Ibid.*
39. *Ibid.*
40. *Ibid.*
41. See *ante*, in this chapter.
42. *Report of the Royal Commission on Dominion-Provincial Relations*, I, 123.
43. See W. N. Sage, "Vancouver: The Rise of a City," *Dalhousie Review*, XVII, 50 ff.

of the early trade were naturally lumber and tinned salmon. As early as 1887, the railway entered into the trans-Pacific trade and established regular steamship services to China and Japan. This service developed steadily and came to capture the lion's share of the high-class passenger traffic, although much of the freight was carried in foreign bottoms. Regular services to Australia were also established. If at one time more had been expected it was because the potentialities of the Suez Canal, as a competitive route to the Far East, had been underrated.

The opening of the Panama Canal made it possible for Vancouver to enter the grain trade and in 1921 there were substantial shipments which increased enormously in volume during the twenties.[44] The "splitting point" for grain depended partly on ocean freight rates which, as we have seen, were abnormally low in the twenties; and partly on railway rates, which, as a result of vigorous agitation, were reduced so as to approach more nearly those charged on shipments by way of the Atlantic ports.[45] In 1922 the Pacific Standard rates were lowered from a level 50 per cent above the prairie rates to a level 25 per cent above those rates.

With the development of the port there was a great growth in population and to the business incidental to a great shipping centre a substantial industrial growth has been added. The city of Vancouver increased its area by the amalgamation with it of the municipalities of Point Grey and South Vancouver. The great metropolitan area of today of course includes other neighbouring municipalities. Population[46] is concentrated in a way not dissimilar to that typical of Australia and it seems likely that this tendency will be reinforced by the hard facts of the economic geography of the province. Some political repercussions are to be expected, for the population of "Greater Vancouver" is already grossly under-represented in the provincial Legislative Assembly.

44. In 1921, 1,251,070 bushels; in 1932, 105,006,925 (*ibid.*, 53).

45. See "Railway Freight Rates in Canada," an appendix to the *Report of the Royal Commission on Dominion-Provincial Relations.* See also *Report*, I, 123.

46. In 1931 the last census year the population of British Columbia was 694,236 and that of Vancouver 246,593. The metropolitan area of Vancouver had a population of 308,340; the southwest corner of the mainland had a population of 379,858. In 1939 the Bureau of Statistics estimated the population of British Columbia at 774,000.

Confidence in an assured and prosperous future developed rapidly and the depression which followed this post-war decade took British Columbians by surprise. They had not, perhaps, been alone in failing to anticipate the depression which brought the prosperity of the twenties to an end. Certainly no financial provision was made in British Columbia for any such contingency. Nor did the educational curriculum of the public schools of the province include any serious attempt to prepare pupils for the economic hardships which they were destined to encounter. But federal policies were not any more far-sighted. When the depression came, it was met by improvised methods, justified, if at all, by the hope that it would not last very long.

Owing largely to the dependence on foreign markets which has been described, British Columbia felt the full force of the depression. Prices in the export markets fell and the resulting unemployment was accentuated by the sharp check to investment which caused a collapse in the construction industry.[47] The problem of relief was intensified by migration from the Prairie Provinces to the mild climate of the coast.[48] In the metropolitan area of Vancouver, which had been growing rapidly, all these influences combined to make the problem of relief particularly acute, and it persisted in spite of the very substantial recovery which took place in the later thirties.

It was during the depression period that British Columbia felt most keenly the pressure of the policies adopted at Ottawa.[49] Three aspects of these policies deserve special attention: immediate relief; monetary policy; and the tariff. The traditional Canadian view has been that relief is a burden which provincial governments must bear either directly or by imposing it on the shoulders of the municipalities. In times of emergency the provincial government should help an overburdened municipality and the federal government should stand ready to help if the financial strength of the province is over-taxed. This doctrine had been applied, on the whole successfully, in the short-lived depression which followed the War of 1914-18. It was applied again ten years later but with

47. *Report of the Royal Commission on Dominion-Provincial Relations*, I, 171 f.

48. A crude estimate of this migration places it at 83,700 from 1931 to 1938 (*Brief submitted by the Province of British Columbia*, 64 f.).

49. *Ibid.*, 273 ff.

much less success.[50] The effect was to force municipalities to incur heavy expenditures at a time when their revenues, based mainly on the taxation of real property, were difficult to maintain. These expenditures were given priority over provision for municipal sinking funds and even for bond interest. Nor was the burden equitably distributed, for the municipality where the burden of unemployment relief was heaviest was likely to experience the greatest difficulty in securing revenue. Nor was the provincial government in a position to offer substantial aid: on the contrary, in order to ensure its own solvency it was obliged early in the depression to withdraw municipal grants which had previously been given. During the later years of the depression the province was practically compelled to assume a larger proportion of the relief, leaving the municipalities to contribute less than 9 per cent of the total outlay.[51]

Canadian monetary policy had been based on the gold standard which preserved parity between the Canadian and the American dollar. When the prices of primary products fell more sharply than those of manufactured goods, it was contended that the burden of the depression would be more equitably spread throughout the nation if the Canadian dollar were allowed to depreciate substantially, so that the export industries, securing better prices (in Canadian dollars), would be better able to meet their fixed costs. It is impossible to enter here into a discussion of this issue, complicated as it was by the large volume of Canadian indebtedness which had to be met in American dollars, and by the weak position of some Canadian export industries.[52] The question entered on a new phase when Great Britain abandoned the gold standard in 1931 and the Canadian dollar was allowed "to find its own level" roughly half way between the old parity with sterling and parity with the American dollar.[53] A further change came in April, 1933, with the departure of the United States from gold. Had this event been foreseen very different policies might have been pursued in Canada. It is very difficult to judge the wisdom of the policies

50. *Report of the Royal Commission on Dominion-Provincial Relations*, I, 162.
51. *Ibid.*, 172.
52. For a full discussion see *ibid.*, 151 ff.
53. *Ibid.*

which were actually followed, because allowance must be made for the fact that no one knew what American monetary policy would be.

The effect of Canadian monetary policy on British Columbia can best be considered in conjunction with Canadian tariff policy. This was directed to maintaining employment in the manufacturing industries by securing the manufacture in Canada of everything which could be made there.[54] It was reinforced by measures designed to protect Canadian industry against competition from countries whose currencies had depreciated. Imports from these countries were given an artificially high valuation for customs purposes. The tariff, which had not changed very substantially over a long period, was sharply increased. The result was that the prices at which the products of British Columbia were sold in the markets of the world fell heavily, while the prices of the products bought for use in British Columbia fell much less.[55] It was easy to argue that British Columbia would have fared better if it had had its own tariff and its own monetary system, as it would have had if its political status had been similar to that of New Zealand. The concessions obtained in the British market by the Ottawa agreement of 1932[56] were important, but it was arguable that similar concessions could have been even more readily obtained by a province which enjoyed tariff autonomy. Analogous contentions have been made at other times by other Canadian provinces, but British Columbia seemed to have been rapidly transformed from a dependent area to a strongly developed export area with an assured future before it. Yet it can hardly be said that public opinion even in British Columbia is thoroughly appreciative of the magnitude of the change or clear as to whether it wishes to give to it any far-reaching political implications.

It also became clear that the prosperity of British Columbia was exposed to two dangers which no federal policies could do much to avert; against which a young community could not be expected to provide; and against which British Columbia did not provide. The first danger was that of depletion. In the case of stands of large trees the date of depletion is not far removed and nothing

54. *Ibid.*, 157 ff.

55. *Brief submitted by the Province of British Columbia*, 276 ff.

56. As regards lumber, see Carrothers, "Forest Industries of British Columbia," 286 f.

can be done to prevent the process. "Coast Douglas fir," says an official report, "has always been a leading export type. It is now being cut from trees, two, three or more centuries old at a rate of one and a half billion board feet a year. Only approximately 18 billion accessible board feet of this type remain, and there is an inadequate area of middle-aged fir."[57] Smaller trees can be replaced by measures of conservation and so preserved as a source of wealth in perpetuity; but the appropriate measures are costly. During the period of hard times at least, the province both from the standpoint of national income and from that of provincial revenue elected to live in part on capital depletion, while complaining that the federal government did so too.[58] The fisheries of British Columbia are considered by the government to be a wastable asset.[59] We are told that: "In the case of halibut and sockeye salmon wasteful methods of exploitation almost resulted in the extermination of these fish. The problem of conservation here was an international one, as the United States fisheries were in both cases interested in the same resources."[60] In both cases satisfactory treaties have been concluded; but it is by no means clear that Canada and the United States can exclude other countries from fishing, in disregard of conservation measures, outside the territorial waters of the two nations. In the presence of the menace of the "floating cannery" or mother-ship, the interests of both countries are identical. Canadians have been able to induce Great Britain to restrain British enterprise interested in halibut; and Americans, taking full advantage of a favourable diplomatic situation, have been able to persuade Japan not to grant licences for vessels desiring to proceed to Bristol Bay in search of salmon. But in neither instance has the legal problem been squarely faced, and both American and Canadian diplomacy are handicapped by the attitude taken by the United States and Great Britain in previous controversies.[61] No arrangement has been made with regard to the conservation of pilchards, and with regard to the herring it is possible that no

57. *Brief submitted by the Province of British Columbia*, 41.

58. *Ibid.*, 43, cited *supra*, 379.

59. *Ibid.*, 52.

60. *Ibid.* See also Gregory and Barnes, *North Pacific Fisheries*, 37 ff.

61. Gregory and Barnes, *North Pacific Fisheries*, 283 ff. For the victory of the British argument in the case of the pelagic seals, see *ante*, chap. XIII.

international arrangement is needed. In all these instances, as in that of the pelagic seals, the problem of conservation, which is technical in character, is complicated by a problem of apportionment, in which each nation seeks to advance the interests of its own nationals. With respect to measures for the conservation of salmon, British Columbia has been more fortunate than the states of Oregon and Washington in not having been forced to elect between the development of electric power and the protection of salmon rivers.

The depletion of mineral wealth is, of course, inevitable and no efforts can be made to conserve it. It would, however, be possible to treat the revenues derived from depletion as capital which should be invested. This has not been done, but again the complaint has been made that a federal income tax on income derived from depletion is inequitable.[62]

It must not be assumed that the provincial government has been acting, or omitting to act, in callous disregard of the interests of posterity. The date of ultimate depletion may be far removed. Resources which seem of the utmost value today may, with changes in technique, become as useless to the white man as they once were to the North American Indian. Most important of all, it has been, and in many quarters still is, an article of faith (which, indeed, no one is in a position to disprove) that abundant undiscovered mineral wealth exists within the vast area of the province.

The second danger lies in the loss of foreign markets which may be closed either by impoverishment or as an act of policy. British Columbians would be hard put to it to consume within the borders of the province the natural products which recent investments have enabled it to produce. While no doubt less exposed than the countries which produce sugar cane have been, or than the wheat growers are today, the province does lie at the mercy of hostile tariffs and other restraints on trade. It can prosper in a world at war, so long as the belligerents still possess the sinews of war, or in a world that is really at peace. But it is in danger in a world where defensive *autarky* is prevalent. And closely allied to the existence of markets is the question of their accessibility, which

62. *Brief submitted by the Province of British Columbia,* 189.

depends on relatively low ocean freight rates. No one would altogether deny the existence of this danger but in practice it gives rise to little uneasiness. People have grown accustomed to it much as many Californians are accustomed to living in an earthquake zone.

From the brief sketch that has been given, it will be seen that the impact of the depression was dissimilar in Canada and the United States. To the ordinary citizen the most marked difference was perhaps that there were no bank failures in Canada and that no depositor lost a dollar or experienced any delay in cashing a cheque. To the government official the leading difference was perhaps that the United States could look, and had to look, to its own policies for positive measures to hasten the return of prosperity; while Canada, with the largest per capita export trade for any country of comparable population, was obliged to frame her policies with a strict regard for what other countries were doing. The United States devalued its currency for domestic reasons and not because of any international strain on its gold holdings. It was able (in spite of constitutional provisions protecting property rights) to defeat the gold clause even in the case of bonds held outside the United States; while Canada did not venture to impair the validity of bonds payable as to principal and interest in foreign currencies, and confined itself to taxing severely the exchange premium in transactions between a Canadian debtor and a Canadian creditor. In one point the resemblance between the courses taken by the two countries was somewhat concealed by their financial methods. Both practised deficit financing, that is, they spent, year by year, far more money than they raised by taxation. But while the American federal deficit reached alarming proportions, the Canadian deficits were scattered among the federal government, the national railway system, the provincial governments, and the municipalities. They were very large in the aggregate, but partly because they were scattered and partly because they appeared as inevitable and not as an indication of a policy deliberately chosen, they attracted less notice and depressed people less. Certainly no one political figure could aspire to have his name associated with them. There was in Canada no counterpart of the American New Deal, and such measures as were attempted were found to be unconstitutional.[63] While the American constitutional provisions were being extensively circumvented by a system of conditional grants which enabled the federal government to "buy control" of state services and entrust its purchase to a strong civil service, Canadians were compelled to proceed to a searching review of their federal system by means of a Royal Commission, and to postpone the political problem of giving effect to any changes which might prove acceptable.[64]

From the point of view of British Columbia the United States appeared during the great depression as a fickle customer who had deserted a foreign source of supply in order to maintain employment at home. As a result of the tax imposed by the United States Revenue Act of 1932, British Columbian exports of lumber to the United States (and other markets reached by water which were, of course, not affected by this tax) fell from 207,586,216 feet board measure in 1931 to 29,528,026 in 1933.[65] When the producers of shingles in Washington and Oregon discussed their code of fair competition under the National Industrial Recovery Act in 1933, after British Columbia had been confined to a quota of 20 per cent of the United States red-cedar shingle consumption, they were keenly sensitive to the danger of British Columbian competition. To avoid a request for total exclusion from the United States market, manufacturers in British Columbia conformed to the minimum wages and maximum hours established in Washington and Oregon, and agreed to maintain the "cost-protection" prices set by the lumber-code authority. In the following year lower wage scales were paid when shingles were produced for the Canadian market and foreign markets other than those of the United States. The quota was raised to 25 per cent in 1934, and even after the National Industrial Recovery Act was found to be unconstitutional this quota was voluntarily observed by the British Columbian manufacturers until the production in Washington

63. For the fate of the "Bennett New Deal" see *Report of the Royal Commission on Dominion-Provincial Relations*, I, 248, and particularly *Attorney-General of Canada* v. *Attorney-General of Ontario* (1937), A.C., 326.

64. For the carefully framed terms of reference of this Commission, see *Report of the Royal Commission on Dominion-Provincial Relations*, I, 9, citing P.C. 1908, dated August 14, 1937.

65. Carrothers, "Forest Industries of British Columbia," 306.

and Oregon was curtailed by strikes.[66] The United States went so far as to abandon by a constitutional amendment the national policy of prohibition, which had been fortified by a constitutional amendment, and so curbed the *wanderlust* of thirsty citizens.

But this view of the United States as an unreliable market was not a perfectly considered judgment. There was little or no American retaliation for such Canadian currency depreciation as occurred while the United States was still on the gold standard. Some British Columbian products always found a market in the United States; gold and silver, lumber and newsprint, for example. Producers of these commodities and those who catered for the tourist trade benefited by the depreciation of the Canadian dollar, the former by better prices, the latter by a larger volume of business. In competitive markets, the British Columbian exporter could compete on favourable terms with his neighbours to the south, owing in part to the depreciation of the Canadian dollar, and later, when the American dollar had also depreciated, to the higher production costs resulting from the New Deal. For instance, British Columbia's share of the exports of lumber from the Pacific Northwest (British Columbia, Washington, and Oregon) to the United Kingdom and the continent of Europe rose from 20 per cent to 90 per cent.[67] Water-borne shipments of lumber to countries other than the United States and Canada showed an advance in British Columbia's share from roughly 16 per cent to 60 per cent.[68] Finally, the trade agreement with the United States, made possible by Mr. Hull's policy, gave substantial, though not excessive, benefits to the lumber industry, in spite of some protests in the states of Washington and Oregon. The first of these agreements was signed on November 15, 1935 and went into effect on January 1, 1936.[69] Concessions made by

66. *Ibid.*, 282 ff. The fortunes of shingles under the trade agreements of 1935 and 1938 are discussed later in this chapter.

67. *Ibid.* Thirty-six million board feet out of 180 million in 1927; 70 million out of 354 million in 1929; but 666 million out of 699 million in 1936 and 648 million out of 700 million in 1937.

68. *Ibid.*; 274,346 million board feet out of 1,942 million in 1927; but 1,043 million out of 1,641 million in 1936.

69. For an analysis of this agreement from the standpoint of Canada as a whole, see F. H. Soward *et al.*, *Canada in World Affairs: The Pre-War Years* (Toronto, 1941), 195 ff., from which this account is taken.

Canada applied only to commodities of which the United States was the principal supplier, in order to avoid the disruption of trade which the extension of these concessions to other nations under the most-favoured nation clause would involve. The concessions obtained by Canada which were of chief importance to British Columbia concerned fish and lumber. In the case of lumber American producers were safeguarded by the imposition of quotas. The second and more extended agreement was made in November, 1938 and took effect on January 1, 1939.[70] Negotiations had been begun in 1937 because the earlier agreement had worked well and these negotiations were merged in the Anglo-American negotiations in order that a three-party agreement might be arrived at which could modify the arrangements made between Great Britain and Canada in 1932 and revised in 1935 and 1937. For fish the maximum concession, viz. 50 per cent of the United States duties, was obtained. Lumber which had already received the maximum tariff concession was affected by removing the United States quota on Douglas fir and western hemlock lumber. In addition Canadian lumber was exempted from the requirement of marking with the country of origin and could, therefore, be used on government contracts. A larger quota fixed at 30 per cent of the United States consumption was provided for shingles, and if this quota were exceeded a duty might be imposed on the excess by the United States. At the same time the British-American agreement provided that those kinds of lumber of which the United States was an important supplier might enter the United Kingdom on terms as favourable as those on which Canadian lumber was admitted to the United States. However in July, 1939, Congress decided not to remove the tax from Canadian lumber. In the case of both these agreements it should be noted that the main Canadian concessions were made by protected industries in Eastern Canada, and that British Columbia therefore benefited as a purchaser as well as in respect of her export industries. It is not possible to use trade statistics as conclusive proof of the value of trade agreements as there is no means of ascertaining what the trade would have been if the agreements had not been concluded. The following table,

70. For an analysis from the standpoint of Canada as a whole see *ibid.*, 212 ff.

however, will serve to show what the exports of logs, lumber, and shingles to the United States have been during the years under review.[71]

Calendar Year	Logs		Lumber		Shingles	
	F. B. M.	Dollars	F. B. M.	Dollars	M.	Dollars
1934	1,143,526	10,520	29,640,000	650,005	1,238,862	3,059,989
1935	96,693,954	970,270	108,755,000	2,149,014	2,842,991	7,590,786
1936	58,905,000	558,419	211,940,000	4,317,218	2,373,601	6,042,516
1937	111,526,000	1,339,438	240,833,000	6,454,324	2,034,278	5,760,874
1938	151,600,000	1,605,444	259,106,000	5,894,785	1,764,664	4,772,960
1939	200,186,000	2,377,088	188,771,000	4,997,534	2,731,851	7,651,937
1940*	157,101,000†	1,975,151	131,728,000†	4,197,877	not available	7,277,000

*Preliminary.   †Water-borne trade only.

If the economic developments of the present century have reflected the political separateness of the Canadian and American sectors of the Pacific Coast rather than the geographical unity of the region, this is even more true of political methods. British Columbia achieved responsible government within a year of her entry into Confederation and has continued to be governed by an Executive Council (or Cabinet) responsible to a single-chamber Legislature, elected for a maximum term of five years and subject to dissolution at any time. Only in special cases have direct appeals been made to the electors by way of plebiscite, and such plebiscites (unless held for local purposes) have been purely advisory in character. The states to the south have experimented much more with direct legislation, and British Columbians have watched with amazement a process by which the electors of the State of Washington have voted to establish old age pensions of $40 a month for their "senior citizens," leaving it to the state Legislature to find by taxation the money needed to match the federal grant.[72] In British Columbia, financial control by the executive still exists on the British model and only a minister of the Crown can propose

71. British Columbia, Bureau of Economics and Statistics, Victoria, *The Trade of British Columbia*, 1935-9.

72. State of Washington, Initiative 141. The pensions were not new but the rules as to eligibility, permissible income, and permissible resources were made very generous.

a measure involving expenditure. Nor are electors in British Columbia charged with the selection of judges or of public officials. The judges are appointed by the federal government for life (subject now to a retiring age) and all provincial officials are appointed by the Lieutenant-Governor, acting on the advice of his ministers. There is no popular demand that more direct methods of democracy should be attempted.

Perhaps a reason for this difference in attitude towards direct democracy is to be found in the existence in British Columbia, as has been the case from the outset throughout Western Canada, of a single-chamber Legislature with no constitutional limitations on the use which it may make of the powers allotted to it under the British North America Act. The electors, choosing an Assembly with these plenary powers, have at least the illusion of complete freedom of action; although they have never developed the political organization necessary to make this freedom of action a reality.

The party system was comparatively late in making its appearance in British Columbia and its development has been interesting. It is perhaps easier for the parliamentary than for the presidential system to operate on a non-party basis; but British Columbian experience prior to the adoption of the party system in 1903 could hardly be cited as an edifying example. When parties were finally recognized, they corresponded roughly to those which competed in the federal field: the Liberals and the Conservatives. Both parties paid lip services to the general popular demands of the day and both, when in office, disappointed in much the same degree the expectations which they had excited. It would require a political leader of genius to detect in either record grounds for believing in the beneficence of either party. But there seems to be a general consensus of opinion that the collective responsibilities of party life did improve political standards and discipline political ambitions.[73] For several reasons it was peculiarly difficult for new parties to emerge. They might, it is true, have a body of principles to unite them, but both the "old-line" parties were sufficiently opportunist to adopt any policy likely to have a popular appeal. The disintegrating disillusionments of the war, the post-war

73. See Edith Dobie, "Party History in British Columbia, 1903-1933," *Pacific Northwest Quarterly*, XXVII, 153-66.

inflation, prosperity, and depression were unquestionably more damaging to established parties in Canada than in the United States, where the use of primaries may have provided an alternative to the formation of new parties, and they were particularly damaging in the western provinces. But the old-line parties in British Columbia had almost impregnable strongholds in the smaller urban and rural constituencies which were enormously over-represented in proportion to their population. When the Co-operative Commonwealth Federation, with a definitely social-istic platform, made a bid for power in 1933, it had a favourable opening; for the government of the day had disintegrated to an extent fatal to its electoral chances. But, although the C.C.F. polled a substantial vote in the election, its parliamentary quota was not proportionate to this vote. Nor was it able in the subsequent election to increase its strength. In 1941 the C.C.F. again had a strong tactical position and succeeded in polling more votes than either of the other parties although far fewer than the two combined. To secure a parliamentary majority a coalition of Liberals and Conservatives was formed which will have an obvious interest in introducing some form of preferential voting.

It may reasonably be asked whether the use of different systems of government—both democratic—has resulted in different solu-tions being found for comparable problems. Before discussing this question we must note that the constitutional powers of a Canadian province are not as extensive as those of an American state. A province, for instance, cannot deal with marriage and divorce, or with the criminal law, or with banks and banking, or with aliens. The results can be seen in the divorce law of British Columbia which, if less strict both in the letter and in practice than the laws of the older provinces, is strict when compared with those of the western American states. They can be seen also in the absence from British Columbia of local banks with small capitalization; and in the inability of the provincial Legislature to enact legislation discriminating between various foreigners on grounds of *nationality*. On the other hand, a Canadian province is not cramped in its legislative powers by any obligation to respect individual rights;[74]

74. Except possibly in cases in which interference with individual rights would imperil parliamentary government in Canada. See *per* Duff, C. J., *Reference re Alberta Statutes* (*The Accurate News and Information Act*), (1938) S.C.R., 134.

for, as we have seen, neither in the federal nor in the provincial constitution, is there any list of things which a provincial government may not do. It is, therefore, possible for a province to enact legislation which is discriminatory on grounds of *race*, and even to withhold the franchise from Canadian citizens on this ground; although there are, in Canada, no barriers to naturalization on grounds of *race* as there are in the United States. There is yet another difference to mention. The federal government in Canada may disallow any provincial legislation within a year of its enactment, while the American federal government has no similar control over state legislation.

To discover the practical results of these differences we cannot do better than consider the problem of Oriental immigration. For the last sixty years this immigration has been disliked by the people of the white races on the Pacific Coast. Before the American act of 1882 prohibited the immigration of the Chinese, Victoria was the leading centre in the Northwest for the distribution of Chinese labourers. After the passage of the act Chinese were smuggled into the United States. In the autumn of 1885, during the temporary business recession, anti-Chinese riots were general along the coast.[75] In Canada the restriction on Chinese immigration took the form of a head tax.[76] The attempts of the Province of British Columbia to act independently and prohibit the immigration, either expressly or by a language test, were defeated by disallowance of the legislation.[77] The attempt to impose disabilities

75. Hansen, *Mingling of Canadian and American Peoples*, 205.

76. 1885 (48-49 Vict., c. 71) $50; 1901 (62-64 Vict., c. 32) $100; 1904 (3 Edw. VII, c. 8) $500. Certain categories—merchants, scientists, students, etc.—were exempt.

77. The persistence of the conflict of views between the Dominion and the Province of British Columbia can be seen from the list of British Columbia Acts disallowed.

1884, c. 3, An Act to prevent the Immigration of Chinese, April 7, 1884

1885, c. 13, An Act to prevent the Immigration of Chinese, March 11, 1886

1900, c. 11, An Act to regulate Immigration into British Columbia, September 11, 1901

1902, c. 34, An Act to regulate Immigration into British Columbia, December 5, 1902

1903, c. 12, An Act to regulate Immigration into British Columbia, March 26, 1904

on the basis of nationality failed[78] because of the incompetence of
the provincial Legislature to legislate concerning aliens. But
certain disabilities were imposed on racial grounds which applied
to British subjects and aliens alike.[79] A somewhat different set of
problems arose in connection with Japanese immigration, which
was not on a serious scale until 1906. Japan was an ally of the
British Empire and Canada had voluntarily accepted the obligations of a treaty containing a most-favoured-nation clause. When
anti-Japanese riots occurred in Vancouver in 1907, the Canadian
government negotiated an agreement with Japan by which the
Japanese government undertook to limit the number who might
receive passports in any one year. This agreement has been revised
from time to time to reduce the number who might receive passports. It was about the same period that immigration from British
India began. In 1910 it was restricted by the test of continuous
voyage. An Order-in-Council dated January 7, 1914, provided,
"From and after the date hereof, the landing in Canada shall be
and the same is hereby prohibited of any immigrant who has
come to Canada otherwise than by continuous journey from the
country of which he is a native or naturalized citizen and upon a
through ticket purchased in that country or prepaid in Canada."[80]
In 1919 an Order-in-Council made an exception for the wives and
minor children of East Indians domiciled in Canada. But the
exclusionist measures taken by the Dominion government against

1904, c. 26, An Act to regulate Immigration into British Columbia, January 20,
    1905
1905, c. 28, An Act to regulate Immigration into British Columbia
        30, An Act relating to the employment on Works carried on under
            Franchises granted by Private Acts
        35, An Act further to amend the Coal Mines Regulation Act, April 28,
            1905, September 30, 1905.
    78. *Union Colliery Company of British Columbia* v. *Bryden*, (1899) A.C. 580.
For an account of this and other cases see Norman MacKenzie and L. H. Laing,
Canada and the Law of Nations (New Haven and Toronto, 1938).
    79. For the right of a province to enact such legislation see *Quong-Wing* v. *The
King*, (1914) 49 S.C.R. 440. For particulars of such legislation in British Columbia,
see H. F. Angus, "The Legal Status in British Columbia of Residents of Oriental
Race and Their Descendants," in Norman MacKenzie (ed.), *The Legal Status of
Aliens in Pacific Countries* (New York, 1937), 27 ff.
    80. P.C. 23. See. H. F. Angus, "Canadian Immigration: The Law and its
Administration," *American Journal of International Law*, XXVIII, 74-89.

Asiatics have never been strict enough to satisfy opinion in British Columbia. Not only has the provincial Legislature attempted to enact stricter measures, it has also used its powers to withhold from Orientals those political rights which British subjects resident in Canada would normally enjoy. There was a good deal to be said for this discrimination in the case of the first generation, whether they acquired British nationality by birth, as the East Indians did, or by naturalization as did many of the Chinese and Japanese; for they did not have a background which would enable them to participate actively and intelligently in the life of a western American democracy. But disqualifications, imposed in terms of *race*, apply equally to the second generation, born in Canada, educated in Canadian schools, and in many cases thoroughly Canadian in outlook. In the United States corresponding difficulties did not arise. The first generation could not vote because they were aliens and could not be naturalized. The second generation could vote because they were Americans by birth and entitled to the constitutional rights guaranteed by the Fifteenth Amendment.[81]

The United States, like Canada, has restricted Oriental immigration, and the Exclusion Act of 1924 forbids the entry of unassimilable aliens. But, in the Pacific Coast states, the presence of Filipinos adds a further complication to the racial question. As in Canada it is the state governments which have shown the greatest hostility. While they have dealt with the situation in different ways, both the Pacific Coast states and the Pacific Coast province have on their hands the social problem of Oriental minorities. Even when legal and political equality exists, *de facto* discrimination is inevitable at the present day. And yet the evil consequences of such discrimination are not hard to predict. By some strange irony the strongest partisans of social planning are not usually prepared to face a situation in which prediction, in general terms at least, is peculiarly easy. And there are still those who speak quite confidently of the repatriation (if one may use this word of the native born) of residents of Oriental race.[82] To act, in sober

81. For a discussion of the legal disabilities and reference to the relevant statutes, see H. F. Angus, "The Legal Status in British Columbia of Oriental Race," 77 ff. For an account of the Japanese population of British Columbia, see C. H. Young and H. R. Y. Reid, *The Japanese Canadians* (Toronto, 1938).

82. See *Brief submitted by the Province of British Columbia*, 353.

earnest, on the model of European deportations, would be another matter.

In the State of Washington discrimination against Orientals has taken a form which has affected Canadians of other races. All aliens have been debarred from owning land except for business purposes. This law made it impossible for the smelter at Trail, British Columbia, to acquire easements which would allow it to discharge smoke in the Columbia Valley, and the damage alleged to have been occasioned by this smoke gave rise to bitter recriminations and to claims which were referred for an advisory opinion to the International Joint Commission.[83]

From what has been said it will be clear that the relations which prevail between Canadians and Americans on the coast do not result either from the economic unity of the region, or from reciprocal admiration for one another's brand of democratic institutions. In fact, it is surprising how little interest is shown by citizens of either country in the political problems of the other. News that possessed some human interest would circulate with marvellous rapidity. But an accurate and matter-of-fact account of legislation and politics excites no interest whatever, except for an infinitely small minority of Americans who rely as a matter of course on the New York *Times* for their information of what may be happening in Canada; and a somewhat larger minority of Canadians who will learn of any happening of sufficient importance to be noticed in prominent weekly or monthly American publications. In spite of this blissful ignorance the relations of the two peoples on the Pacific Coast are cordial and remarkably friendly. But the reason for friendly relations must be sought in cultural and social intercourse, made possible in the first instance by similarity of language and enormously strengthened by similarity in living standards. This intercourse takes many forms, of which the more important may be briefly noted.

It is no longer business or economic activities which are most prominent in bringing about these contacts; and we must look to certain relatively recent inventions, developed in a high degree by the relatively wealthy population of the Pacific Coast. First in importance comes the automobile which makes a holiday visit to

83. See Corbett, *Settlement of Canadian-American Disputes*, 70 f.

the neighbouring country something within the means of people of very moderate incomes. Far more than half of the population of British Columbia lives within easy driving distance of the borders of the United States (if we make allowance for a short ferry journey for those who live on Vancouver Island). Not only is this true but the scarcity of good roads leading north and east makes it almost an inevitable choice that the car should frequently be turned southwards; and a route through the United States may often form the best means of access from the coast of British Columbia to the interior or from the interior to the coast. Pending the completion of the Trans-Canada Highway it is almost a matter of necessity to use American roads if the journey is to be prolonged to Eastern Canada. Indeed, it is recognized as a necessity by as matter-of-fact a body as the Foreign Exchange Control Board. In attracting Americans northwards, British Columbia must rely on its charms alone (although for a time the enforcement of prohibition in the United States was sufficiently effective to add another incentive). The scenery, the summer climate, the fishing and (for some) the big game, and perhaps the novelty of a country which at a pinch can be counted as "foreign" do draw large numbers northwards; just as the somewhat complementary attractions of California draw many British Columbians south. Shopping may be an added inducement to travel as it is possible to take back $100 worth of purchases free of duty.[84]

The automobile is rivalled in importance, from the standpoint of promoting contact and knowledge, by two other recent inventions: the moving picture and the radio. In both cases the influence is one-sided and British Columbians learn far more about Americans than Americans do about British Columbia. But it remains none the less true that all people on the Pacific Coast of North America see the same pictures and listen to the same programmes at about the same time. In British Columbia the radio programmes, at least, are largely diluted from British and Eastern Canadian sources but American programmes are often repeated to Canadian stations and are heard directly as well.

There are, of course, many other channels of intercourse. American periodicals are freely read in Canada: British Columbian

84. These statements require some modification in war-time.

students often pursue their post-graduate studies in the United States and find that, for specialists, there is a better labour market south than north of the international boundary. Service clubs are mostly international and make a point of emphasizing their international character.

It will have been noticed that American influences on Canada are far and away more potent than Canadian influences on the United States. There are more Canadians teaching in the universities of the Pacific Coast states and in their summer sessions than there are Americans teaching in the University of British Columbia. If a university teacher influences the outlook of those who attend his lectures or his seminars this Canadian influence exceeds the American. But to offset this circumstance is the fact that many Canadians have received all, or a large part, of their post-graduate instruction in the United States. It is possible to imagine an Americanization of British Columbia, but certainly not a Canadianization of the United States.

How, we may well ask, has British Columbia retained a separate identity at all? About the fact of this identity there can be little doubt. One has but to attend a meeting where attention is turned to world affairs to feel that there is a very great difference in outlook between the two peoples. To answer this question we must look east across the Rockies and even across the Atlantic to consider Canadian and British influences which have acted and continue to act on British Columbia, and which may well be powerful enough to create a British Columbian identity capable of self-preservation even in the insidious environment of the Pacific slope.

The first of these tramontane influences is settlement. British Columbia has always had a special attraction for settlers from the British Isles and the present population is largely of British stock. An influential element comes from Eastern Canada. Hitherto few of the men who have governed the province and who have occupied positions of leadership in it have been born and educated in British Columbia.

The second influence is the strong material vested interests which depend on the maintenance of the *status quo*. Business enterprises have been built up behind tariffs and in dependence on trade routes. Neighbouring districts in the same geographical region are likely to be keen competitors in many respects, and this is certainly true of British Columbia and the neighbouring State of Washington. To remove political barriers, artificial as these may seem, would impair the fortunes of many citizens in both countries. And closely related to these material interests are the strong moral vested interests that demand the maintenance of any nation as a going concern.

Then, too, a difference of world outlook, once established, is in some degree at least, self-perpetuating. For the American everything external to the United States is foreign. The Canadian can hardly feel that any corner of the English-speaking world is completely foreign to him, and in addition to his dependence on foreign trade there is much in his life to keep before his eyes the importance of the historical links which keep these wider associations alive.

The aim of this chapter has been to show how the naturally predatory economy of the nineteenth century, followed by the nation-building processes which have been deliberately employed to weld each region of the Pacific Coast into a great transcontinental federation, has produced two communities which are friendly rather than intimate. Their goodwill towards each other is as evident as is their ignorance of each other's political life. Nothing has occurred to disturb their good-natured tolerance, and, as far as they are conscious of it, they are disposed to regard it with pride. Their wider loyalties lead them into different company and give them different outlooks on the major world problems. Yet in the presence of any practical danger they would readily co-operate in self-defence. They might even unite in self-defence, though they are not at all eager to do so. They are prone to a certain self-righteousness, as if their good relations merely reflected their good sense, and not the absence of great differences in living standards or real conflicts of interest which if present would make it really creditable to be friendly. Perhaps, to some extent, they are aware of common characteristics which distinguish them both from their compatriots in the Middle West or on the eastern seaboard. But they are both patriotic enough to see these differences through a diminishing glass. They are both unsophisticated enough not to be ashamed of possessing one of the few joint histories which can be brought up to date and yet have a happy ending.